ARTISTS

BRYNLEY ODU DAVIES

** TROLLEY **

FOREWORD

In the ever-evolving tapestry of contemporary art, there exists a profound desire to capture the essence of the present moment—a moment that transcends the ordinary and crystallises the extraordinary. Through the lens of Brynley Odu Davies, we embark on a visual journey, one that began in 2020 and spans the last three years, documenting over 200 contemporary artists across the United Kingdom in their sanctuaries of creativity.

Brynley Odu Davies's artistic odyssey began as a response to the unforeseen disruption brought about by the Covid-19 pandemic. Faced with the suspension of his career as a music photographer, Brynley turned his lens toward the vibrant community of South London-based artists. Little did he know that this decision would set in motion a creative pilgrimage, guiding him through the length and breadth of the United Kingdom.

In this remarkable and diverse archive that Brynley has meticulously crafted, we find ourselves immersed in the heart of the UK's emerging arts scene. As you turn the pages of this book, you will be transported to the inner sanctums of these artists. You will witness the intimate connection between the artists and their work, a connection that Brynley has masterfully preserved.

What distinguishes Brynley's work is his distinctive style, one that captures authenticity and truth in its purest form. His photographs, often bathed in the gentle embrace of natural light and presented with minimal editing, have an enduring, timeless quality. In each portrait, he captures not just the physical presence of his subjects but also the very essence of their being.

These photographs are empowering in their simplicity. They are more than just images; they are windows into the souls of the artists themselves. Through Brynley's lens, we witness a precise moment in time—a moment that encapsulates not only the artist's life but also their artistic journey. It is a testament to the resilience, creativity and originality of the individuals who shape our contemporary art landscape.

Ell Pennick, founder and director of Guts Gallery

Hector Campbell: Having developed an interest in photography at a young age, you first studied it academically at Bath College before completing a BA in Digital Photography at Ravensbourne University. What ignited that initial interest in photography? How did art education nurture your passion?

Brynley Odu Davies: I was drawn to imagery from a young age. I remember looking at Robert Doisneau's photograph *Les enfants de la place Hébert* during my teens and just being amazed by the image. Looking at those people in Paris, dressed in a certain way, I could envision what Paris looked like at that time. It felt like I was connecting to history at that moment. Capturing a particular period, and the people of that period, had such a strong pull for me. I wanted to do that myself, to document people at a particular moment in time, and to capture how they are as people at that time.

Studying photography at college, and extra courses like graphic design and art history, also taught me a lot about the history of the photographic art form. I remember going on a trip to Lacock Abbey near Bath, where I grew up, and learning about the invention of photography. Even just being able to sit in a classroom and study photographs was exciting for me. I was always a little obsessed with images, with portrait photographs, and I could sit for hours at the computer studying them in college and later university.

I also think you develop a kinship with arts education, and I have been lucky to have had lots of teachers who loved art, loved photography, and nurtured that love within me. I had a great art history teacher at Bath College called Sally. We would have classes once a week, and I remember just sitting there and soaking up the history of each art movement, what they meant and who was involved. All of these classes, and my own continued research into the history of portrait photography, allow me to engage with the artists I am photographing. I have references to draw from and have a better understanding of what they are doing, and the direction of their work.

Hector: Post-graduation, you began working widely within the music industry, documenting gigs and photographing emerging bands and musicians. How did your experience of the music scene influence and inform your current work photographing visual artists?

Brynley: The music world was competitive. I first started by going backstage at festivals, where I would see these famous musicians just walking around. I would build up the courage to approach them and ask to take a photograph, but as soon as I got close there would be other photographers, blocking my moment of bravery and trying to get in there and photograph the musicians themselves. When I changed direction to photographing visual artists, I kept that competitive spirit, imagining that there was somebody behind me also ready to shoot the artists I was about to shoot. That competitiveness made me want to work harder and harder. In reality, I was lucky as it seems now that nobody else was documenting these artists, but that competitive spirit within me was useful and kept driving me to keep photographing.

Hector: When the pandemic lockdown sadly put paid to live music events, you pivoted to photographing artists in their studios, the first being Bradford-born London-based painter Conor Murgatroyd. How did that first photo shoot come about? Was it always important to you to photograph these visual artists in their own studios?

Brynley: I spent lockdown in Bath with my parents and grandmother, and when I returned to London I was walking down the street one day and Conor caught my eye. He just looked so interesting and cool. He had previously staged an exhibition at a local pub, and I remember seeing his early work on the walls and enjoying it. I reached out to him to see if he wanted to be photographed, and when I got to his studio he had all this artwork that he had been doing over the last few months, loads of it, just sitting there. It felt special, like I was entering his own little world. And when I started shooting, as I hadn't taken photographs in a while due to lockdown, it felt even more special. It was a new direction for me, and I embraced it.

It felt easy early on, and entering these artists' studios felt like a safe space, both for them and for me. I like to think I'm a naturally friendly and open person, non-judgemental and keen to just observe the artists and witness their talent. I always go in with open eyes and an open mind, excited to meet the artist and take their photograph. The artists have respected this approach, and it has allowed me to be embraced by that community.

Hector: I understand that at the outset of the project, you outlined a certain set of rules for yourself, including using the same camera with an option of just two lenses; positioning the artist as being physically taller than or above their artworks; and photographing in natural light. Could you expand upon these early rules? Did you introduce further rules or guidelines as the project progressed?

Brynley: Shooting with the same two lenses was something I found important early on. Before lockdown, I had only shot with a 50mm lens, so when I got a 35mm and then a 24mm I felt that with them I could capture everything I needed to capture. All I had to do was move my feet, get into some odd positions and I could cover the whole scene.

I have always studied photography and images, and knew that when I took images I wanted to empower my subject. I think shooting directly on or from below gives this feeling, it is something I picked up on early on and continued to use as a tool. I think that the more you shoot while adhering to a few simple rules, your images slowly become more distinctive as your own. Also, the more you shoot, the more you learn what you don't want to shoot. I can see an image and know quickly if it's something I would shoot or not. Not to limit myself, but to know what it is I find visually stimulating.

Capturing somebody in a way that shows respect to them is something I am always keen to do. I don't want to take images that make people look bad, I want them to look like themselves and uplift them simultaneously. I like the idea that by having respect for my subject, they hopefully also have respect for me too in that process.

Hector: On the advice of a former lecturer, you eventually expanded your search for emerging artistic talent out of London, travelling the length and breadth of the British Isles to photograph artists living and making work outside of the capital. What did you discover about those artistic communities that exist outside of London? How was the diversity of representation maintained as an important part of the overall project?

Brynley: I would meet with my old lecturer, Geraint, every six months or so since graduating. Just meet for a coffee and a chat about photography, and he would give me advice. In our first meeting after starting the project, he told me to look outside of London, to respect a wider scene and show people what was happening outside of London. That felt important, so I used money I had saved and invested it back in myself and the project, travelling to shoot artists in other cities.

I started with Scotland, and immediately noticed that artists in other parts of the country had a different feel to their work. If they had studied in Glasgow, for example, I could see a particular subtlety in the style of their work. The more I travelled, the more I felt like London is the centre of things with all the galleries, art schools and opportunities. But I also recognised that the internet and social media were allowing artists outside of London to finally get a look in.

I photographed Louise Giovanelli in an old mill in Salford, Manchester just as she was about to head to New York for an exhibition, and then a few months later she was signed to White Cube. There is talent everywhere, and I'm really glad I went out and searched for it. I photographed so many amazing artists, had brilliant conversations with them and learnt more about the wider artistic community as time went on.

Hector: As the series documents artists within their own individual studios, invariably surrounded by finished artworks or works-in-

progress, your resultant photographs can offer an insight into both the artists themselves, and their practices. Have you begun to notice any notable comparisons, or differences, between the two?

Brynley: Absolutely. The artists I'm drawn to tend to live through their art practices, creating their own worlds and universes through the art they make. Often I go to a studio and they are surrounded by all the amazing work they have spent weeks or months making, and the same paint would be on the floor, on the walls and their clothes, covering everything. It feels very special to enter those spaces, it is always a real privilege. The fact that they're creating these artworks that may be sold and end up in faraway places, maybe never to be seen by the artist again, is bittersweet. I'm there to document not only the artist but also the artworks they have been putting their heart and soul into. I often capture their final moments surrounded by those artworks before they disappear into the world.

Hector: To date, you have photographed over two hundred visual artists, with the occasional few featuring multiple times over repeat studio visits. What draws you back to certain artists' studios? Is this series something you hope to keep returning to, as these artists' burgeoning careers progress?

Brynley: I develop a rapport with certain artists, a connected energy that makes creating images together feel effortless. I remember photographing Daisy Parris a few times at the start of the series, when they were based in Croydon. I would message them and we would meet up, shoot and chat, engaging in beautiful conversation. I think I grew a lot from meeting these artists and having these interesting conversations, but also from letting myself be vulnerable and express myself to sometimes complete strangers. By shooting artists repeatedly, like Daisy, you again get to document the newest artworks they are creating. It's a chance to catch up, but also with a purpose. I remember Daisy saying 'Work hard whilst you are young' at one of our earliest encounters, and I took that to heart.

I used to photograph a lot of musicians at the early stages of their careers, and then wouldn't see them again as they blew up and their careers took off. I was documenting them as they emerged, and then waving goodbye. However, with visual artists, I could maintain those relationships because at whatever stage of their career, they'll always be in the studio making work.

Hector: Social media, and especially Instagram, has been instrumental in the documentation and dissemination of the series, as well as exposing you to the wider artistic community at large. What are your thoughts on Instagram as a tool for creatives and photographers?

Brynley: When I started travelling around the UK more for the project, Instagram was a great tool for connecting with many of those regional artists. With the multiple pandemic lockdowns, everyone was spending more time on their phones, but also more time than ever making art. Artists were increasingly open to sharing their work online, and galleries too realised they had to embrace social media and online resources. This led to greater awareness of young artists, and collectors were spending more time at home willing to spend money on art instead of a two-week holiday somewhere abroad. It felt like an art boom was happening, with Instagram connecting people and making the whole scene more accessible.

Every morning I would log on and search out new artists, just messaging people and creating my own database of all these artists based around the UK. All done entirely through Instagram. And then a lot of those artists also knew each other through social media, and I could act as a connector between artists I was photographing. If I had already photographed an artist that another artist liked and respected, it made it easy to facilitate shoots. I hope I made some artists feel seen within that community and network, and that I have facilitated further connection and conversations amongst artists.

Hector: Finally, this book must mark a culmination of the Artist Portraits series. Does this also mean the start of a new chapter for you as a photographer? Or will you still be pursuing the project going forward?

Brynley: It's definitely a culmination for sure. I've been hoping to make a book of all these photographs since almost the start of the project back in 2020. It's been a long time coming, finally realised thanks to some dedication on my side and a lot of love and support from my family and friends.

I think photographing artists is something I will always do. They are such interesting, unique and brilliant people, and I will always treasure the friendships I have made throughout the process of this project. I don't see myself stopping, there are always new people to meet and more photographs to take. I just hope that when I'm old, I can look back and see all the images I have made as important documentation of these artists who went on to do great things and who contributed to pushing culture forward.

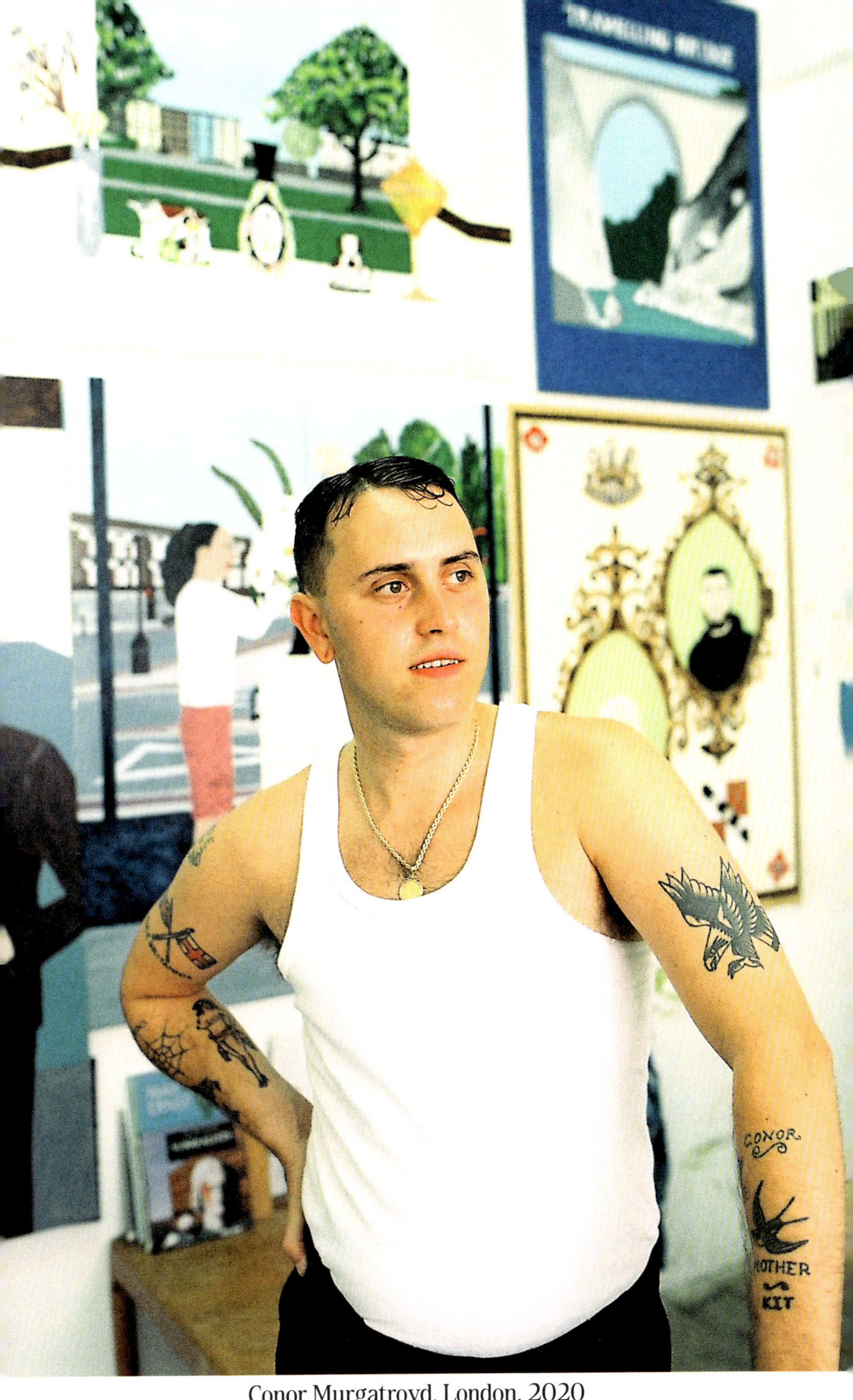

Conor Murgatroyd, London, 2020

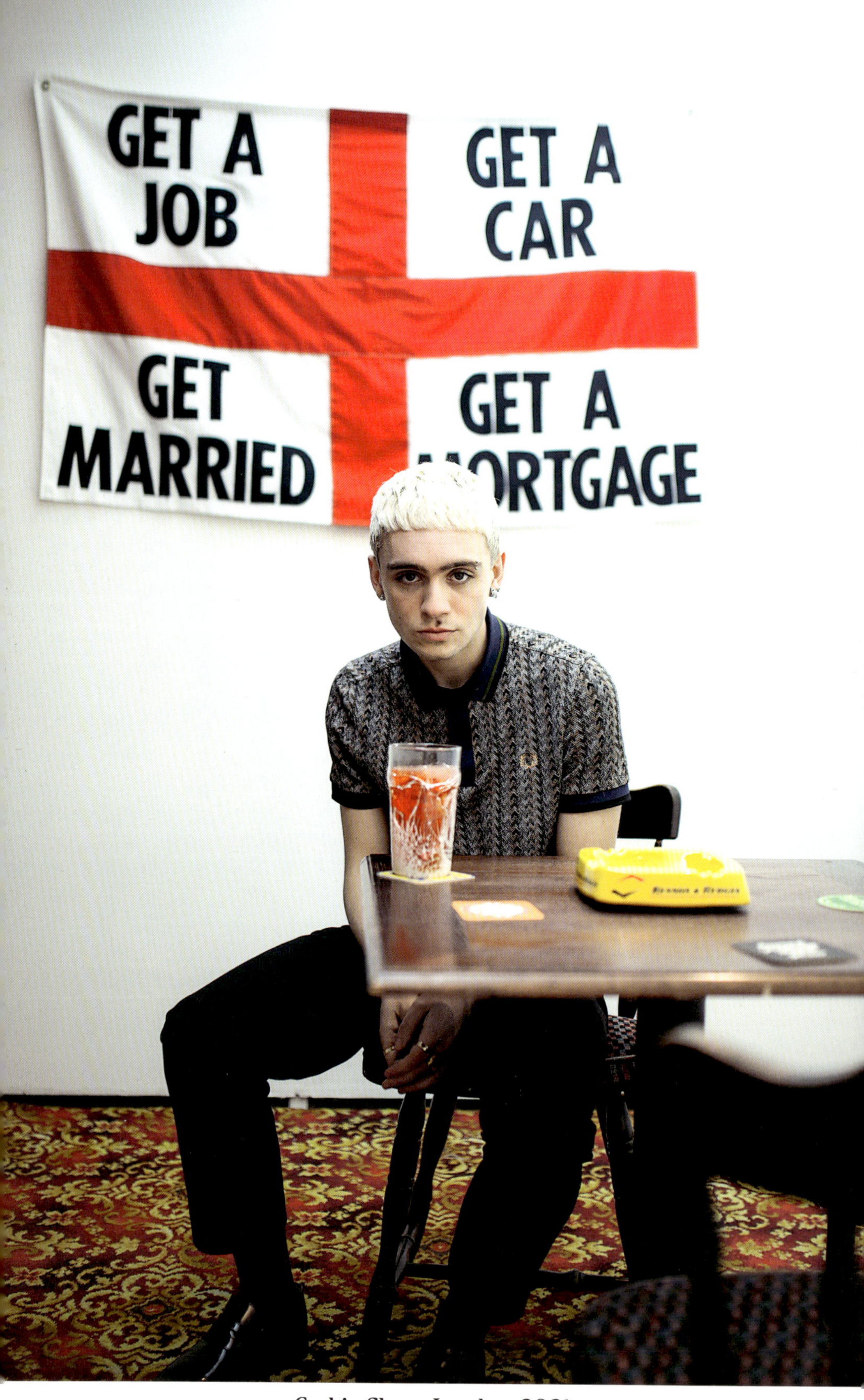

Corbin Shaw, London, 2021

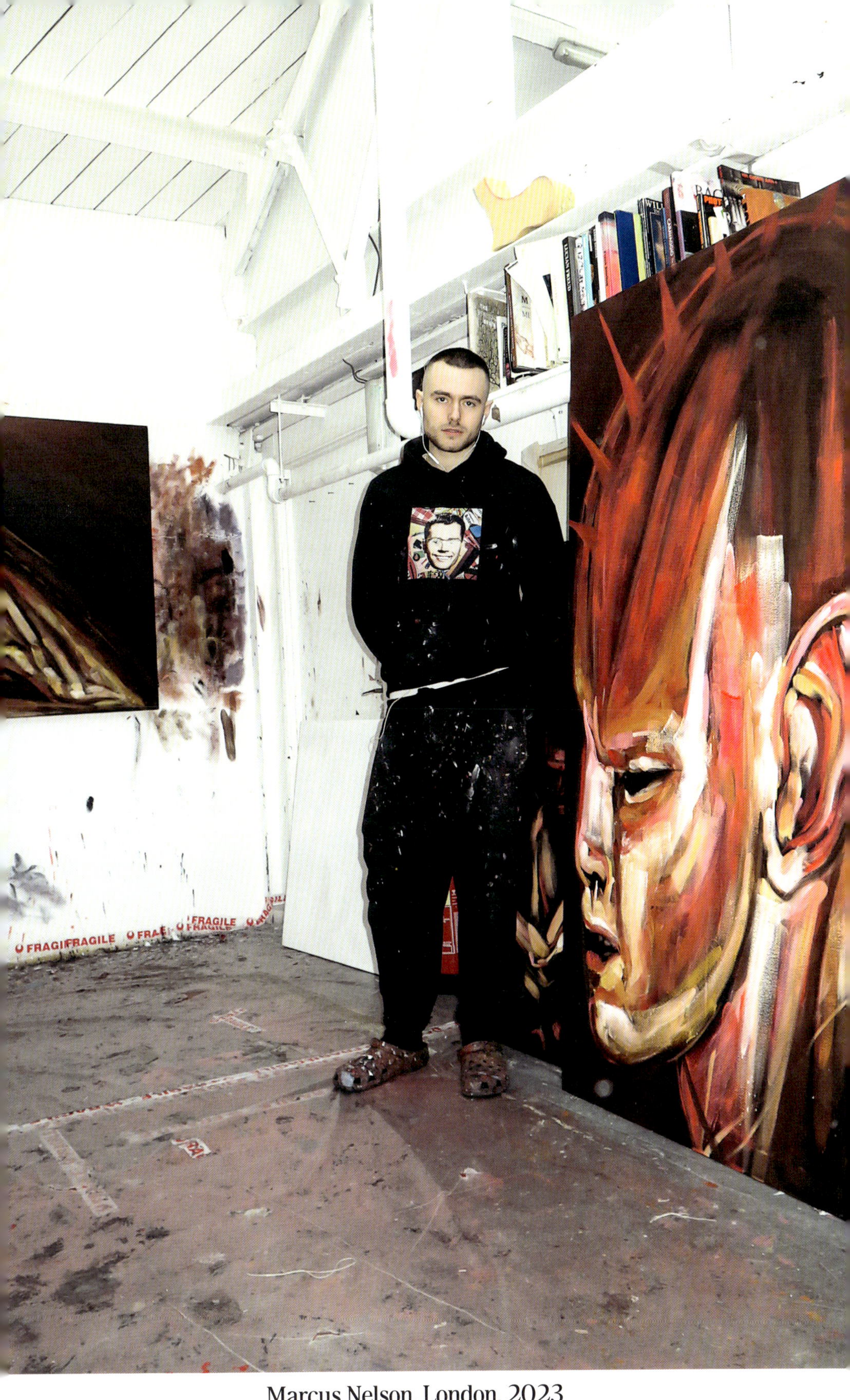

Marcus Nelson, London, 2023

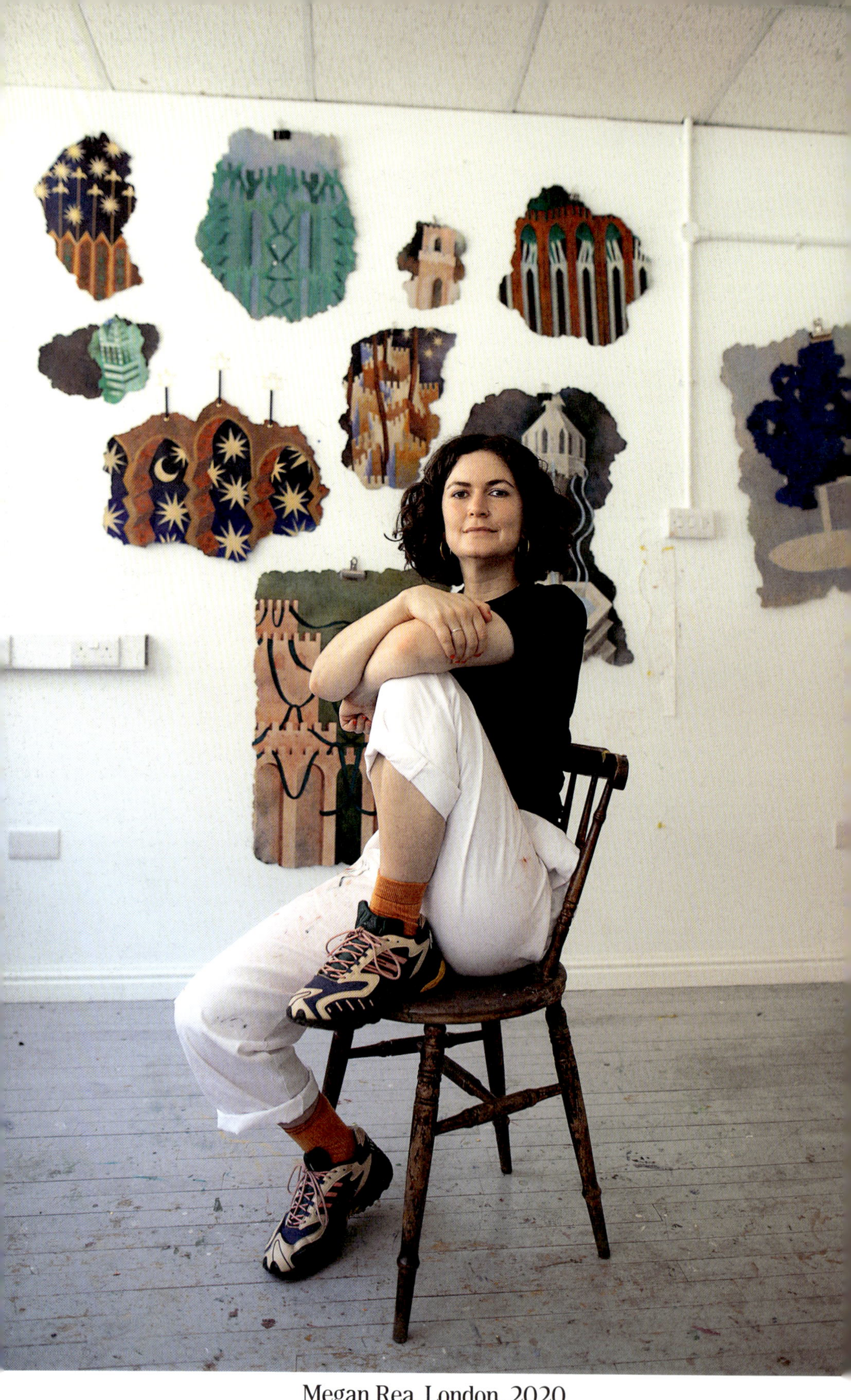

Megan Rea, London, 2020

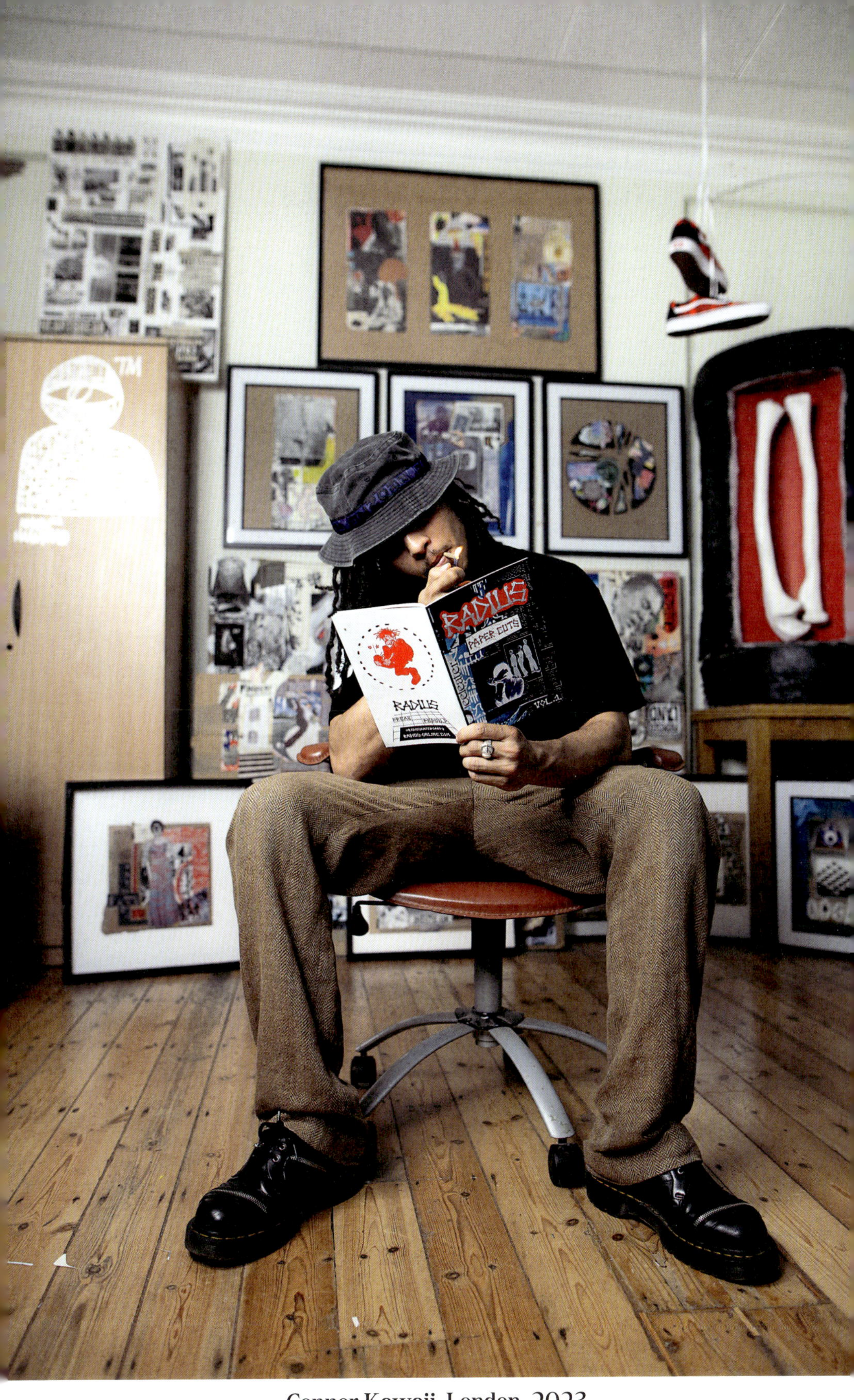

Connor Kawaii, London, 2023

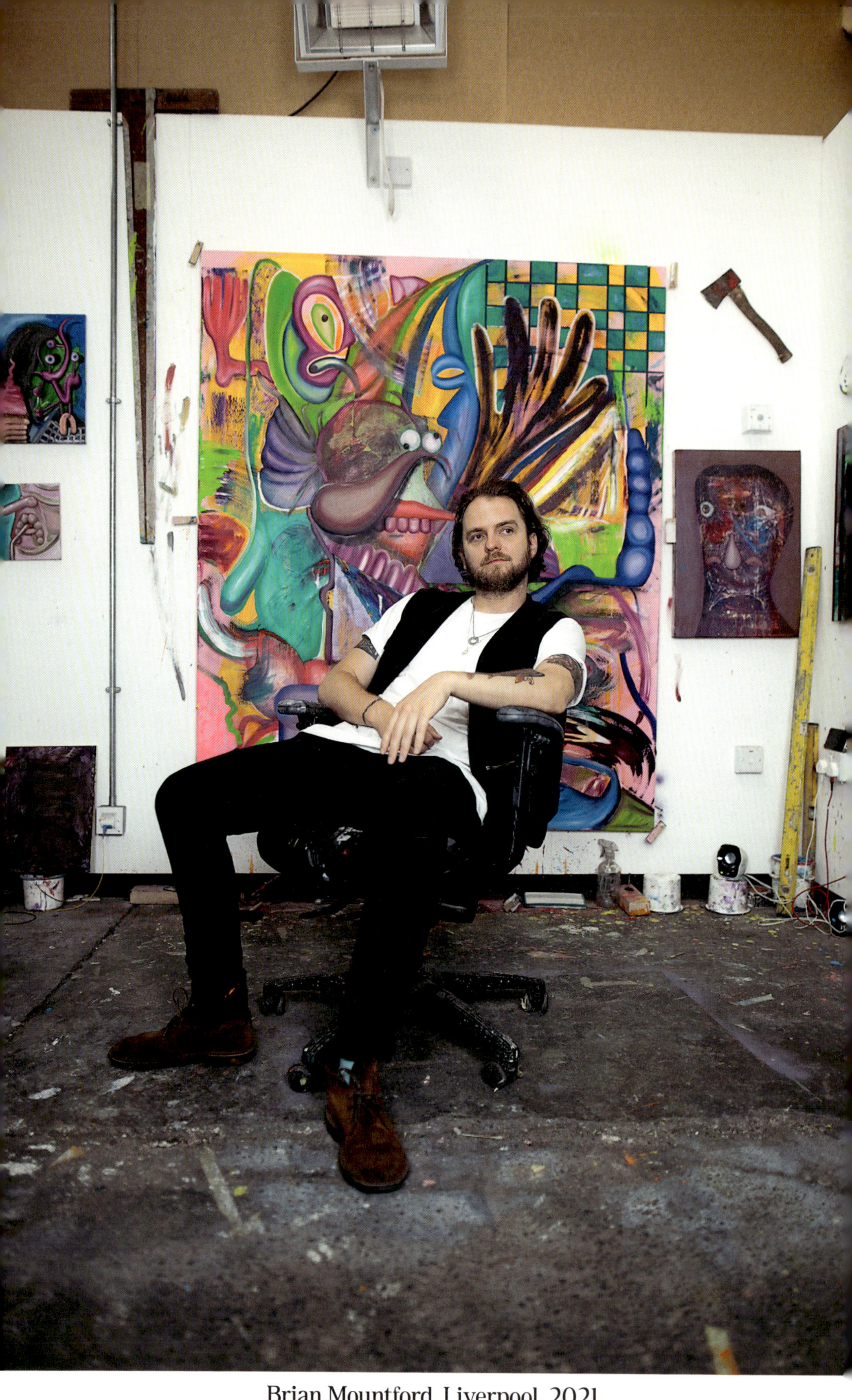

Brian Mountford, Liverpool, 2021

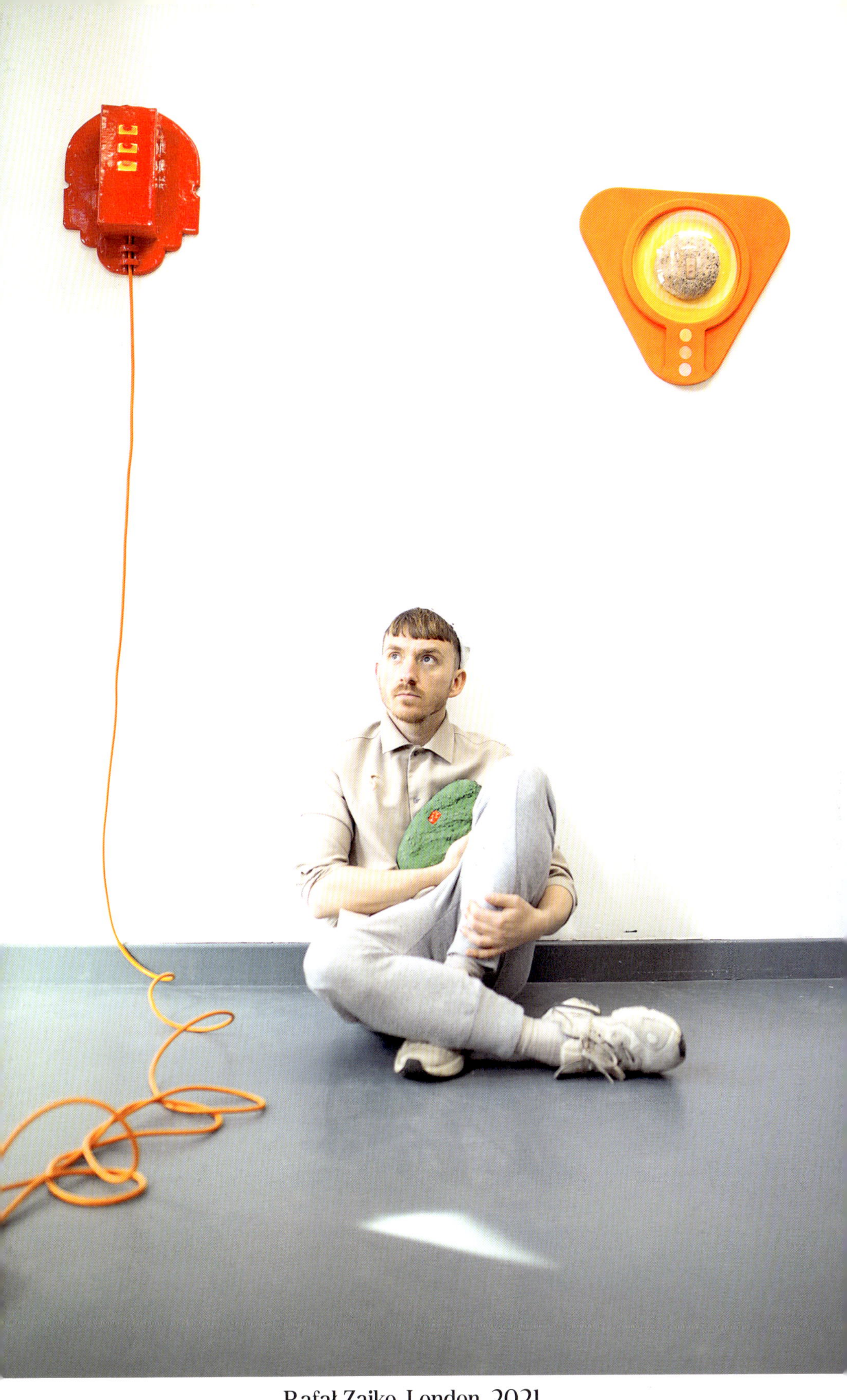

Rafał Zajko, London, 2021

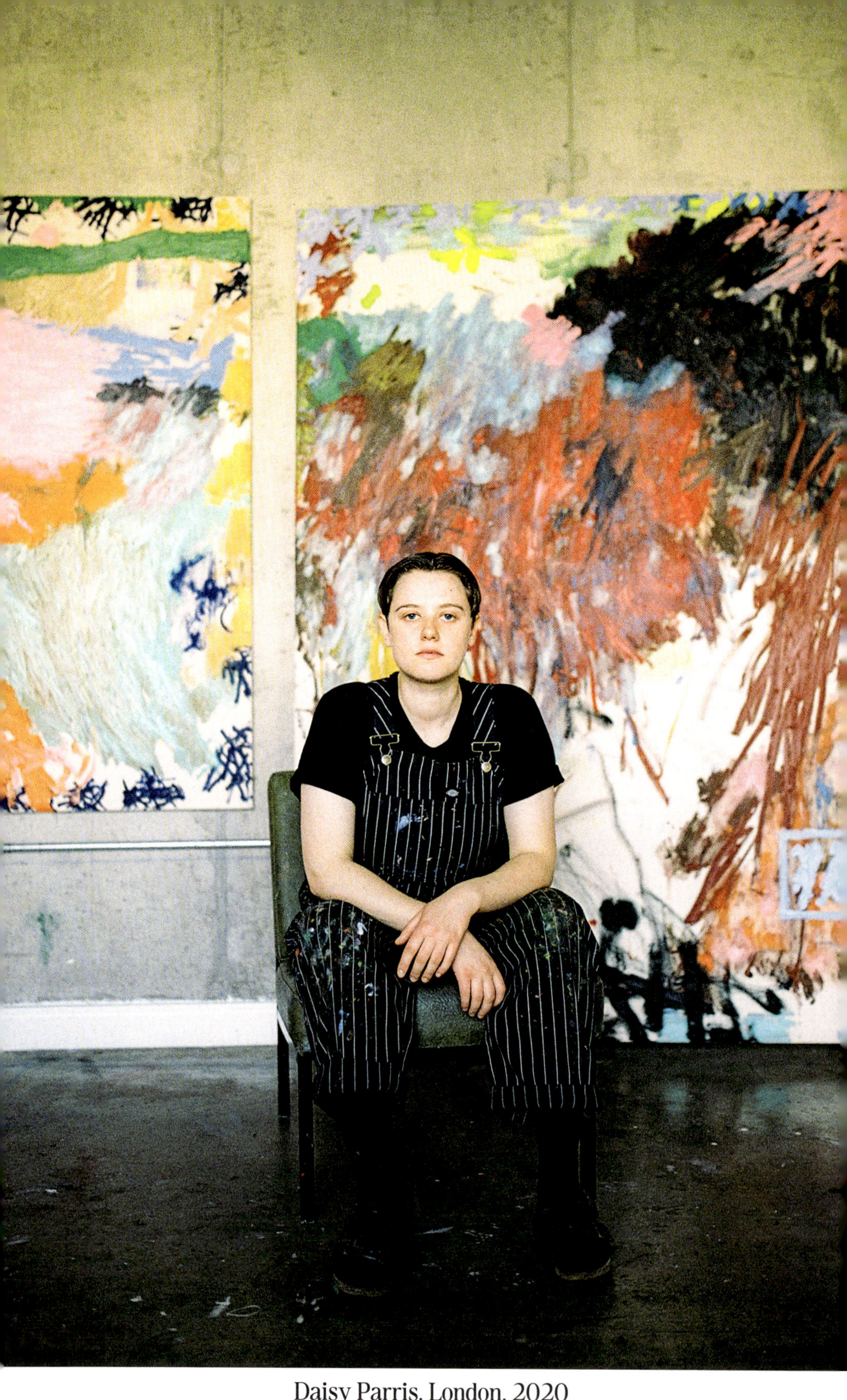

Daisy Parris, London, 2020

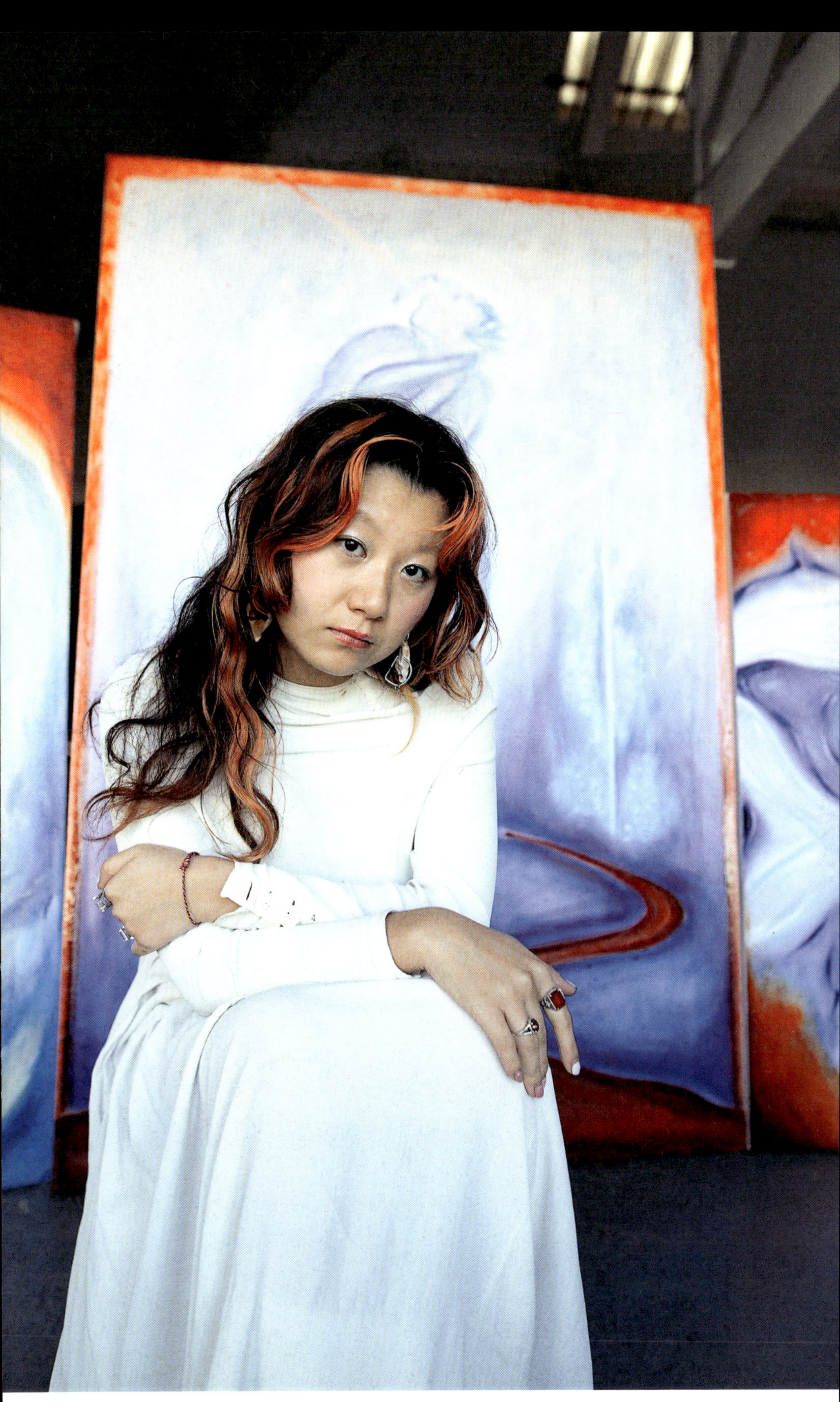

Salomé Wu, London, 2021

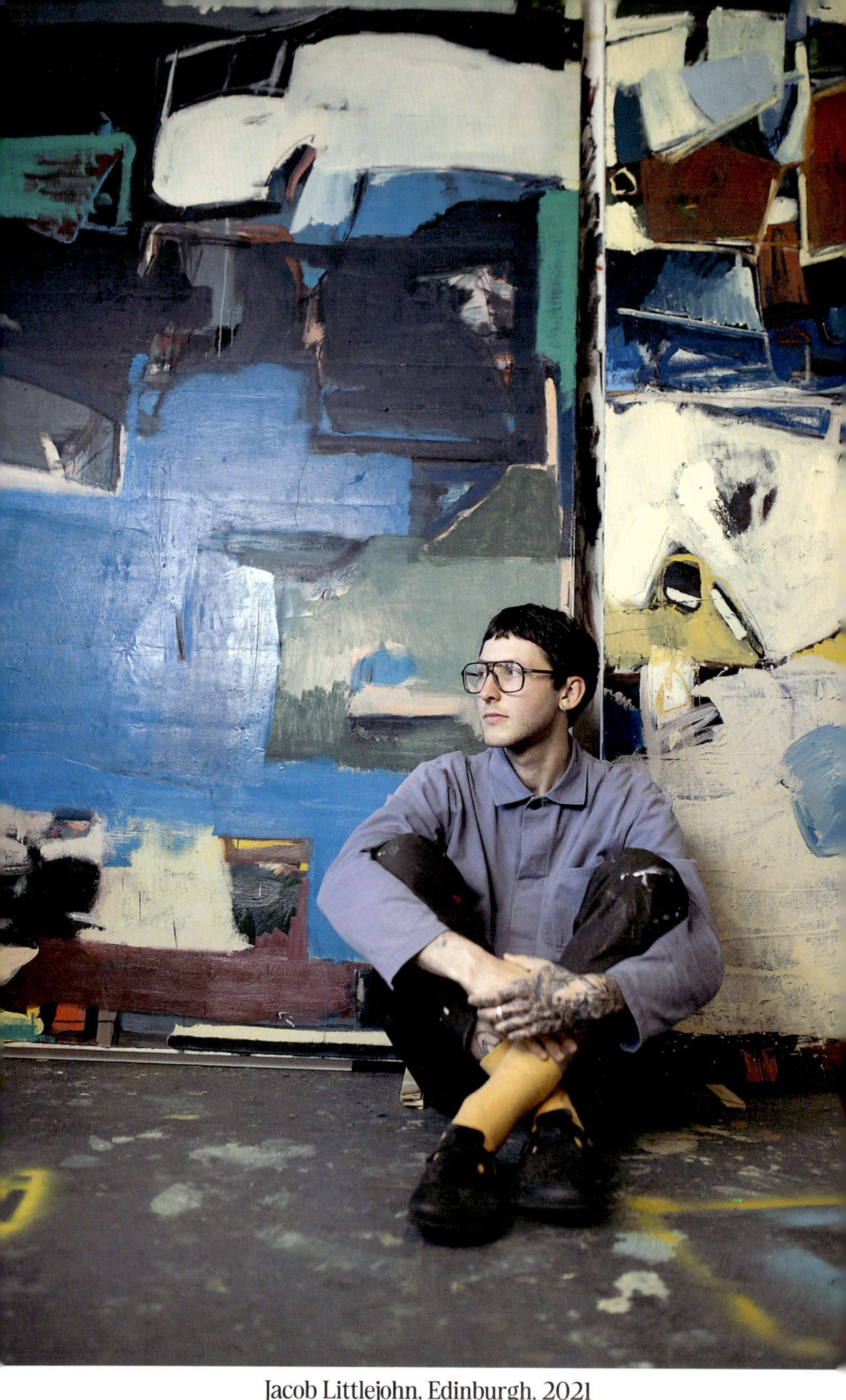

Jacob Littlejohn, Edinburgh, 2021

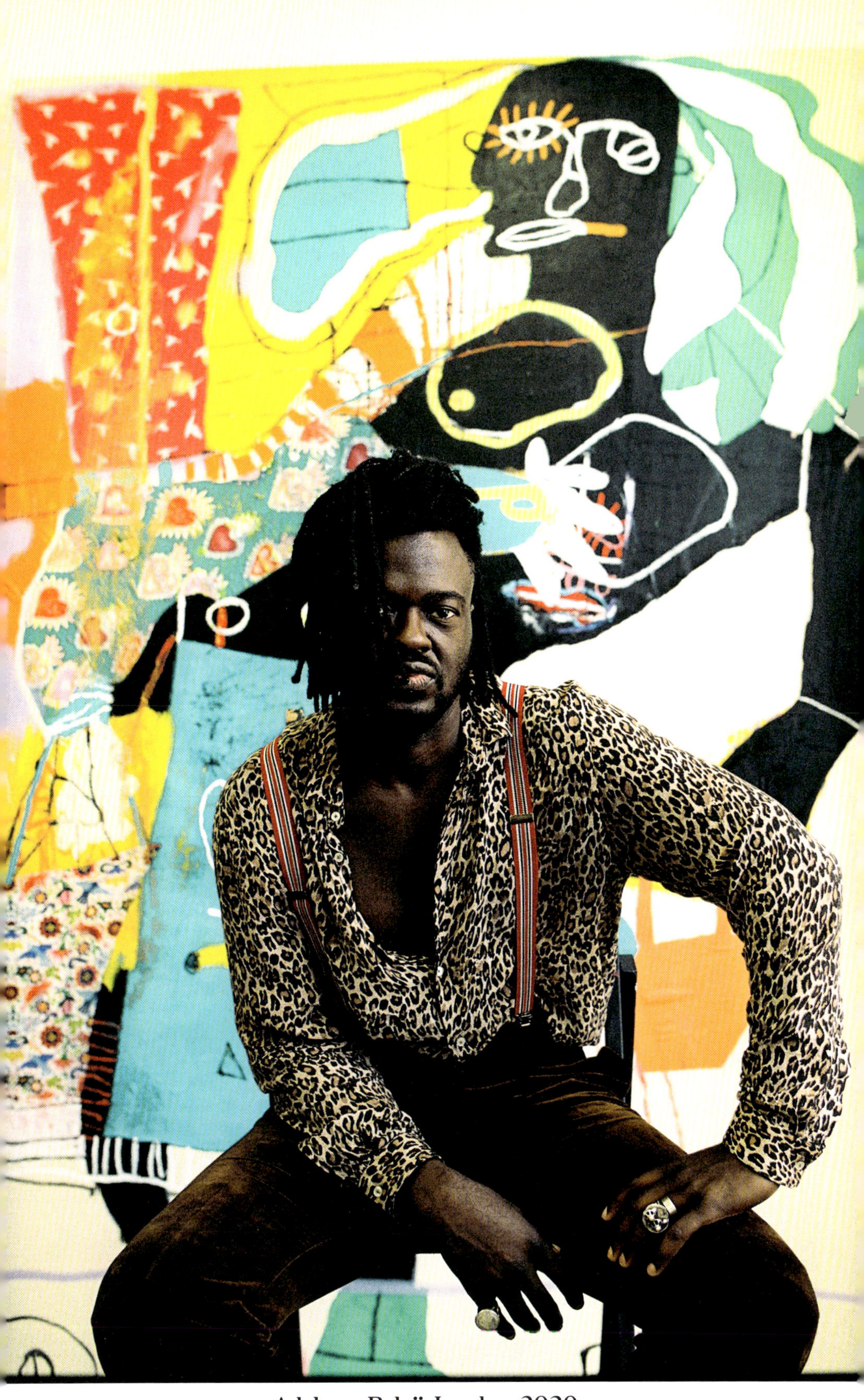

Adebayo Bolaji, London, 2020

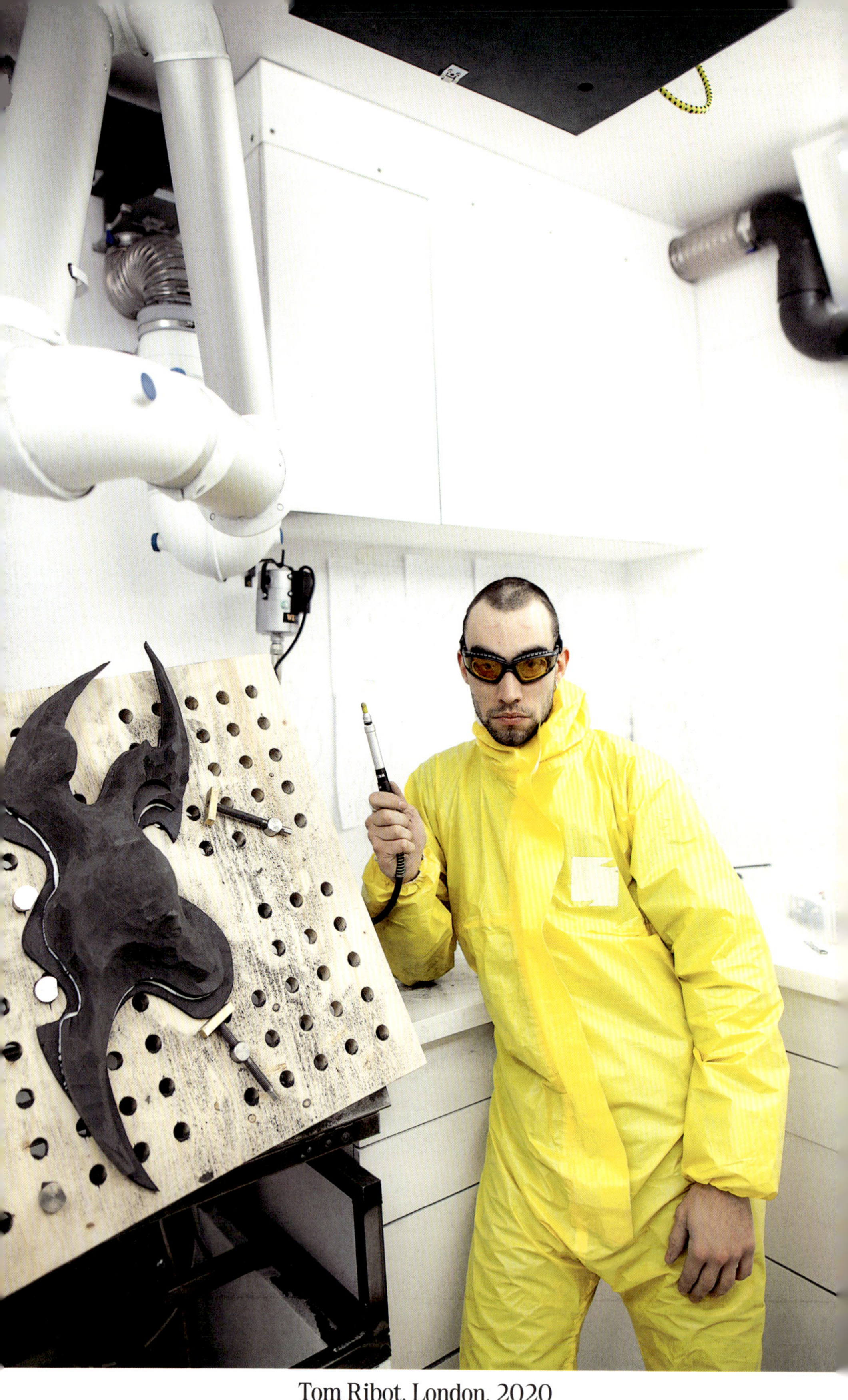

Tom Ribot, London, 2020

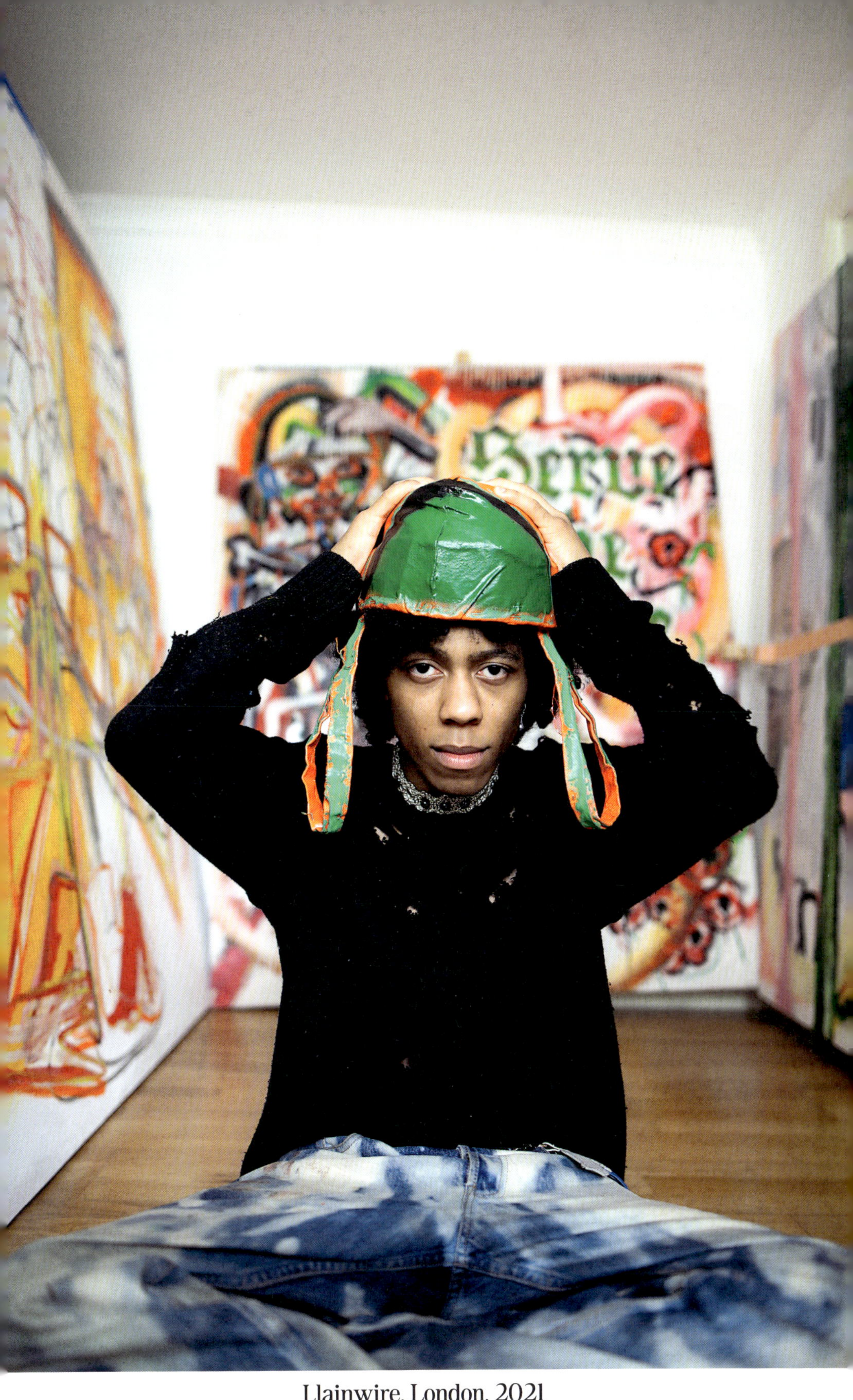

Llainwire, London, 2021

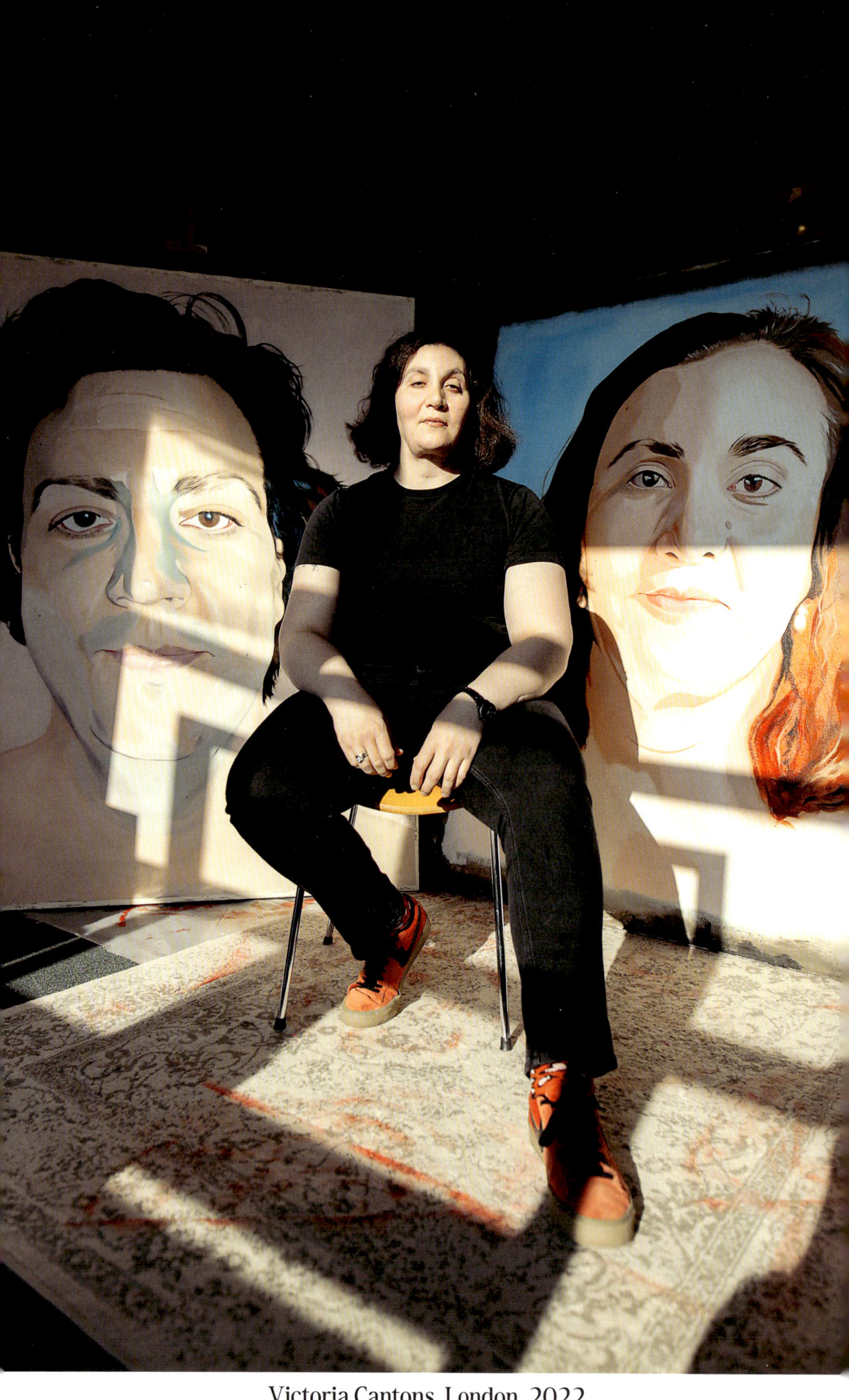

Victoria Cantons, London, 2022

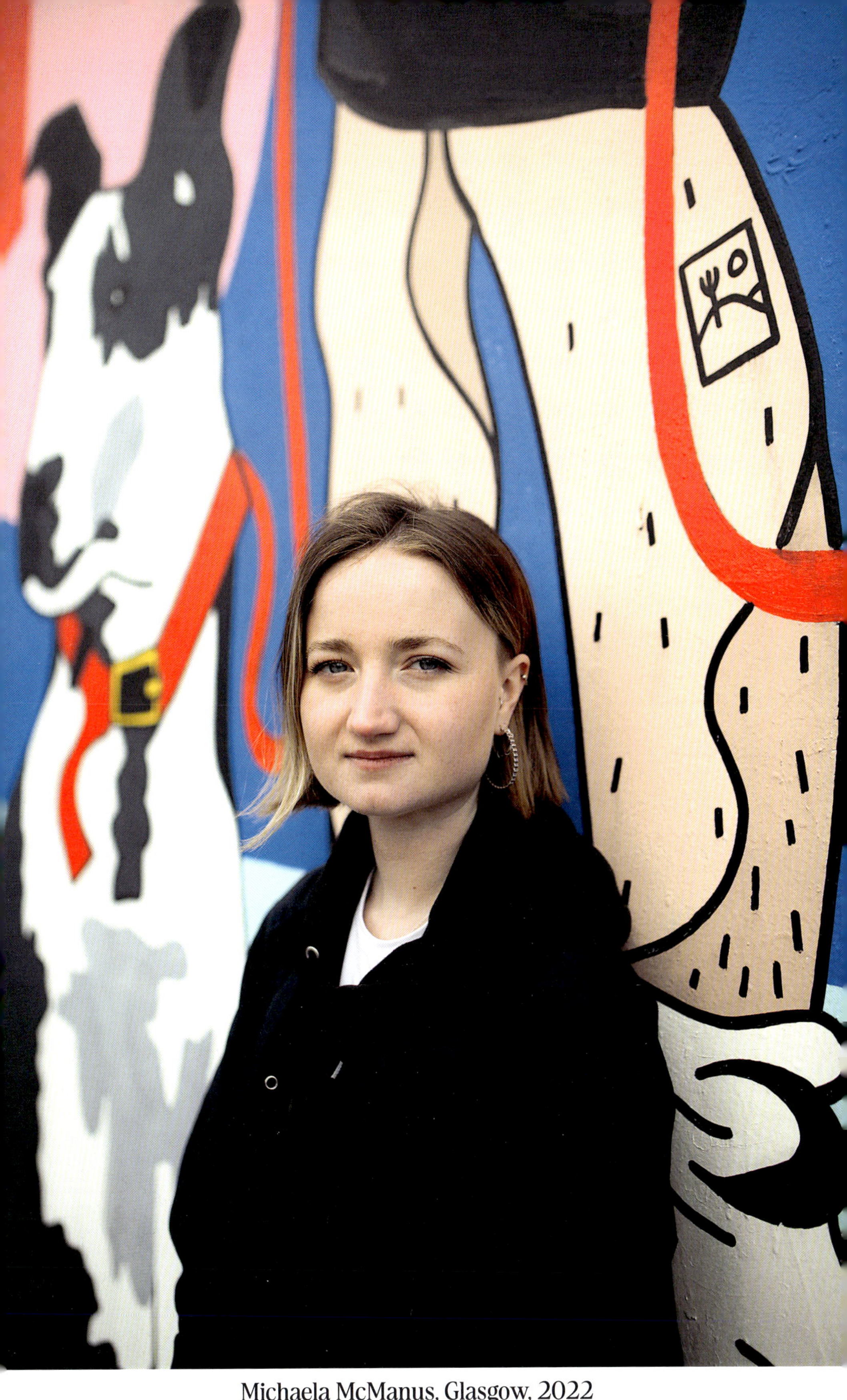

Michaela McManus, Glasgow, 2022

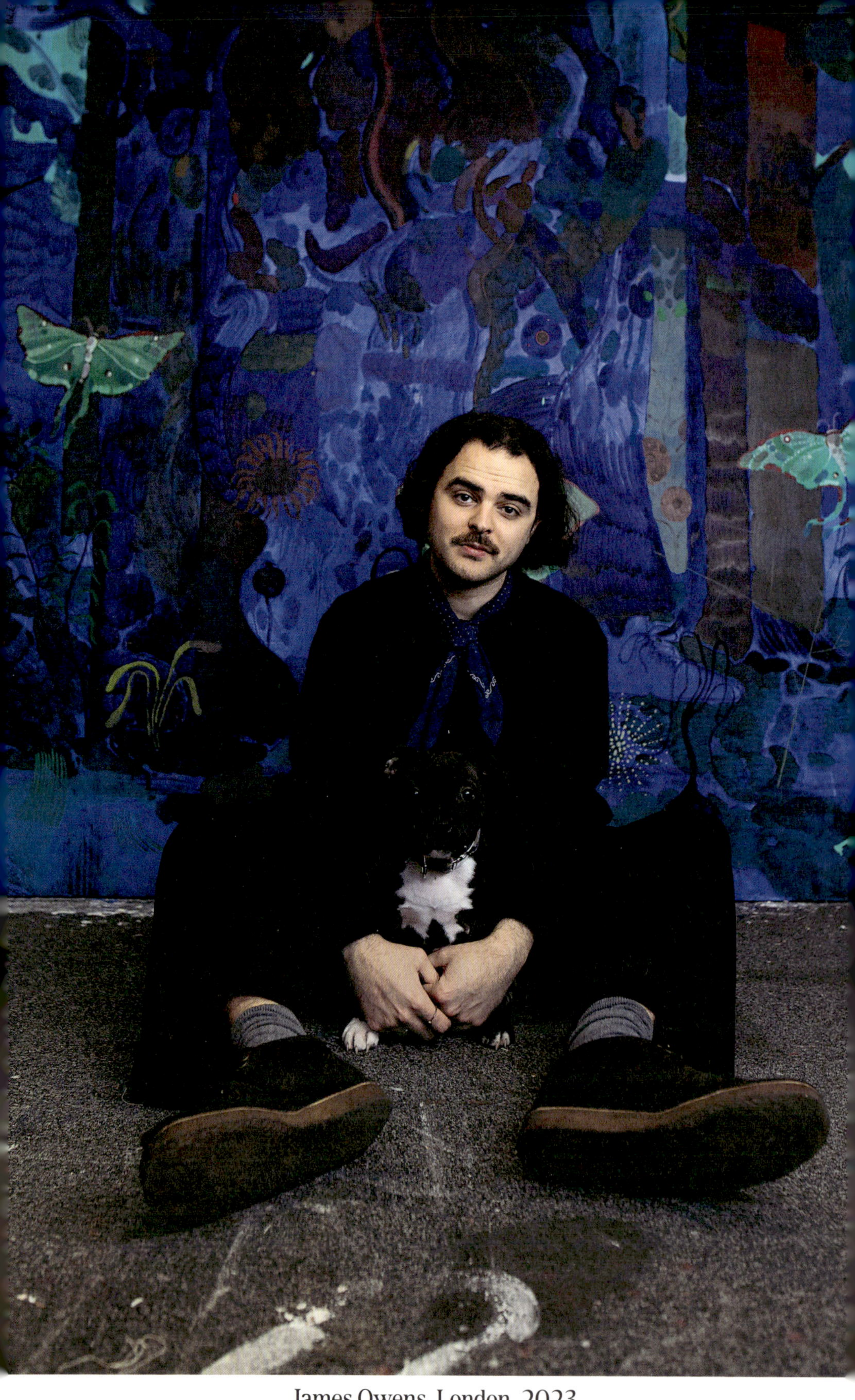

James Owens, London, 2023

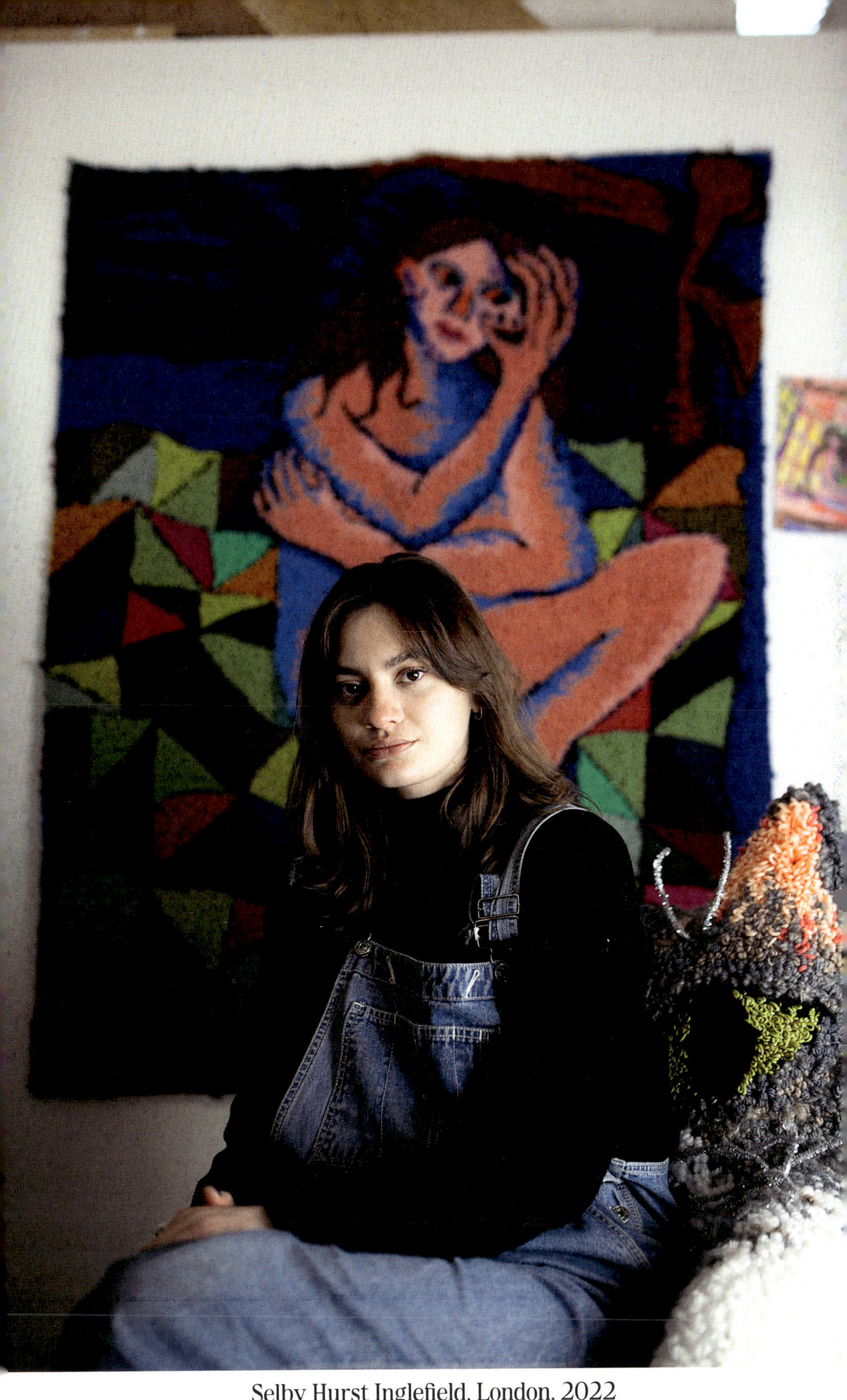

Selby Hurst Inglefield, London, 2022

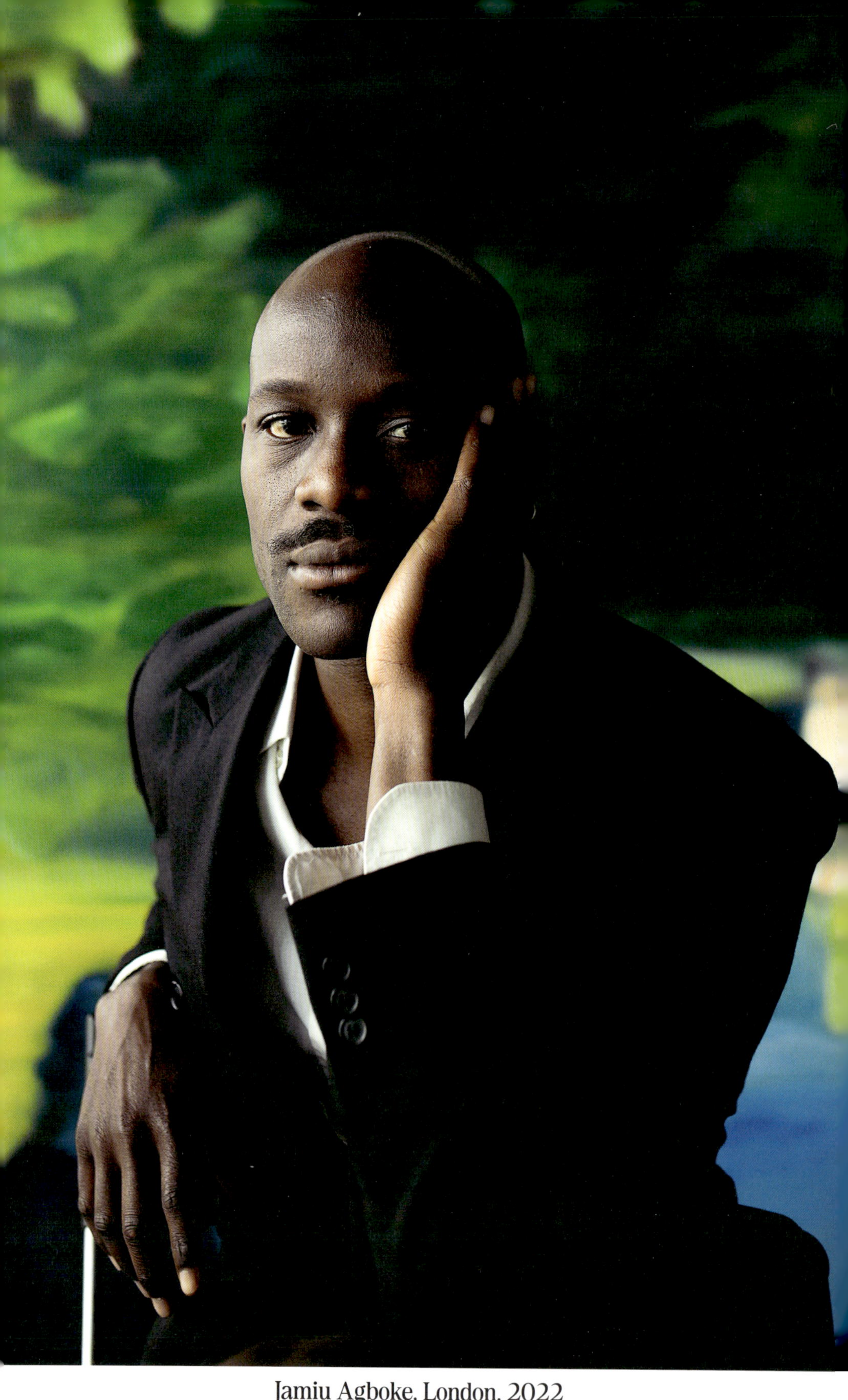

Jamiu Agboke, London, 2022

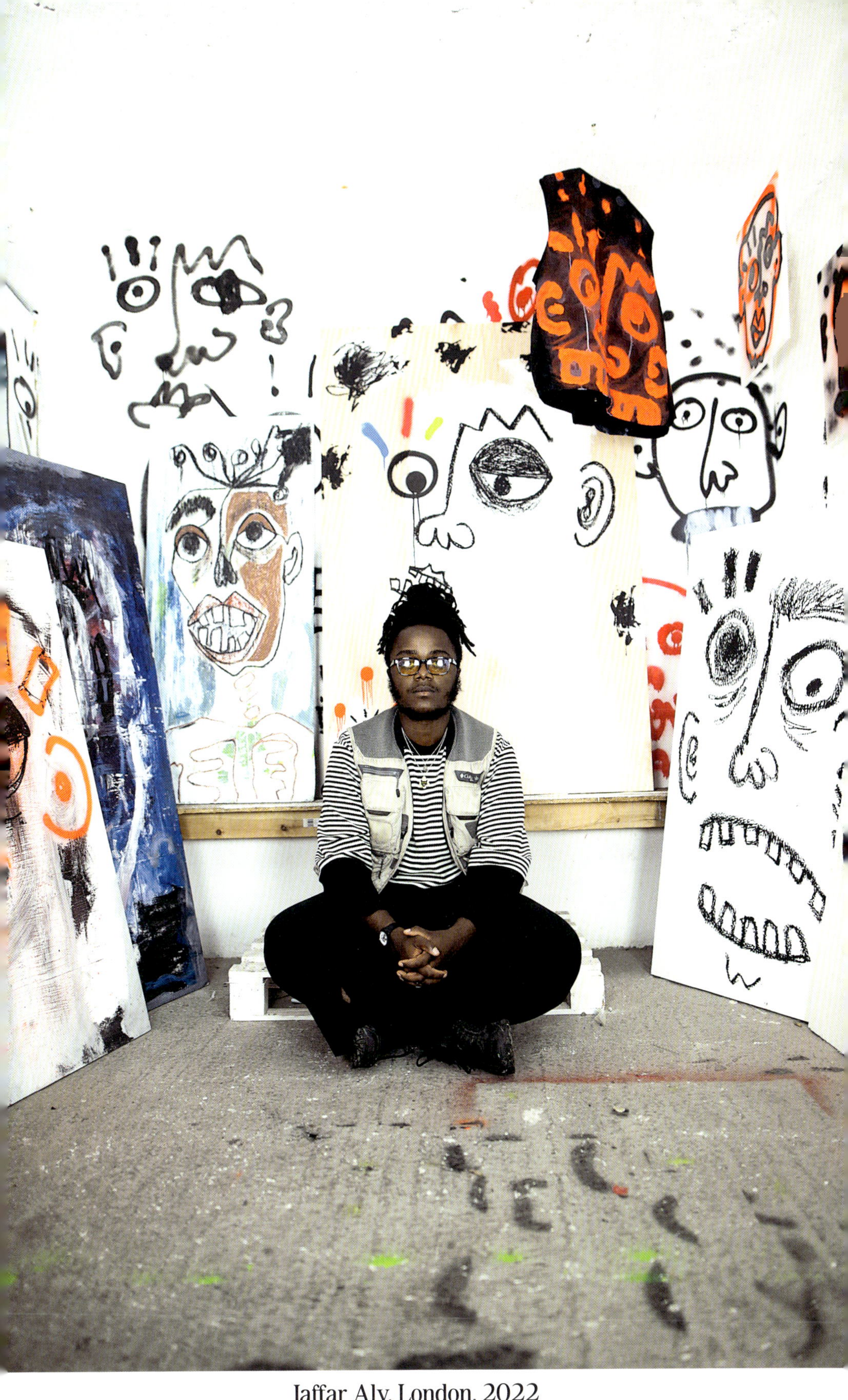

Jaffar Aly, London, 2022

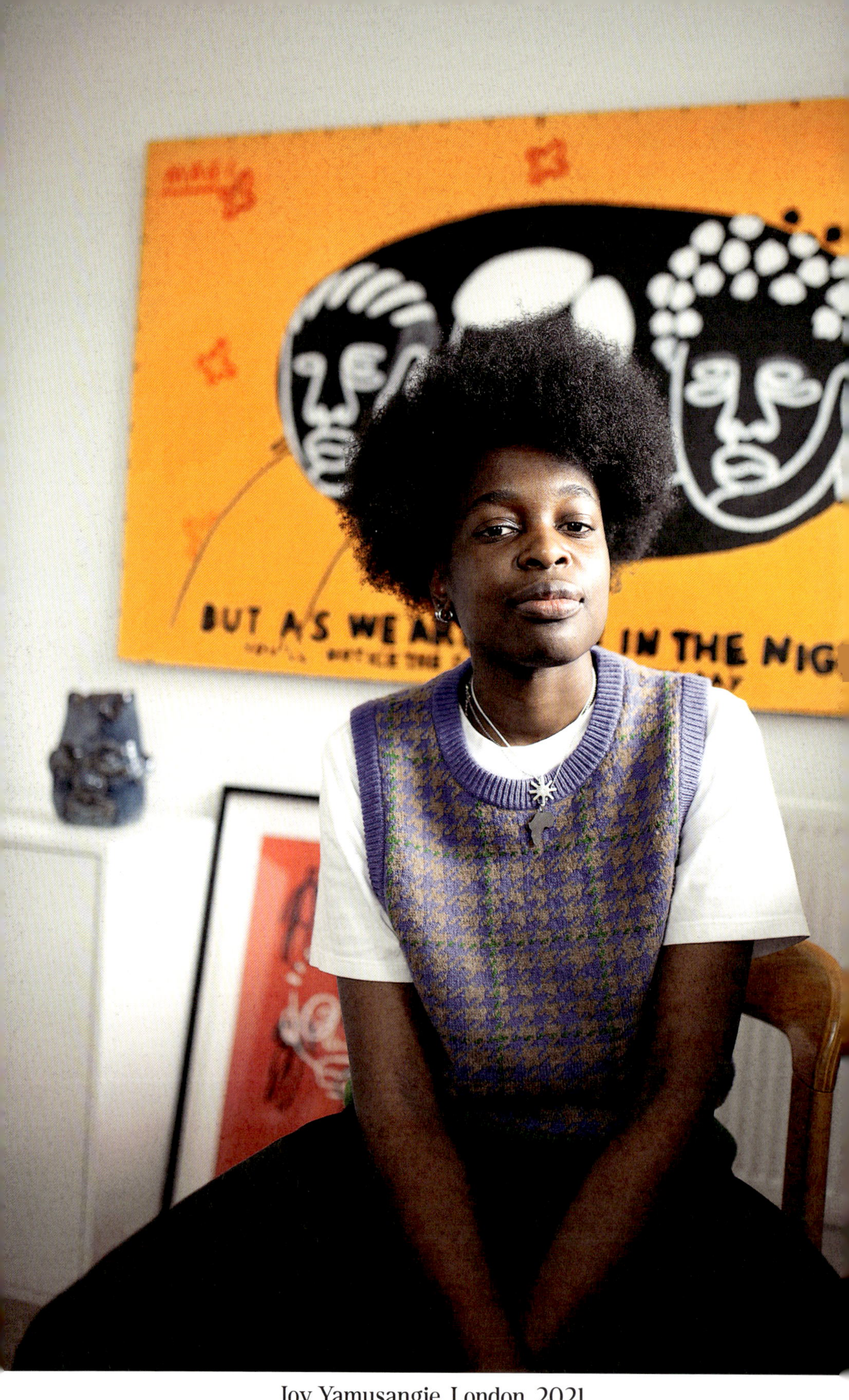

Joy Yamusangie, London, 2021

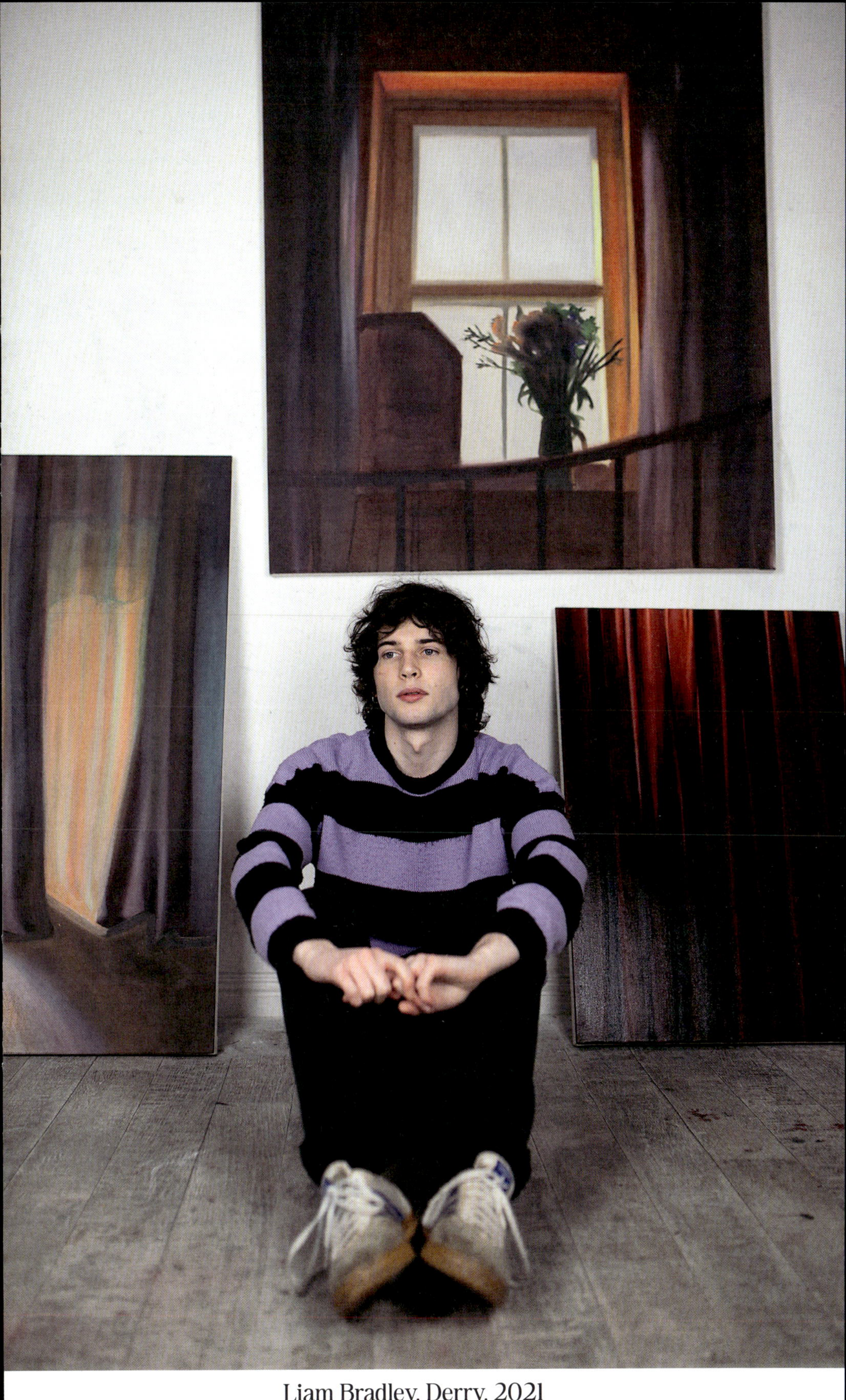

Liam Bradley, Derry, 2021

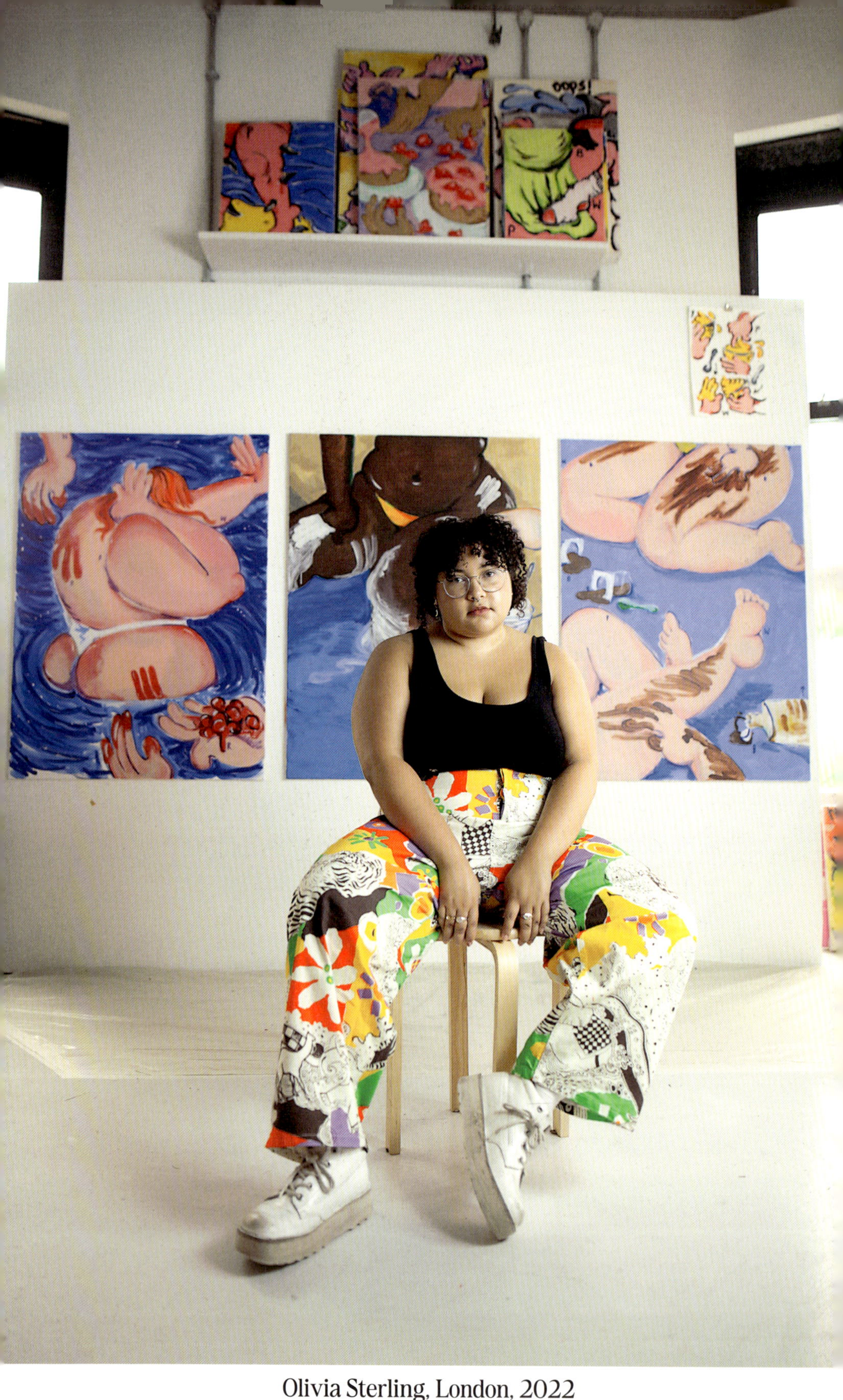

Olivia Sterling, London, 2022

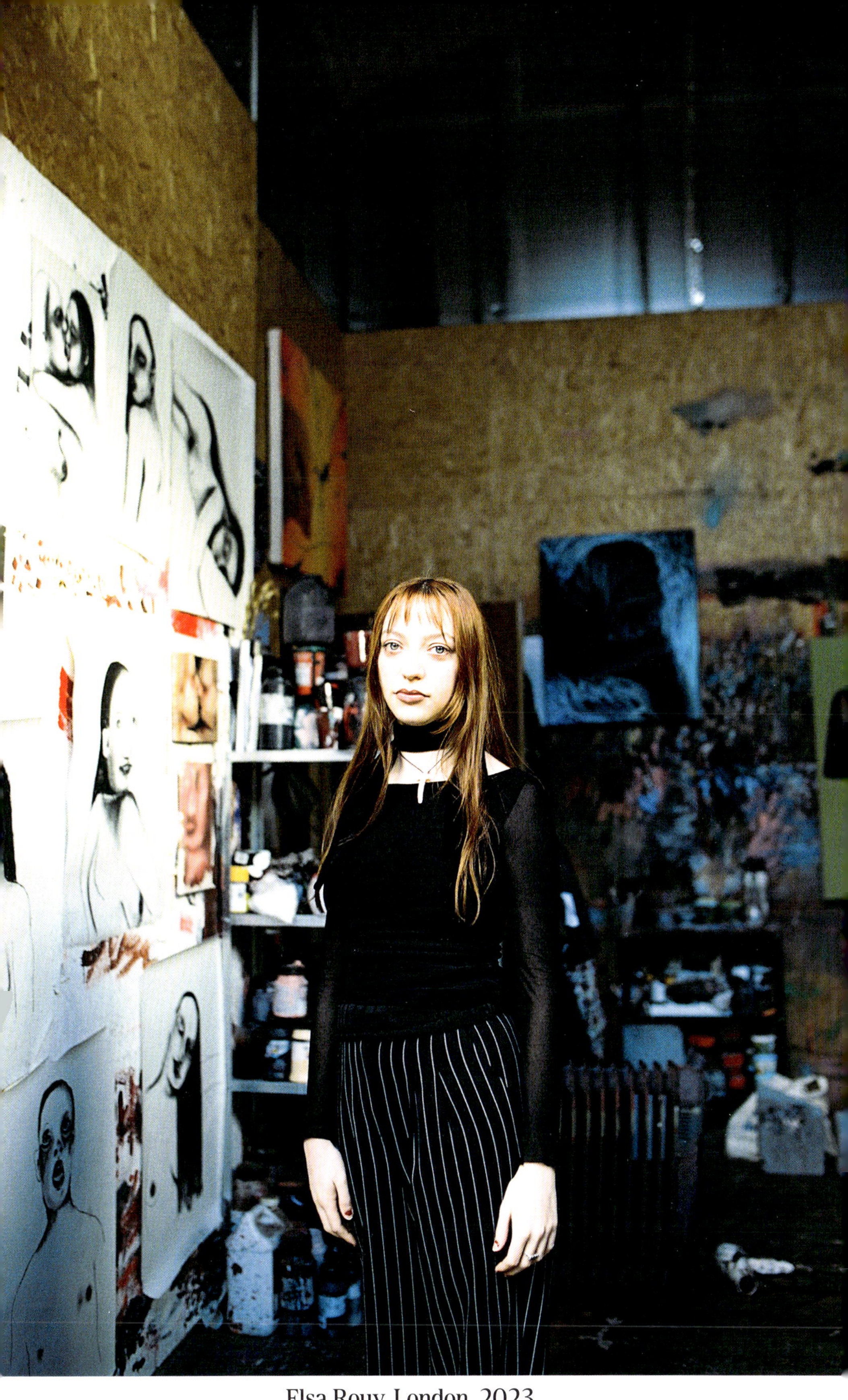

Elsa Rouy, London, 2023

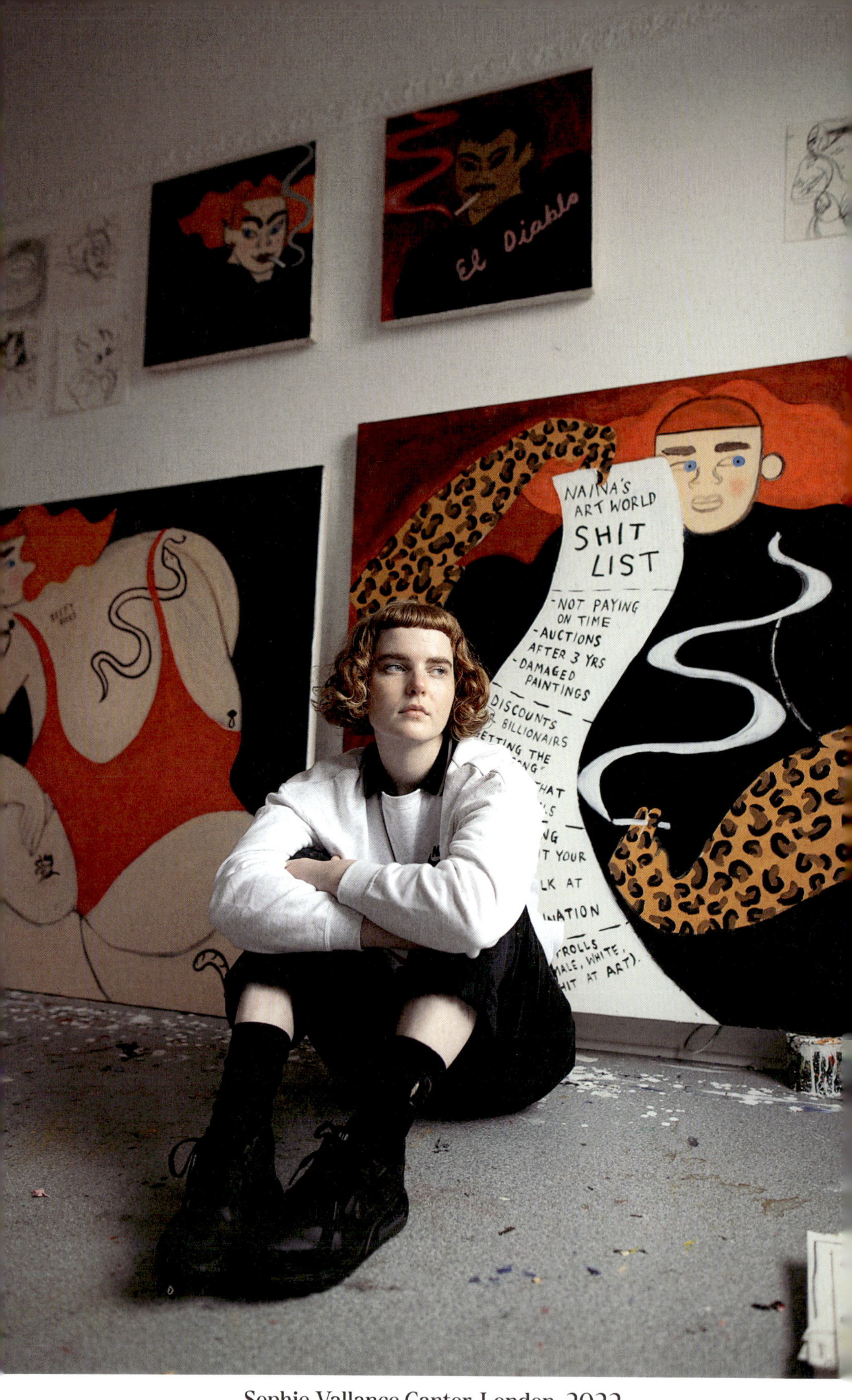

Sophie Vallance Cantor, London, 2022

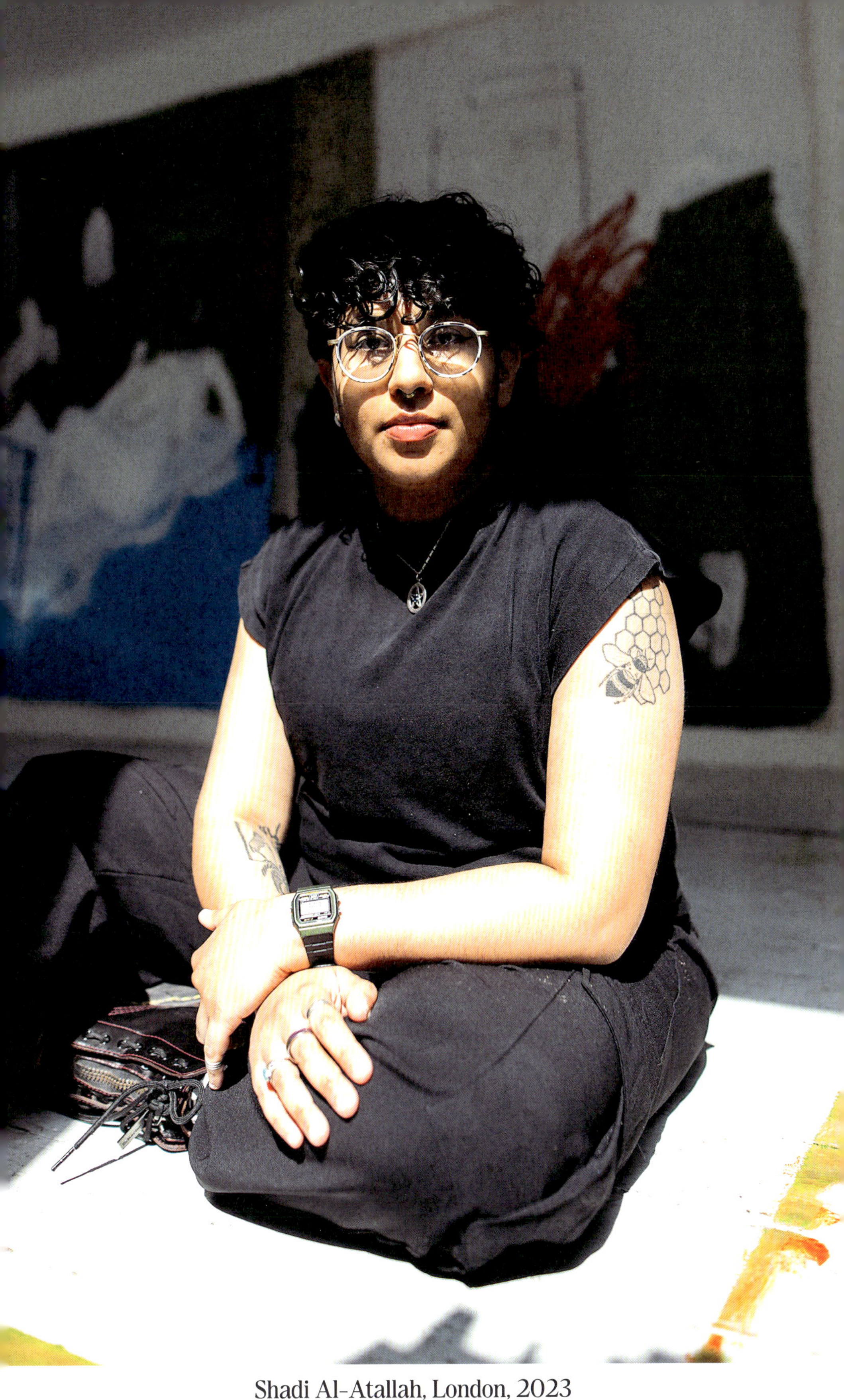

Shadi Al-Atallah, London, 2023

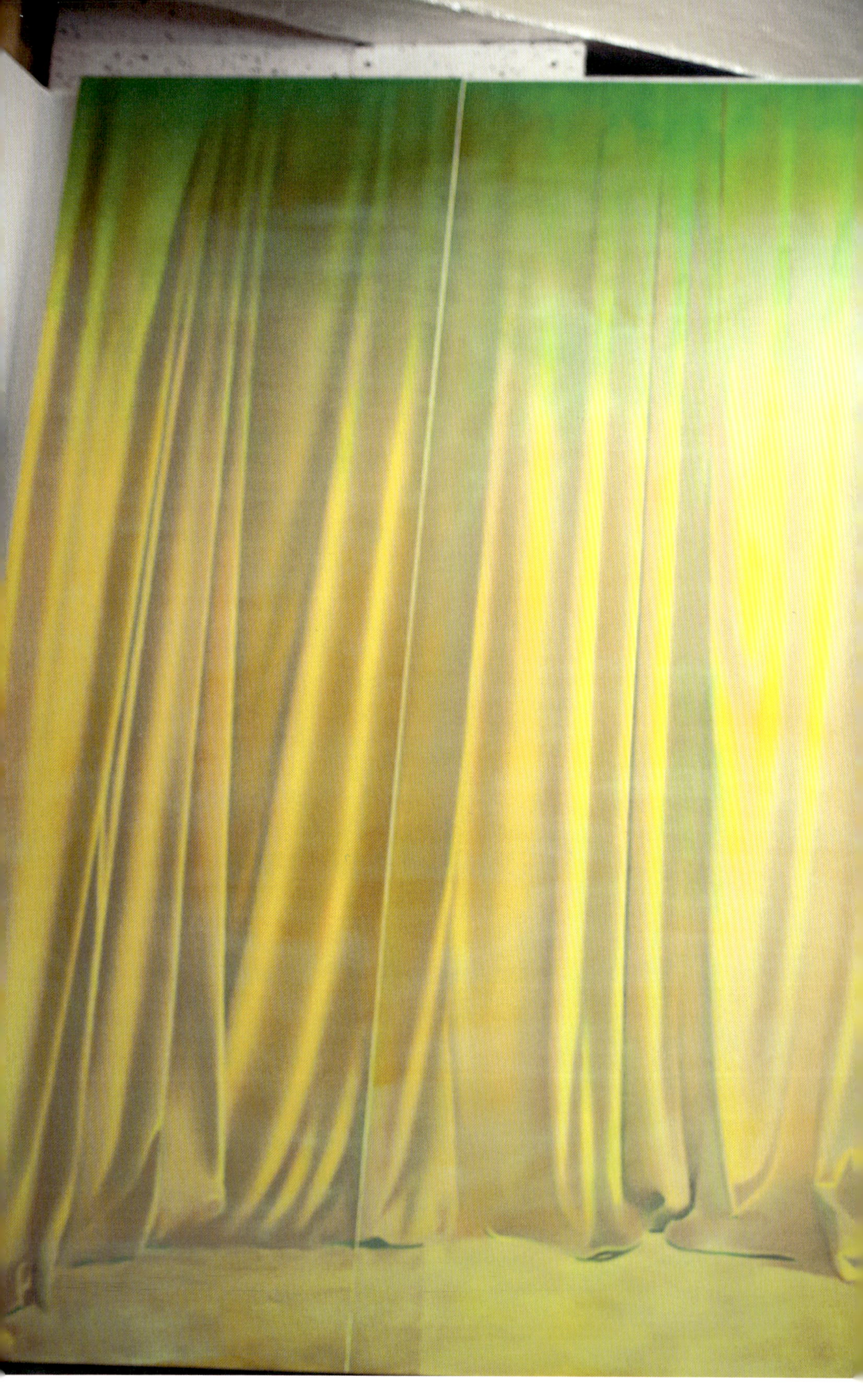

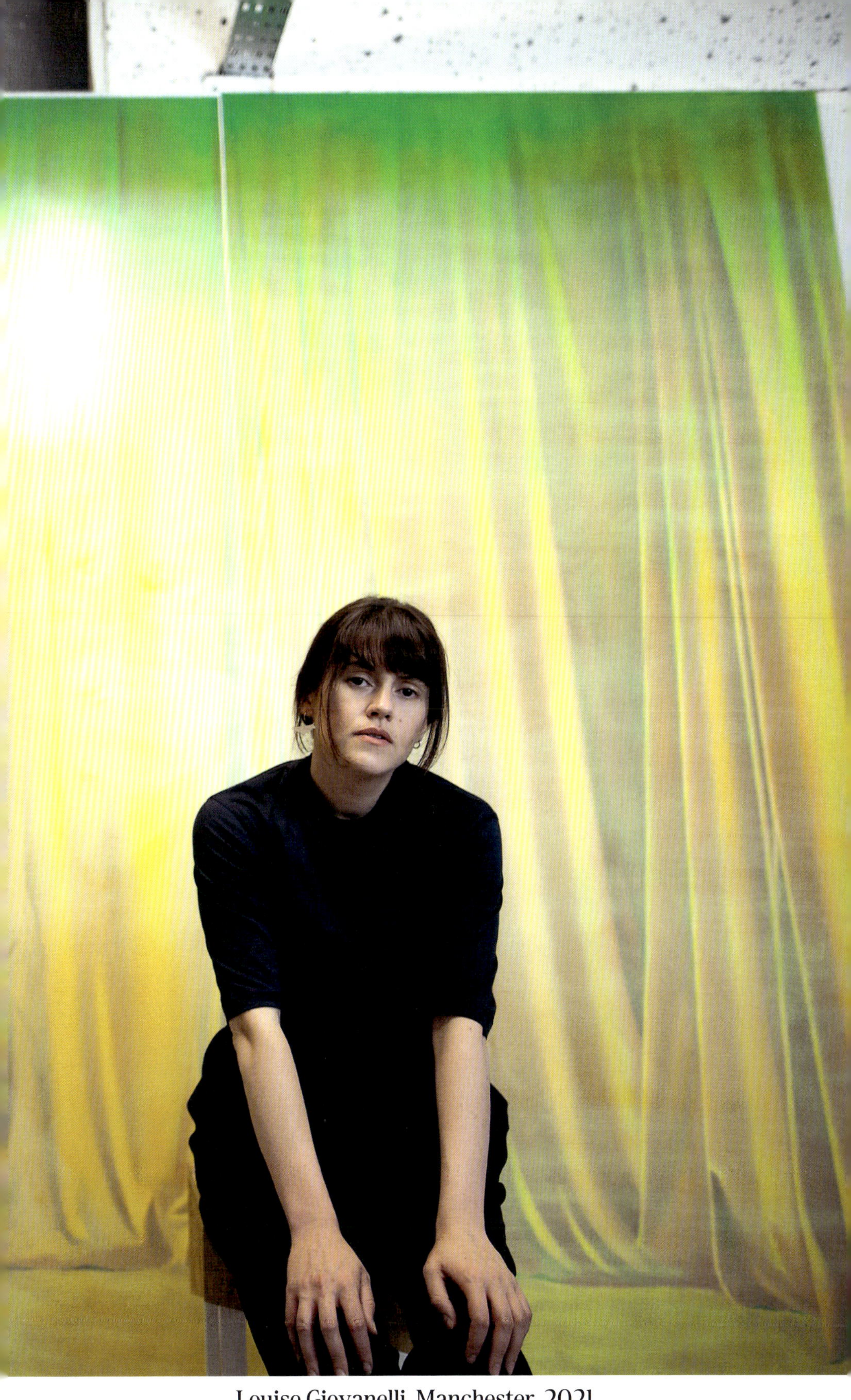

Louise Giovanelli, Manchester, 2021

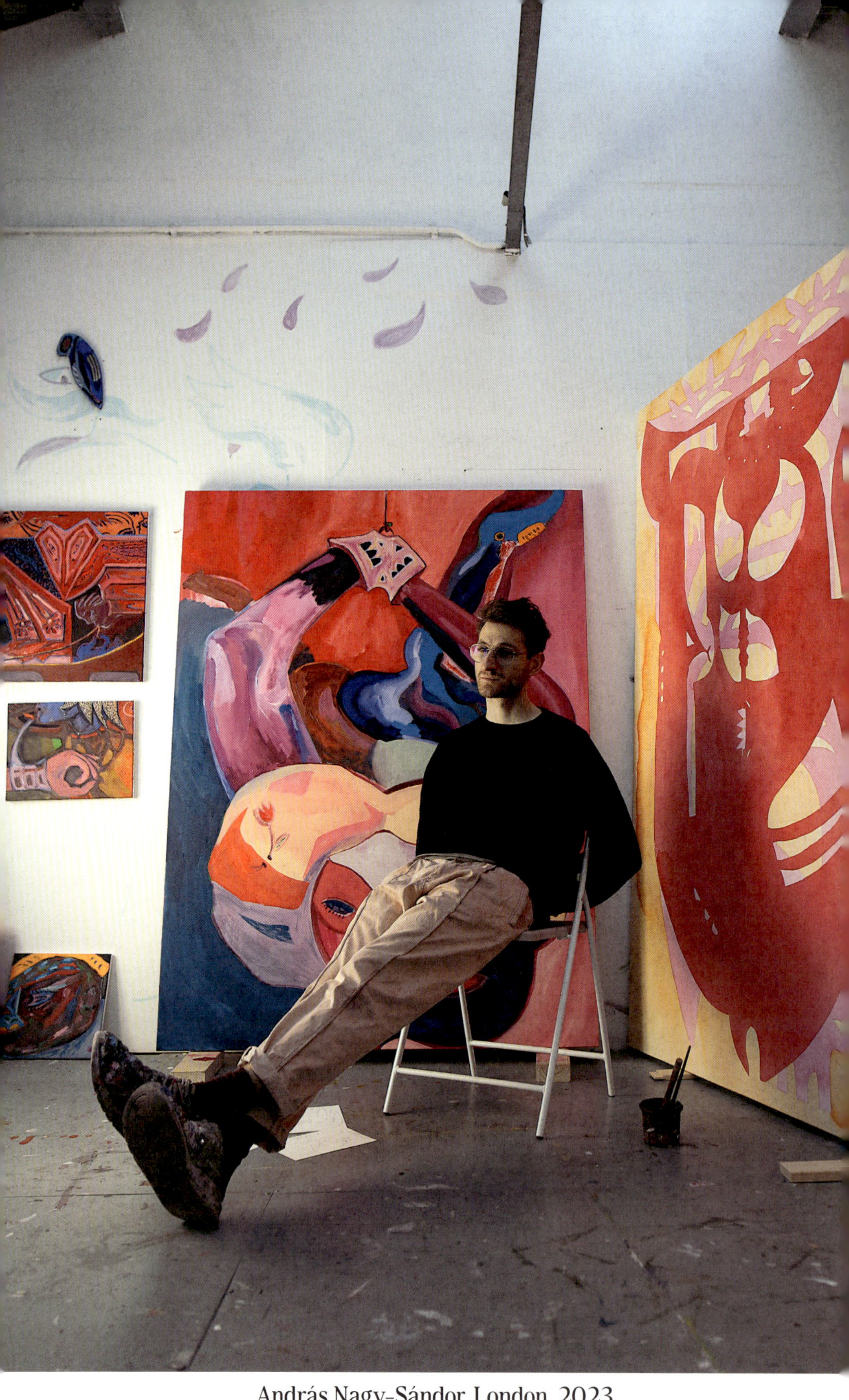

András Nagy–Sándor, London, 2023

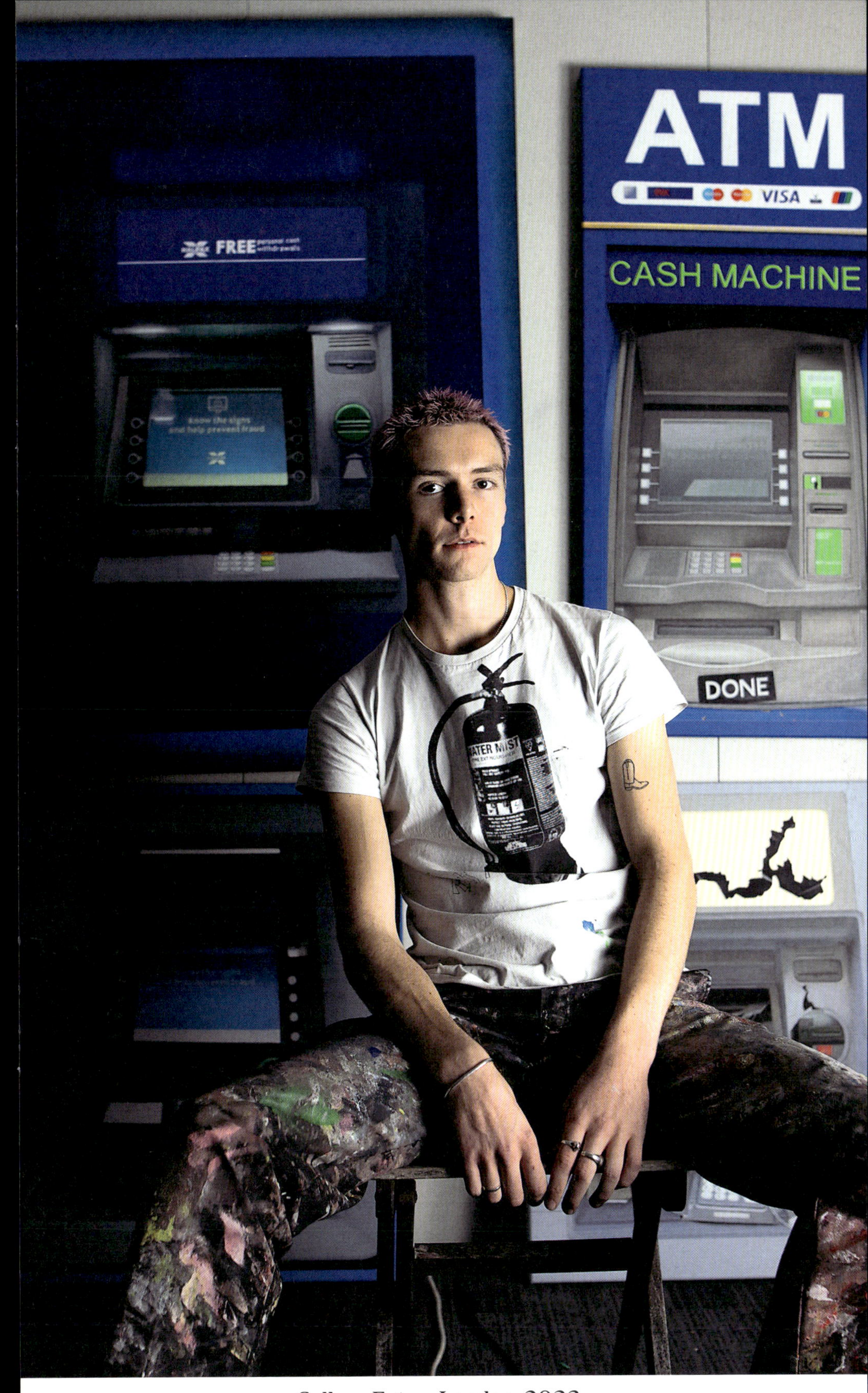

Callum Eaton, London, 2023

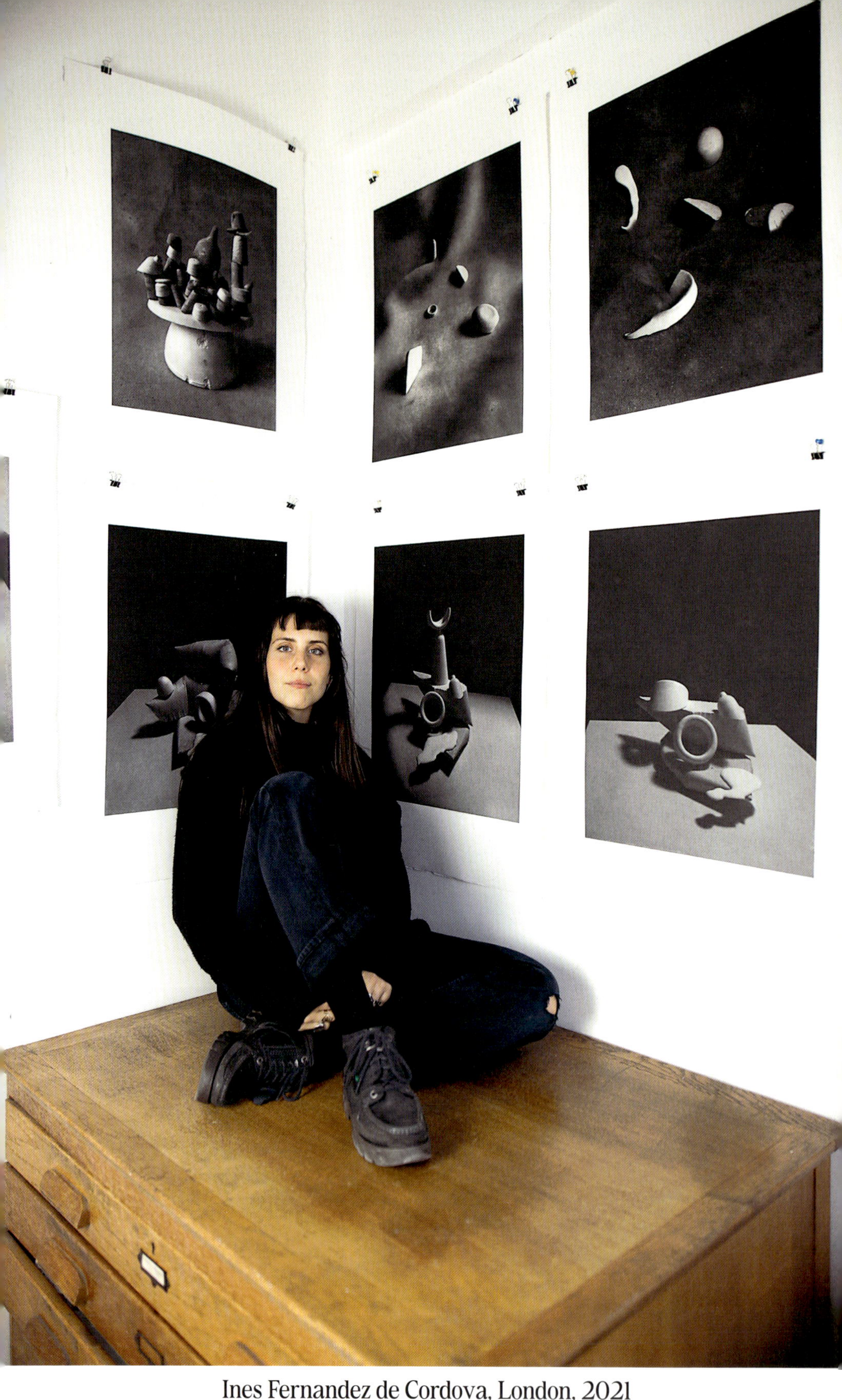

Ines Fernandez de Cordova, London, 2021

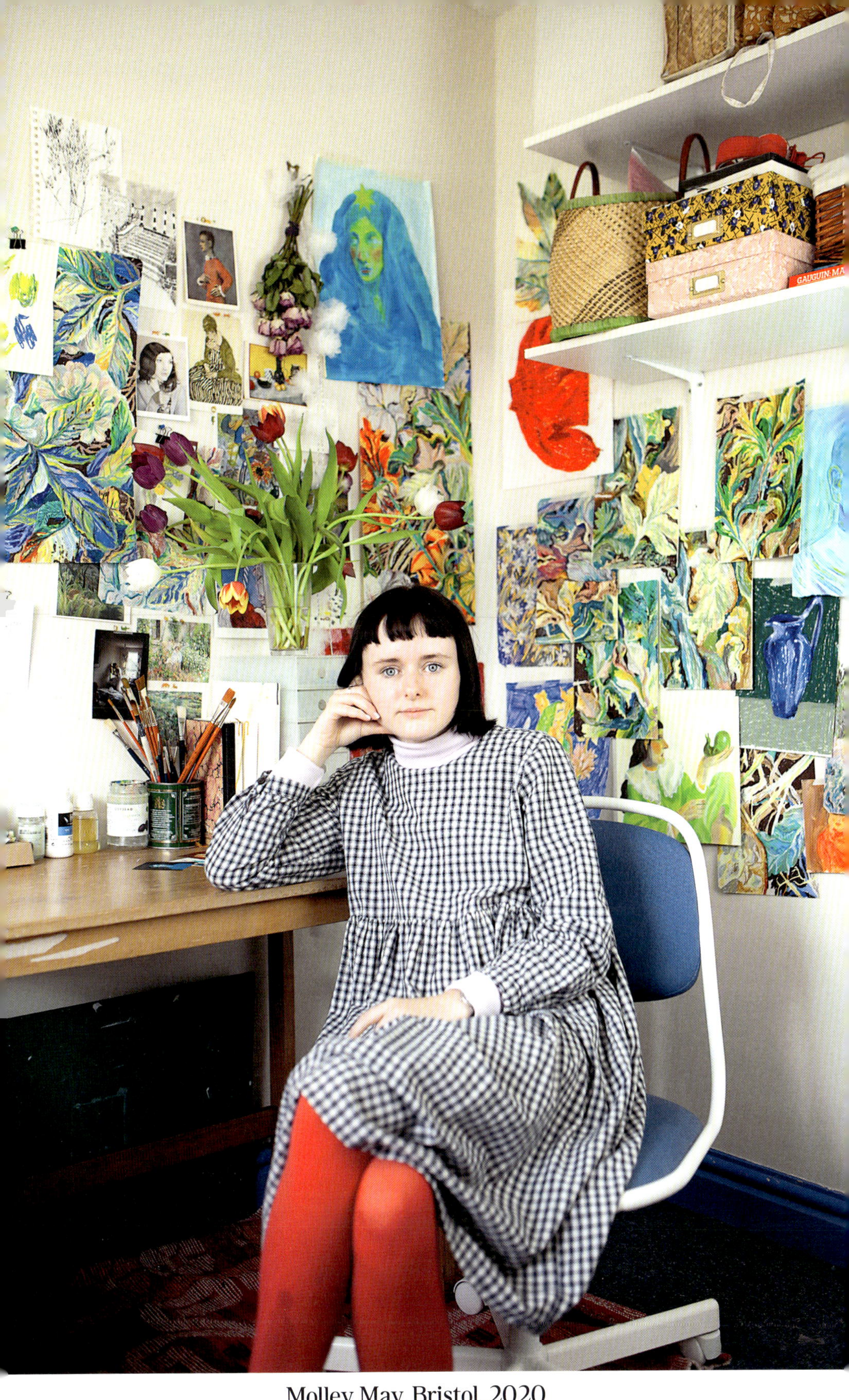

Molley May, Bristol, 2020

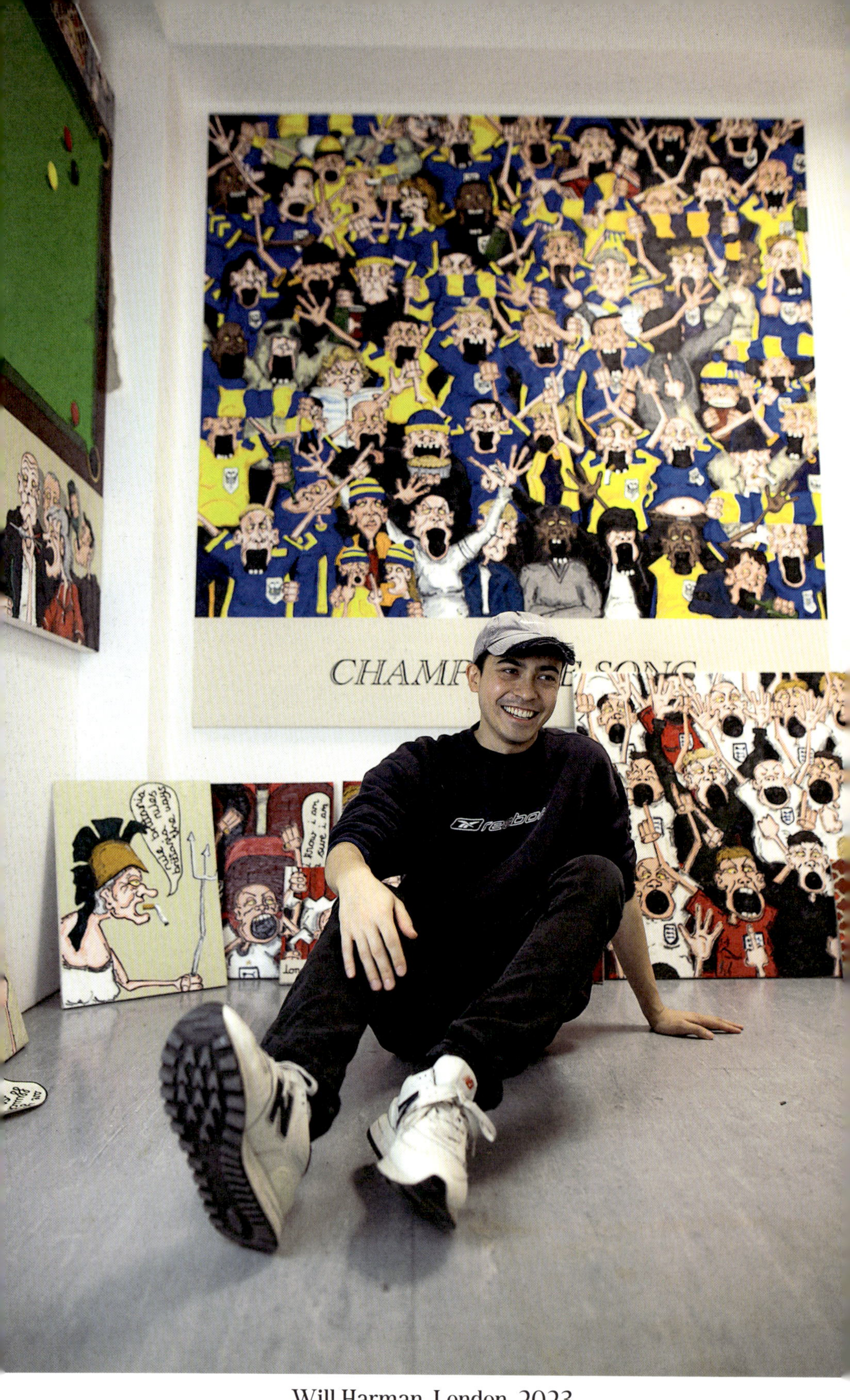

Will Harman, London, 2023

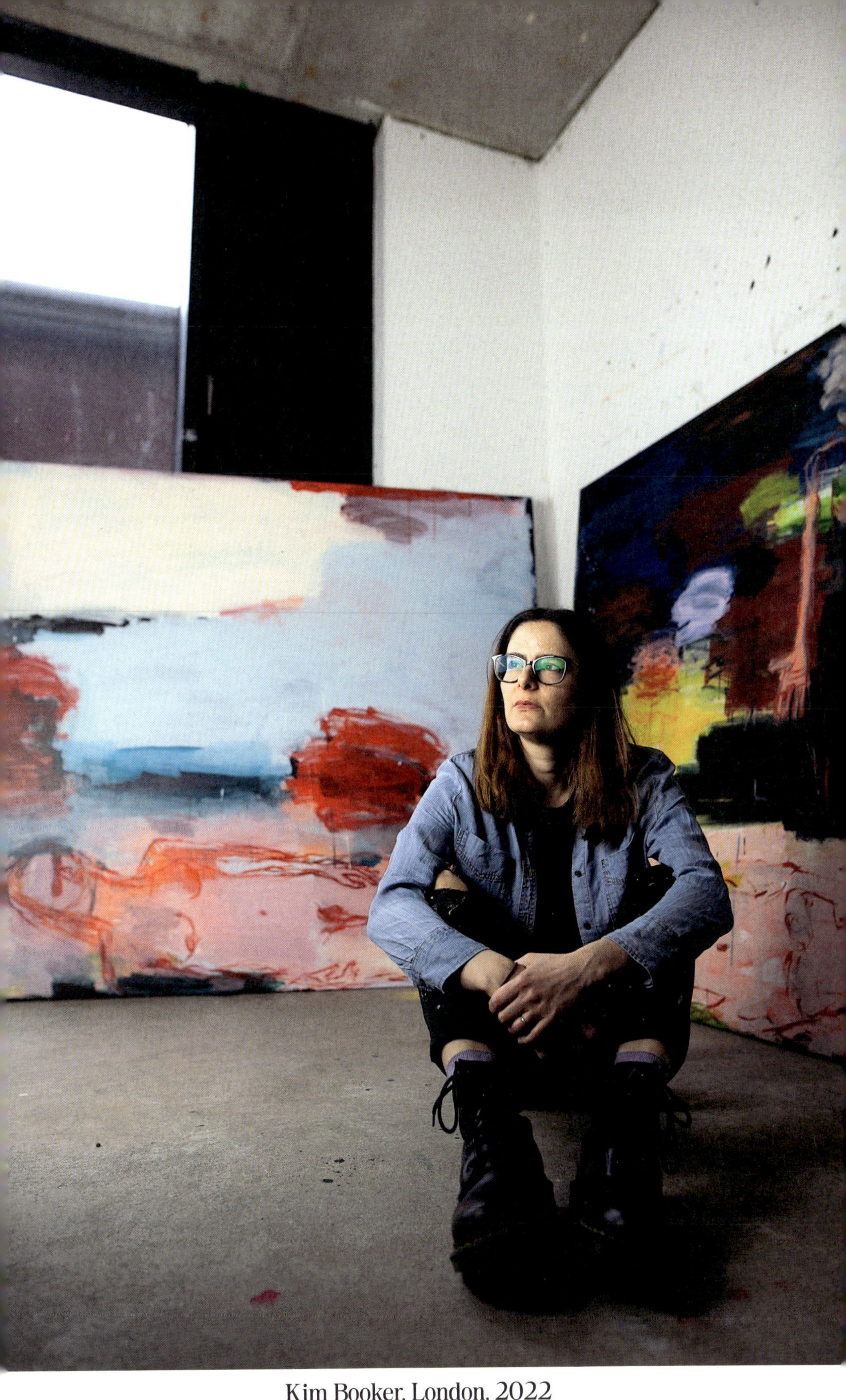

Kim Booker, London, 2022

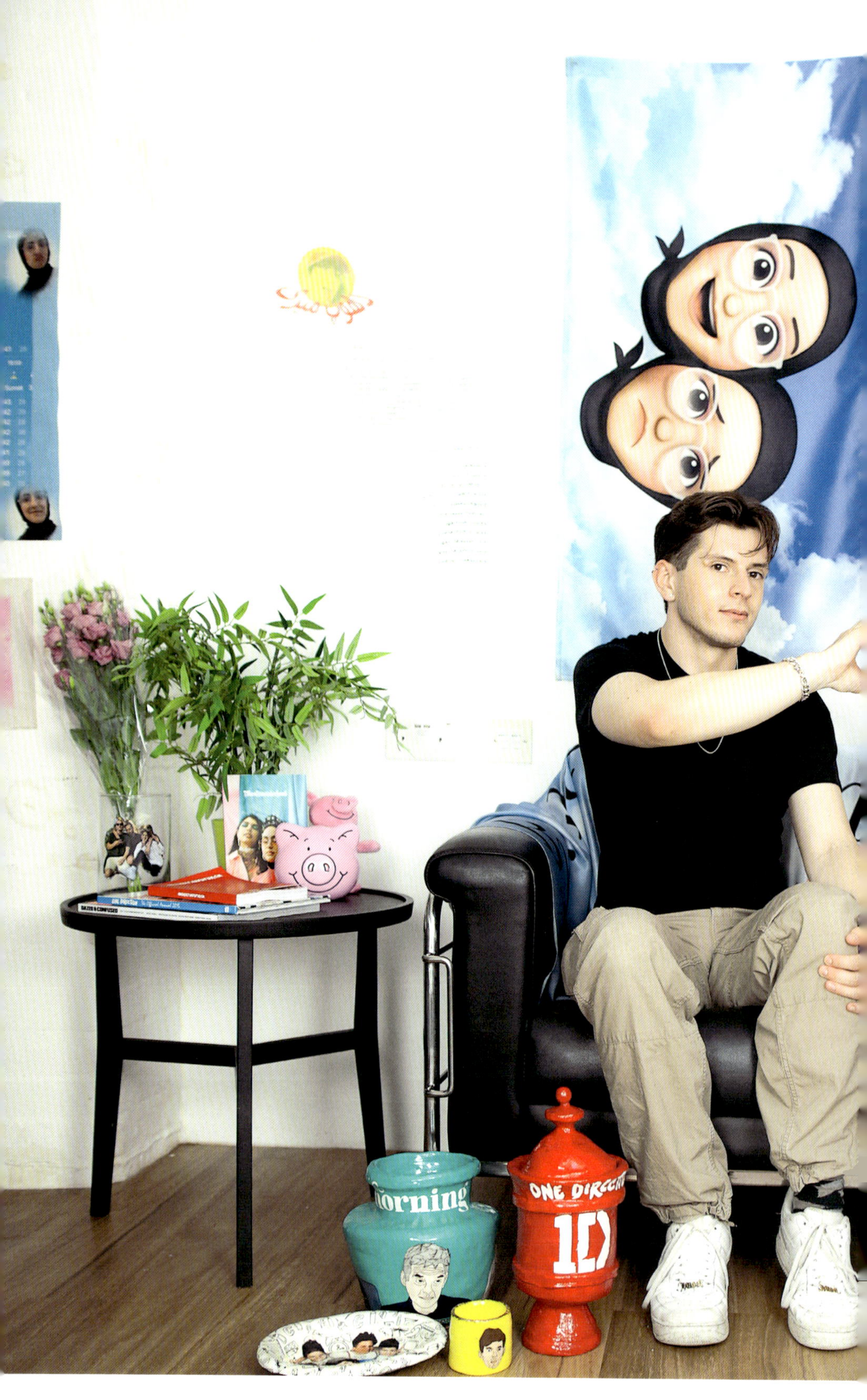

orning
ONE DIRECTION
1D

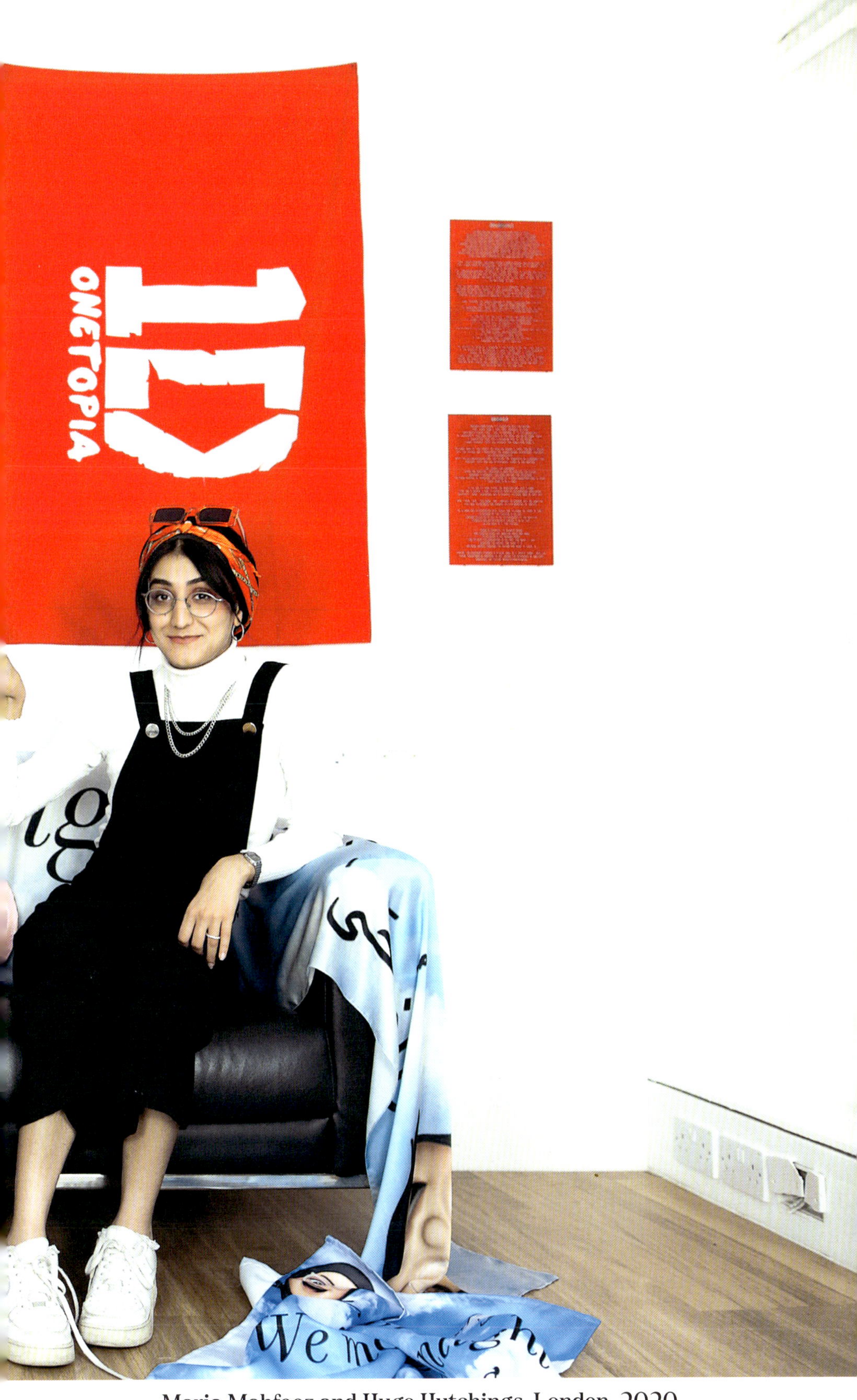

Maria Mahfooz and Hugo Hutchings, London, 2020

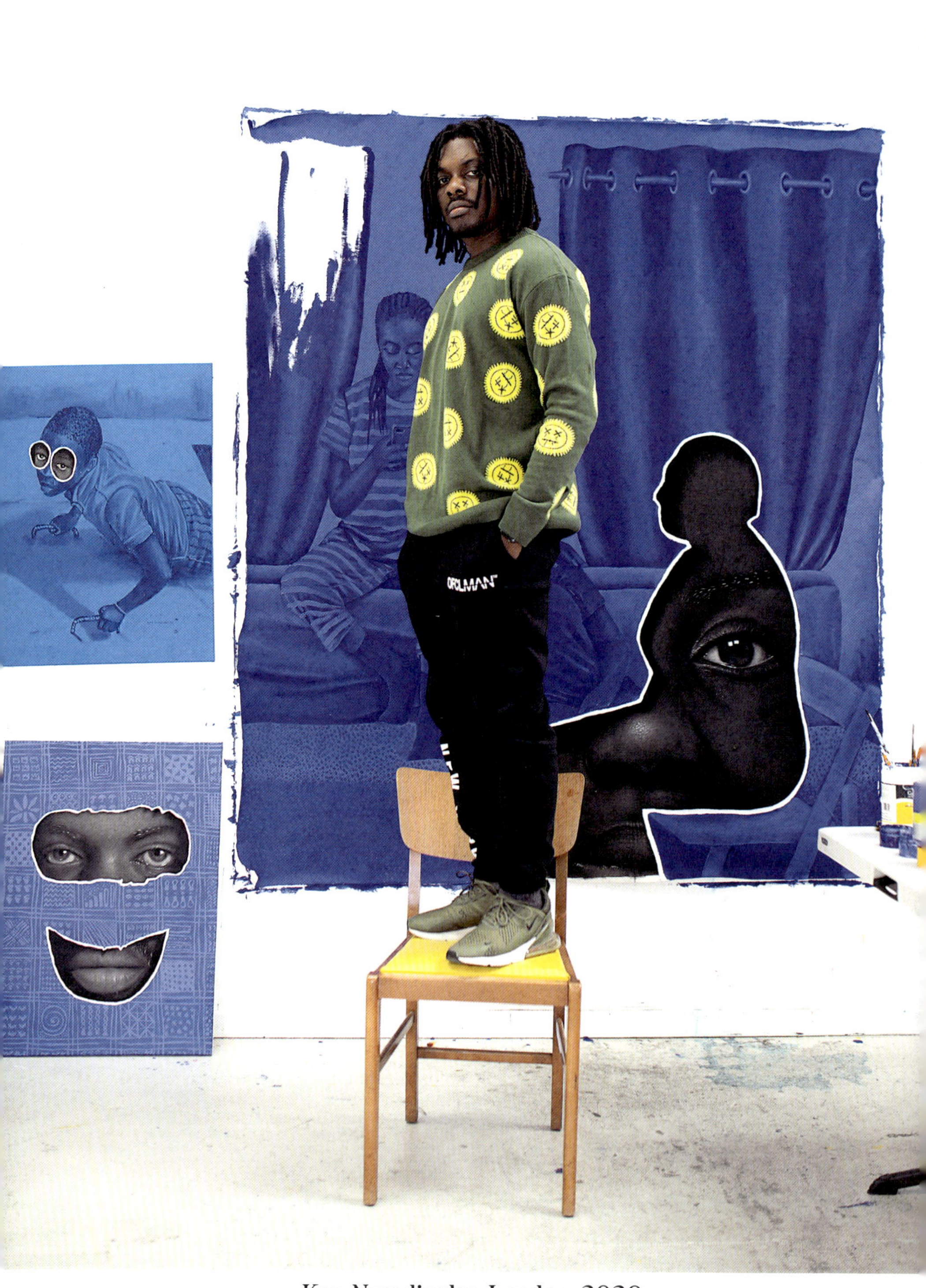

Ken Nwadiogbu, London, 2020

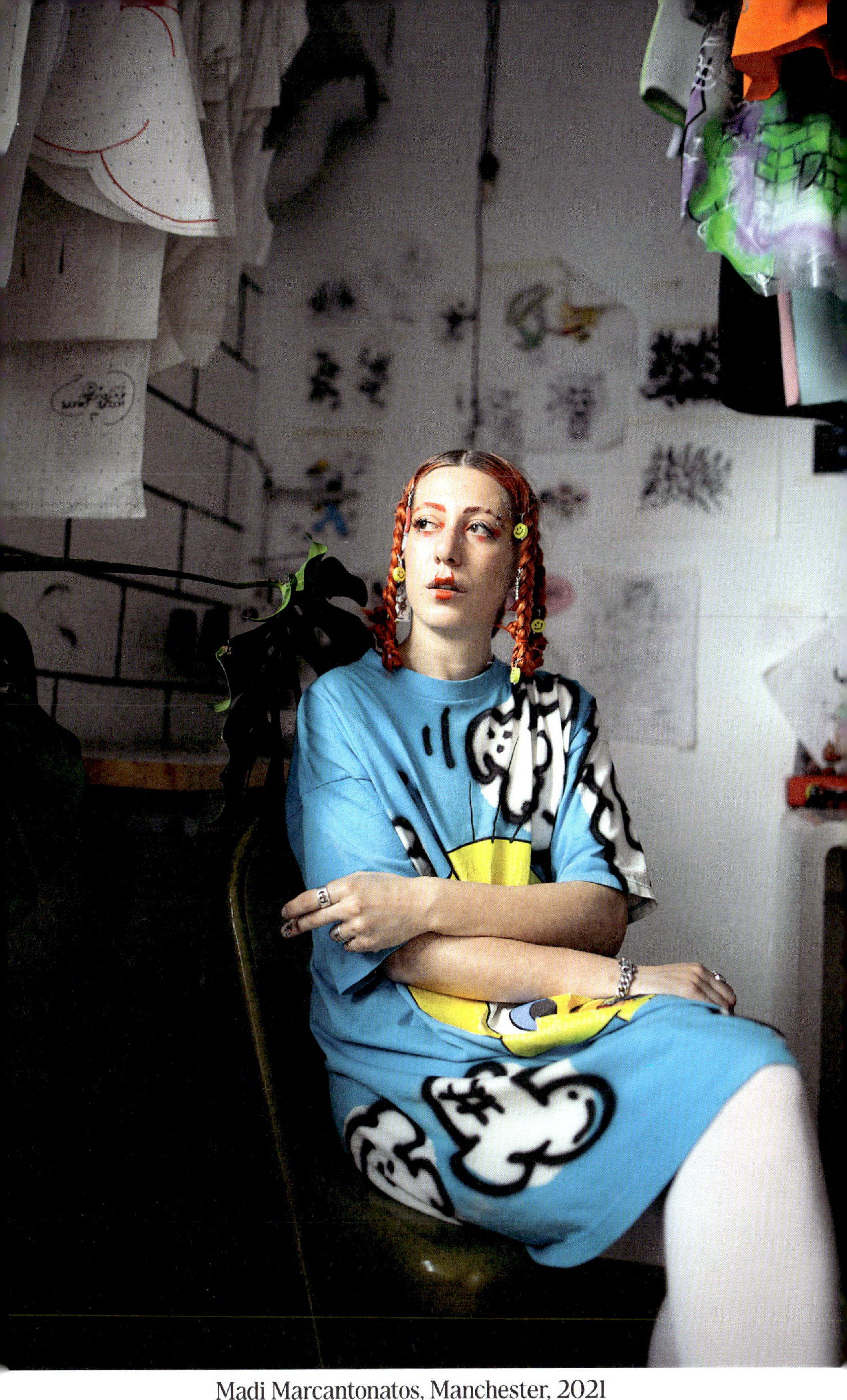

Madi Marcantonatos, Manchester, 2021

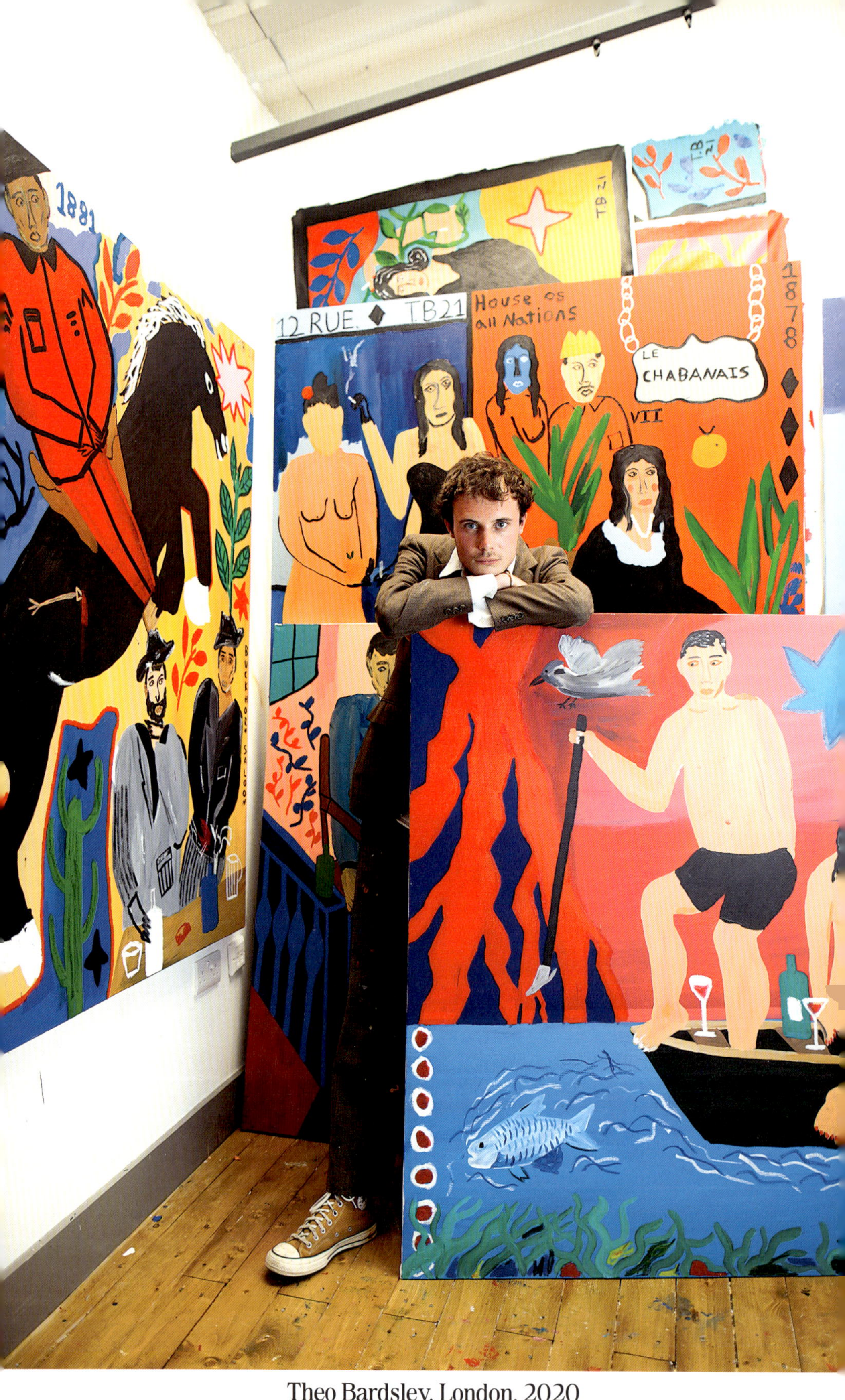

Theo Bardsley, London, 2020

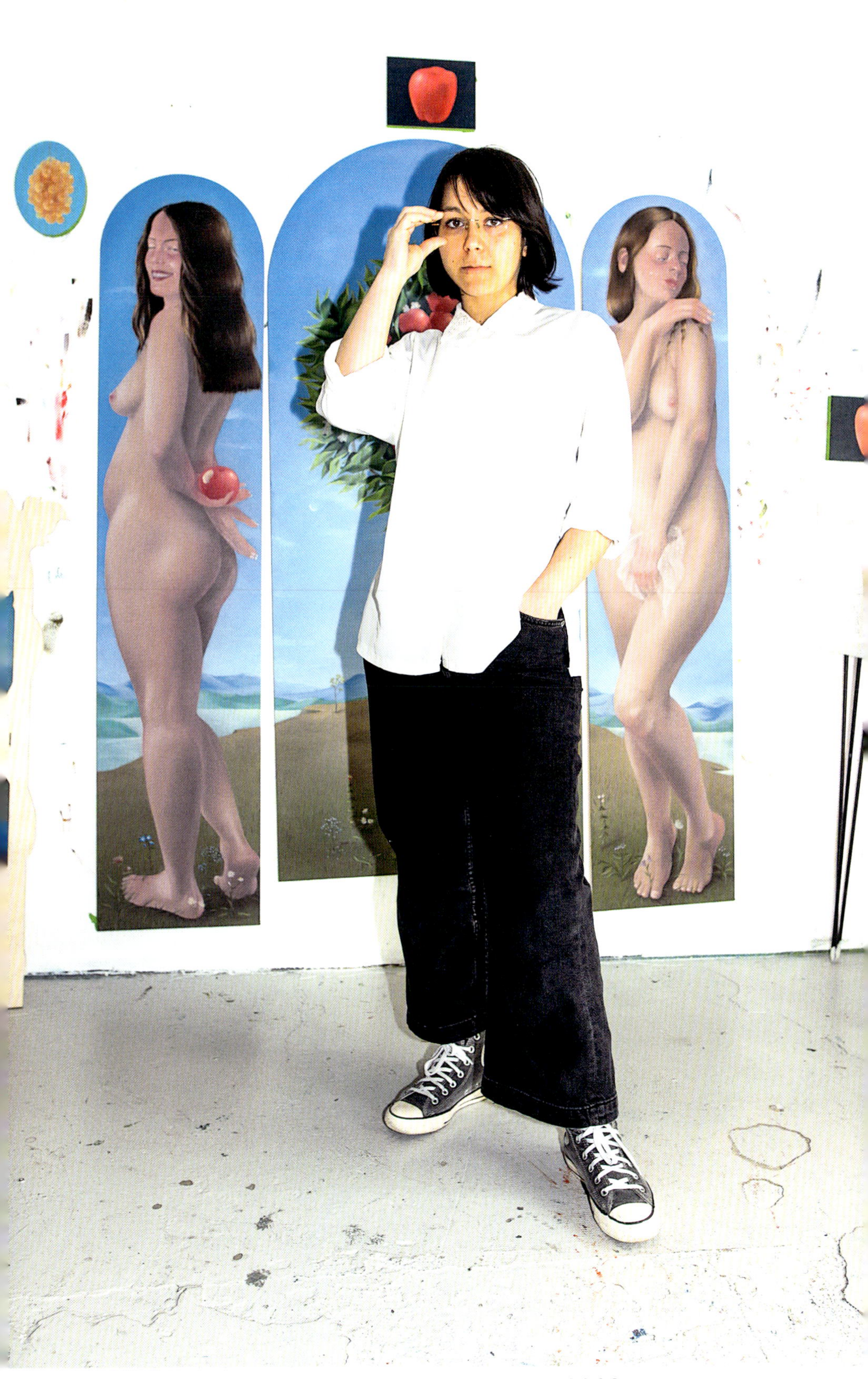

Natalia González Martín, London, 2022

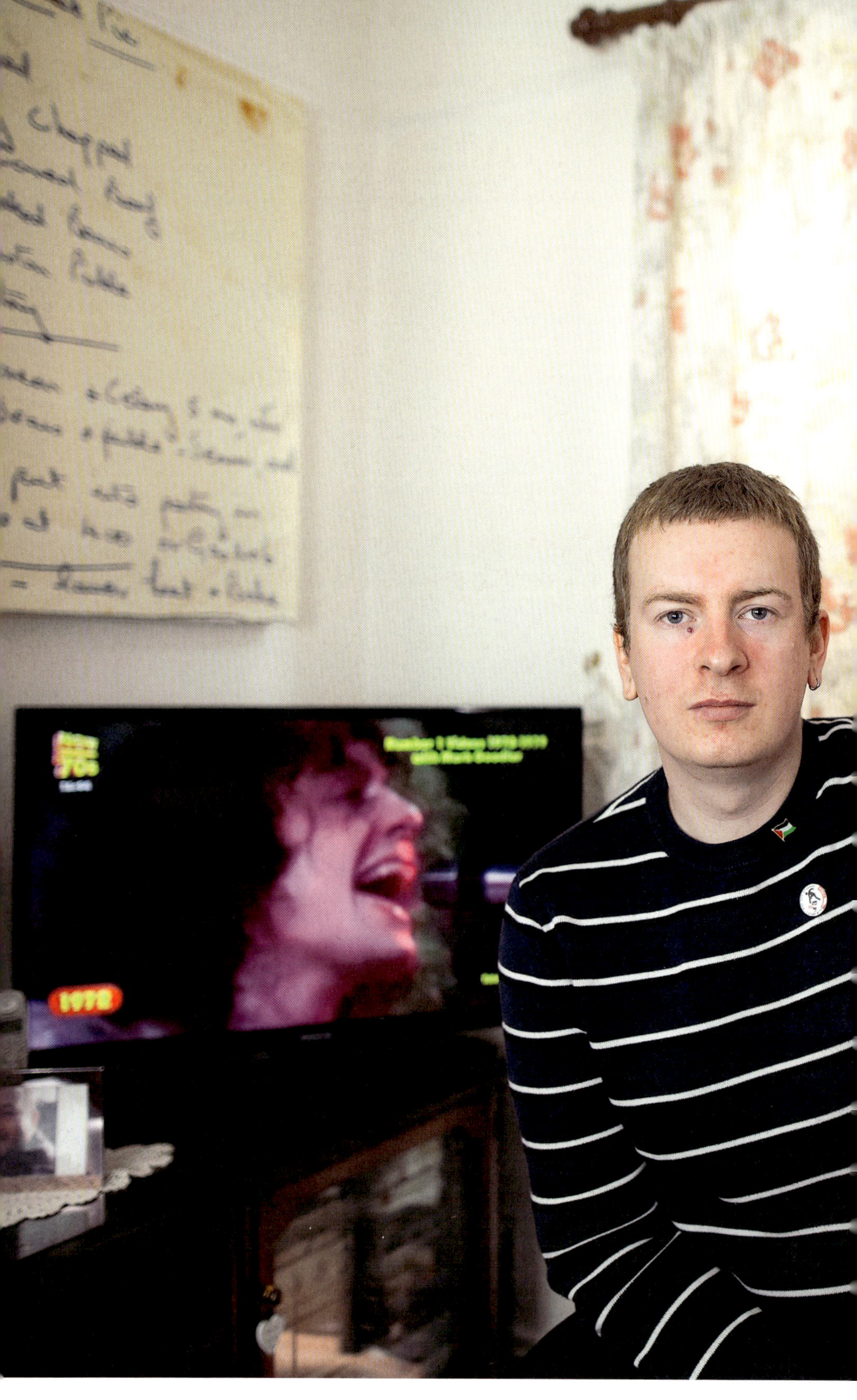

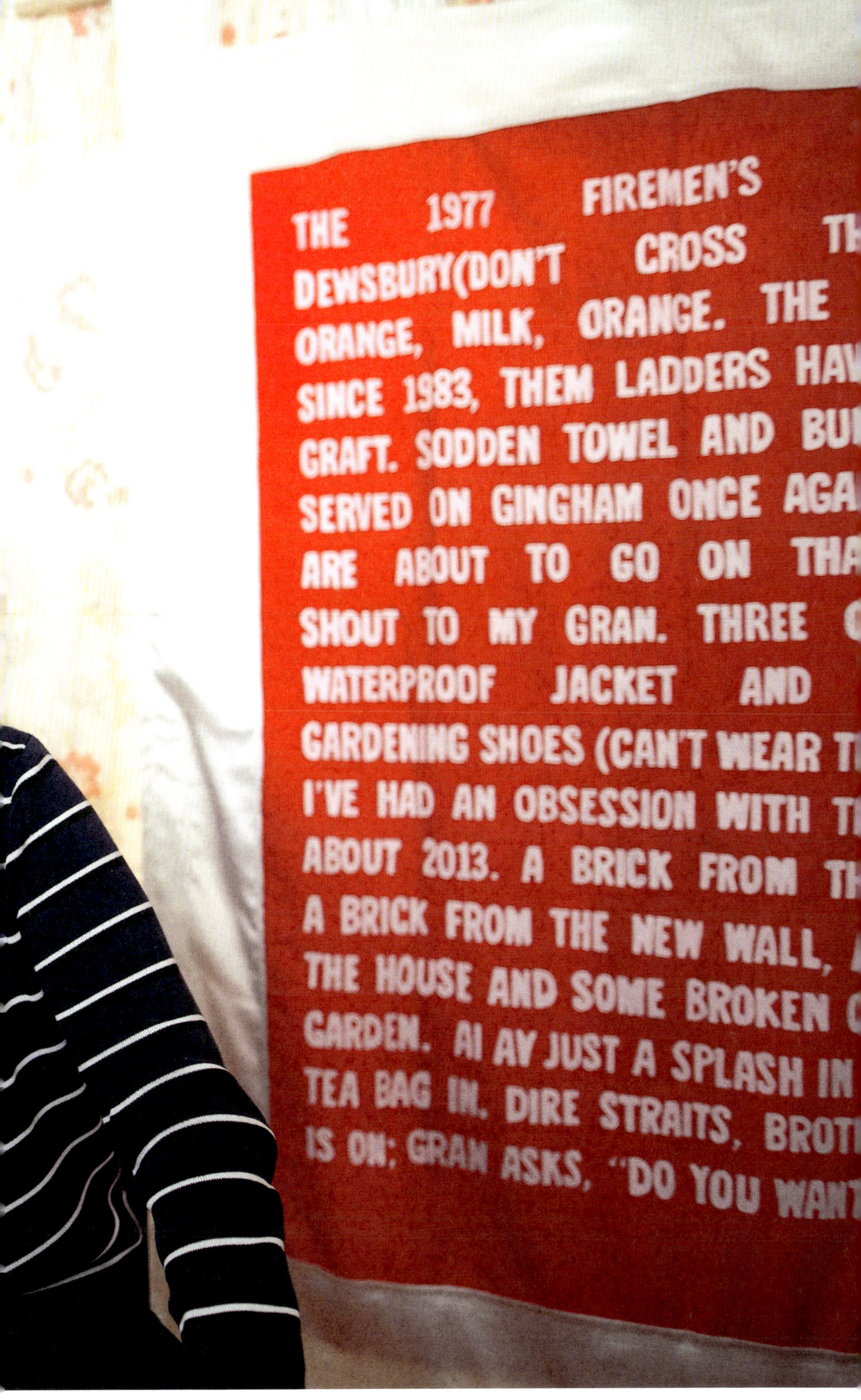

Jim Brook, Dewsbury, 2021

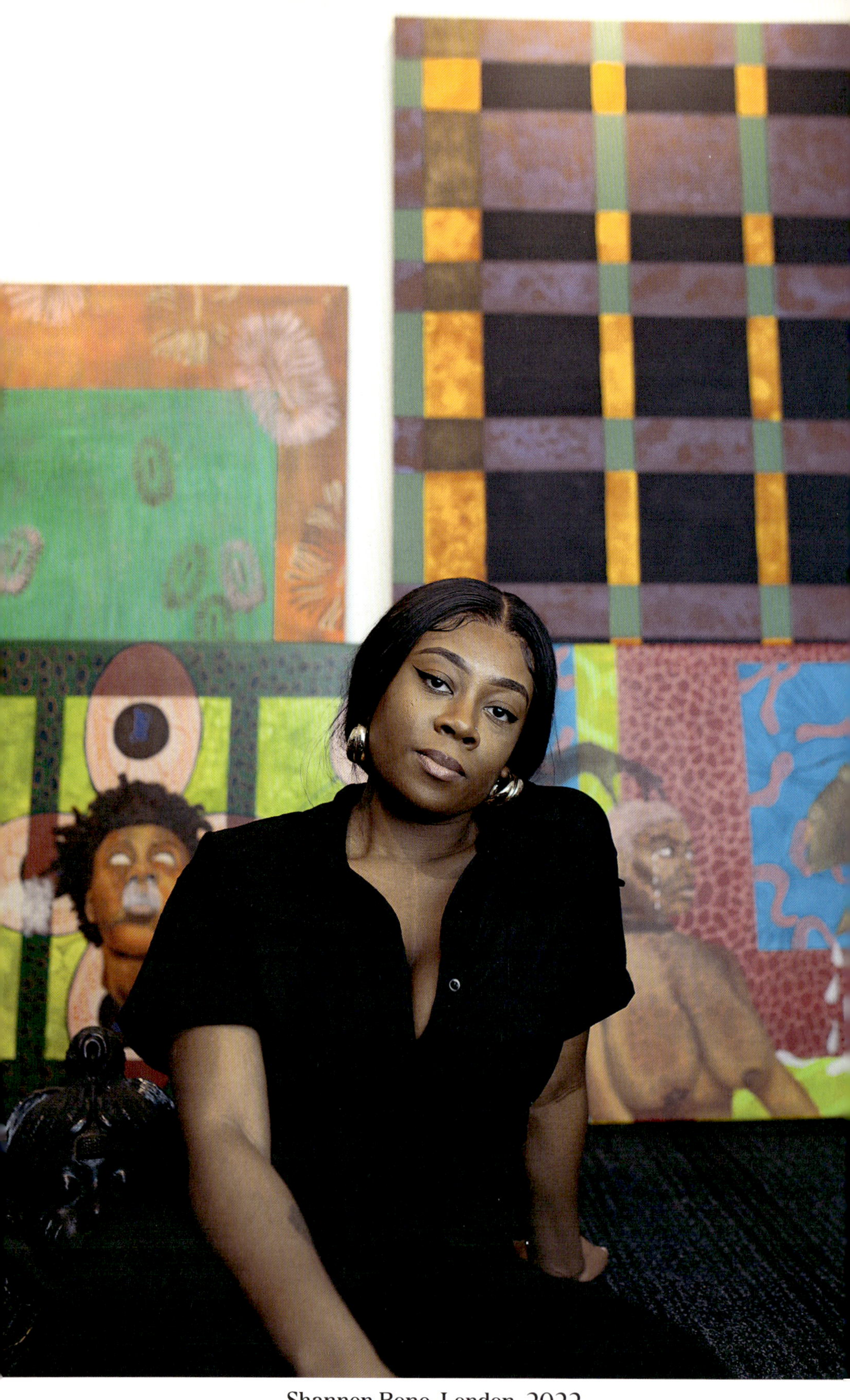

Shannon Bono, London, 2022

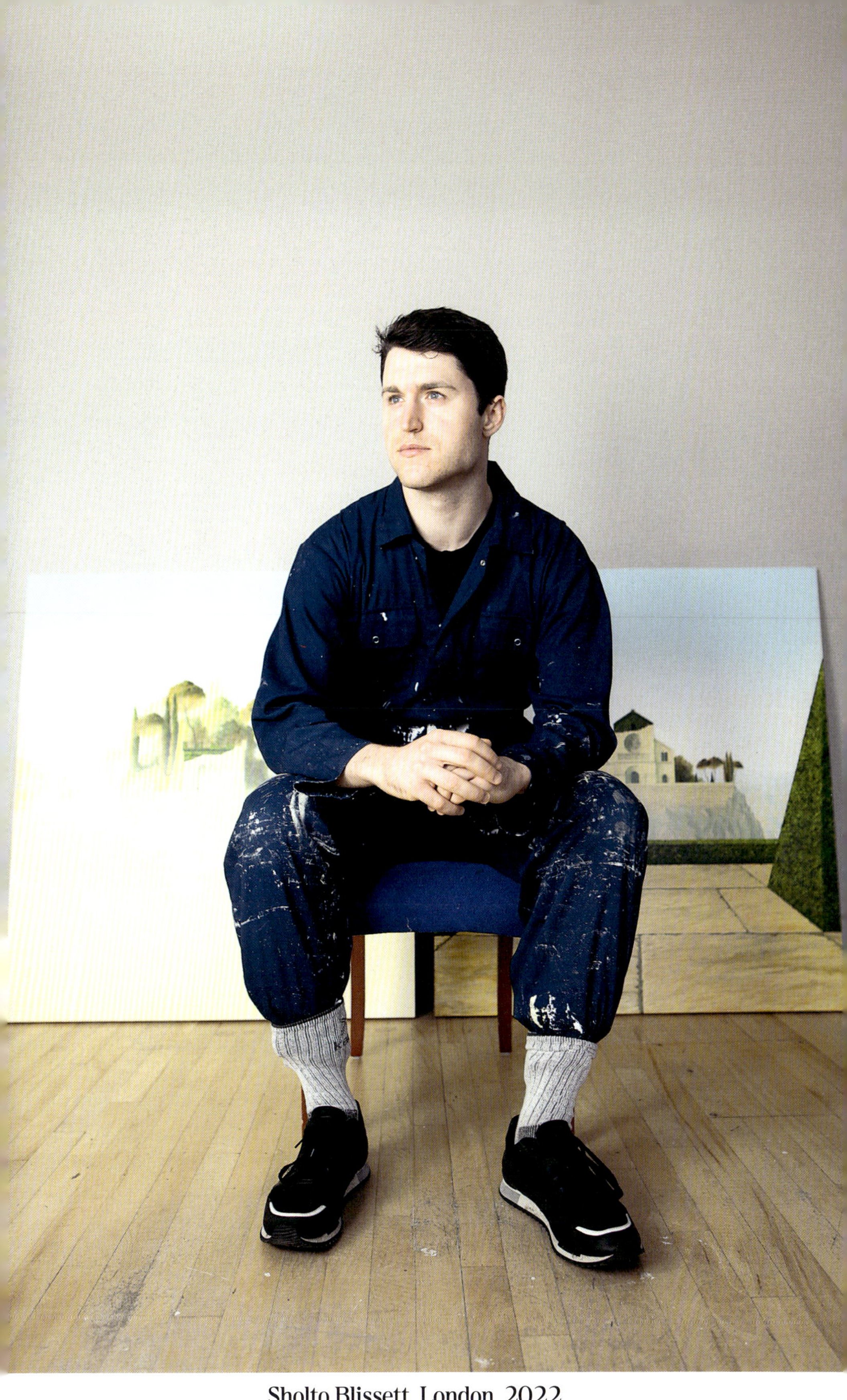

Sholto Blissett, London, 2022

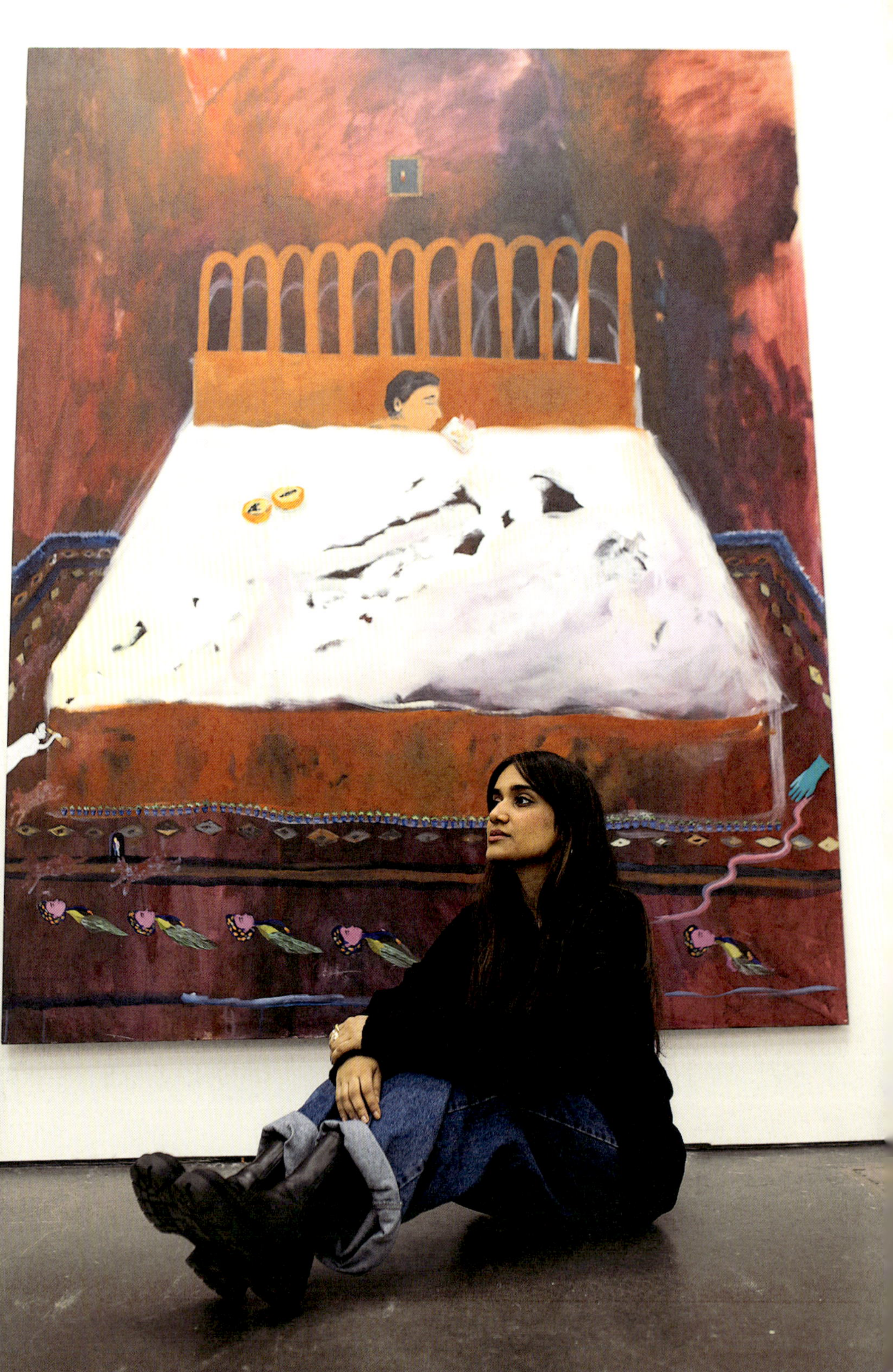

Nooraian Inam, London, 2023

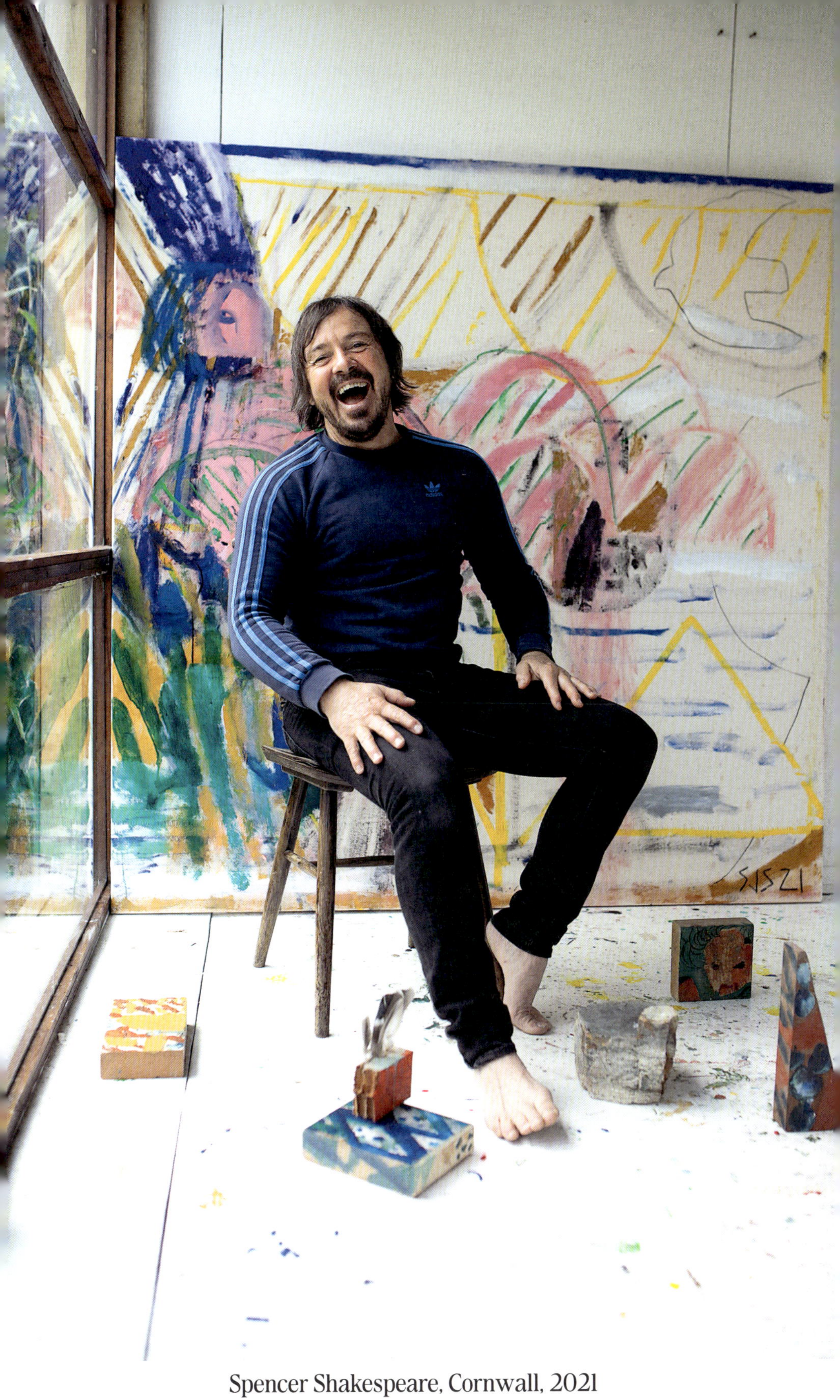

Spencer Shakespeare, Cornwall, 2021

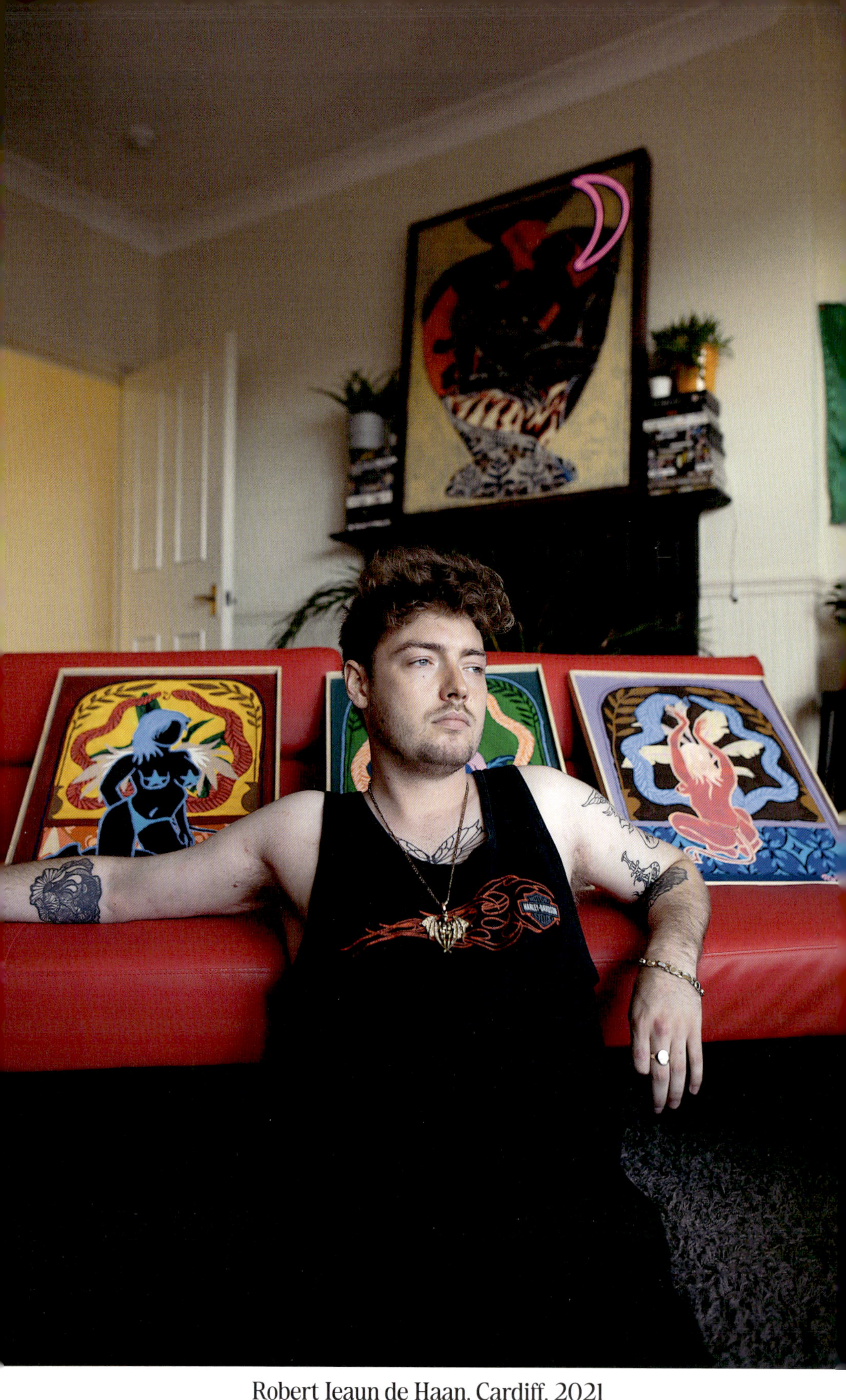

Robert Ieaun de Haan, Cardiff, 2021

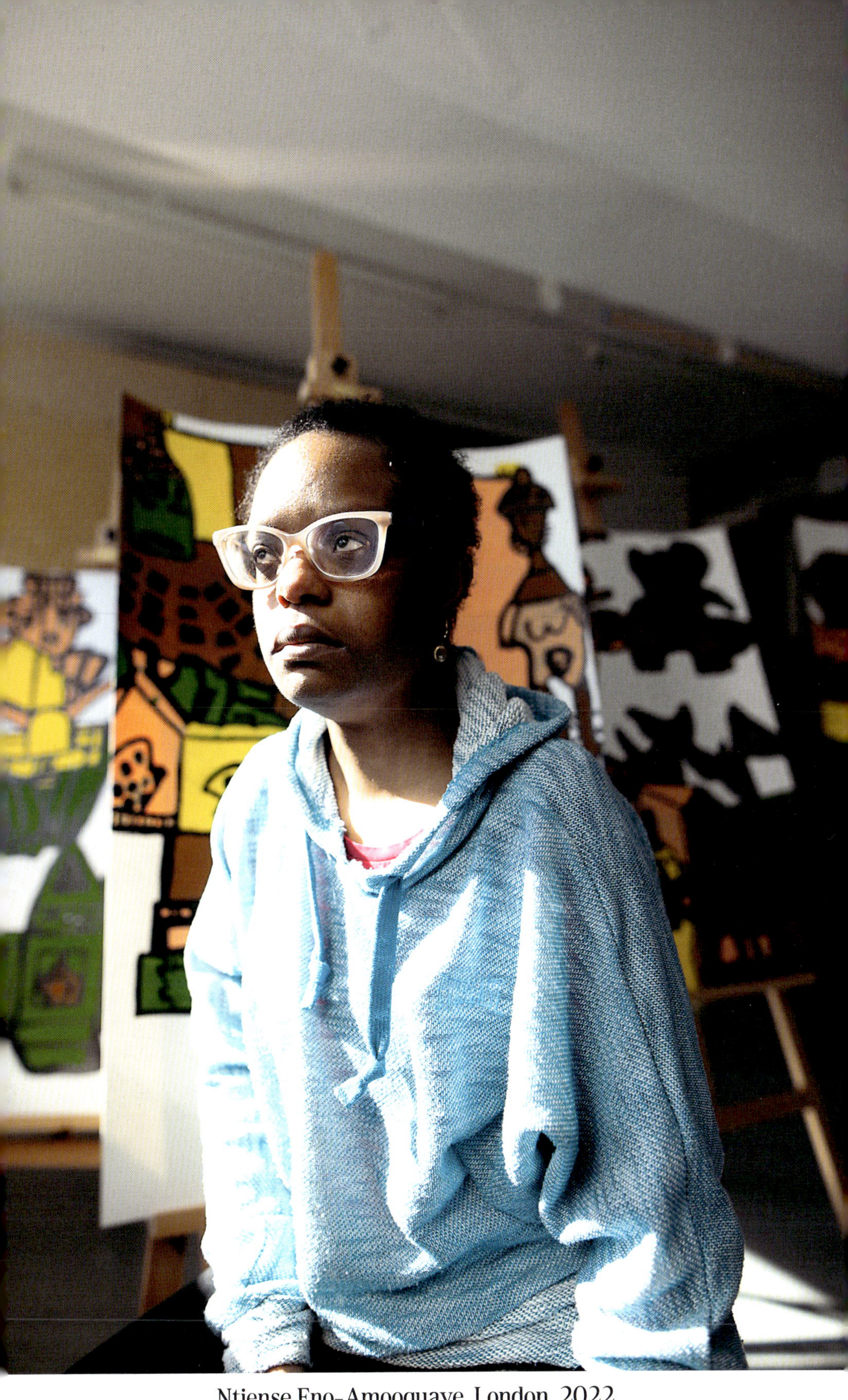

Ntiense Eno–Amooquaye, London, 2022

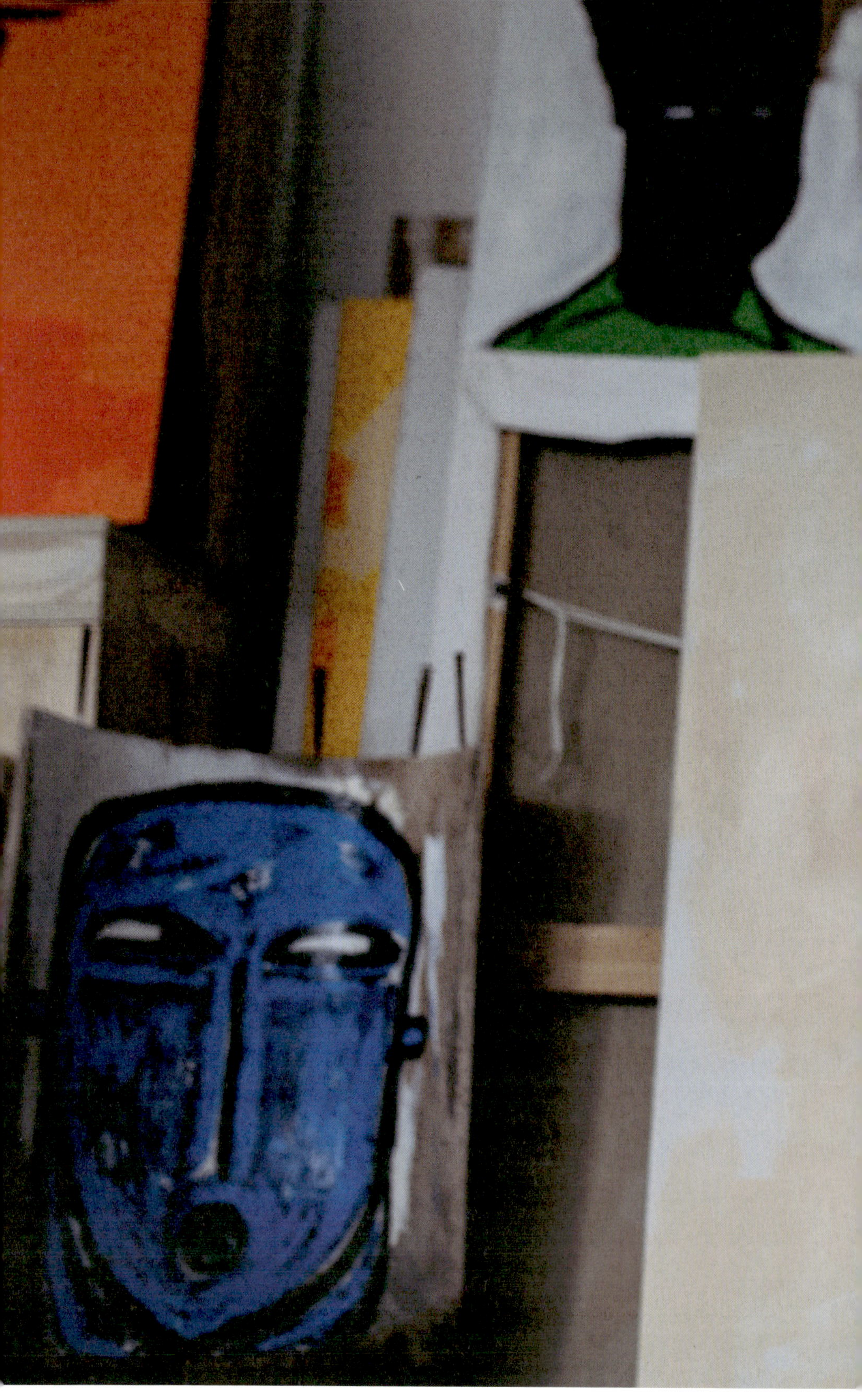

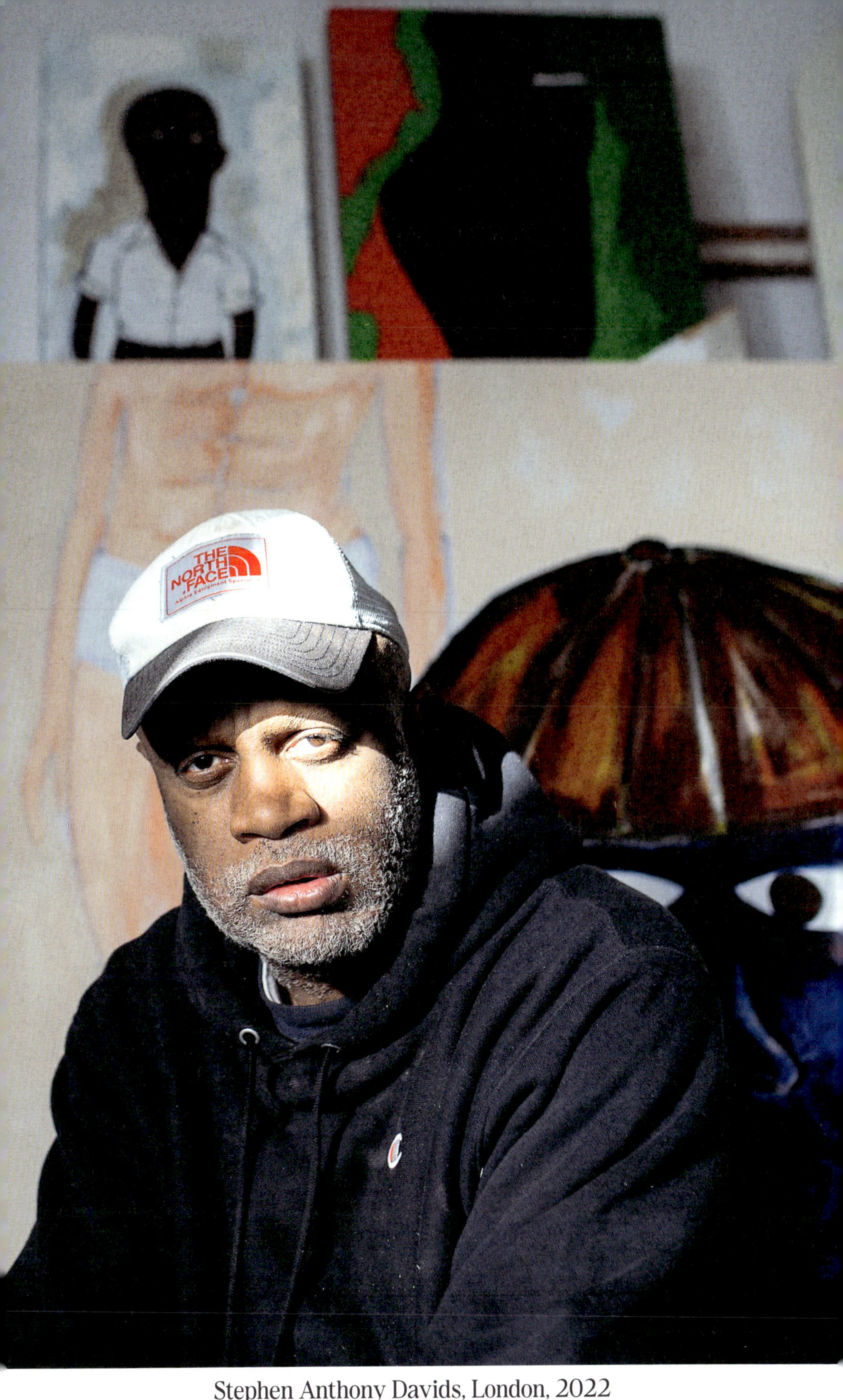

Stephen Anthony Davids, London, 2022

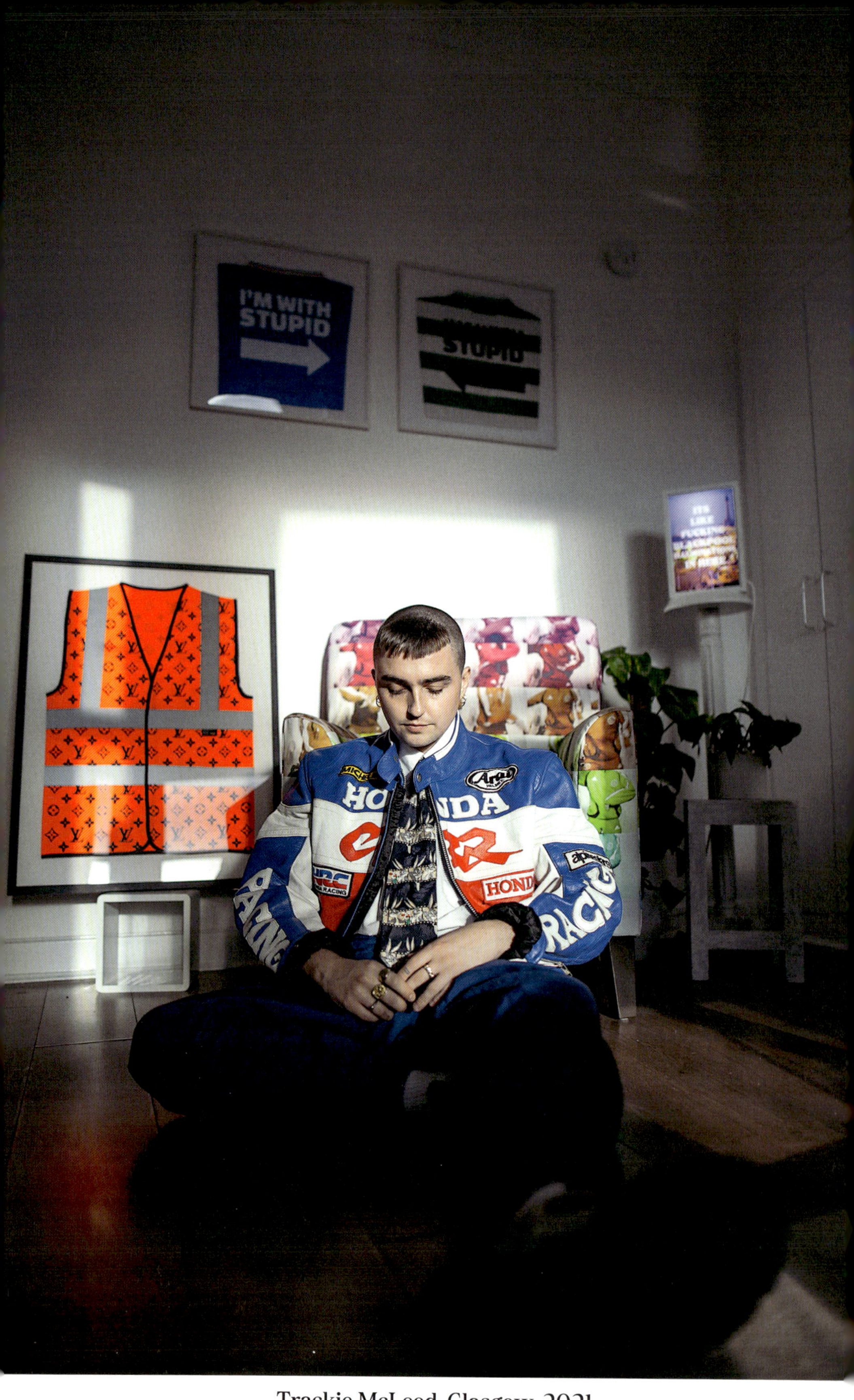

Trackie McLeod, Glasgow, 2021

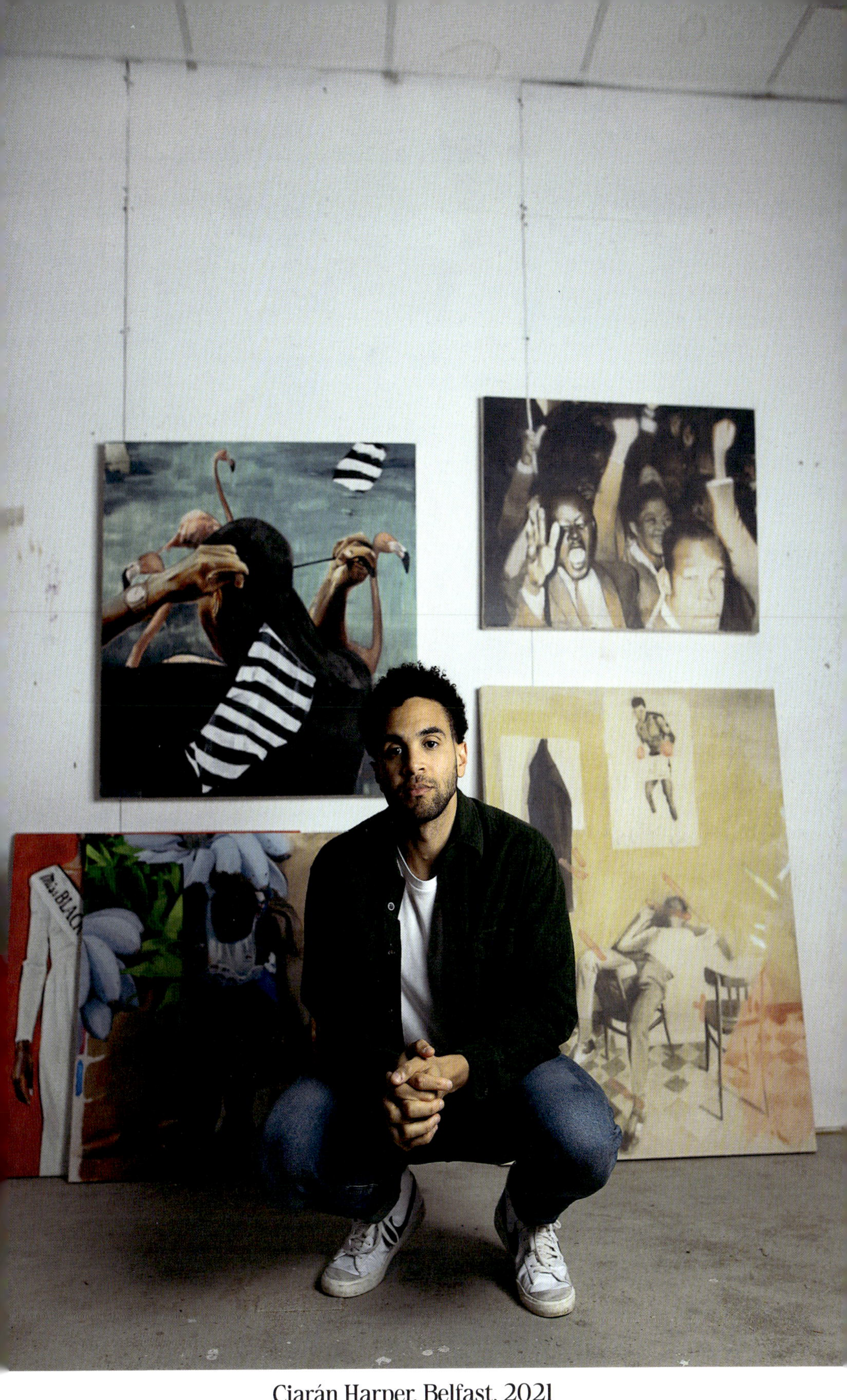

Ciarán Harper, Belfast, 2021

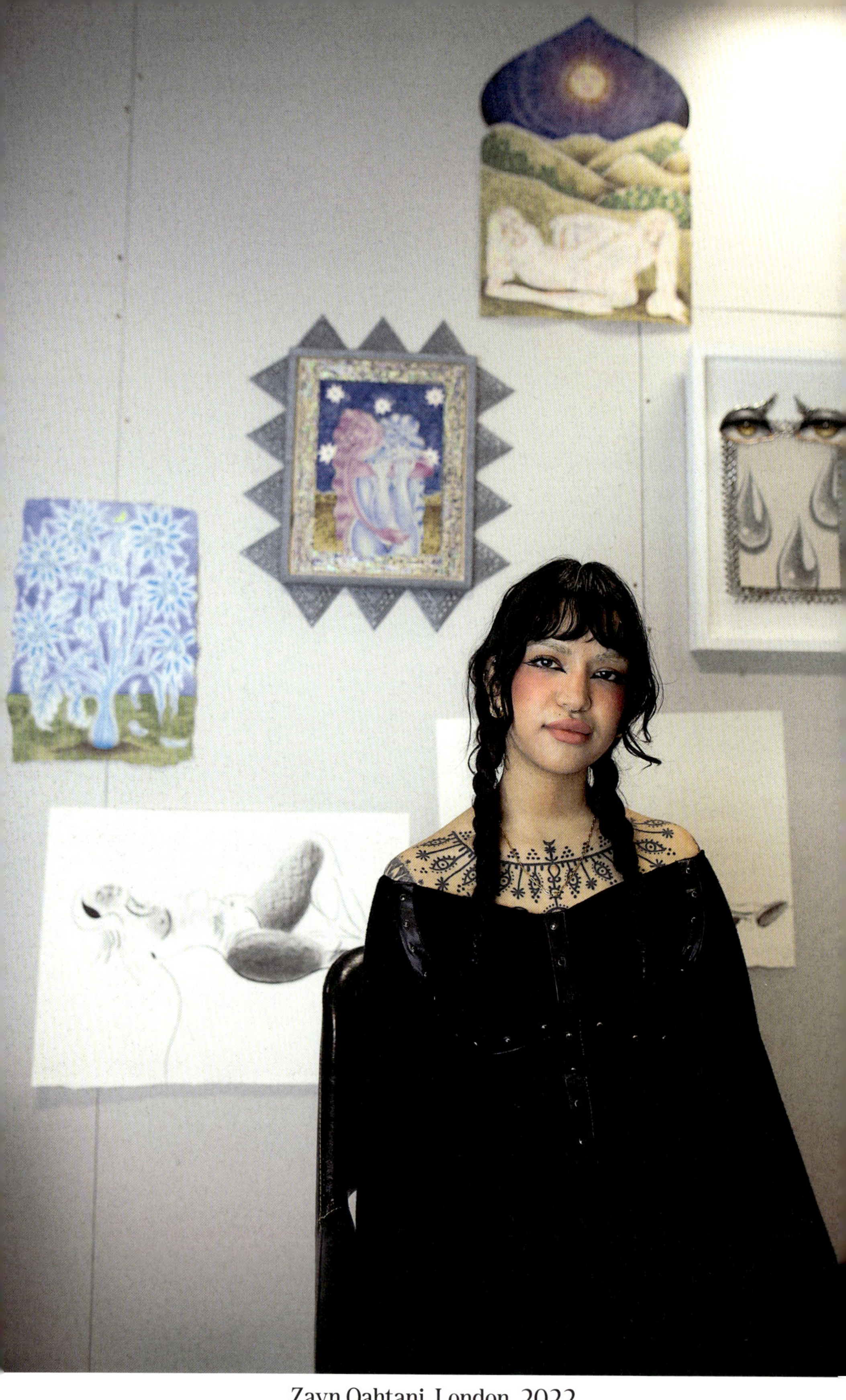

Zayn Qahtani, London, 2022

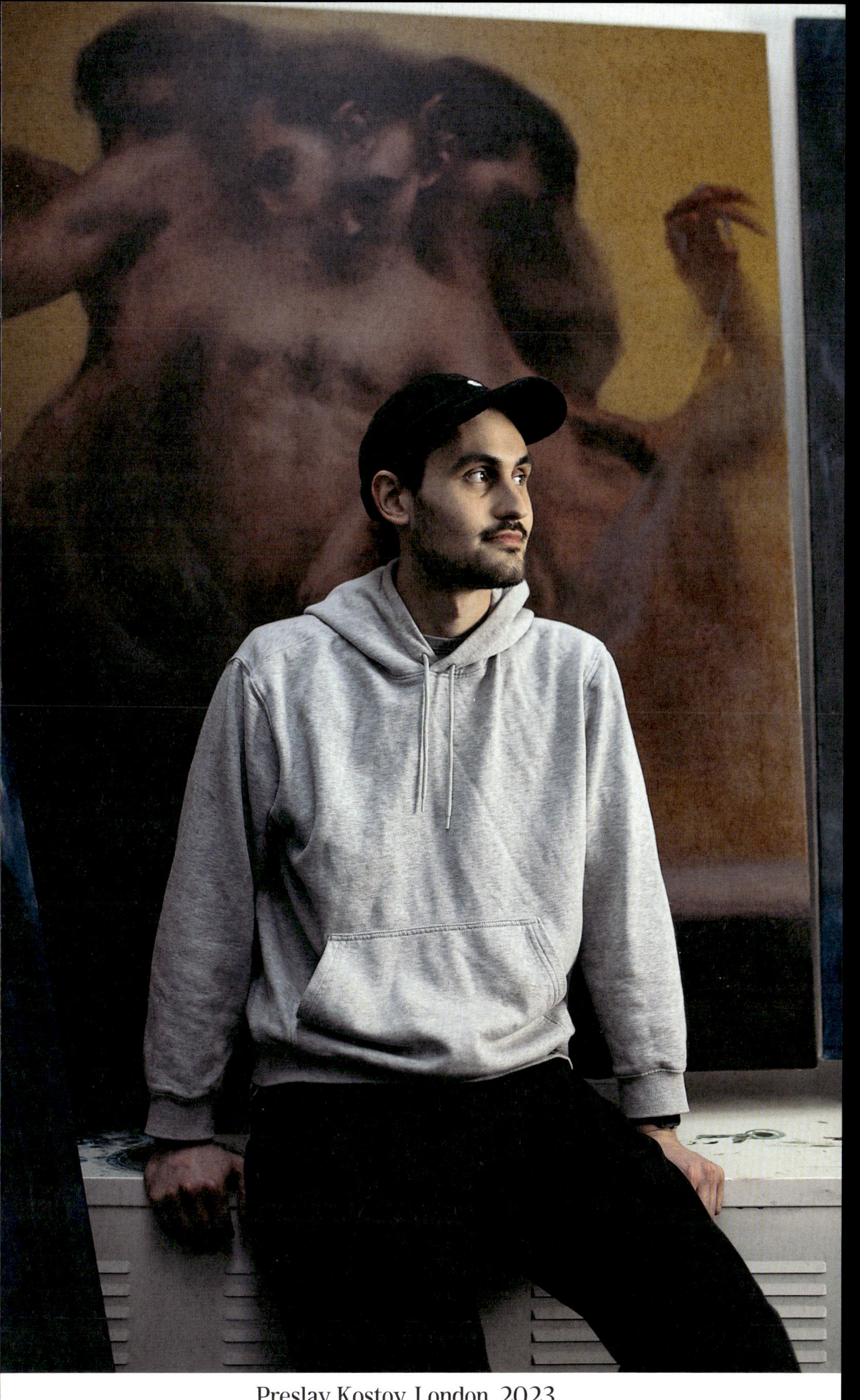

Preslav Kostov, London, 2023

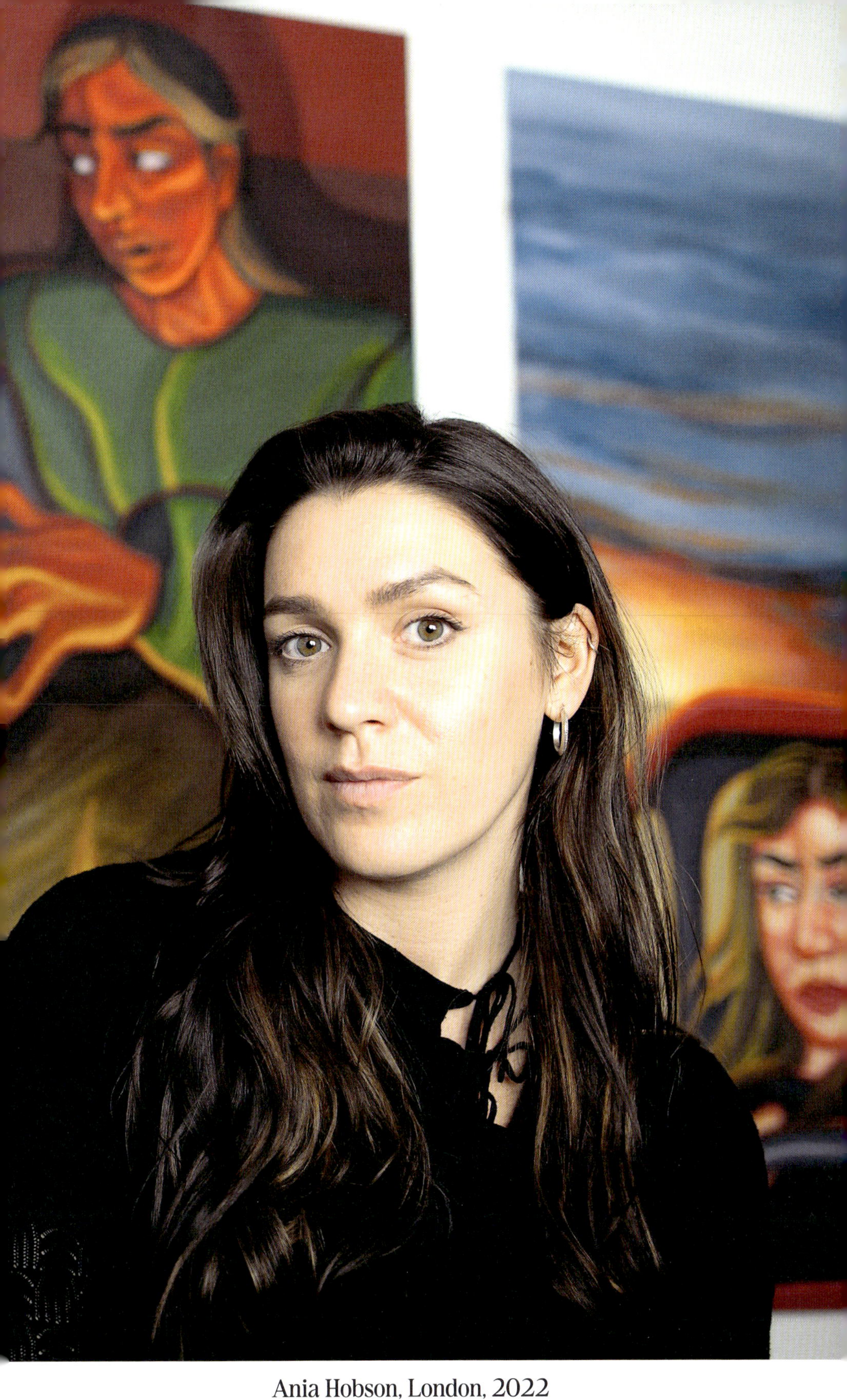

Ania Hobson, London, 2022

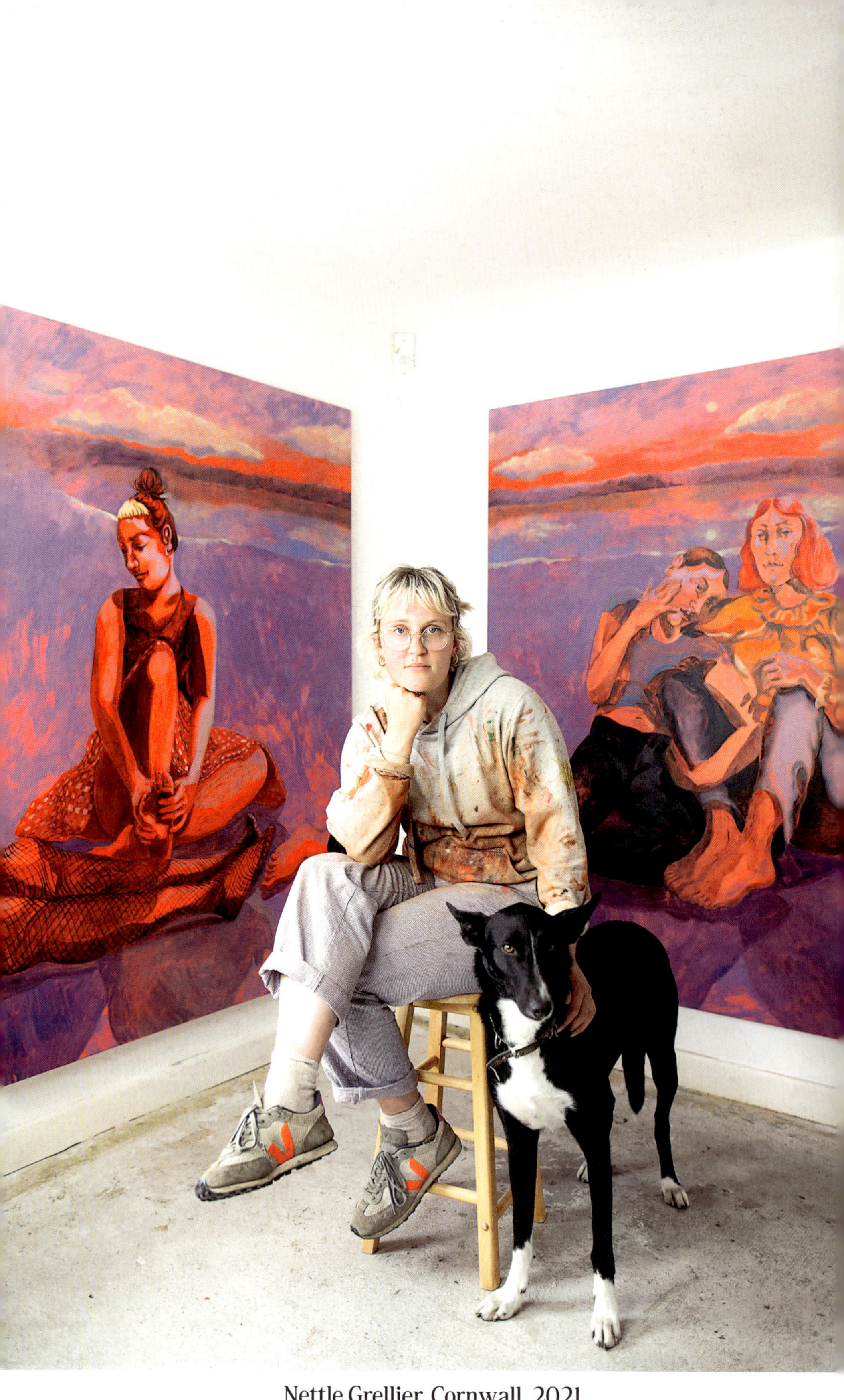

Nettle Grellier, Cornwall, 2021

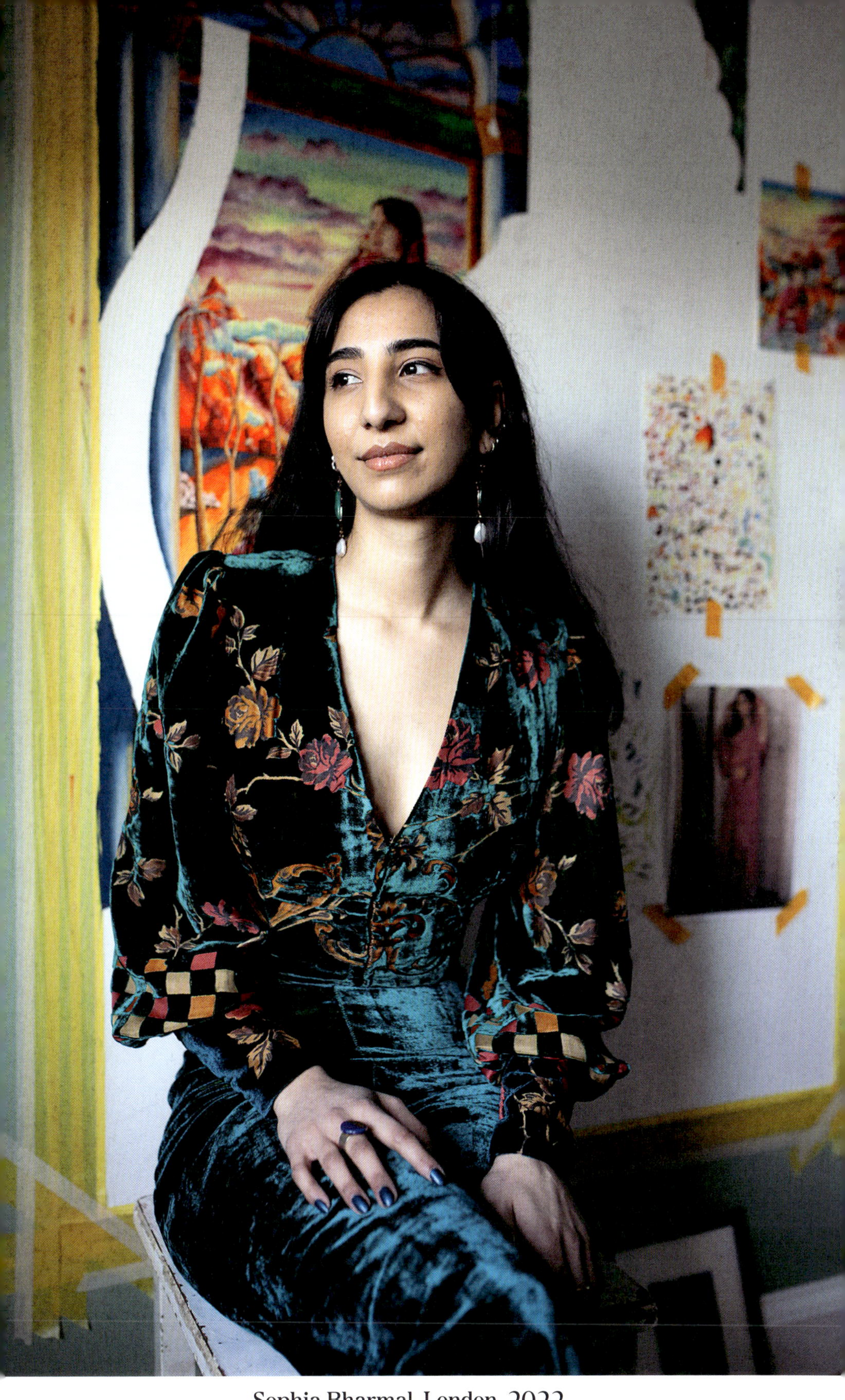

Sophia Bharmal, London, 2022

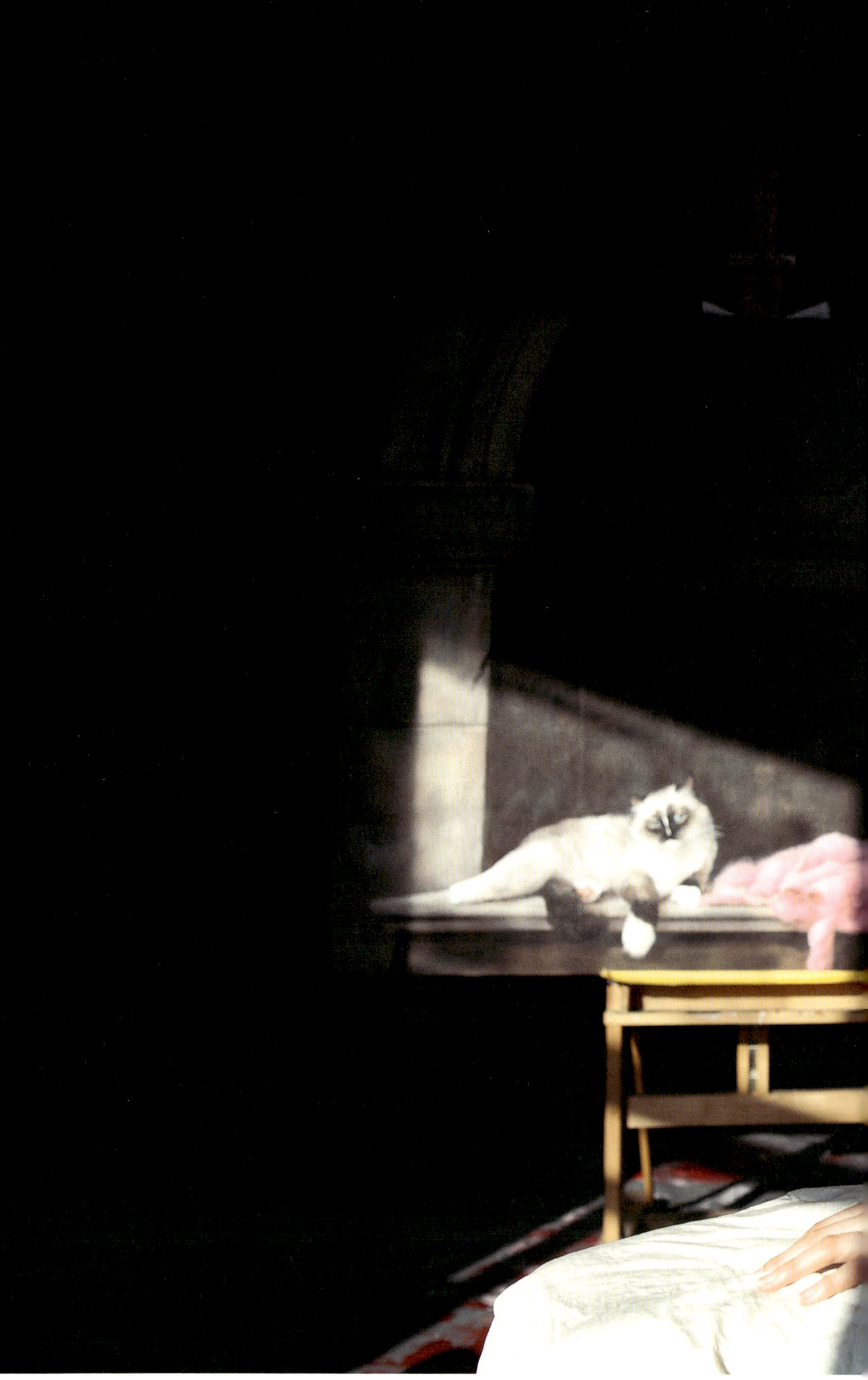

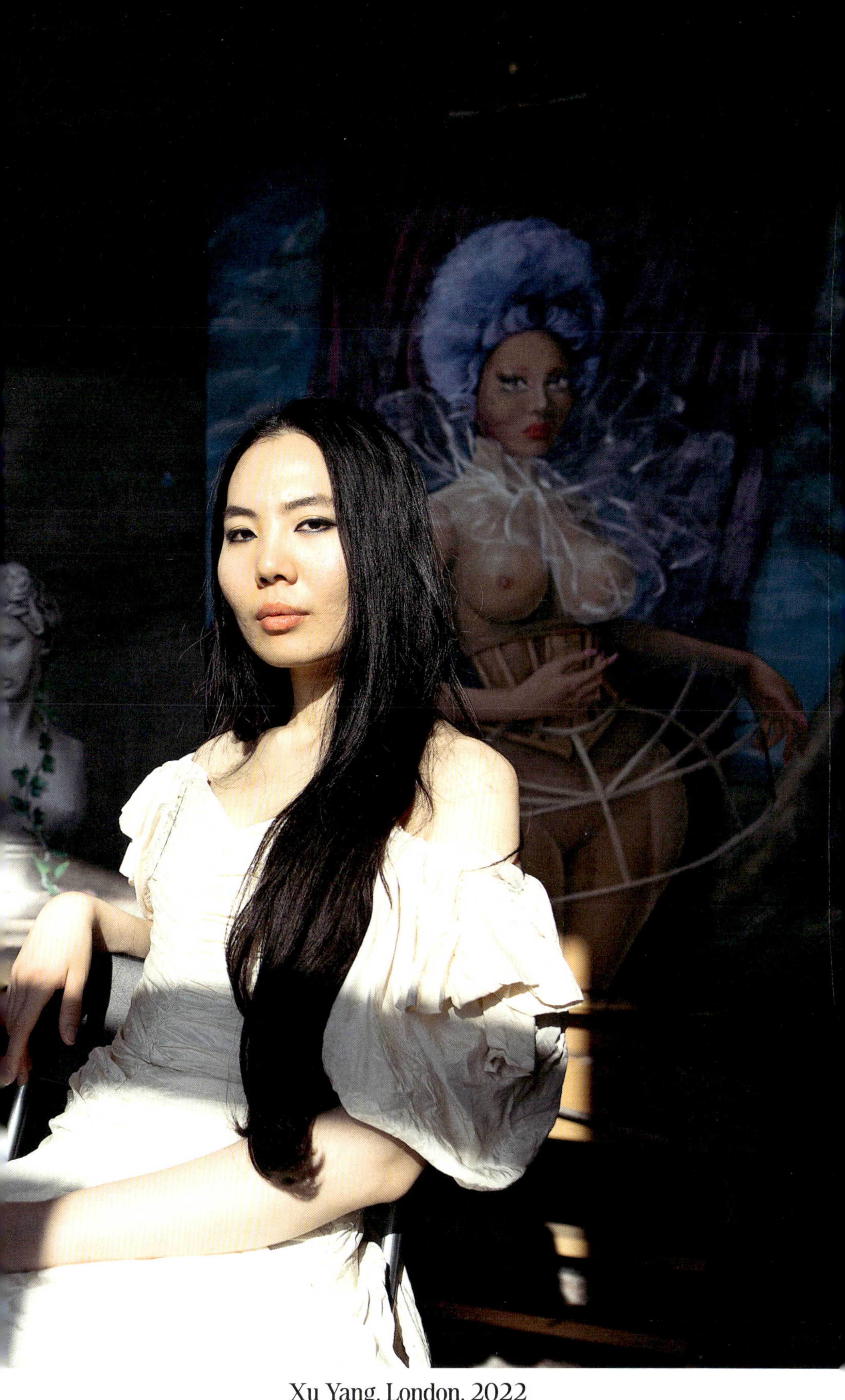

Xu Yang, London, 2022

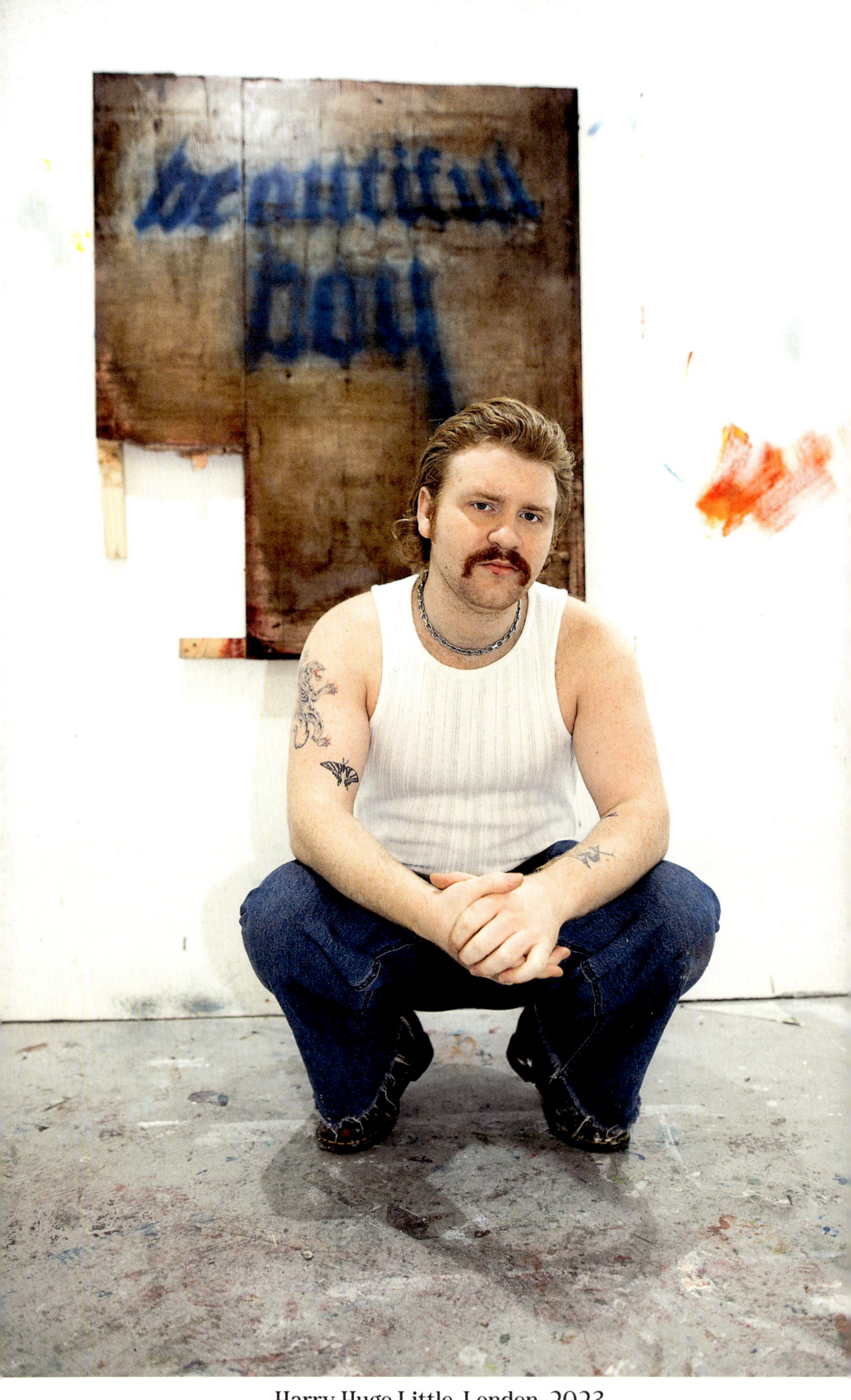

Harry Hugo Little, London, 2023

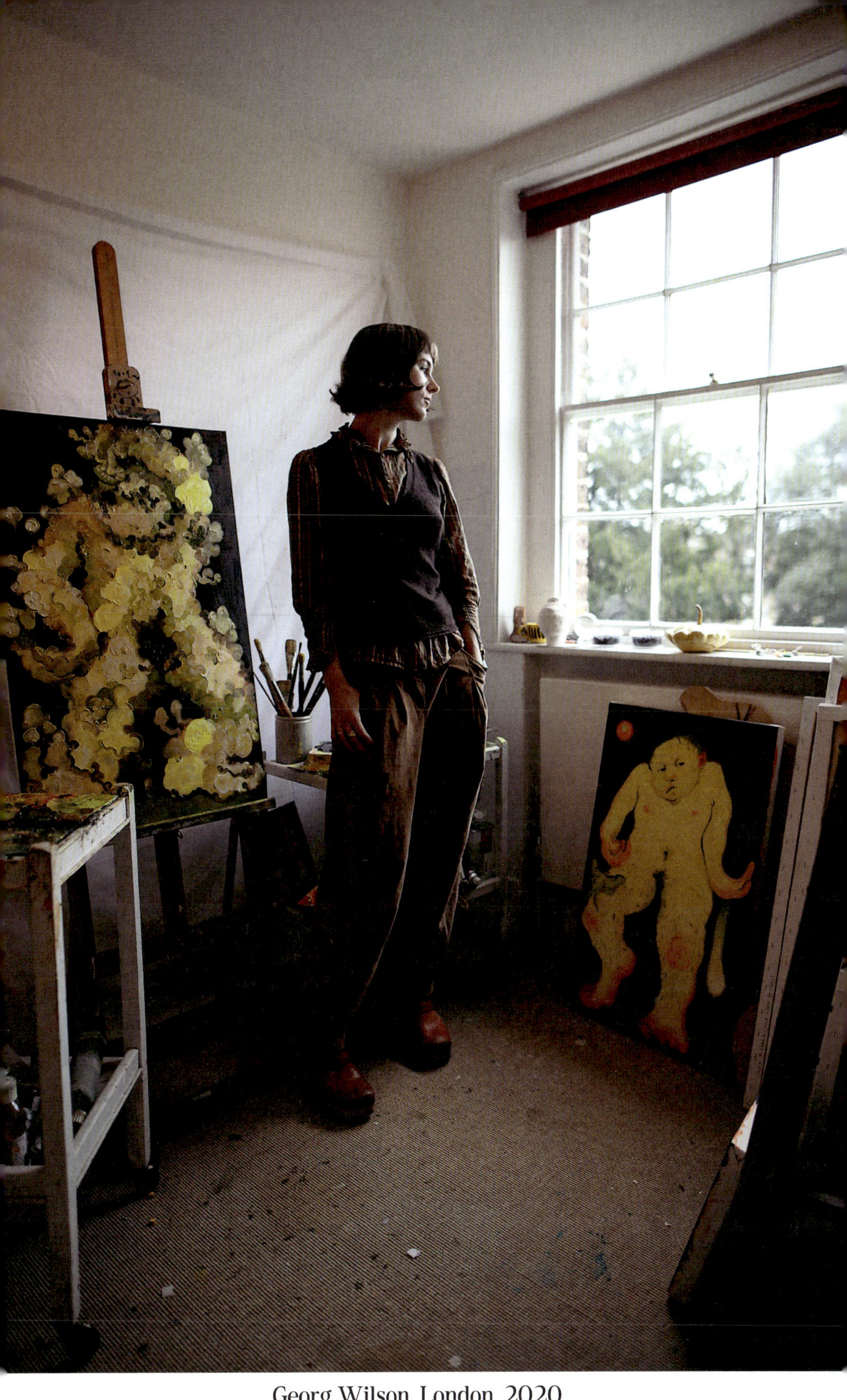

Georg Wilson, London, 2020

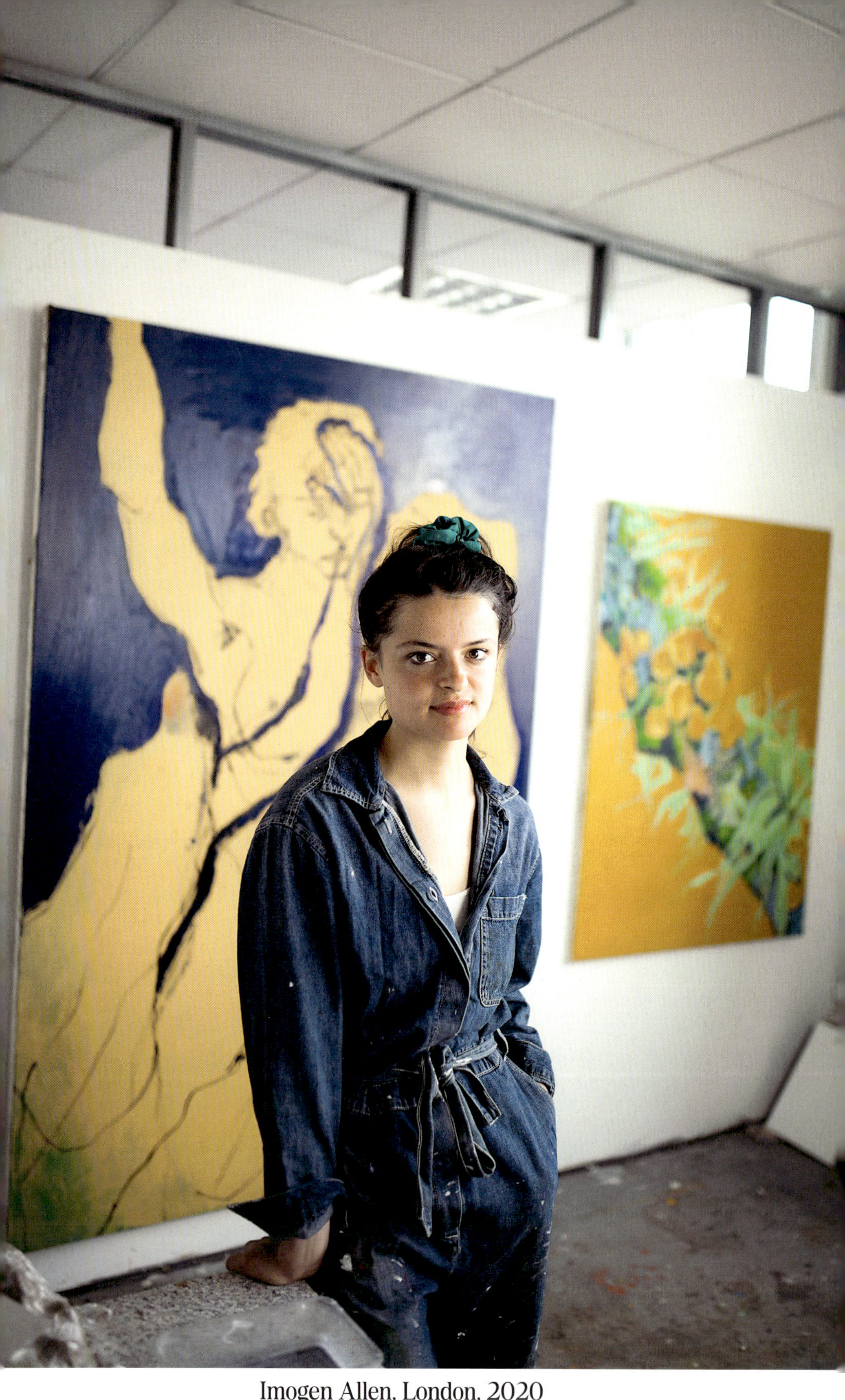

Imogen Allen, London, 2020

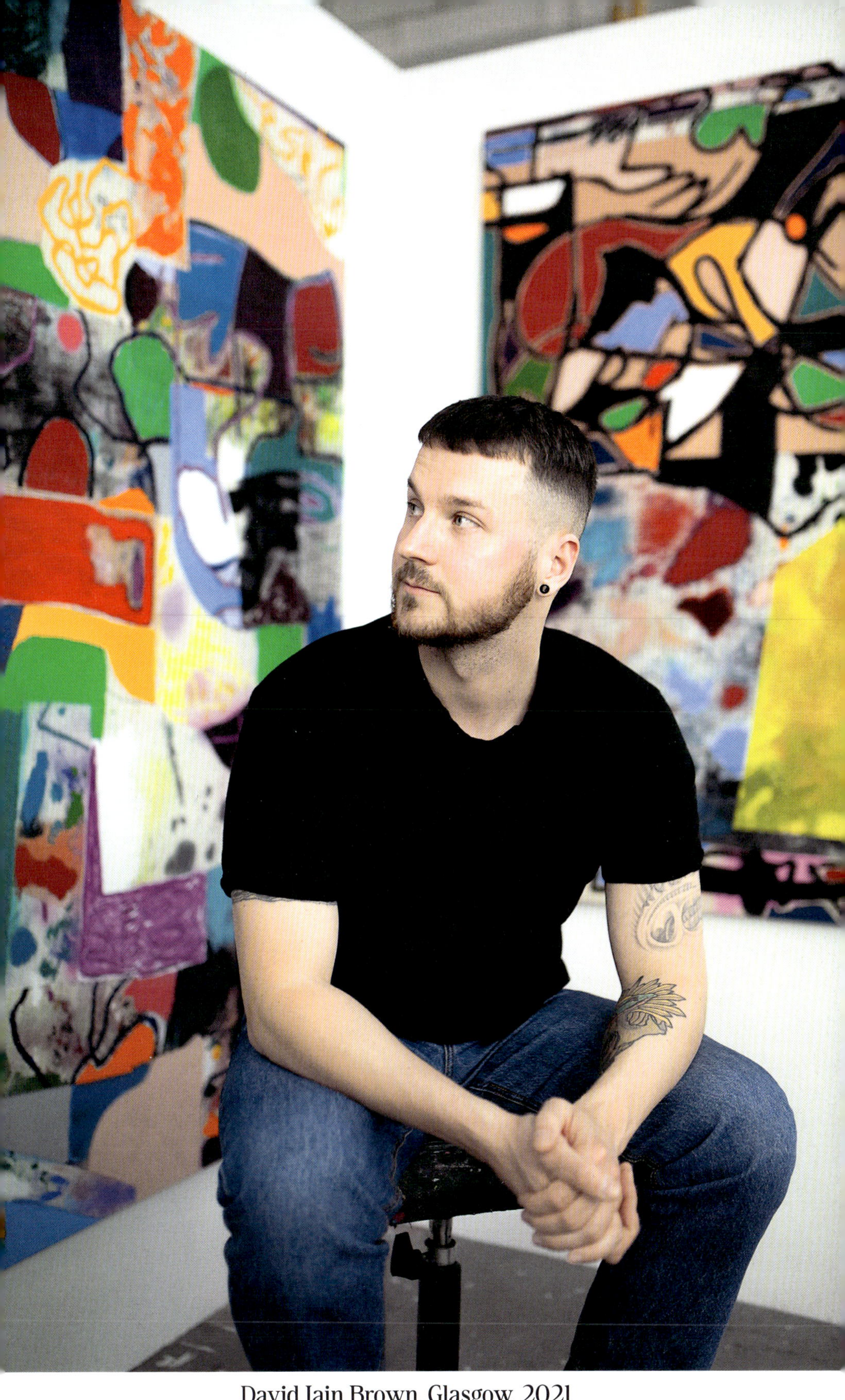

David Iain Brown, Glasgow, 2021

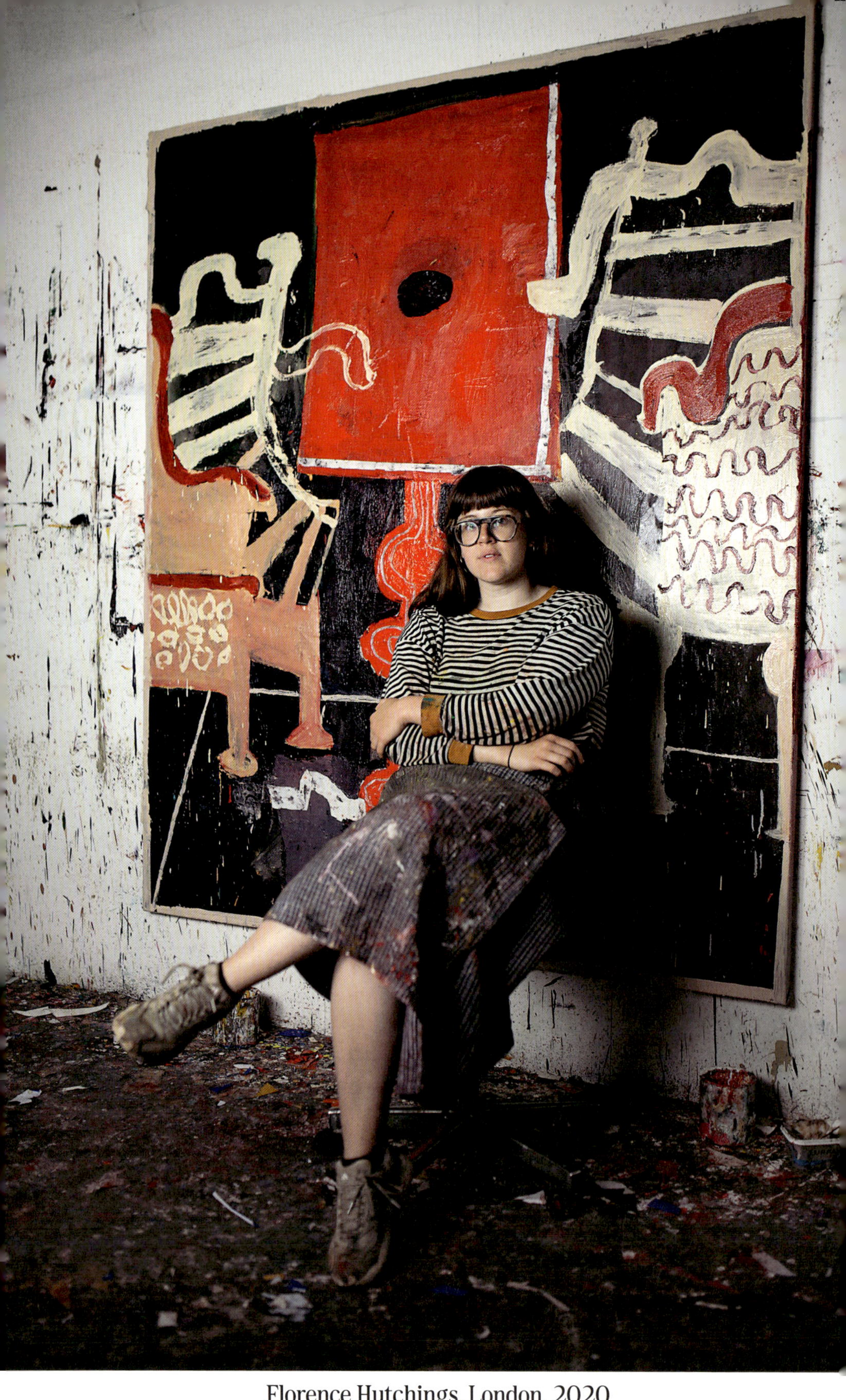

Florence Hutchings, London, 2020

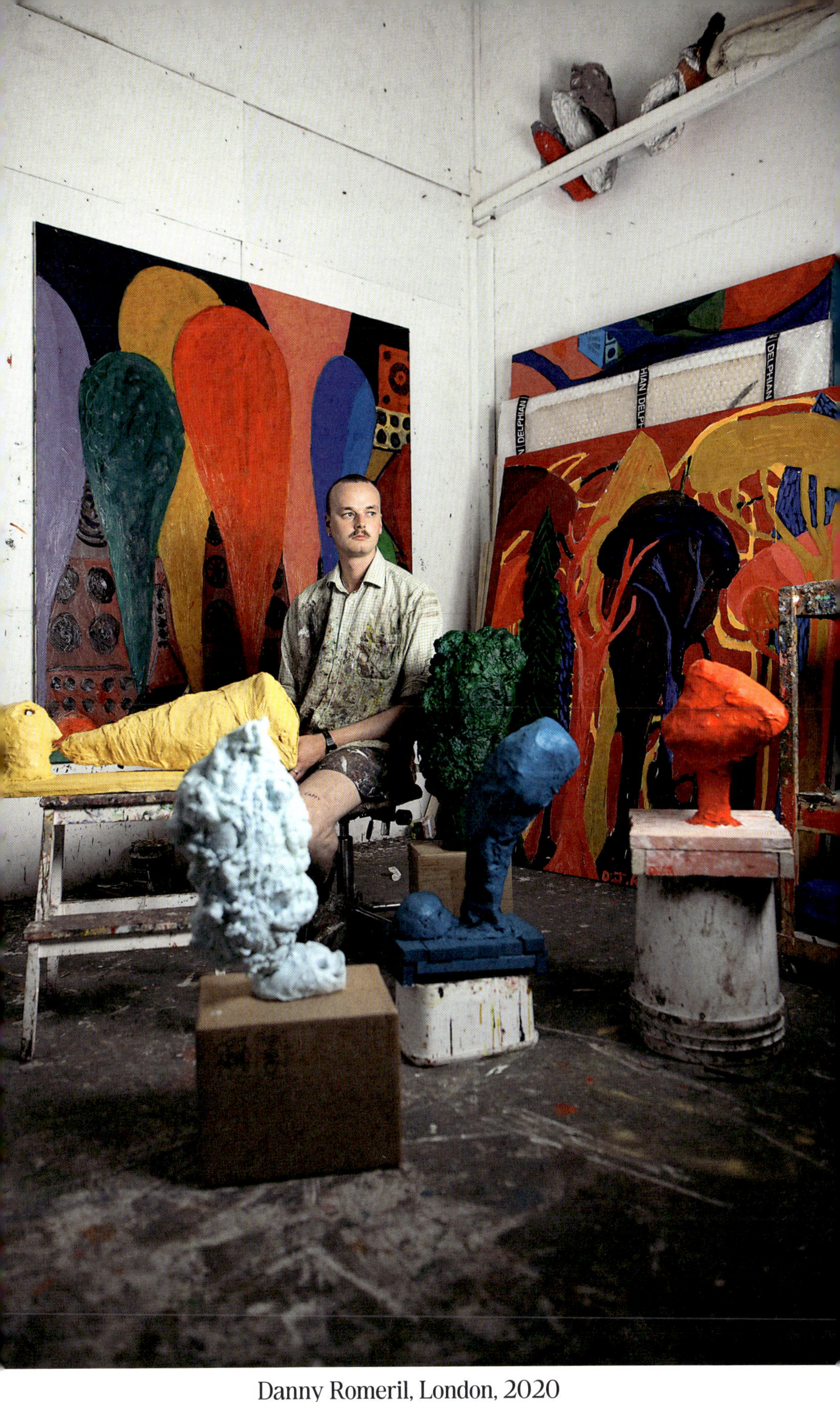

Danny Romeril, London, 2020

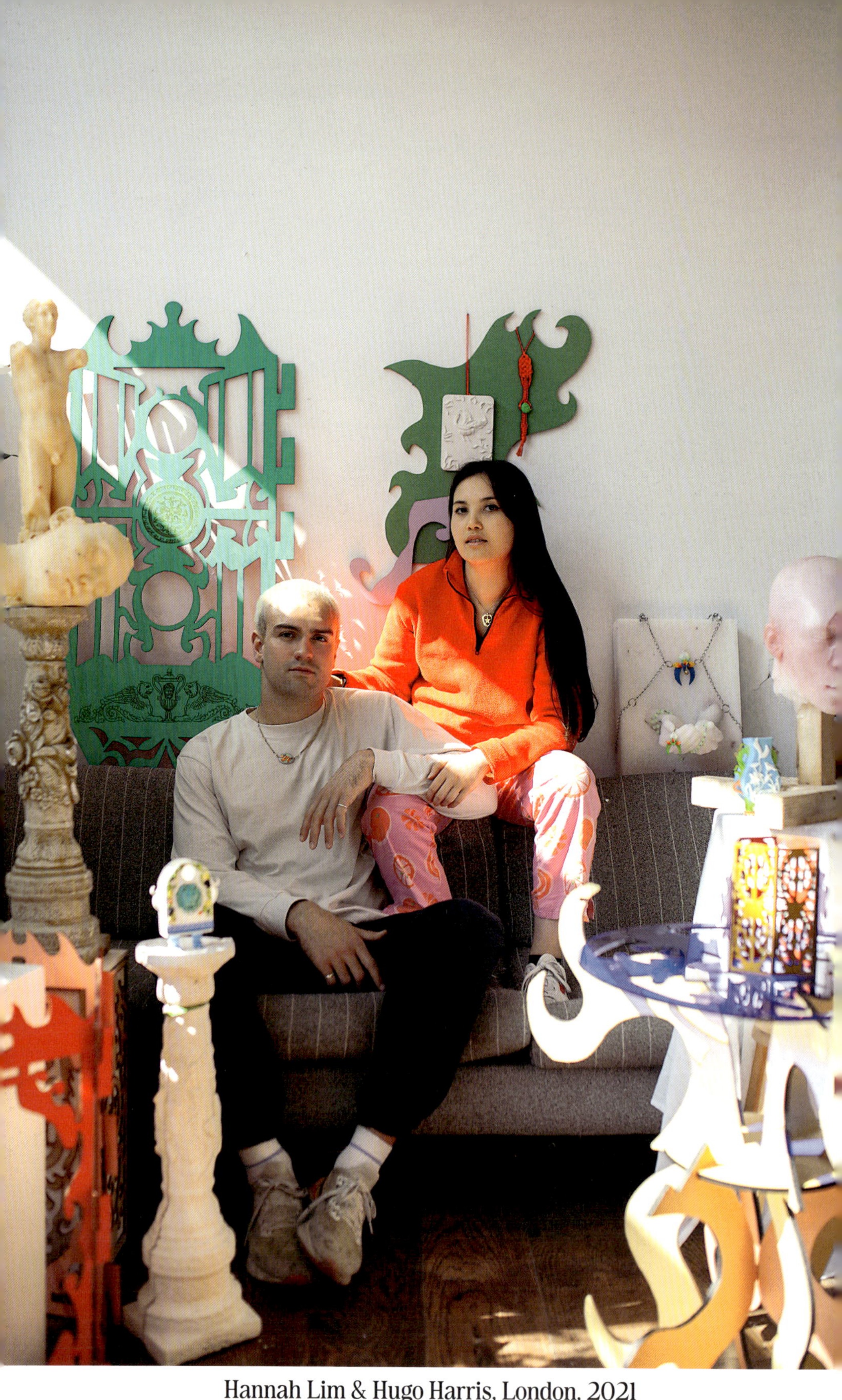

Hannah Lim & Hugo Harris, London, 2021

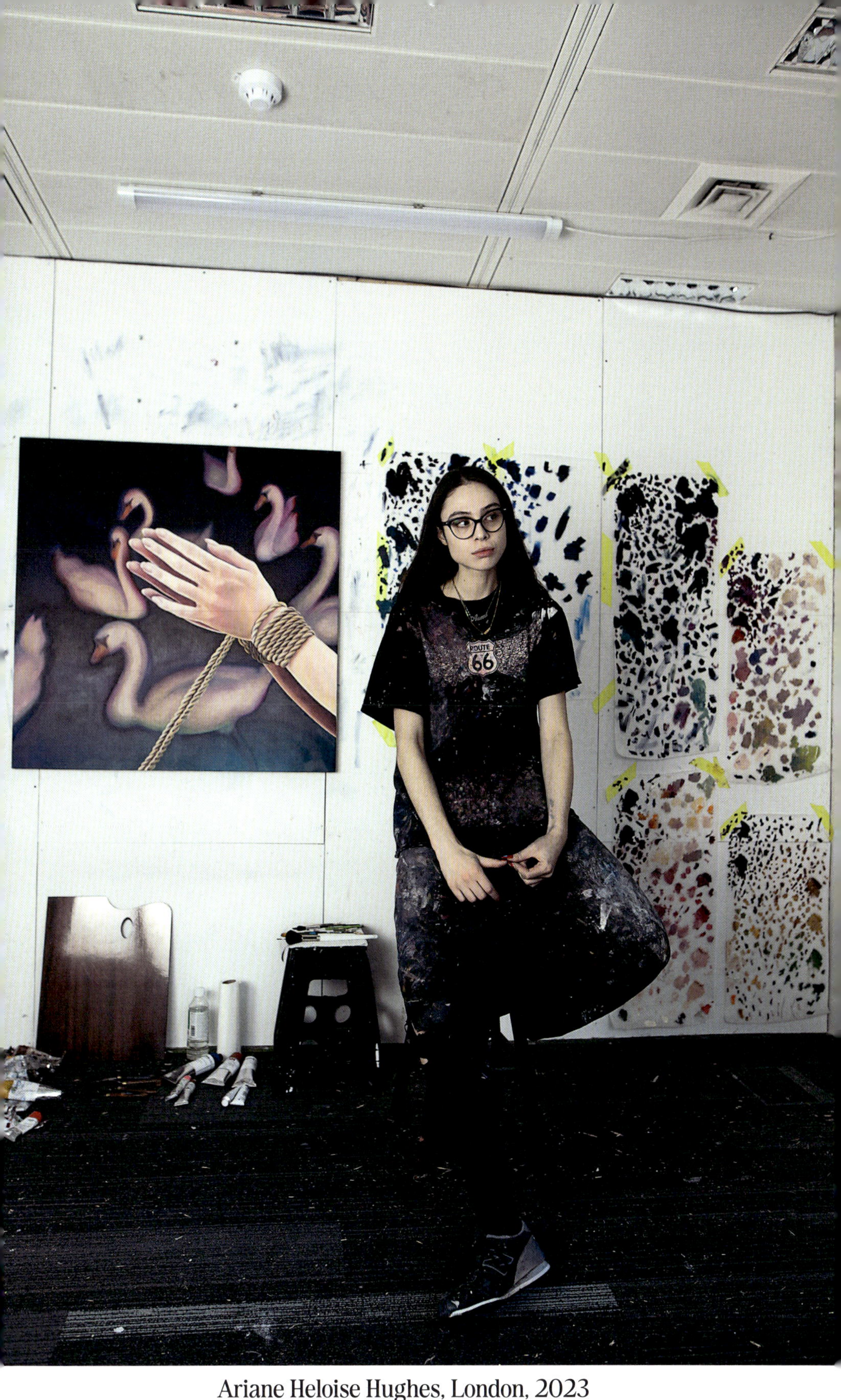

Ariane Heloise Hughes, London, 2023

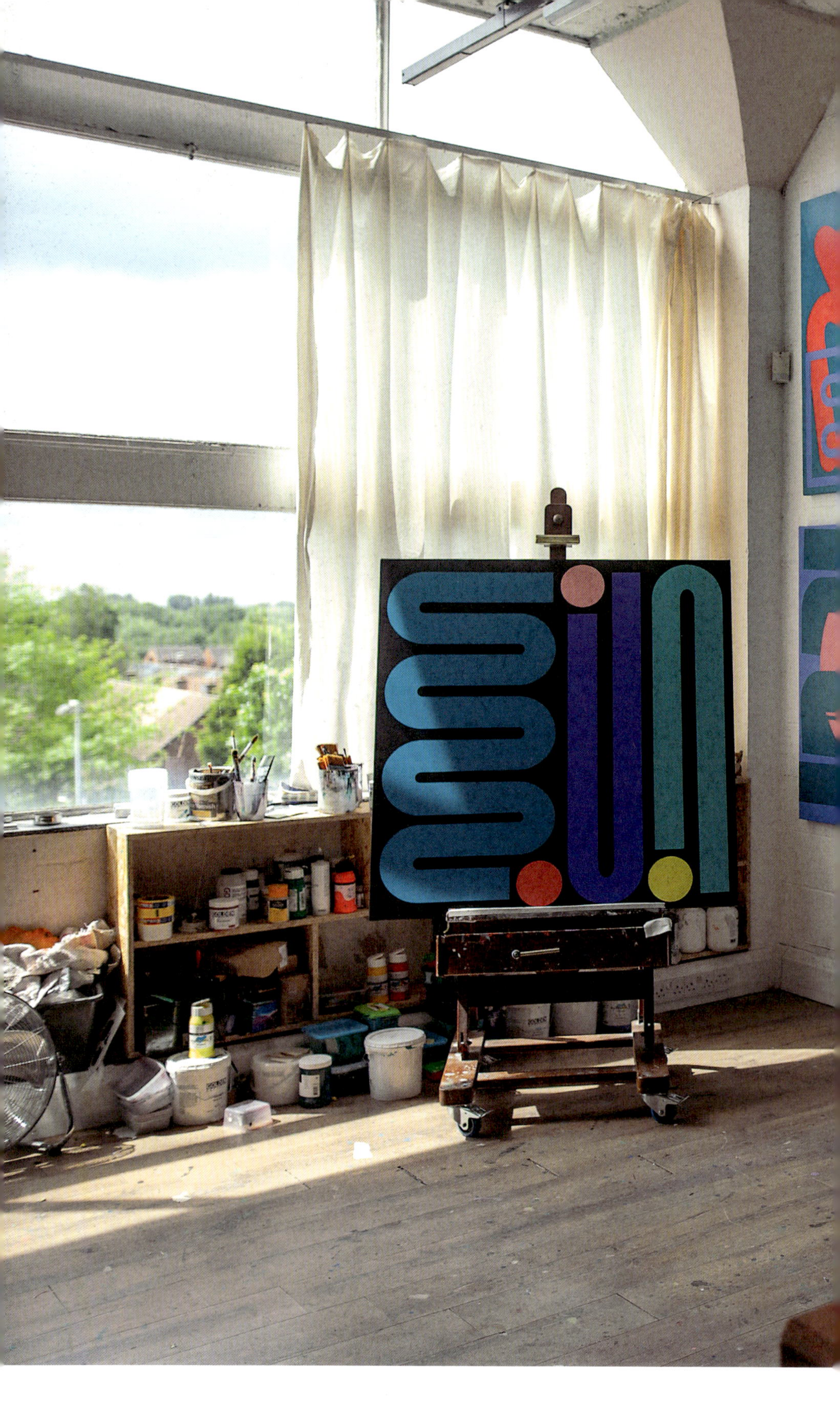

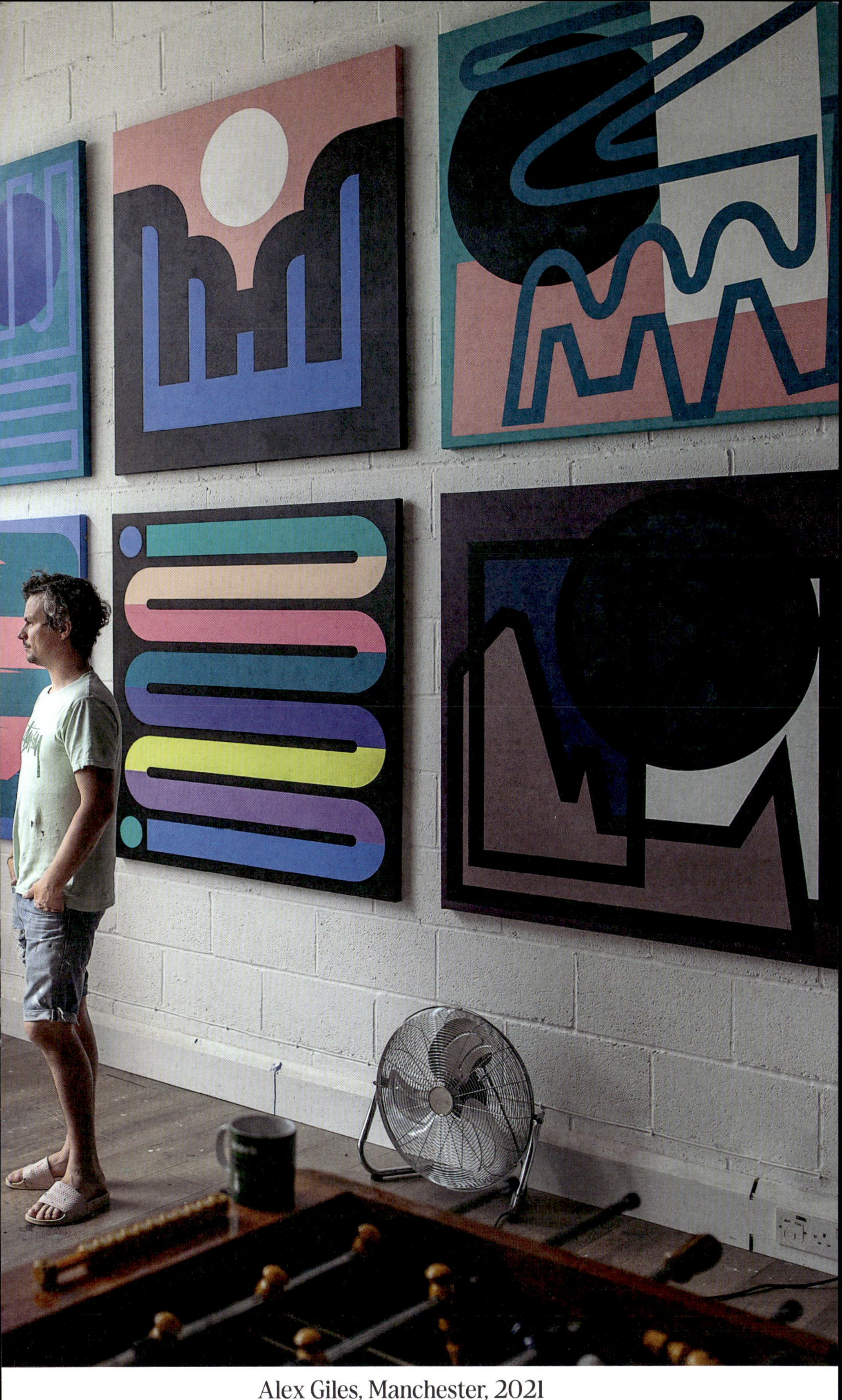

Alex Giles, Manchester, 2021

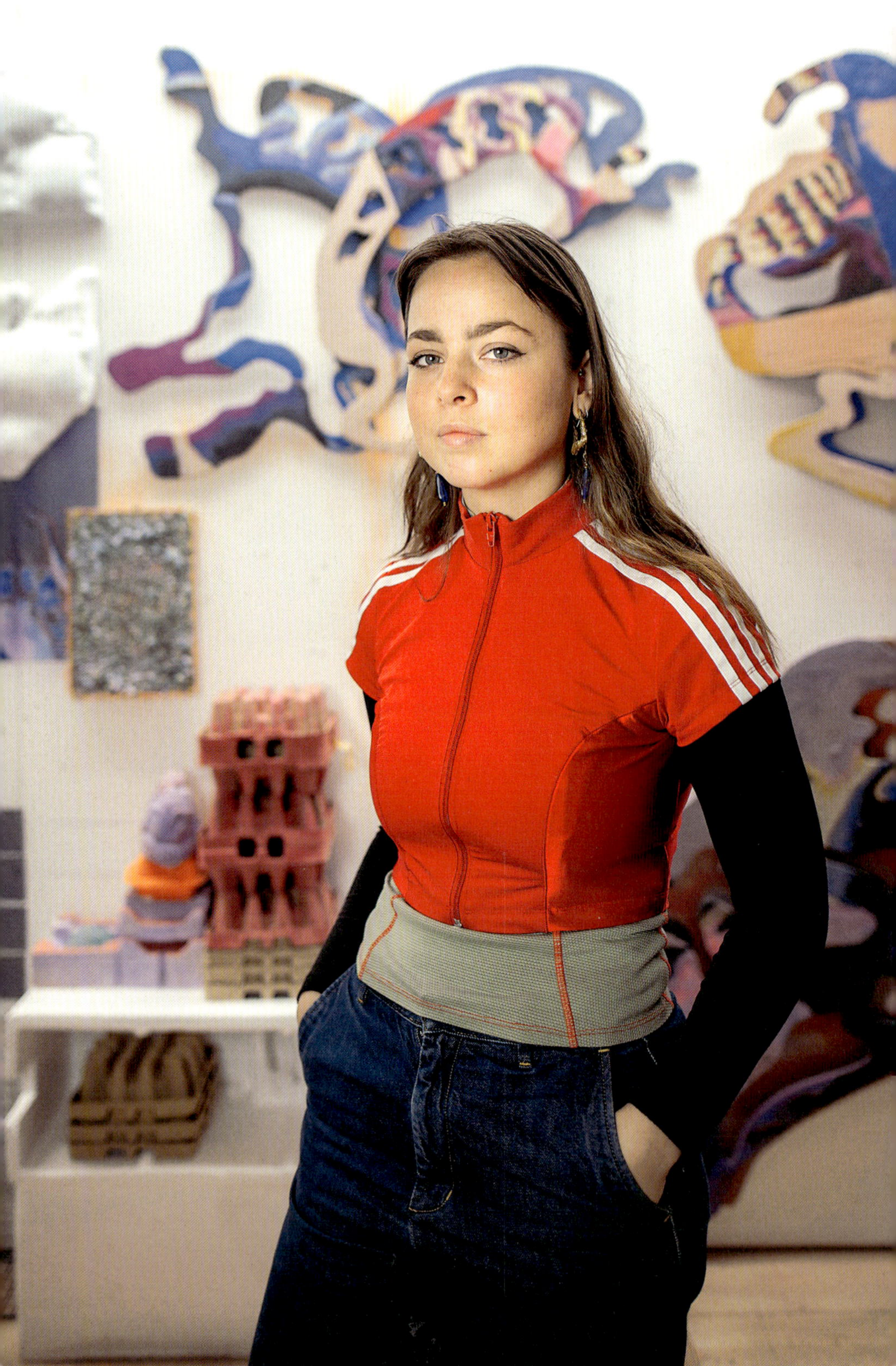

Alia Hamaoui, London, 2022

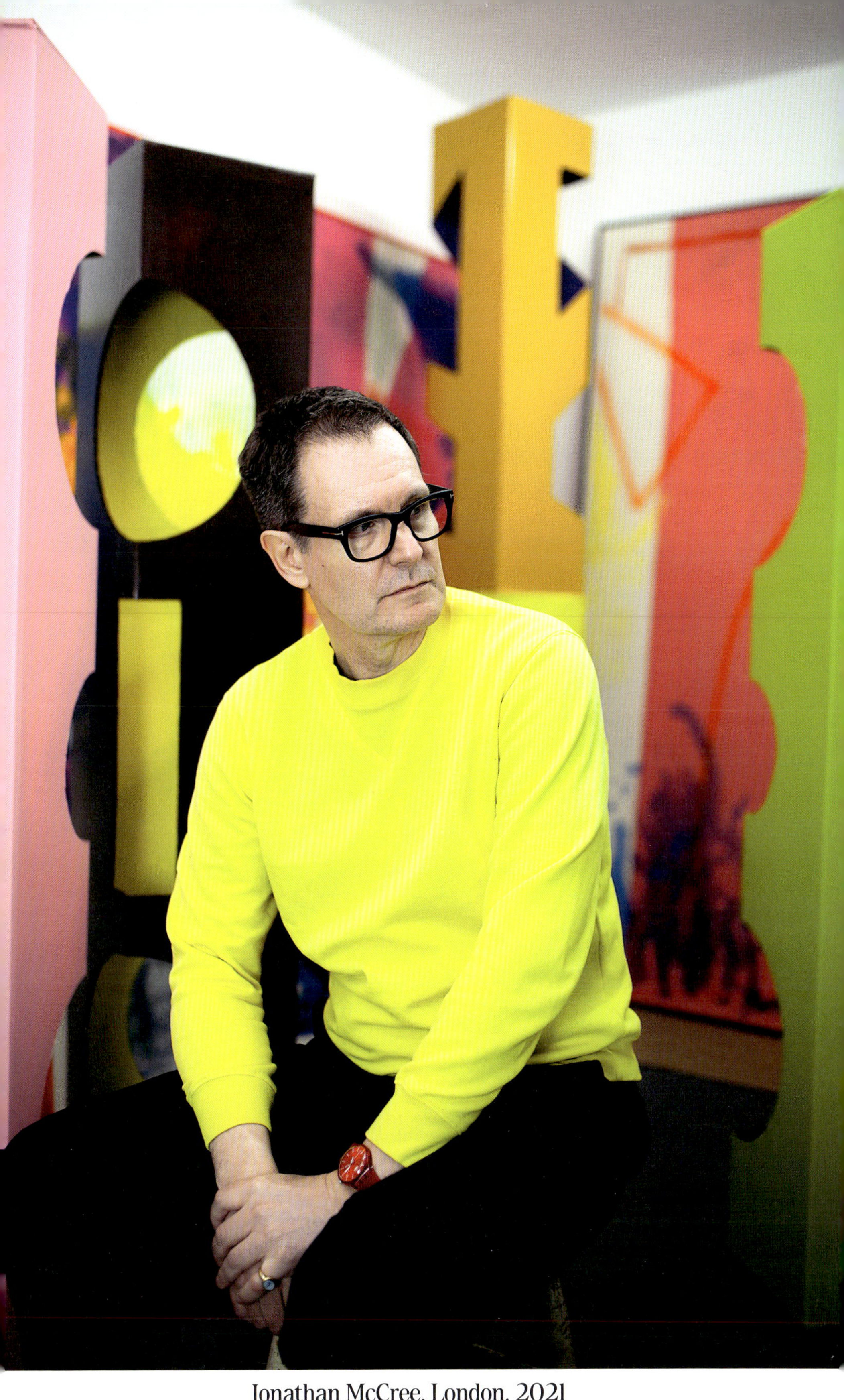

Jonathan McCree, London, 2021

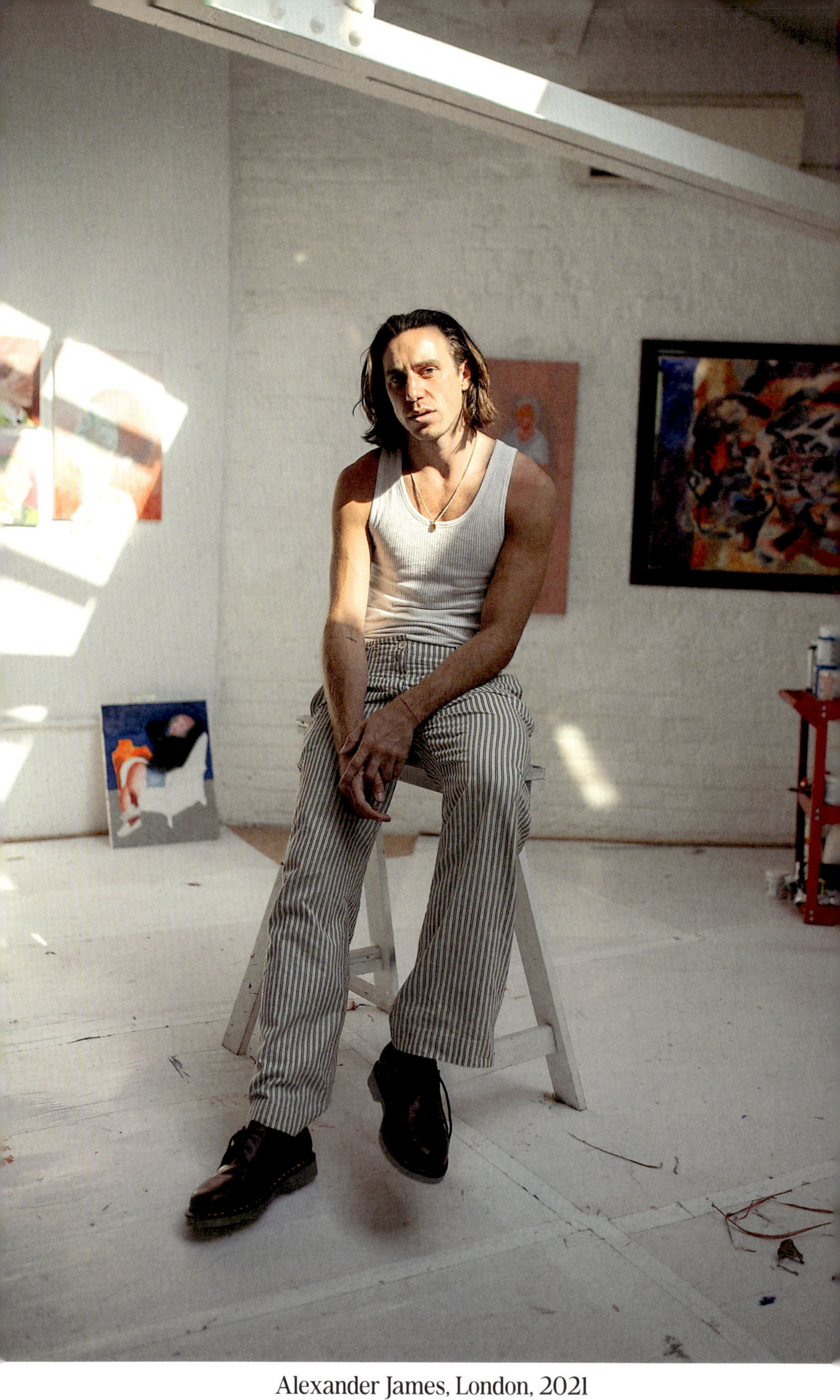

Alexander James, London, 2021

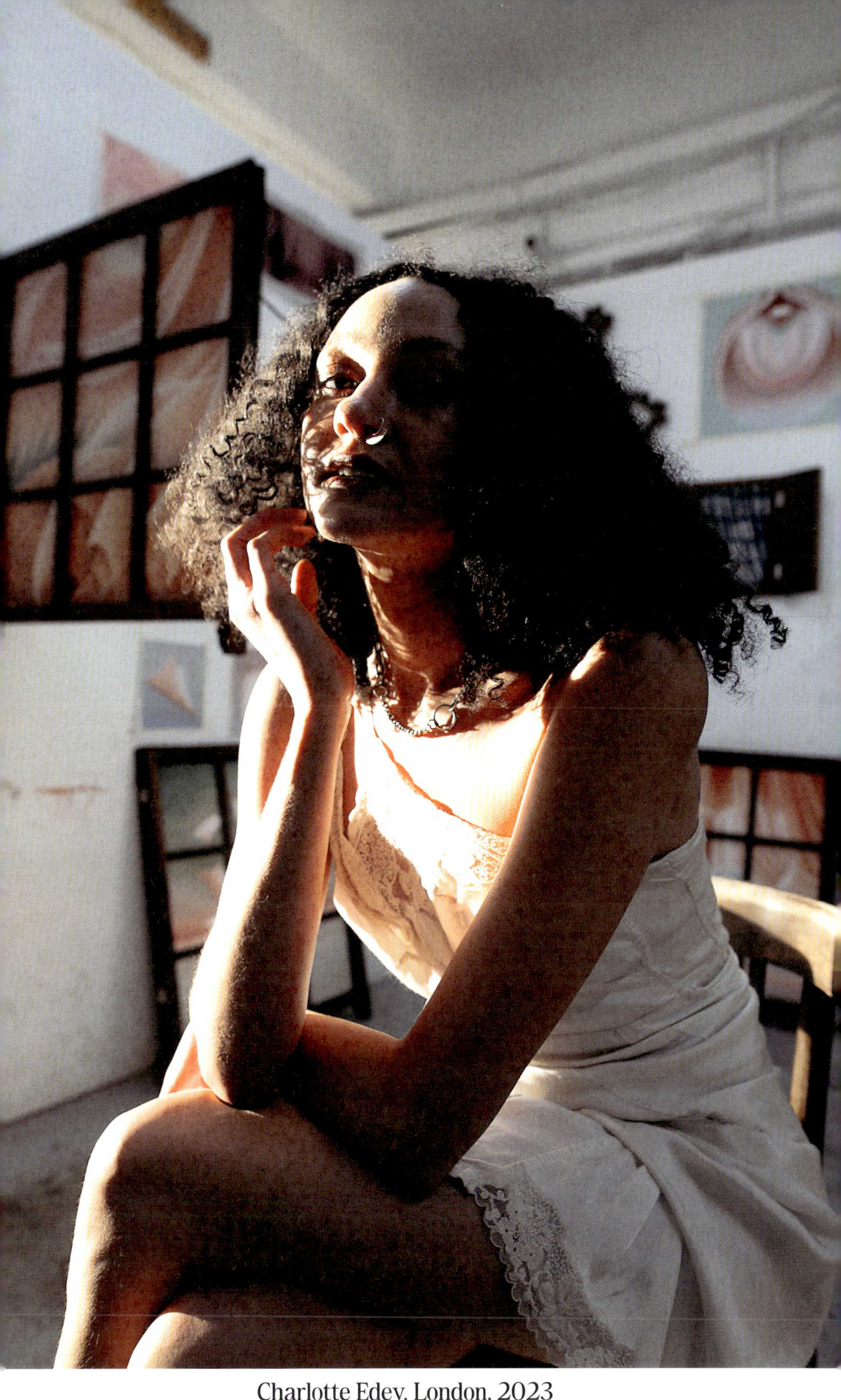

Charlotte Edey, London, 2023

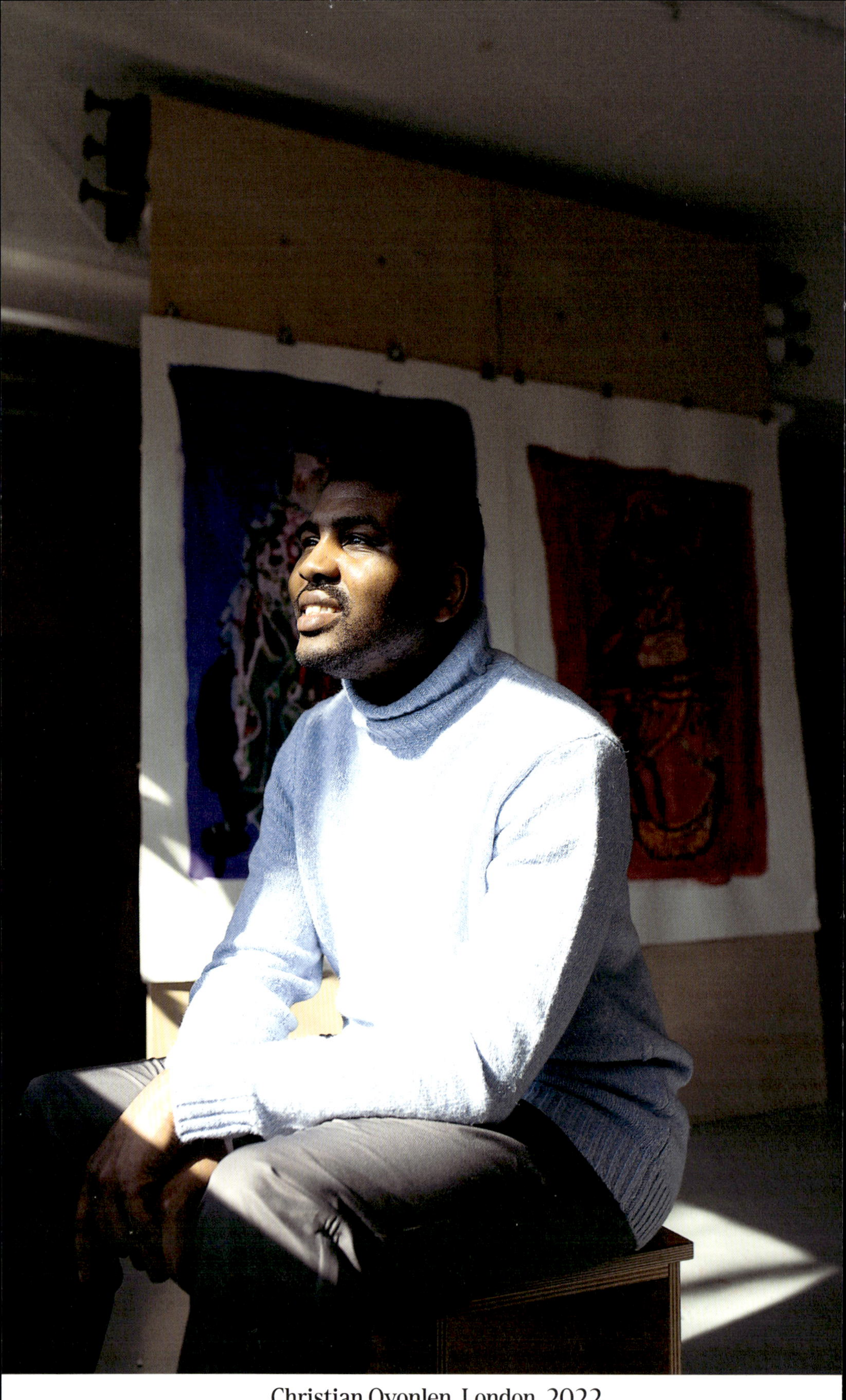

Christian Ovonlen, London, 2022

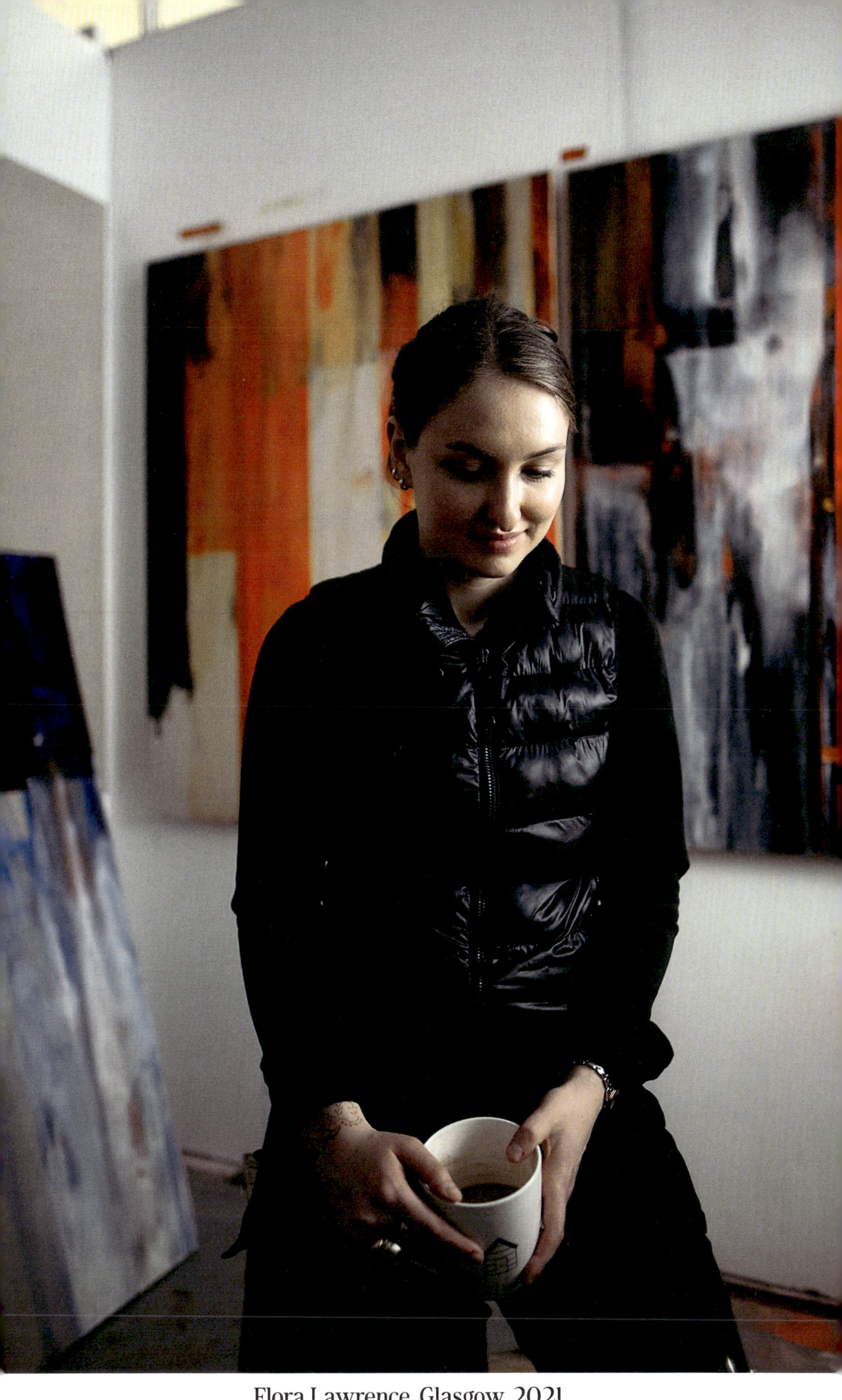

Flora Lawrence, Glasgow, 2021

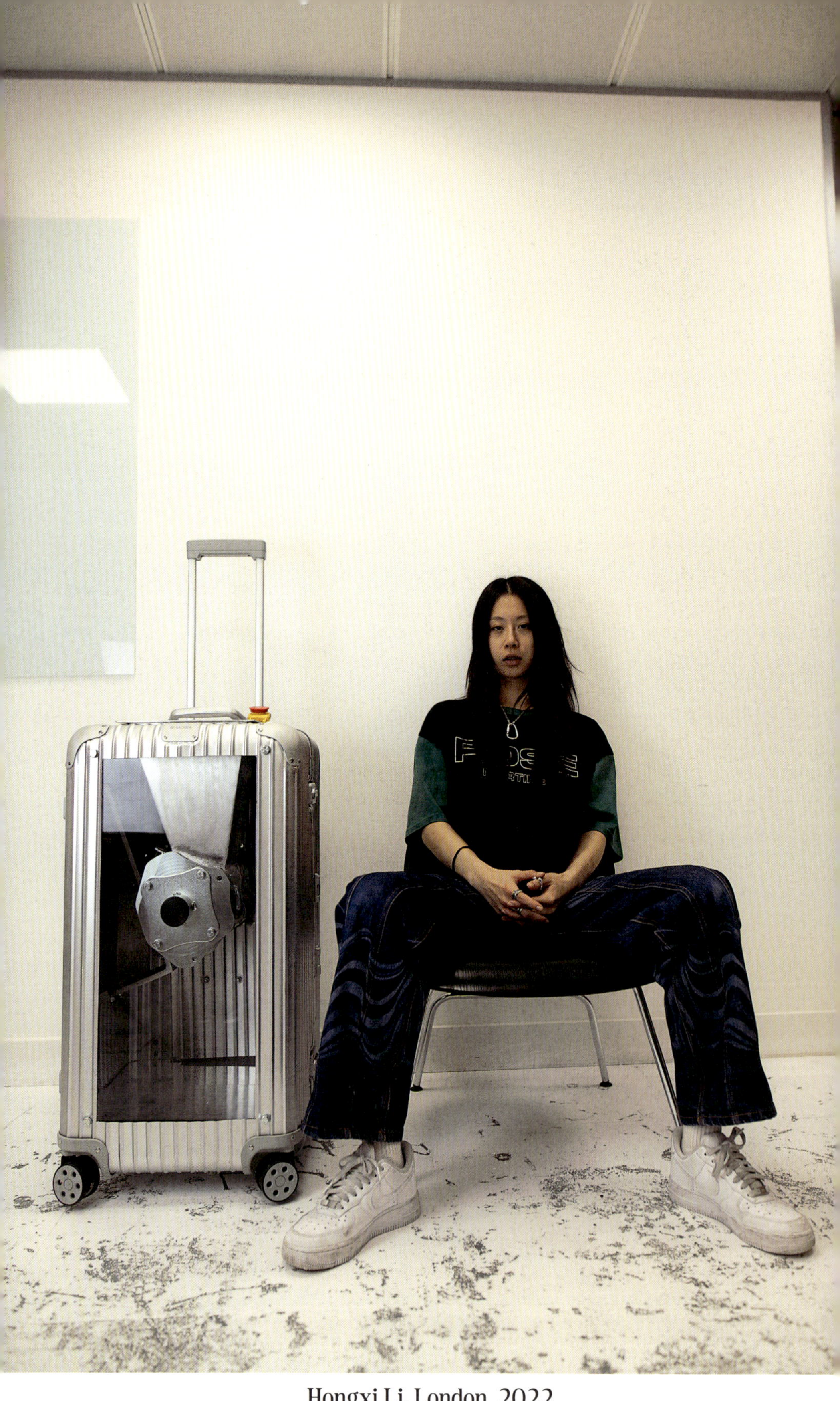

Hongxi Li, London, 2022

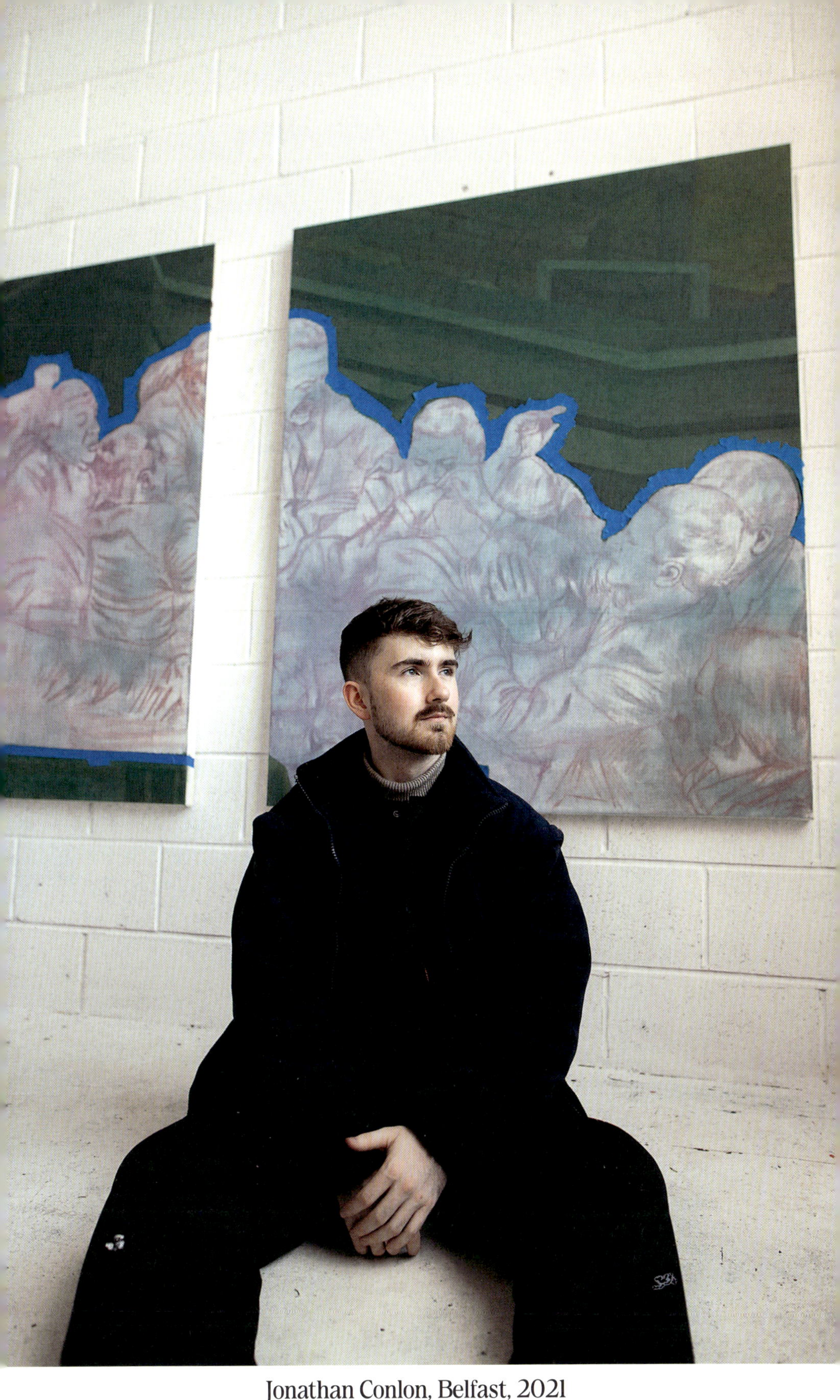

Jonathan Conlon, Belfast, 2021

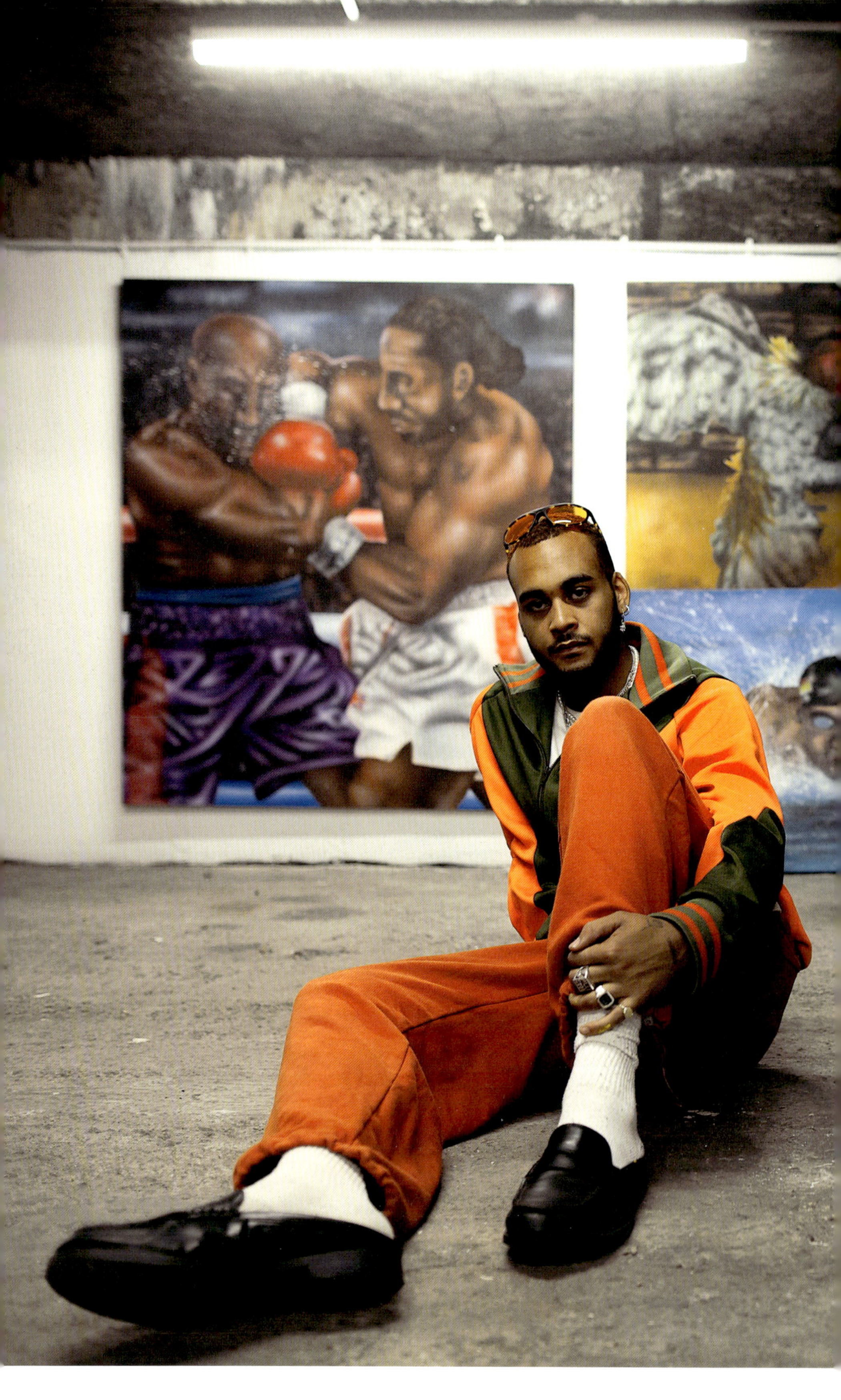

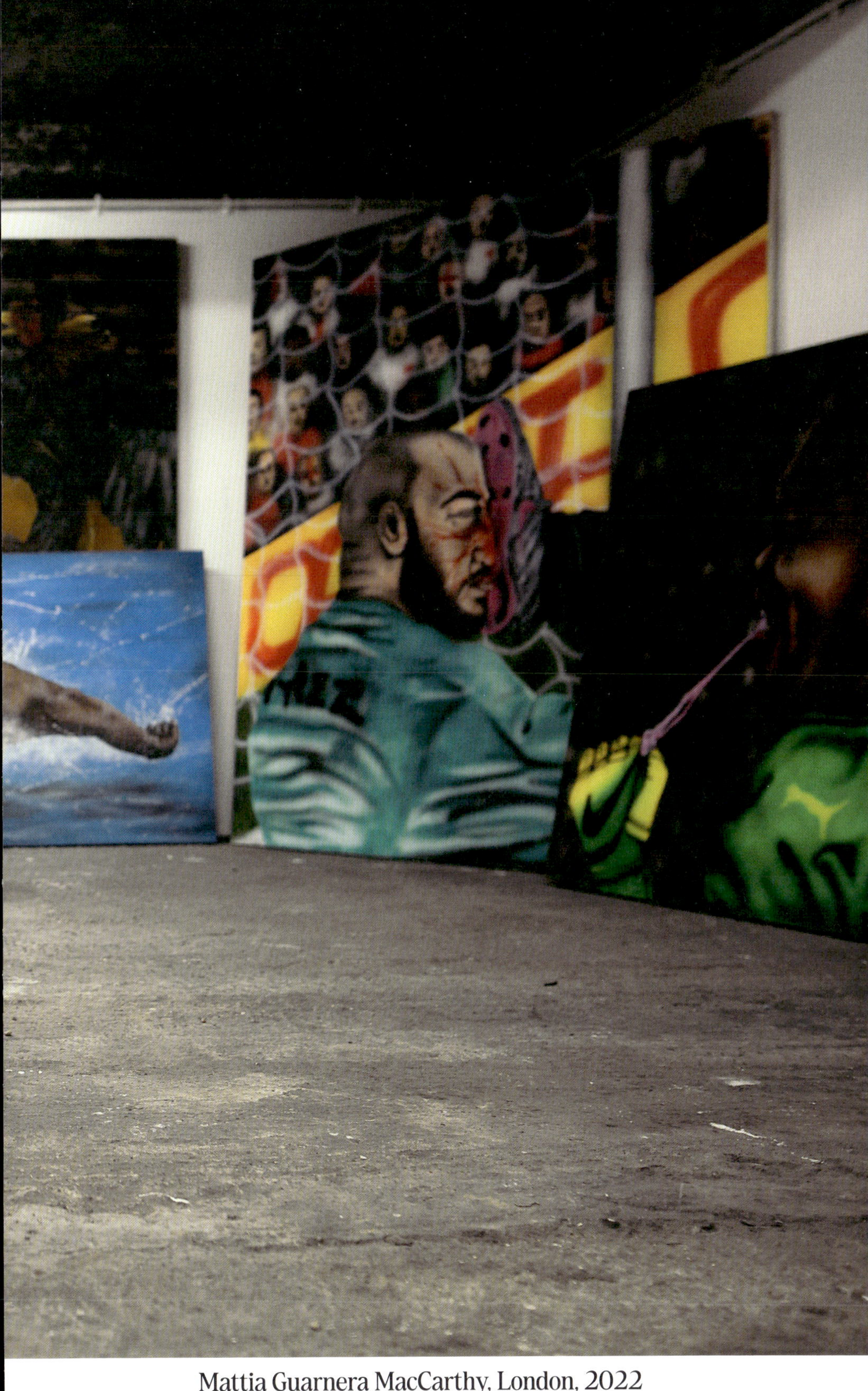

Mattia Guarnera MacCarthy, London, 2022

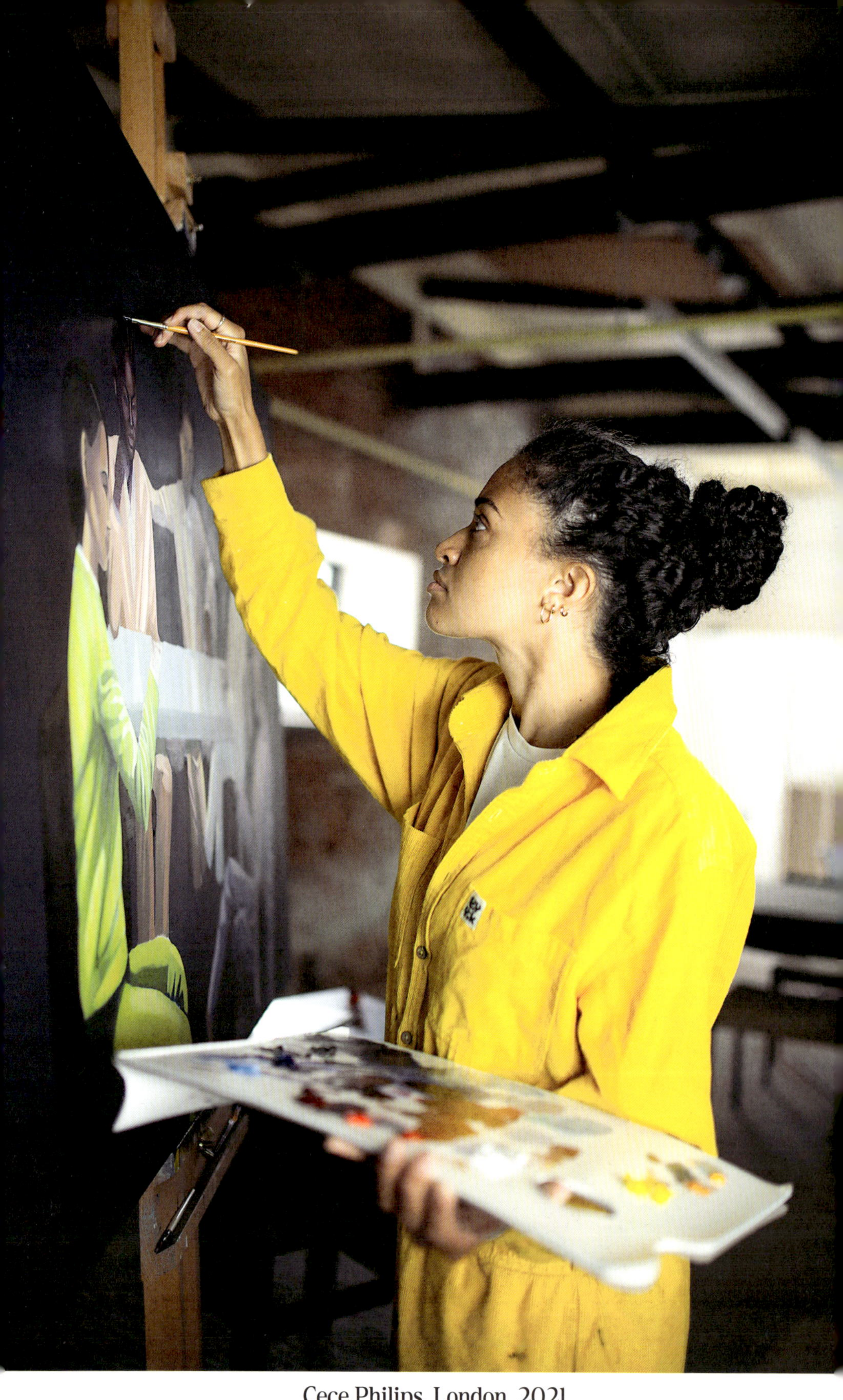

Cece Philips, London, 2021

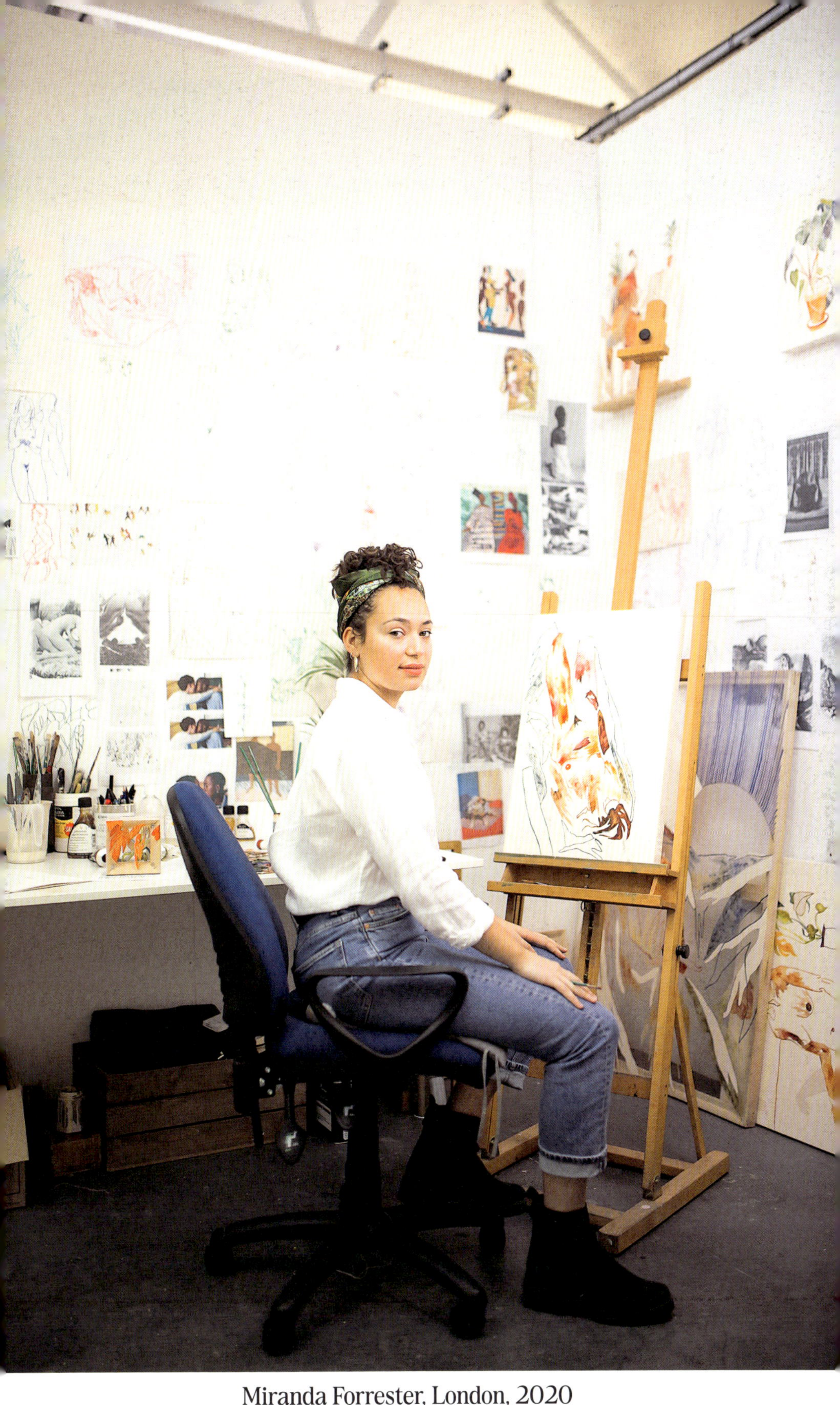

Miranda Forrester, London, 2020

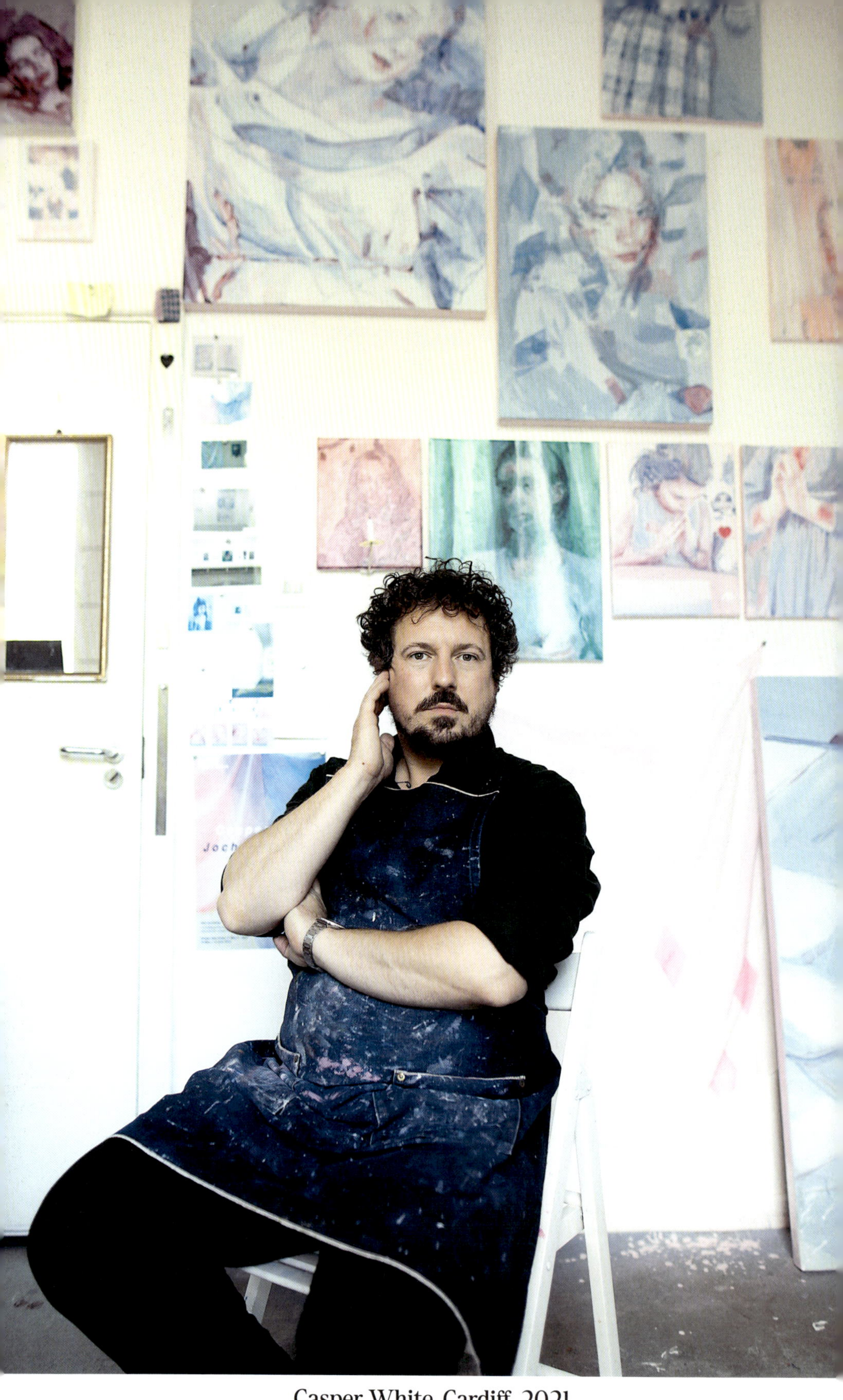

Casper White, Cardiff, 2021

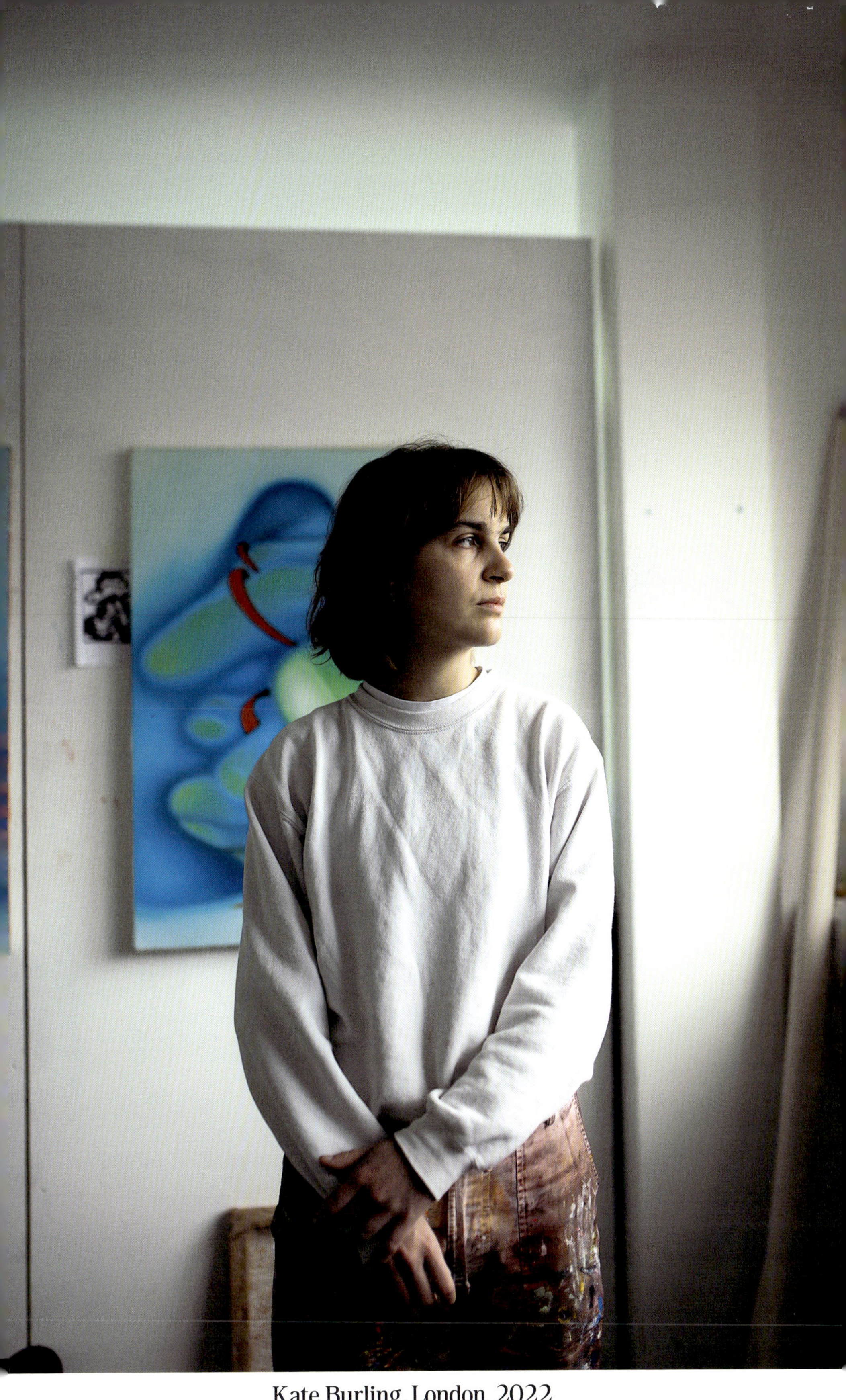

Kate Burling, London, 2022

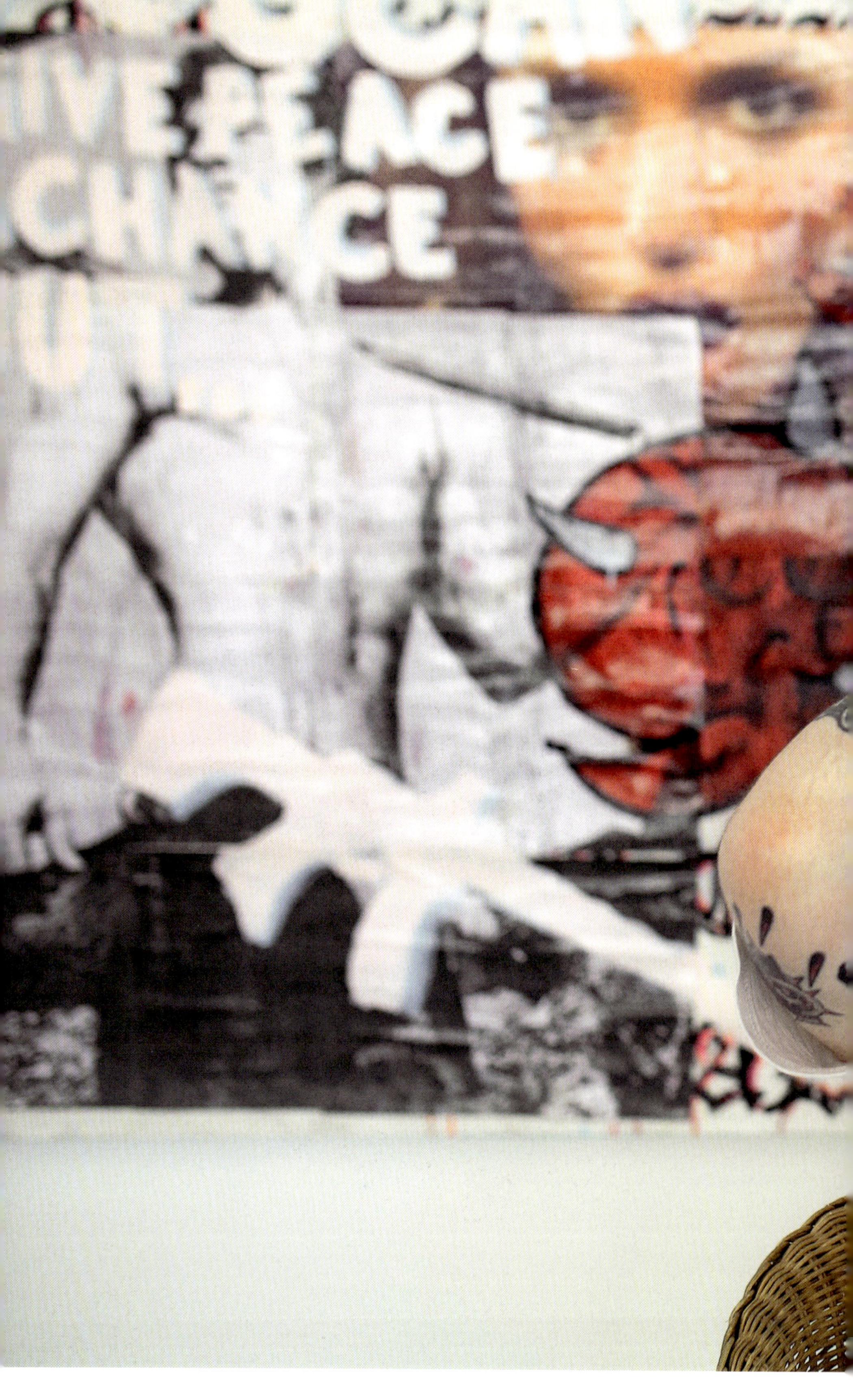
CAN
PEACE
PEACE
CHANCE
CE

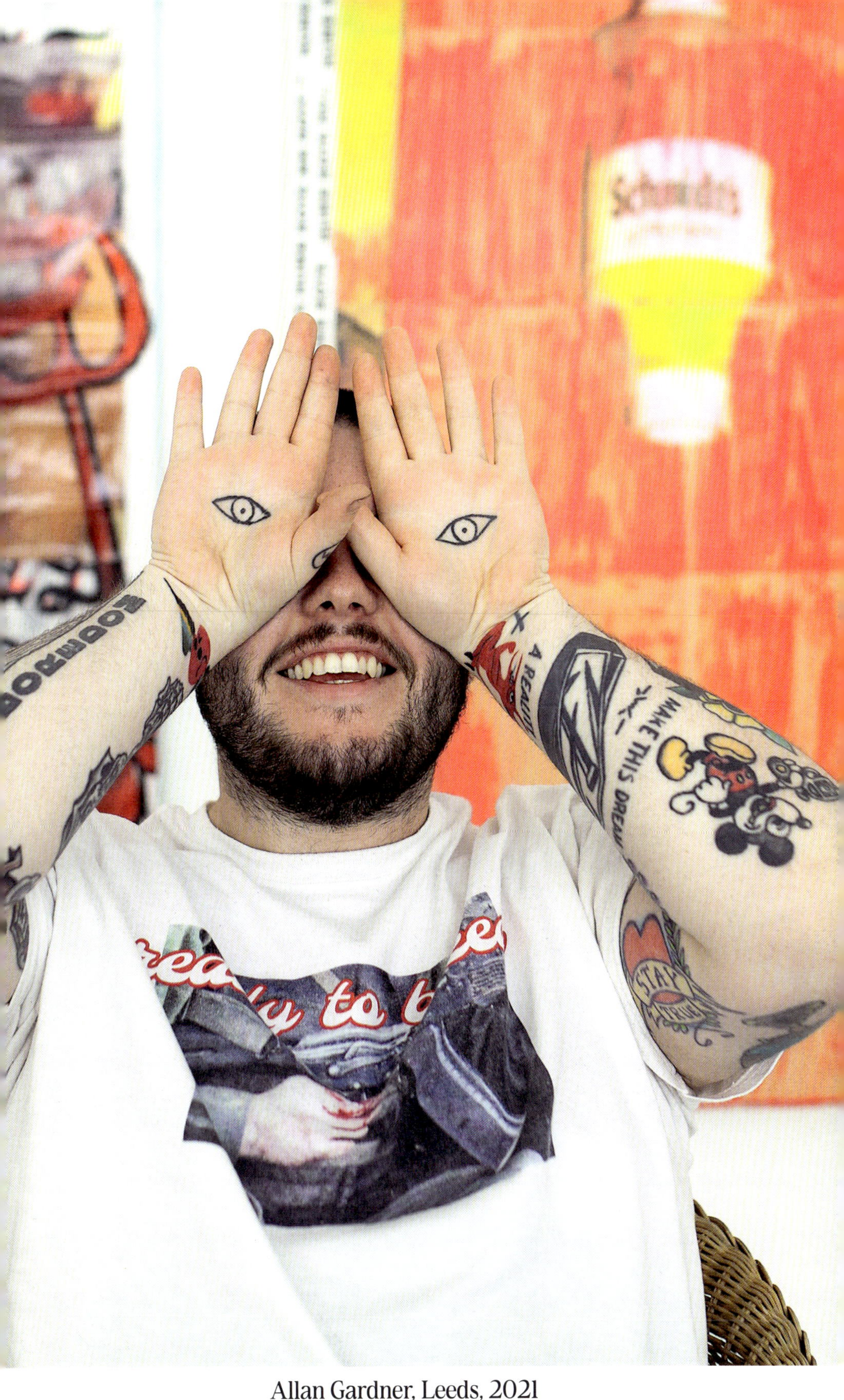

Allan Gardner, Leeds, 2021

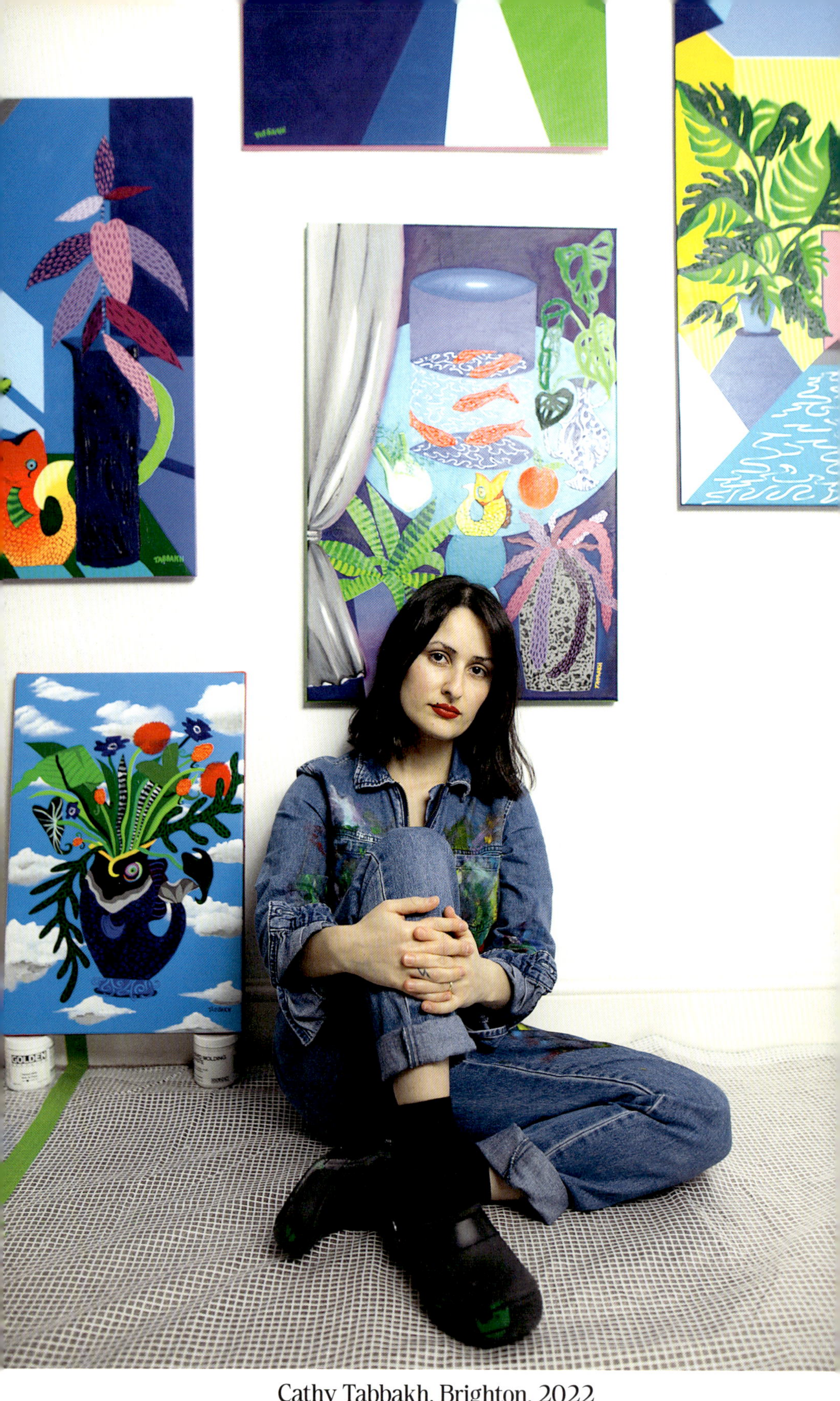

Cathy Tabbakh, Brighton, 2022

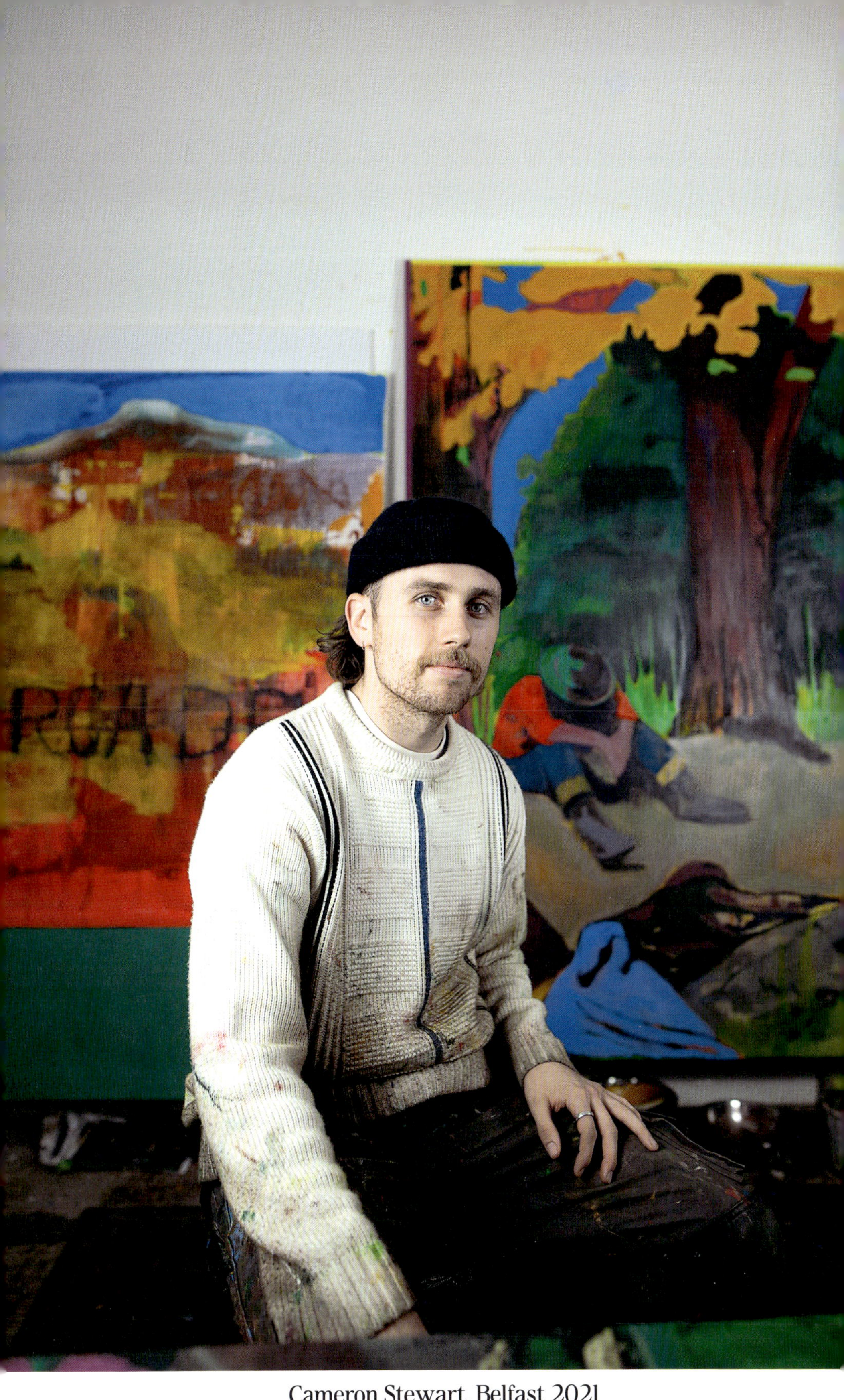

Cameron Stewart, Belfast 2021

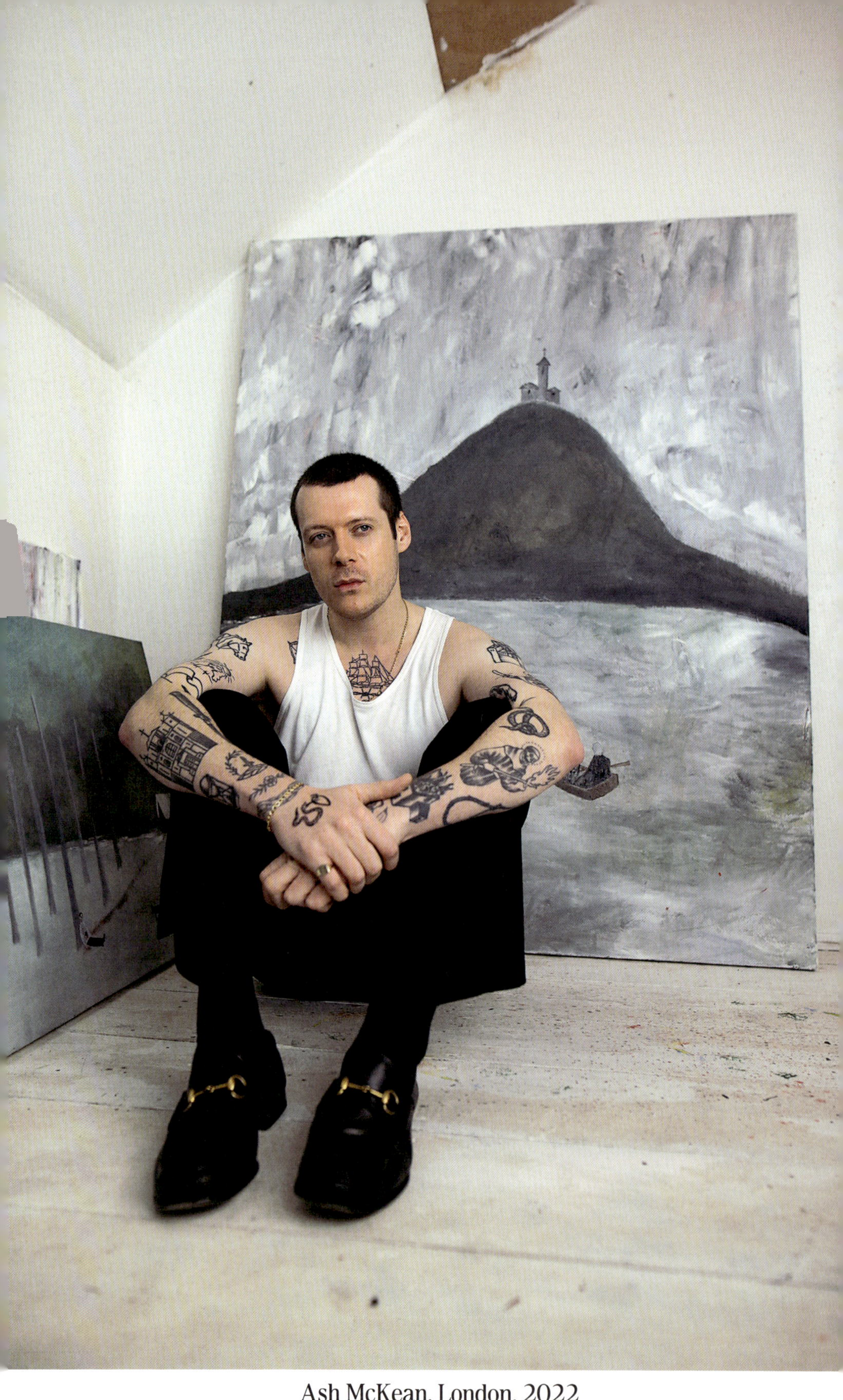

Ash McKean, London, 2022

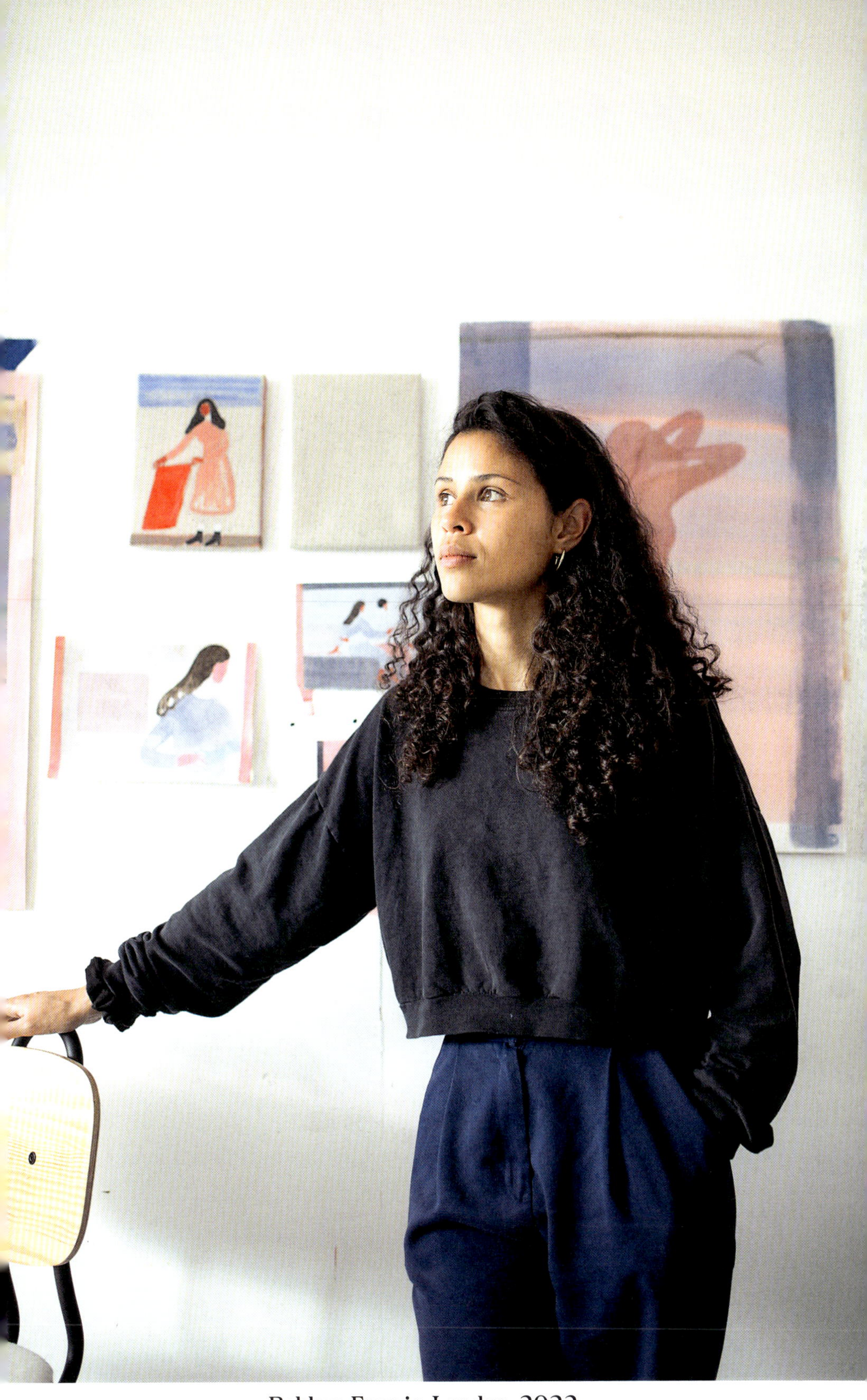

Bobbye Fermie, London, 2022

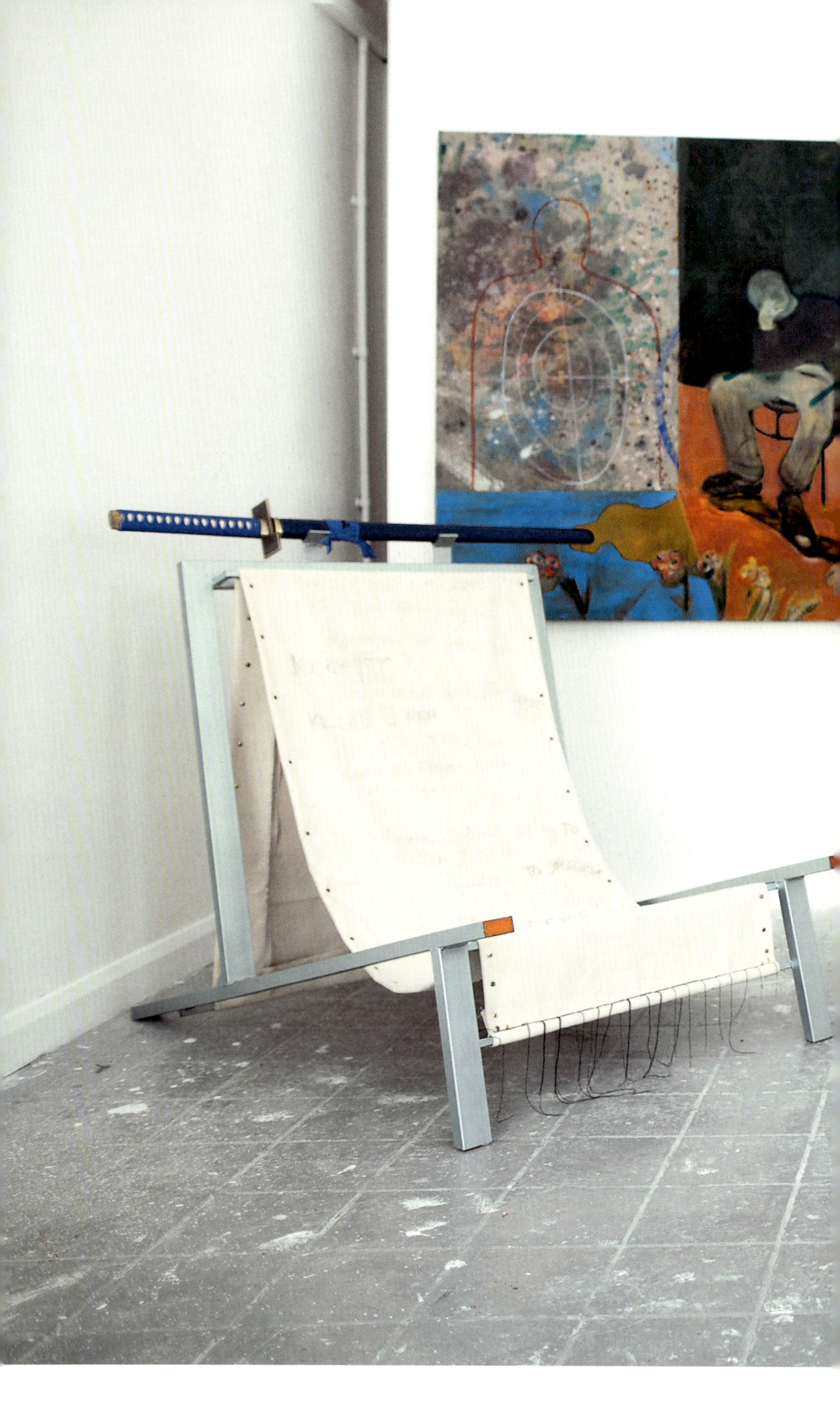

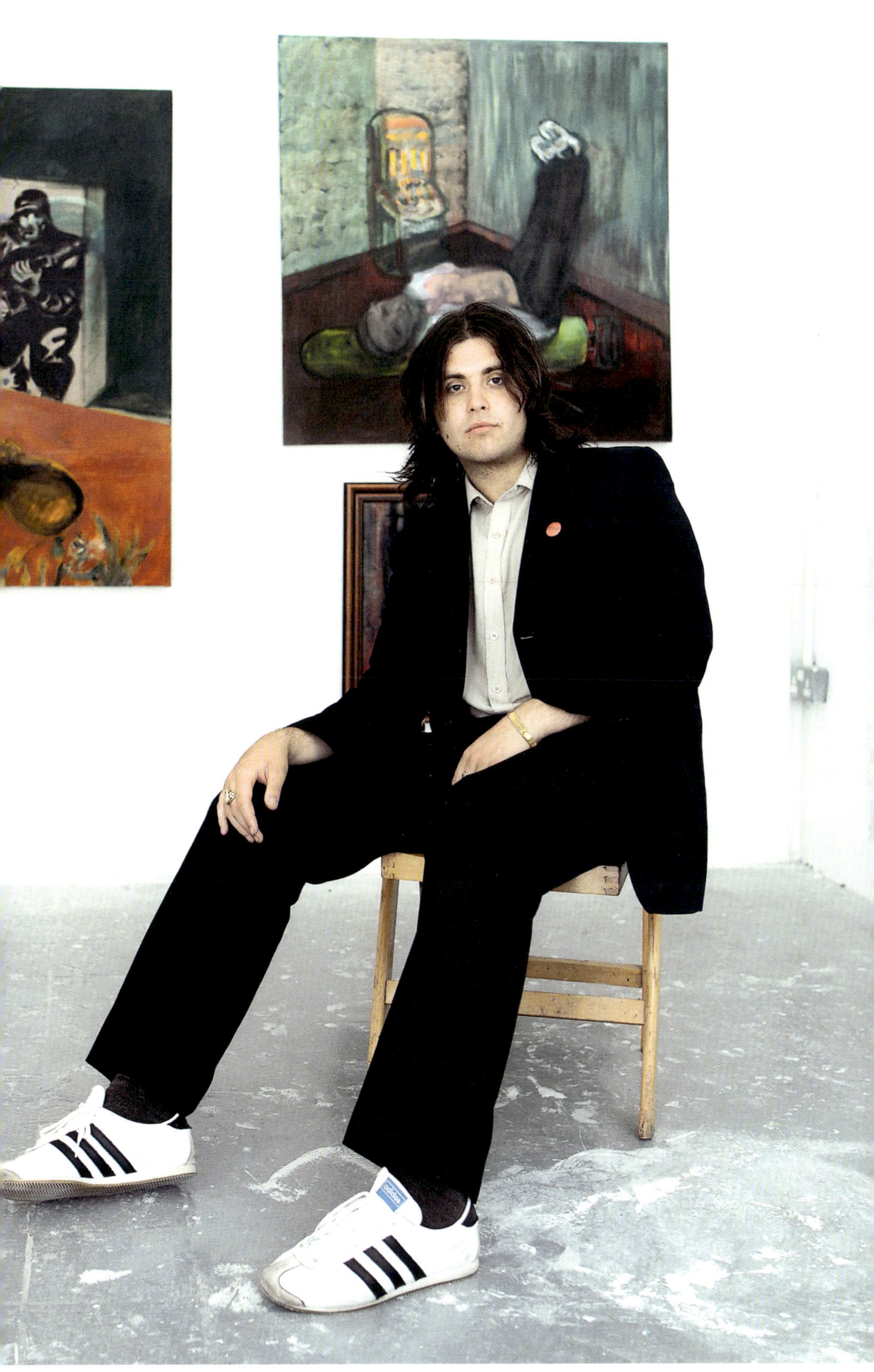

Harley Roberts, Leeds, 2021

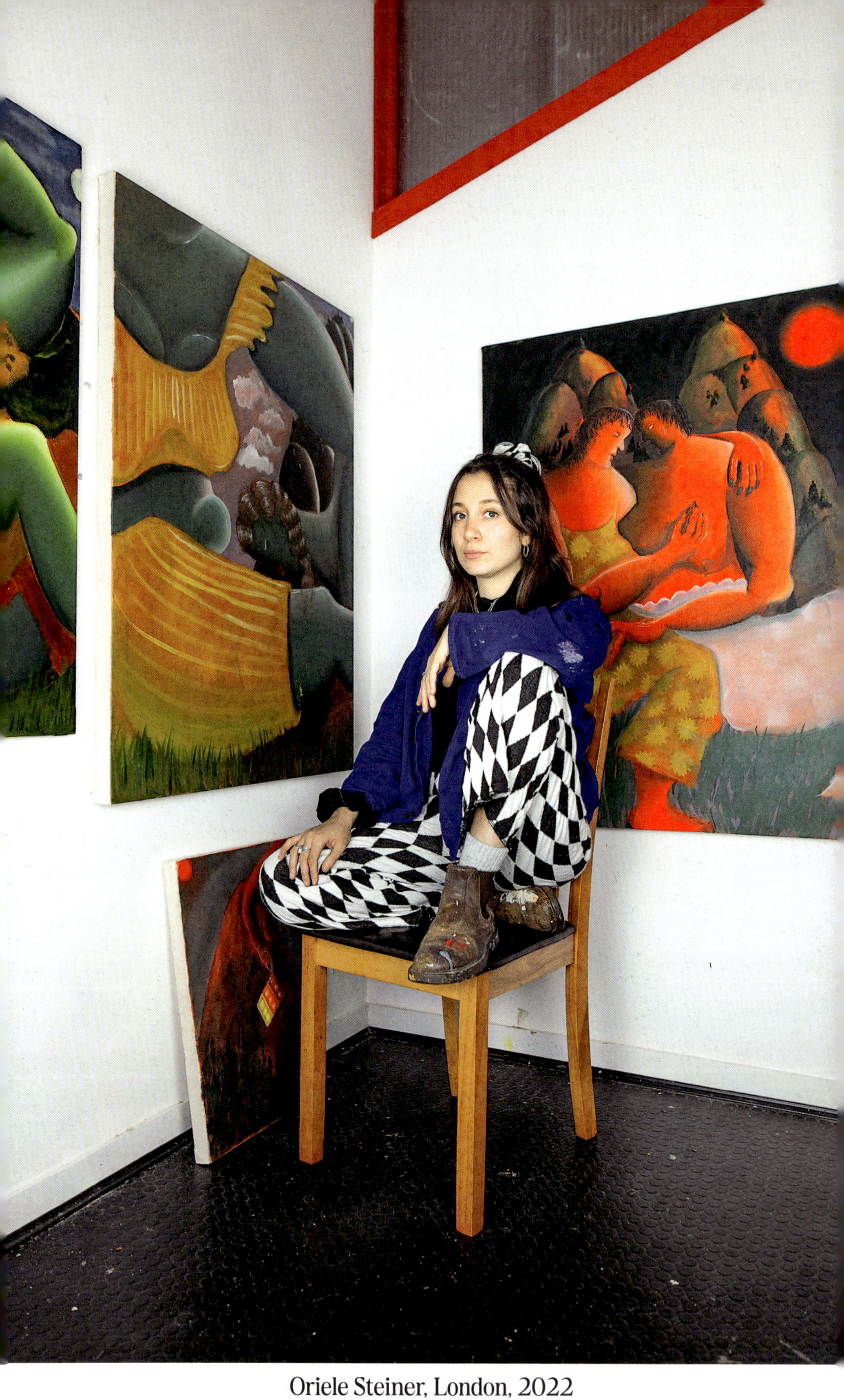

Oriele Steiner, London, 2022

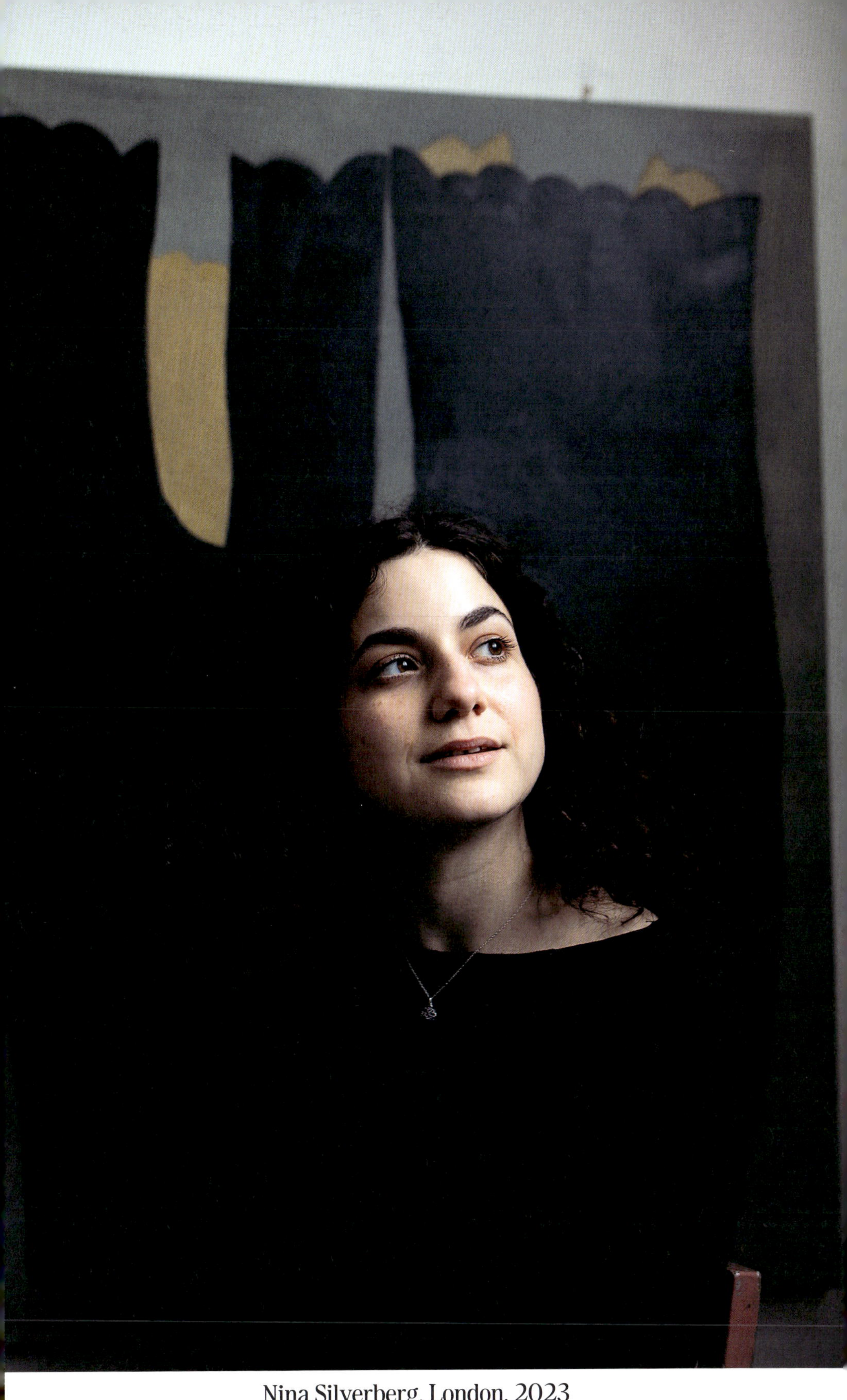

Nina Silverberg, London, 2023

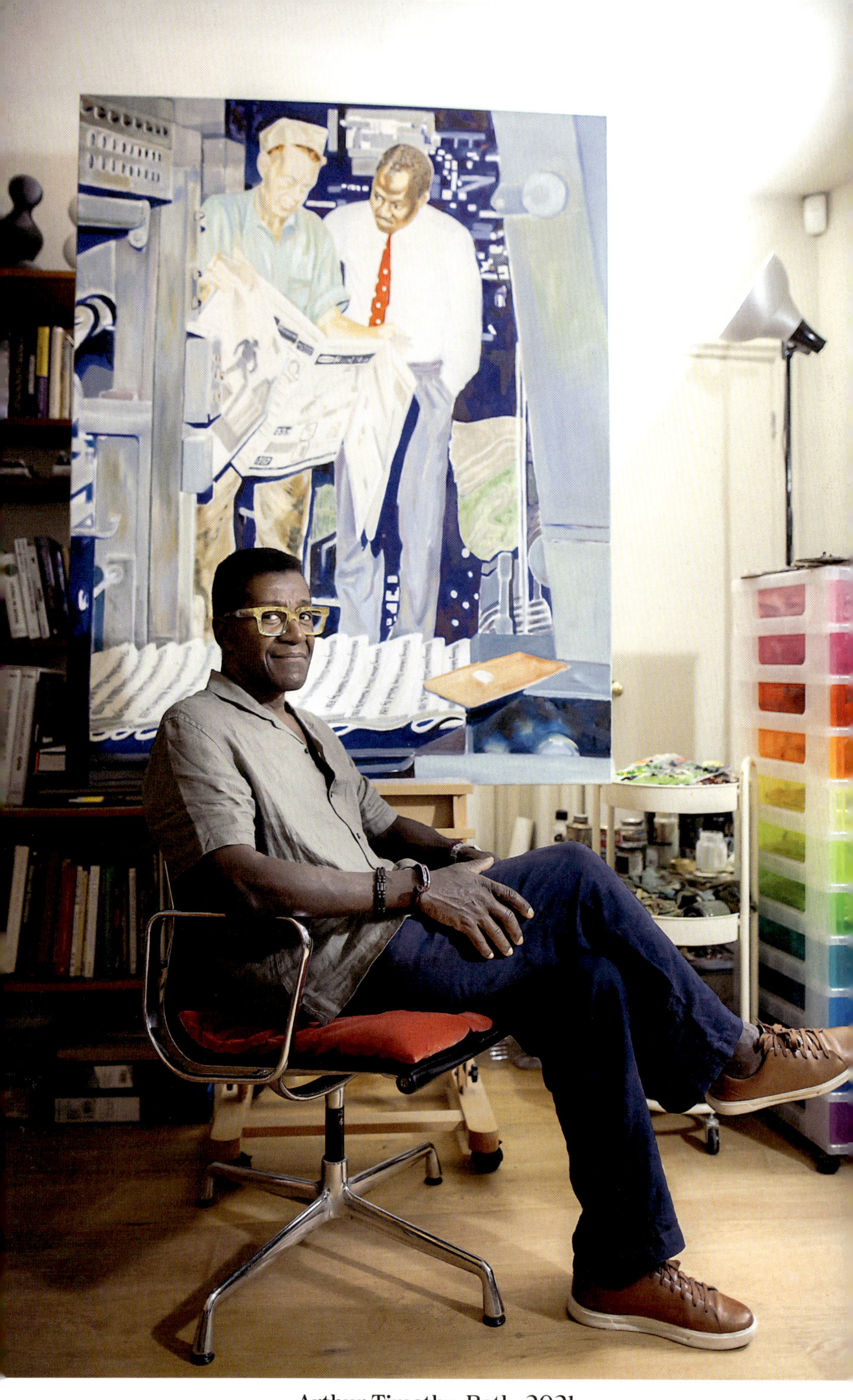

Arthur Timothy, Bath, 2021

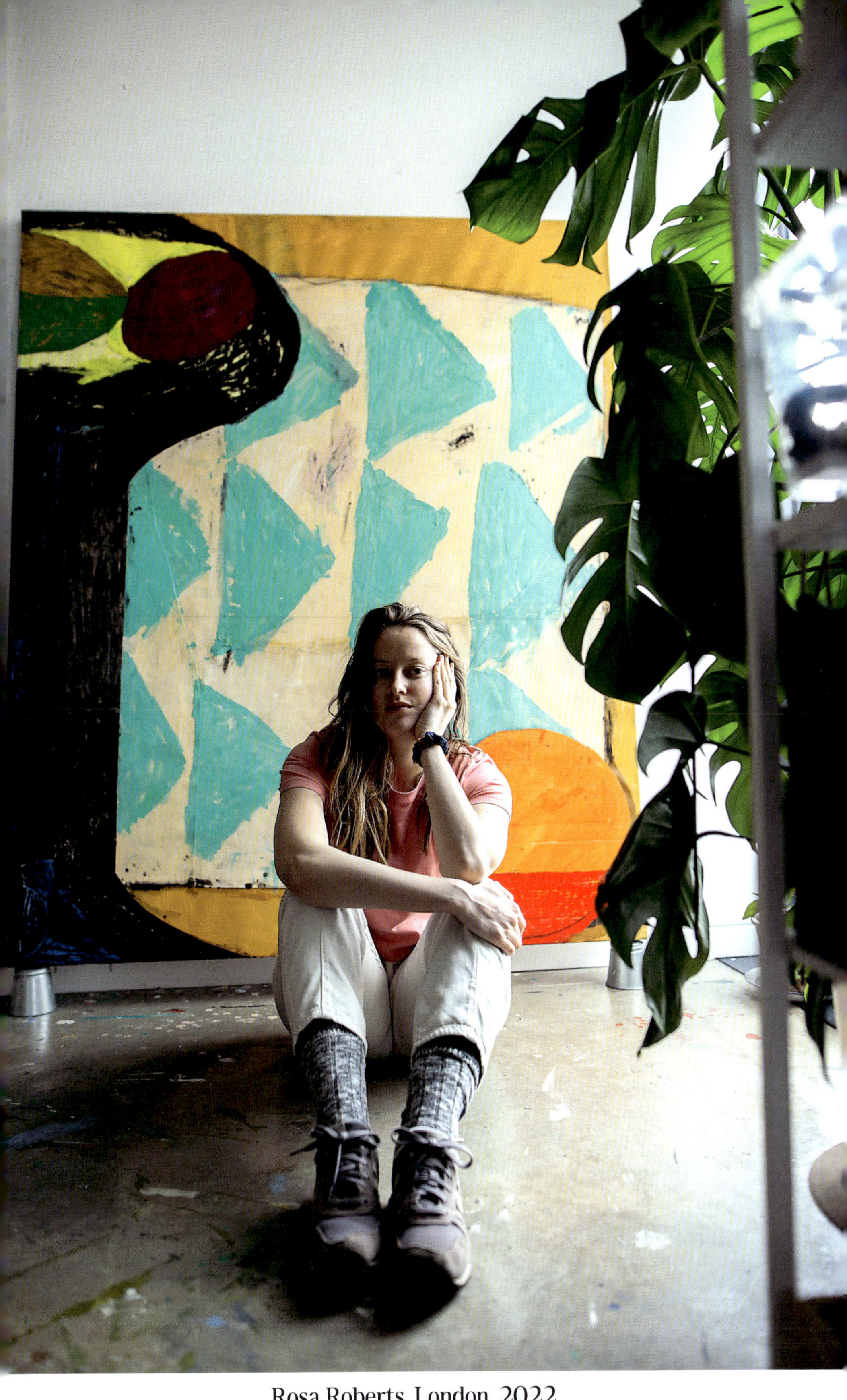

Rosa Roberts, London, 2022

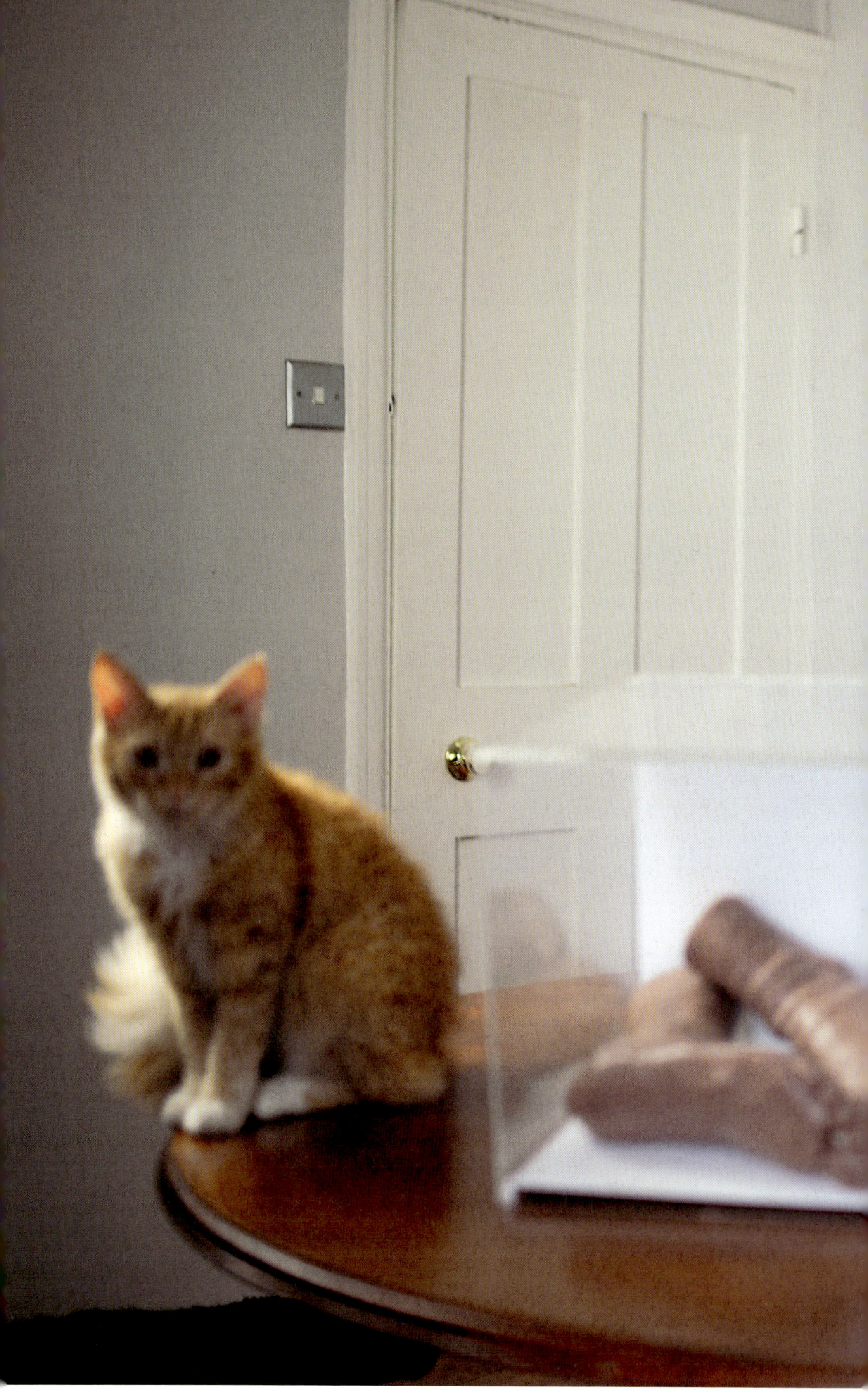

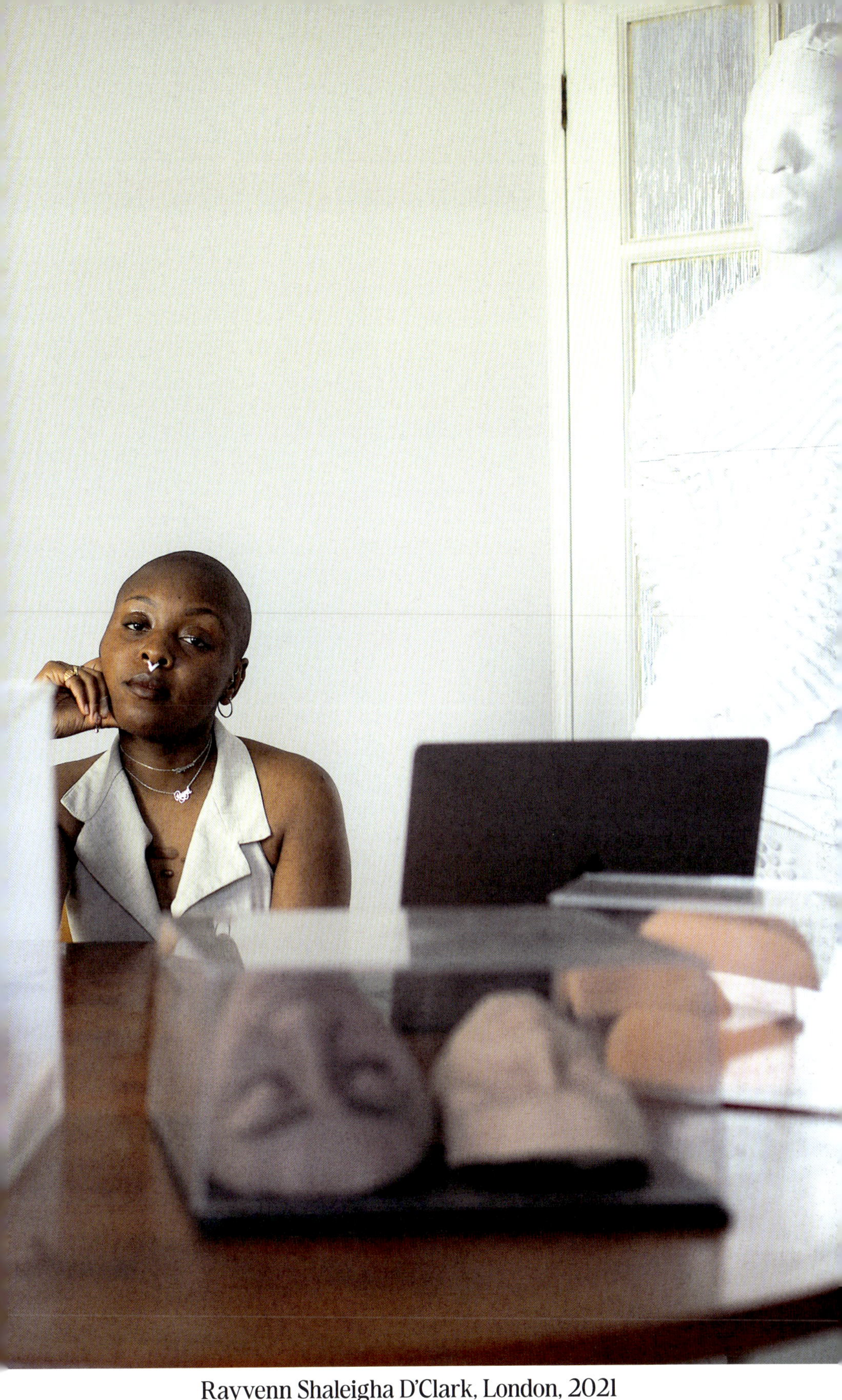

Rayvenn Shaleigha D'Clark, London, 2021

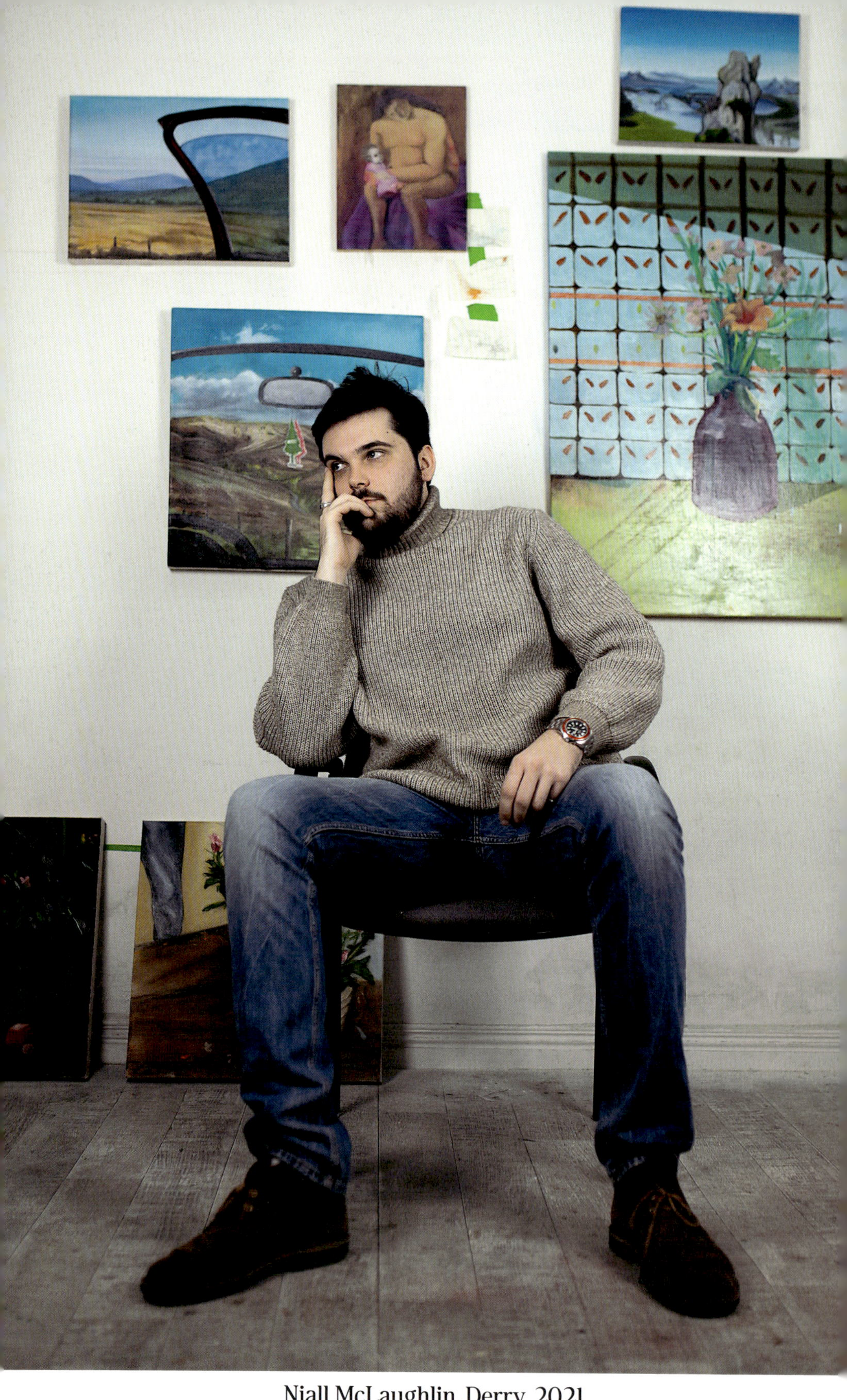

Niall McLaughlin, Derry, 2021

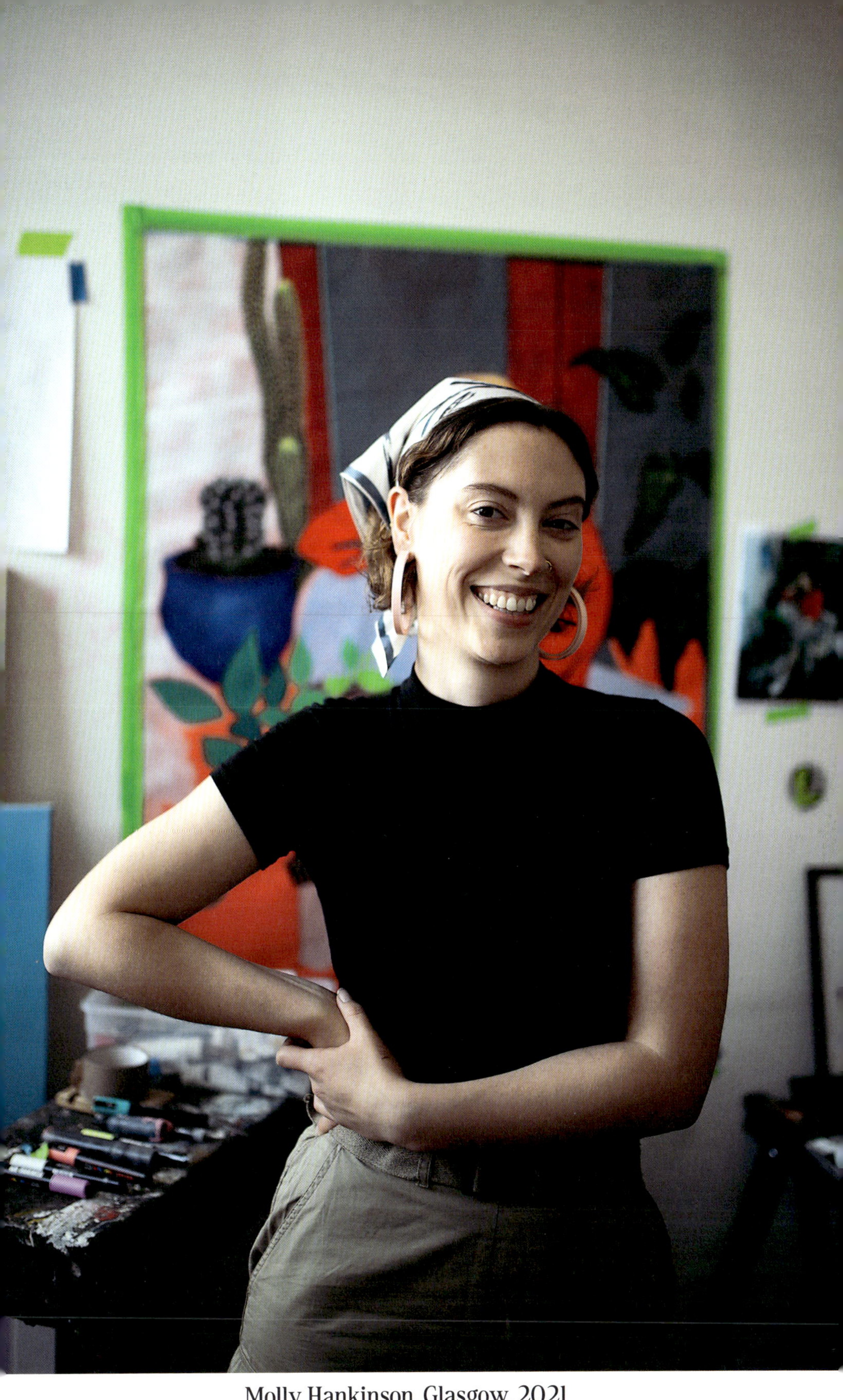

Molly Hankinson, Glasgow, 2021

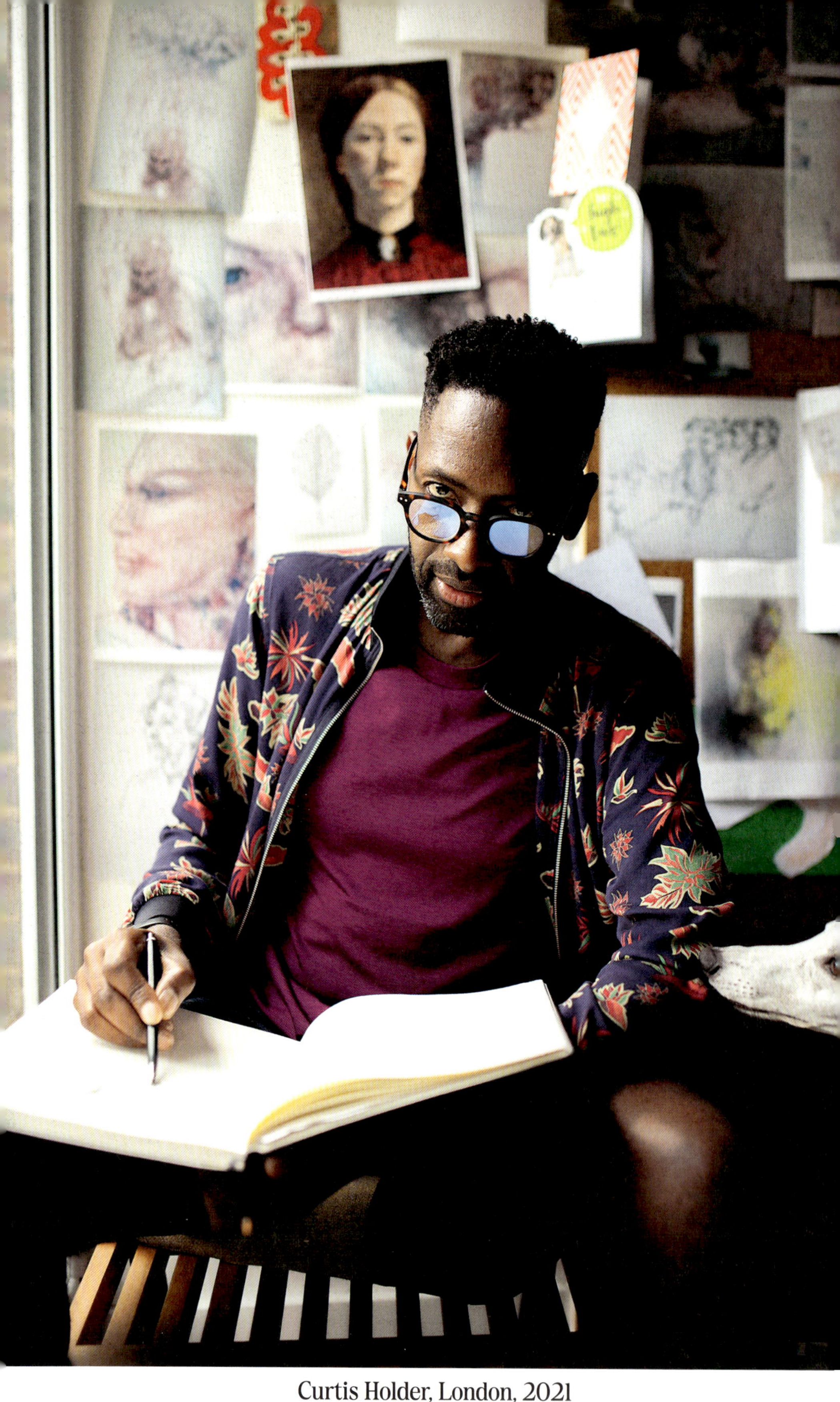

Curtis Holder, London, 2021

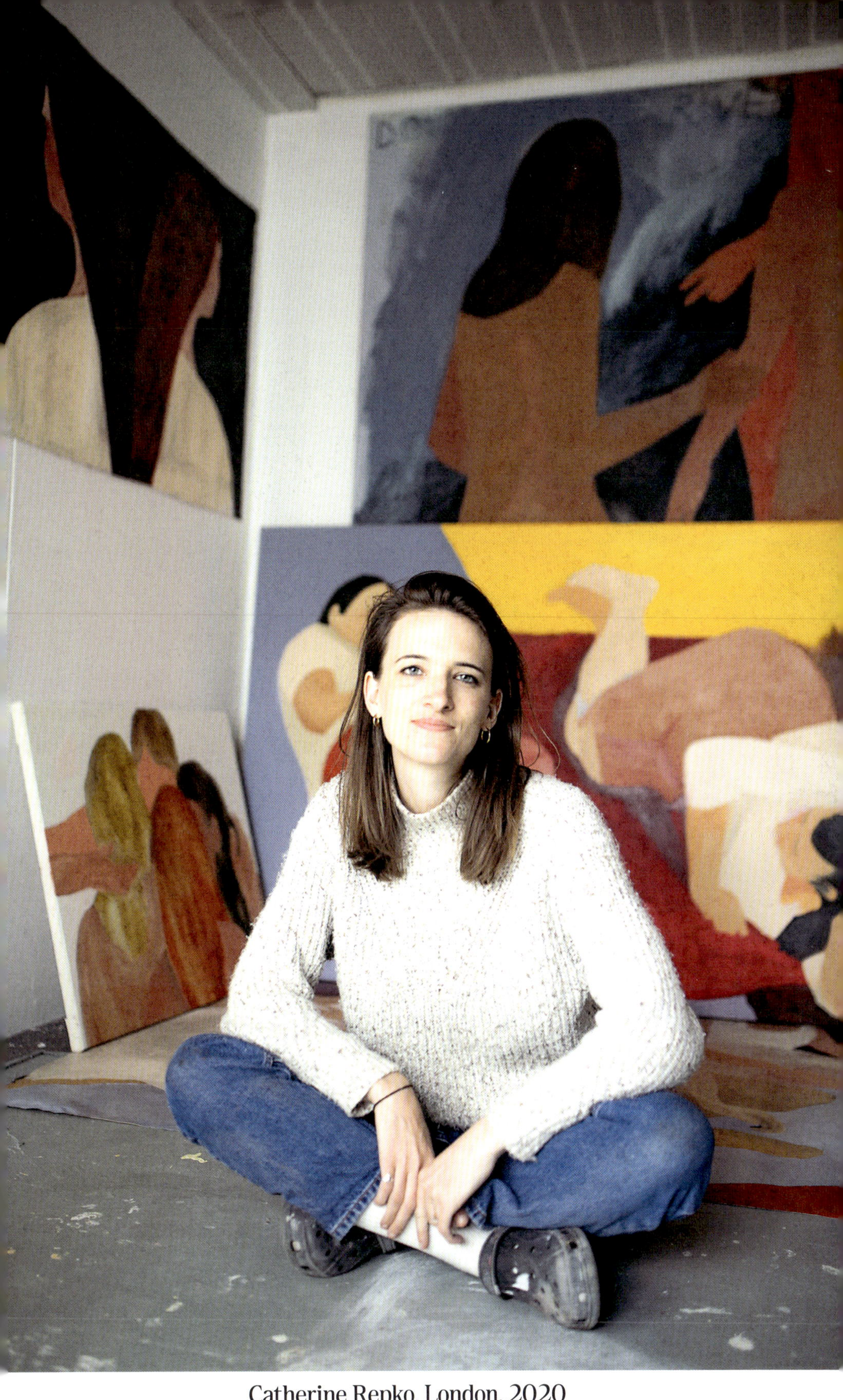

Catherine Repko, London, 2020

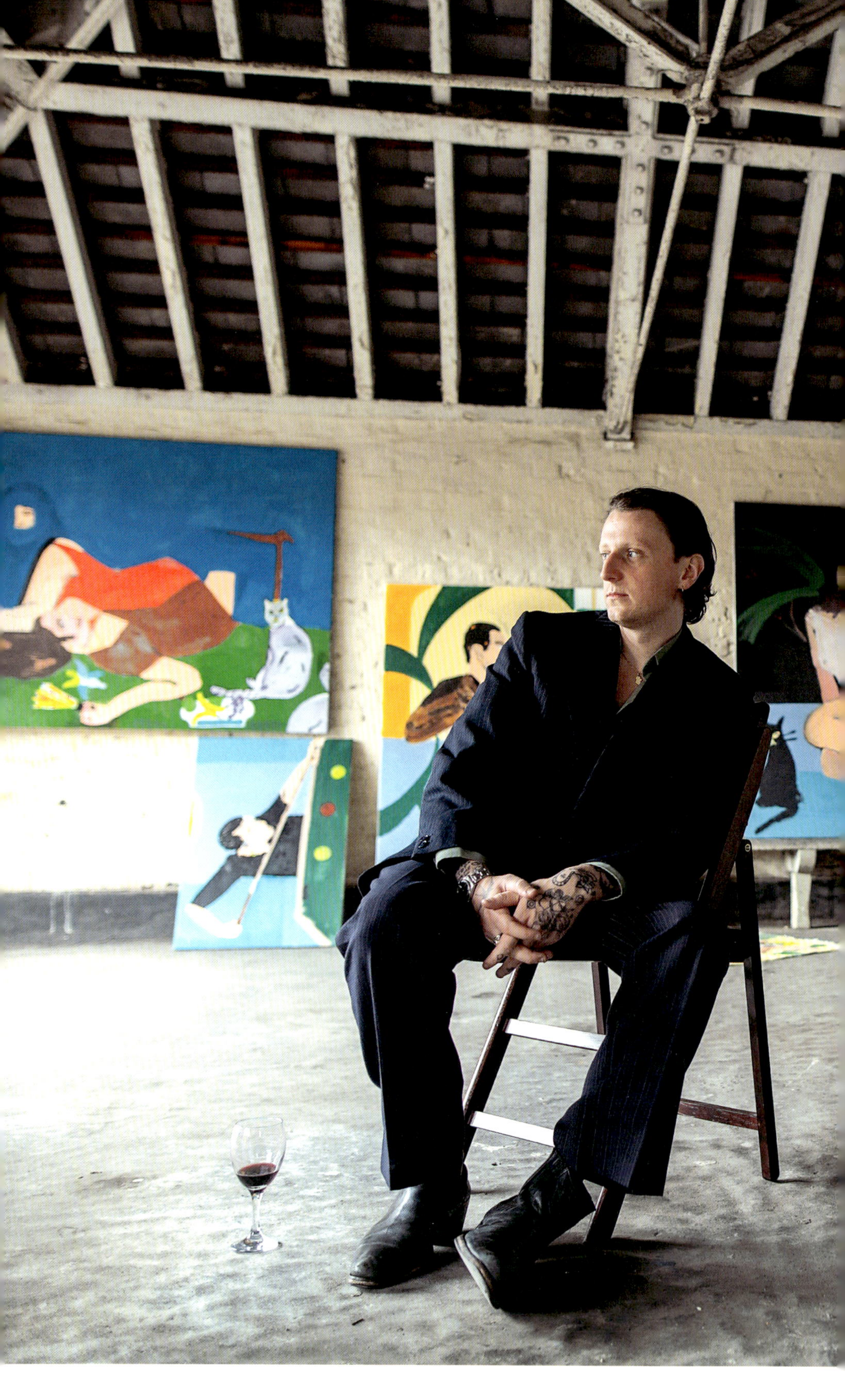

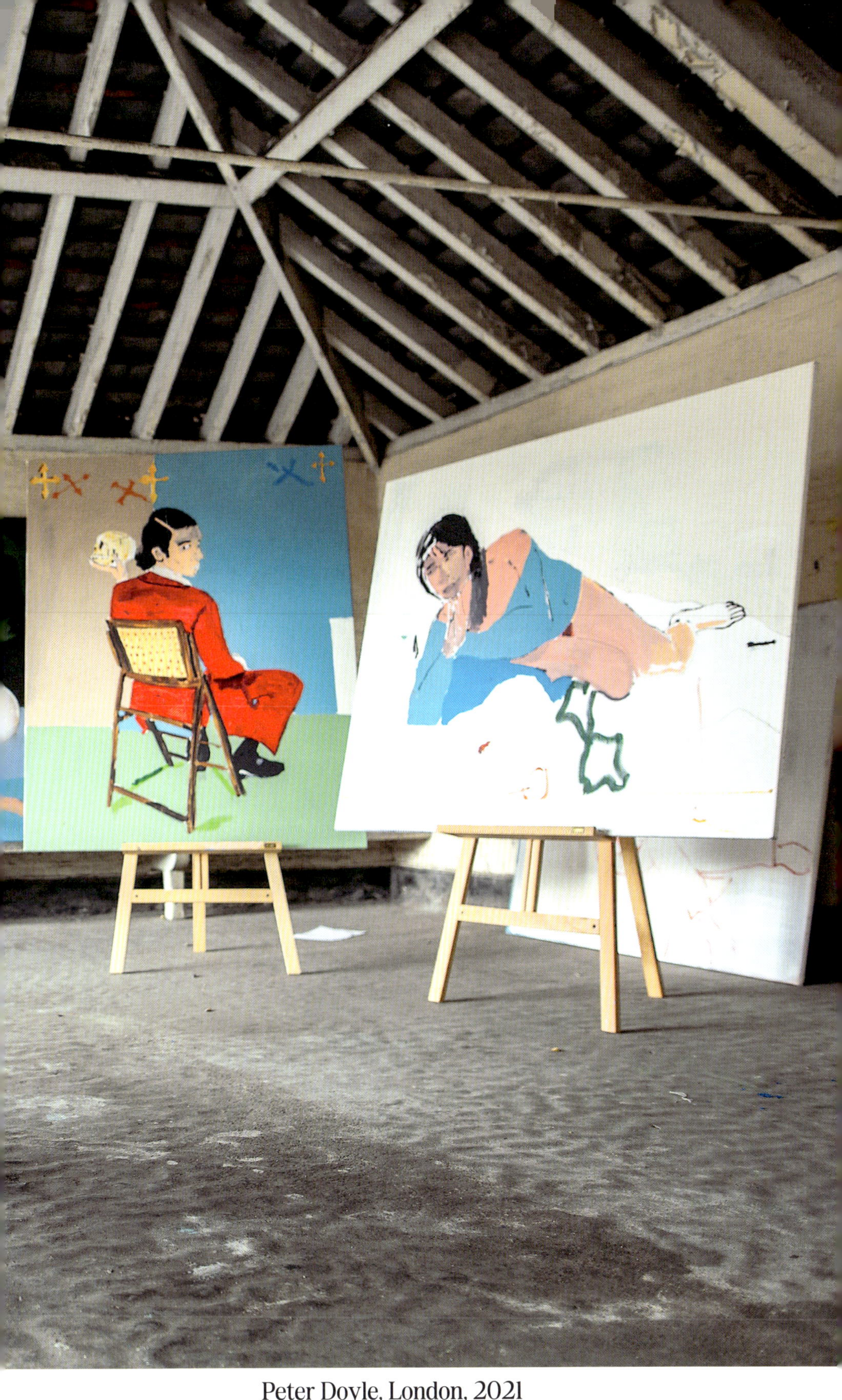

Peter Doyle, London, 2021

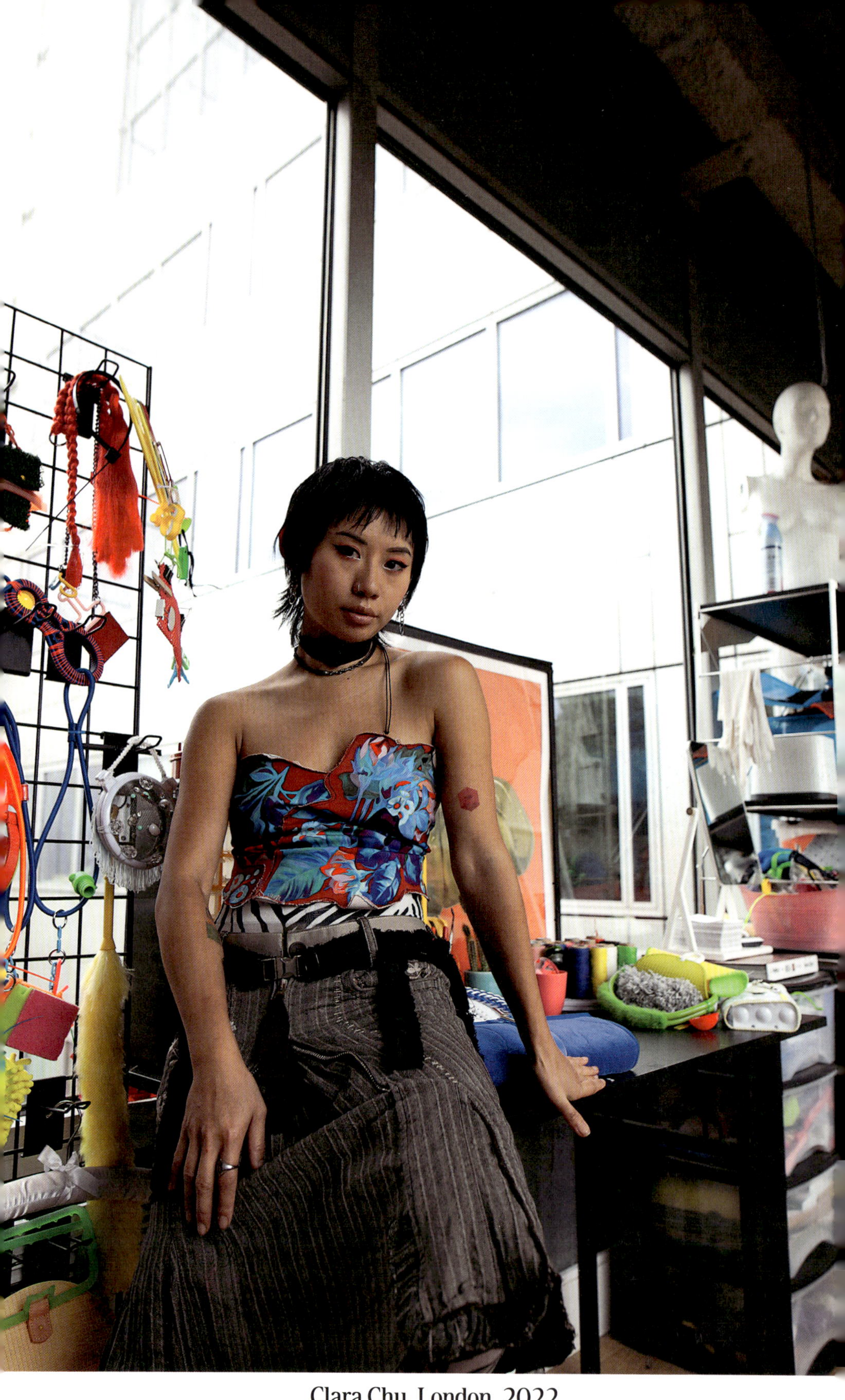

Clara Chu, London, 2022

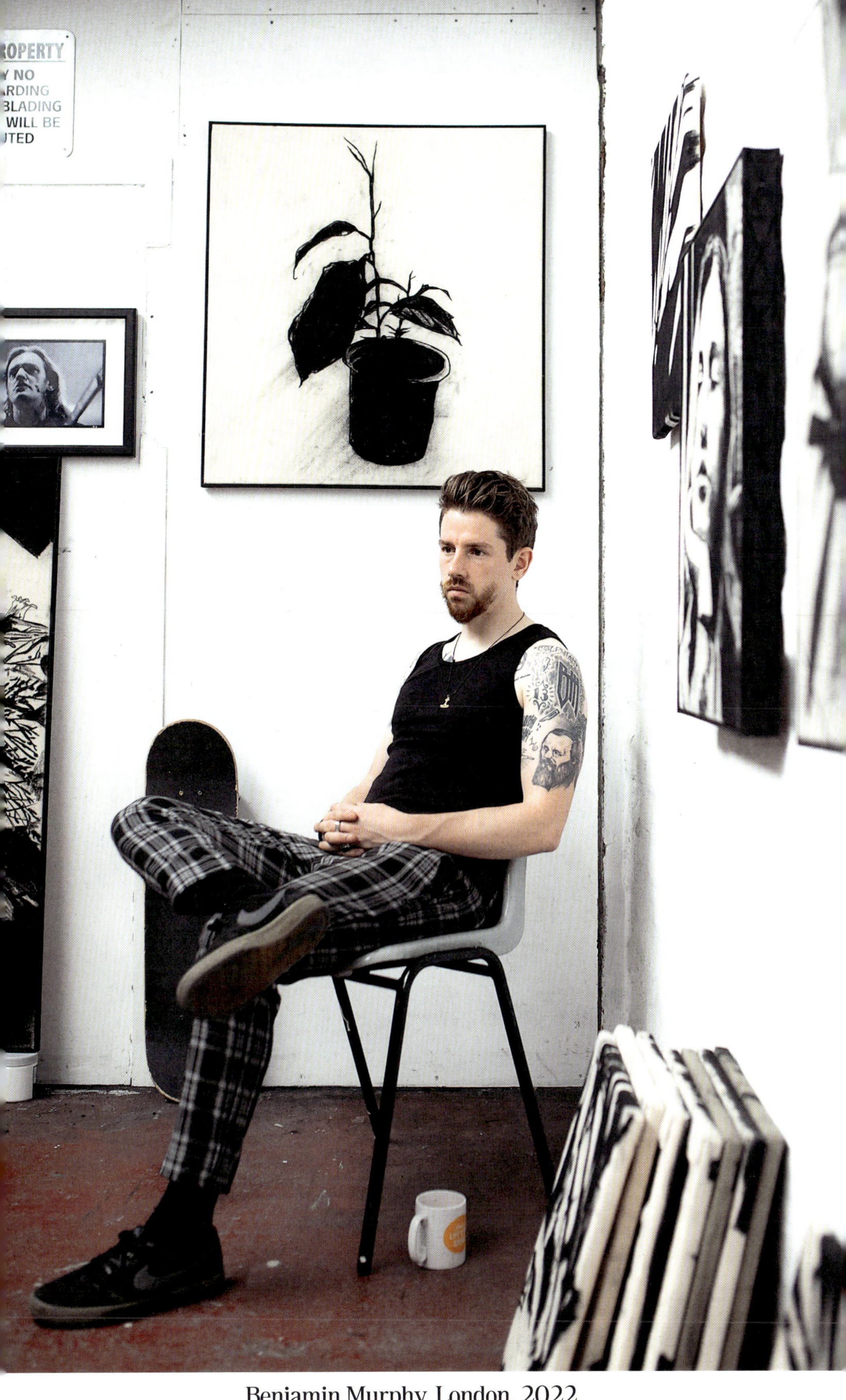

Benjamin Murphy, London, 2022

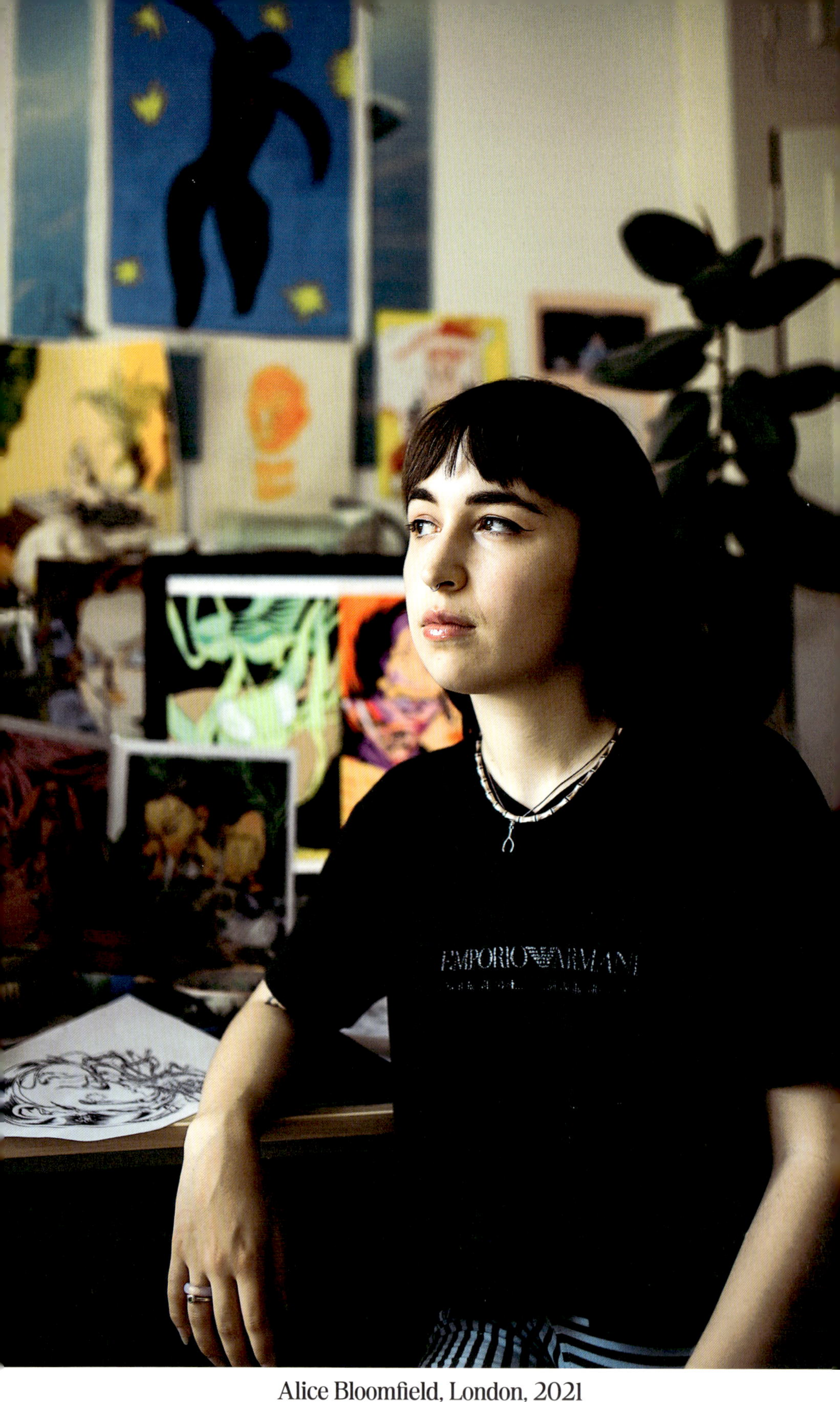

Alice Bloomfield, London, 2021

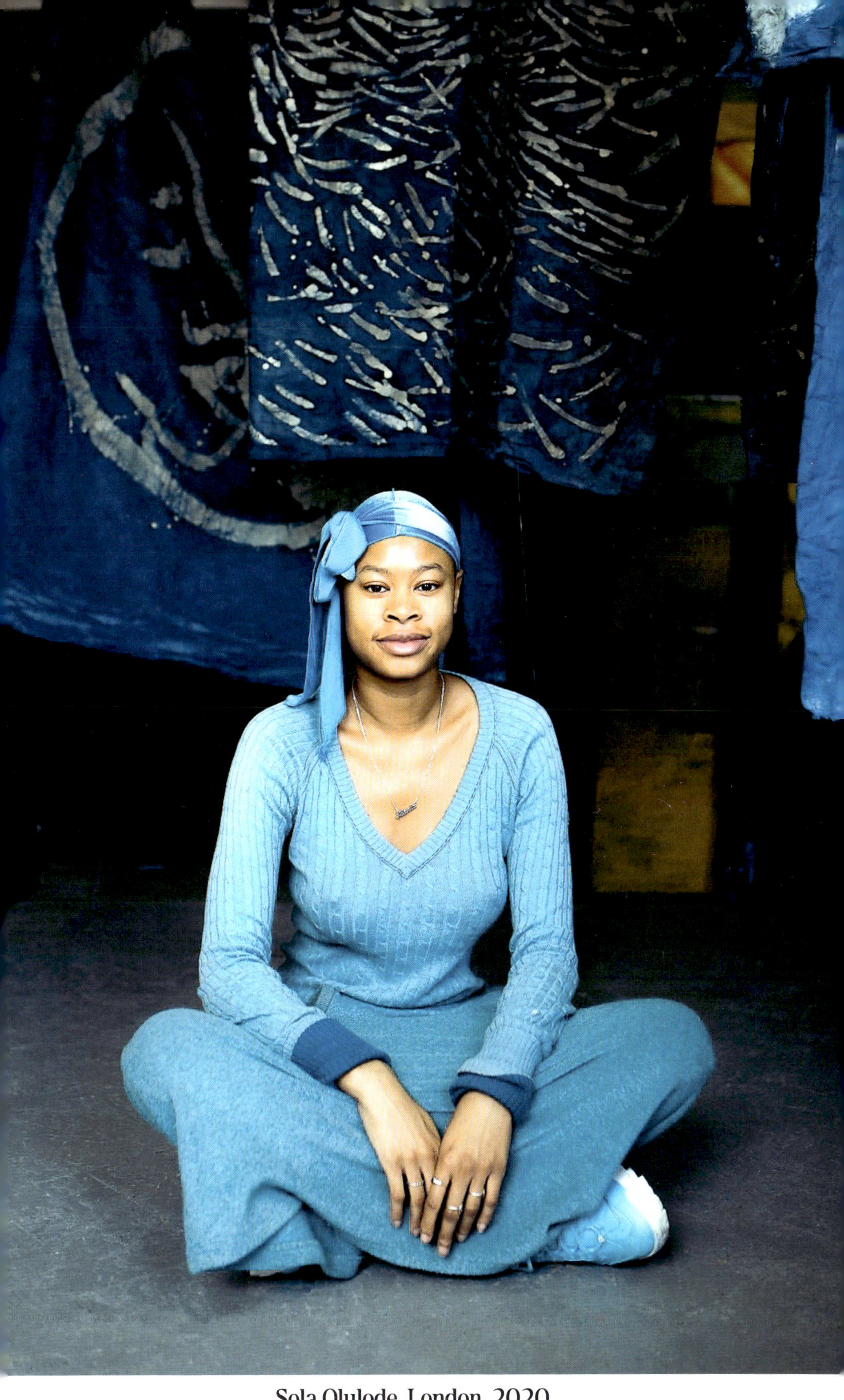

Sola Olulode, London, 2020

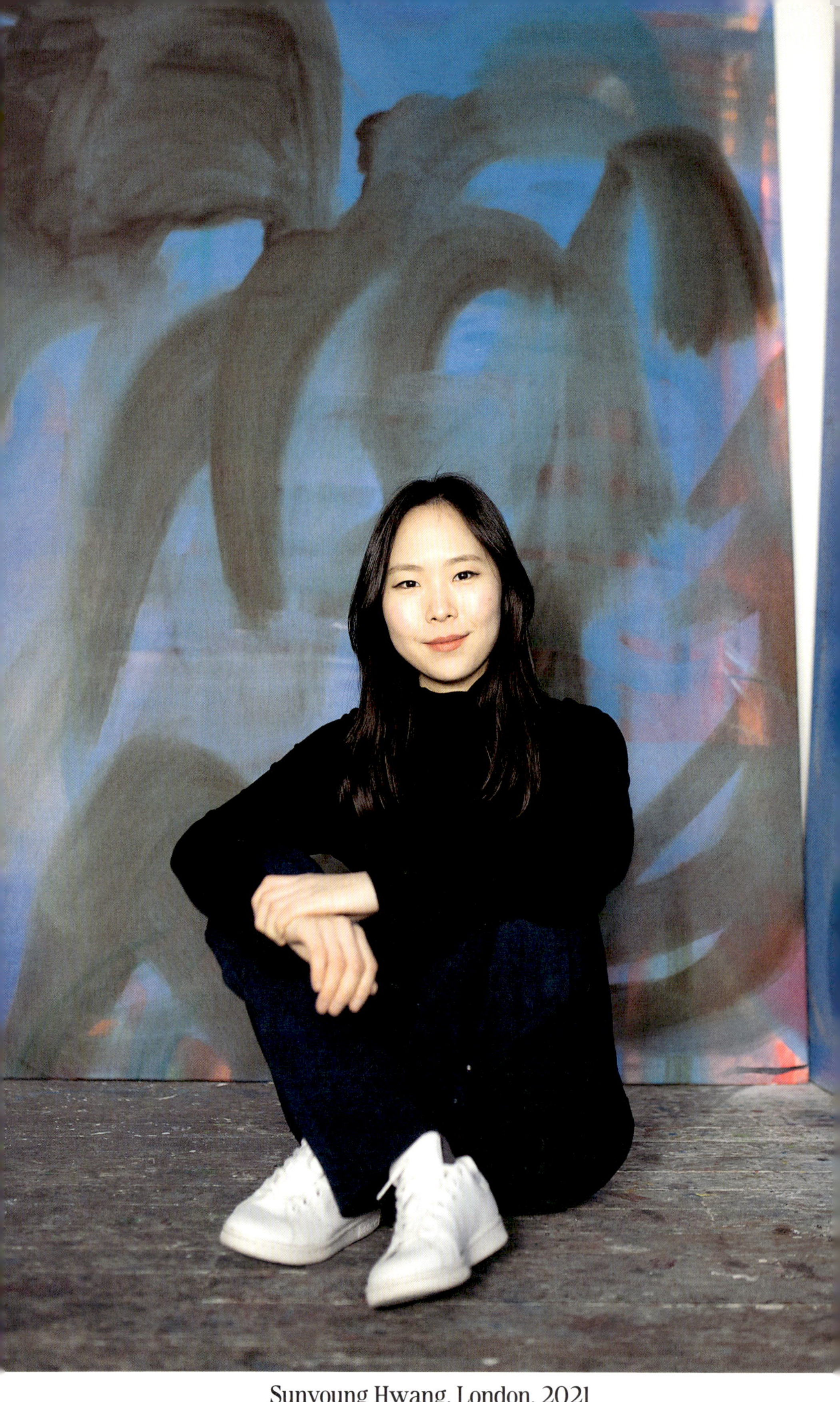

Sunyoung Hwang, London, 2021

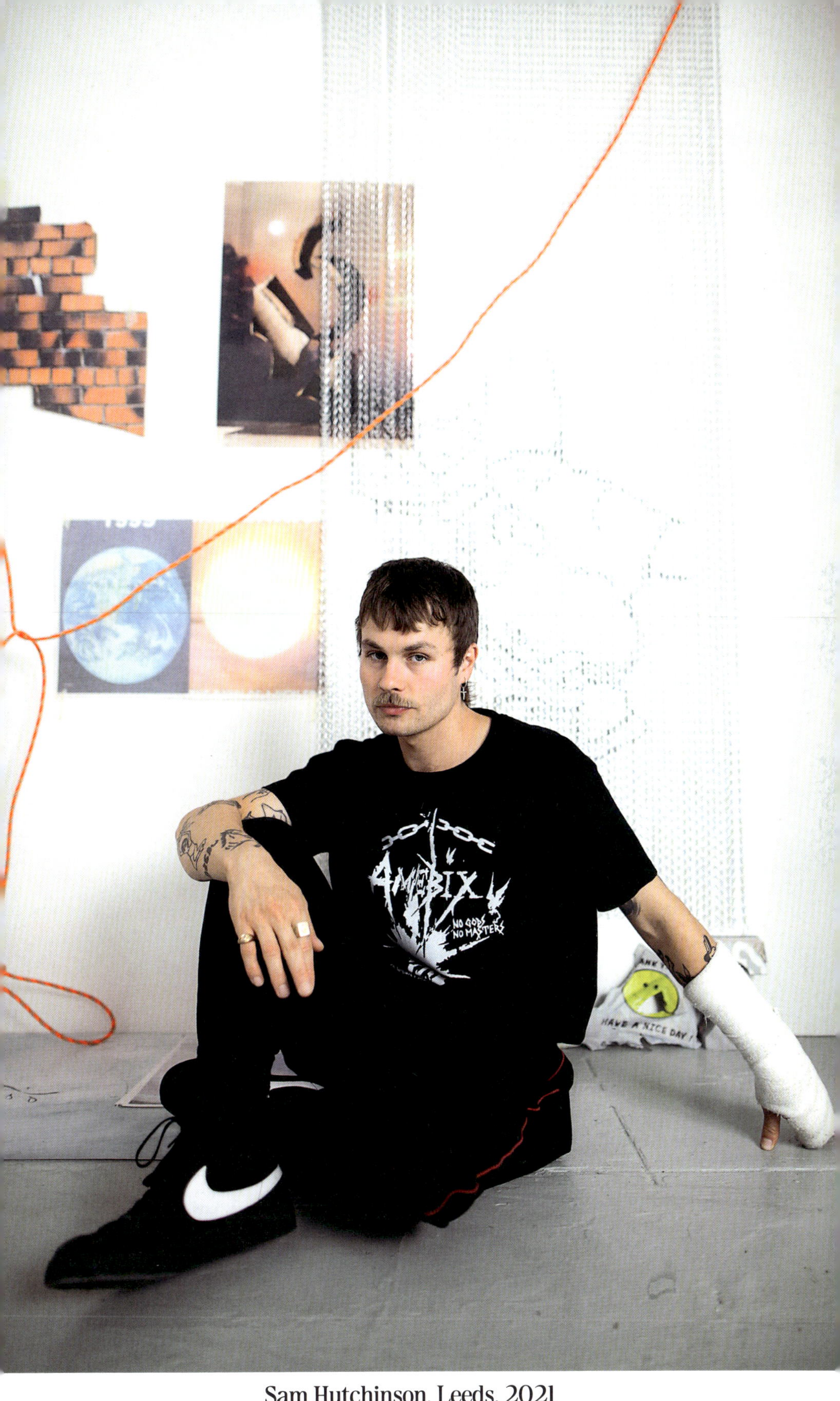

Sam Hutchinson, Leeds, 2021

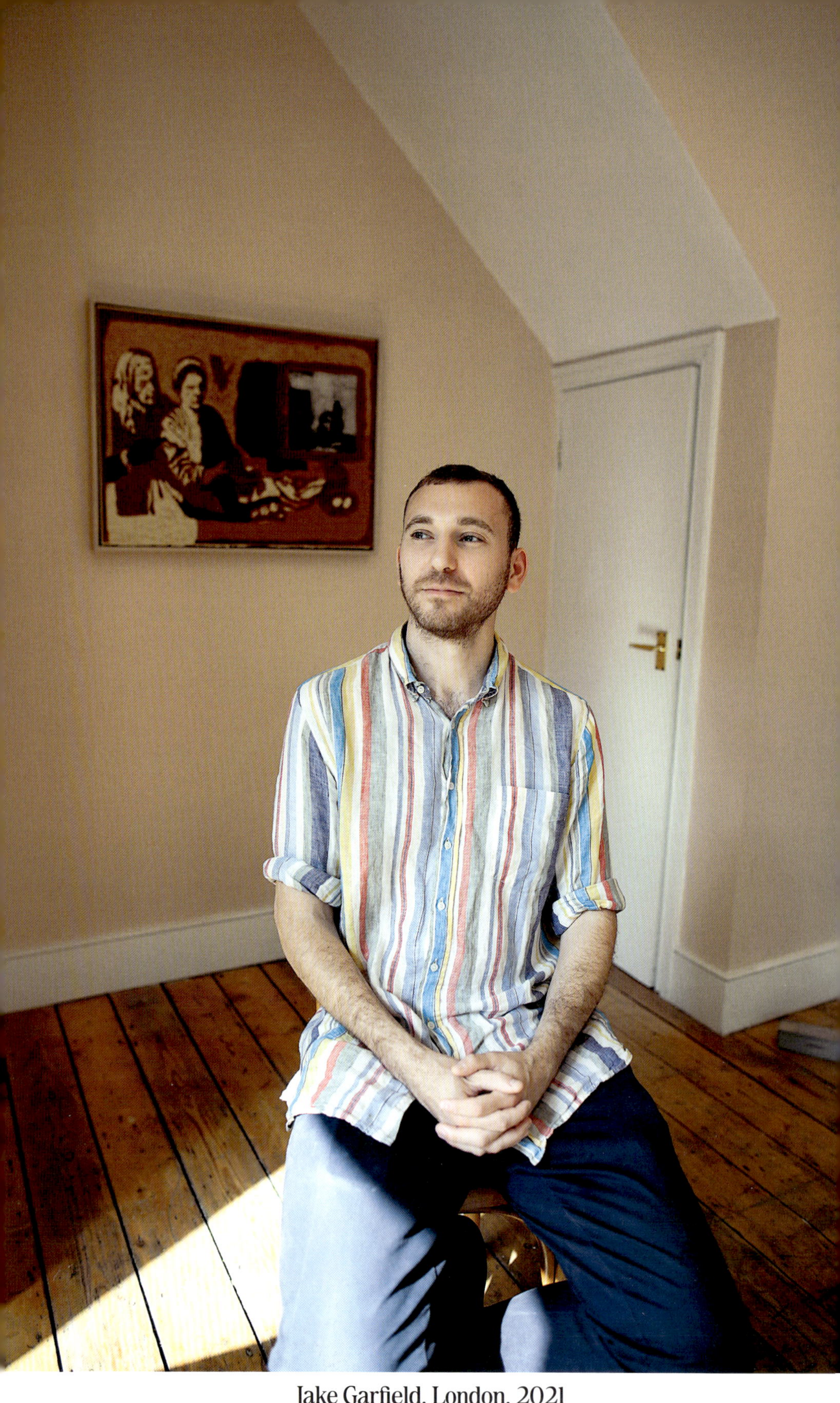

Jake Garfield, London, 2021

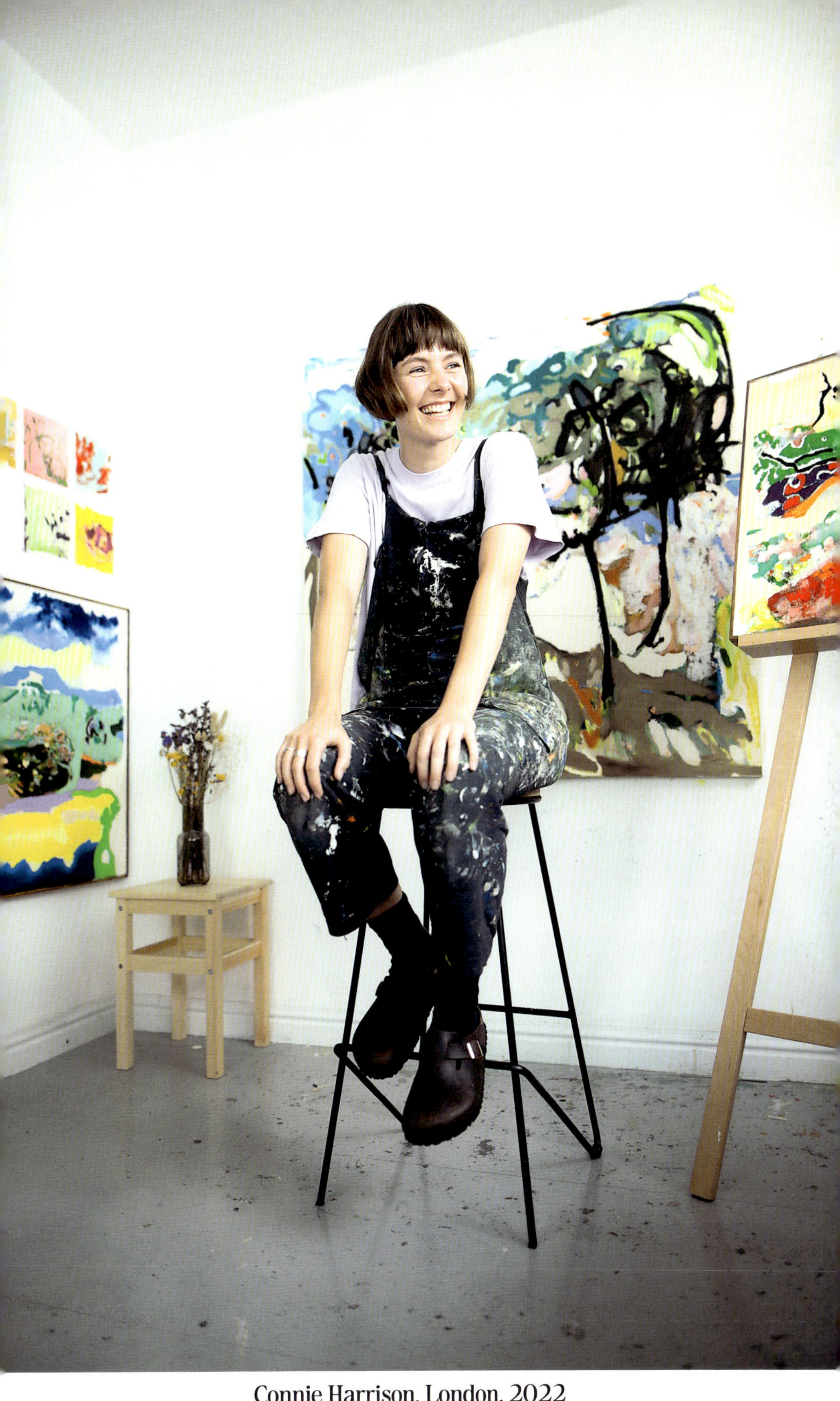

Connie Harrison, London, 2022

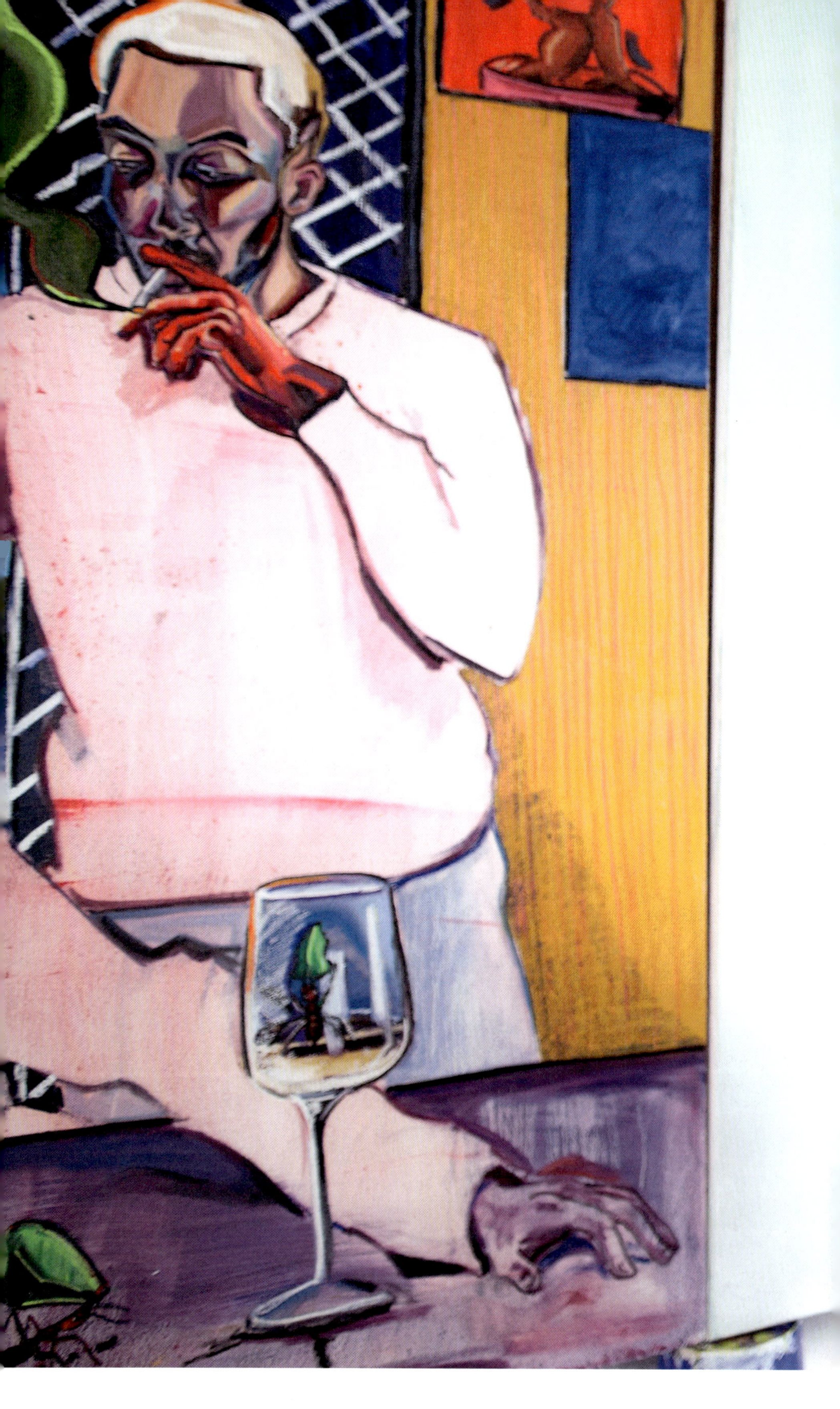

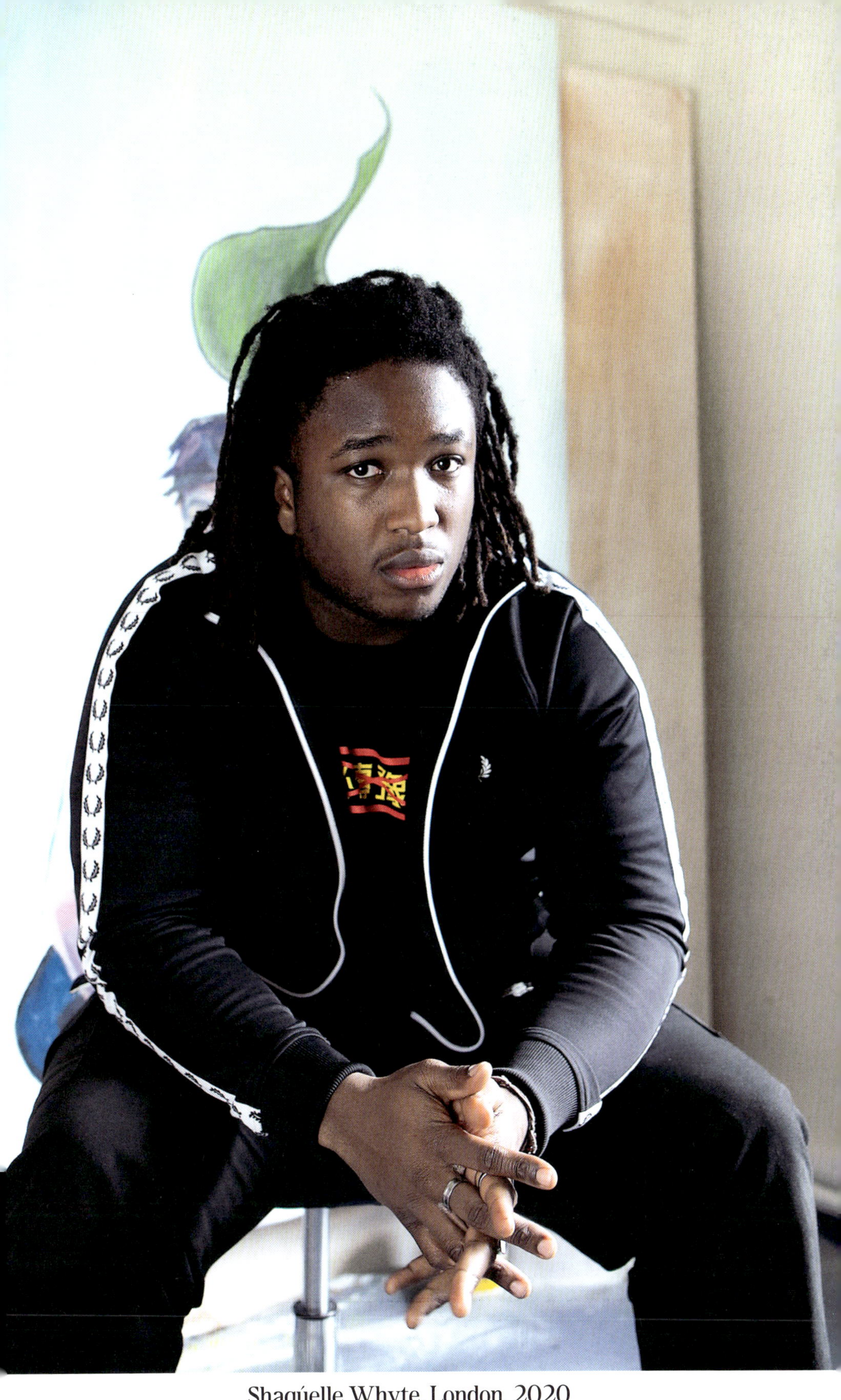

Shaqúelle Whyte, London, 2020

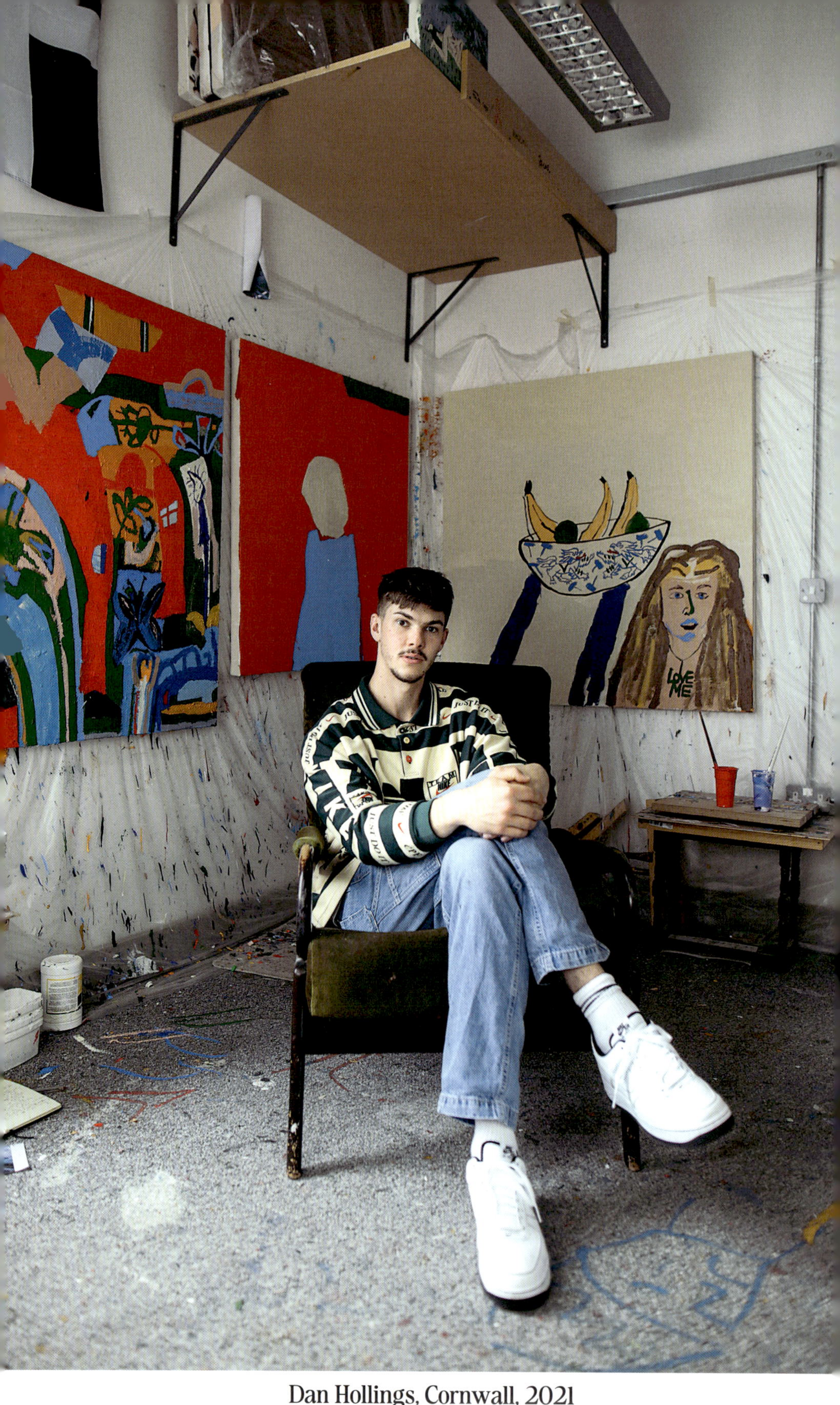

Dan Hollings, Cornwall, 2021

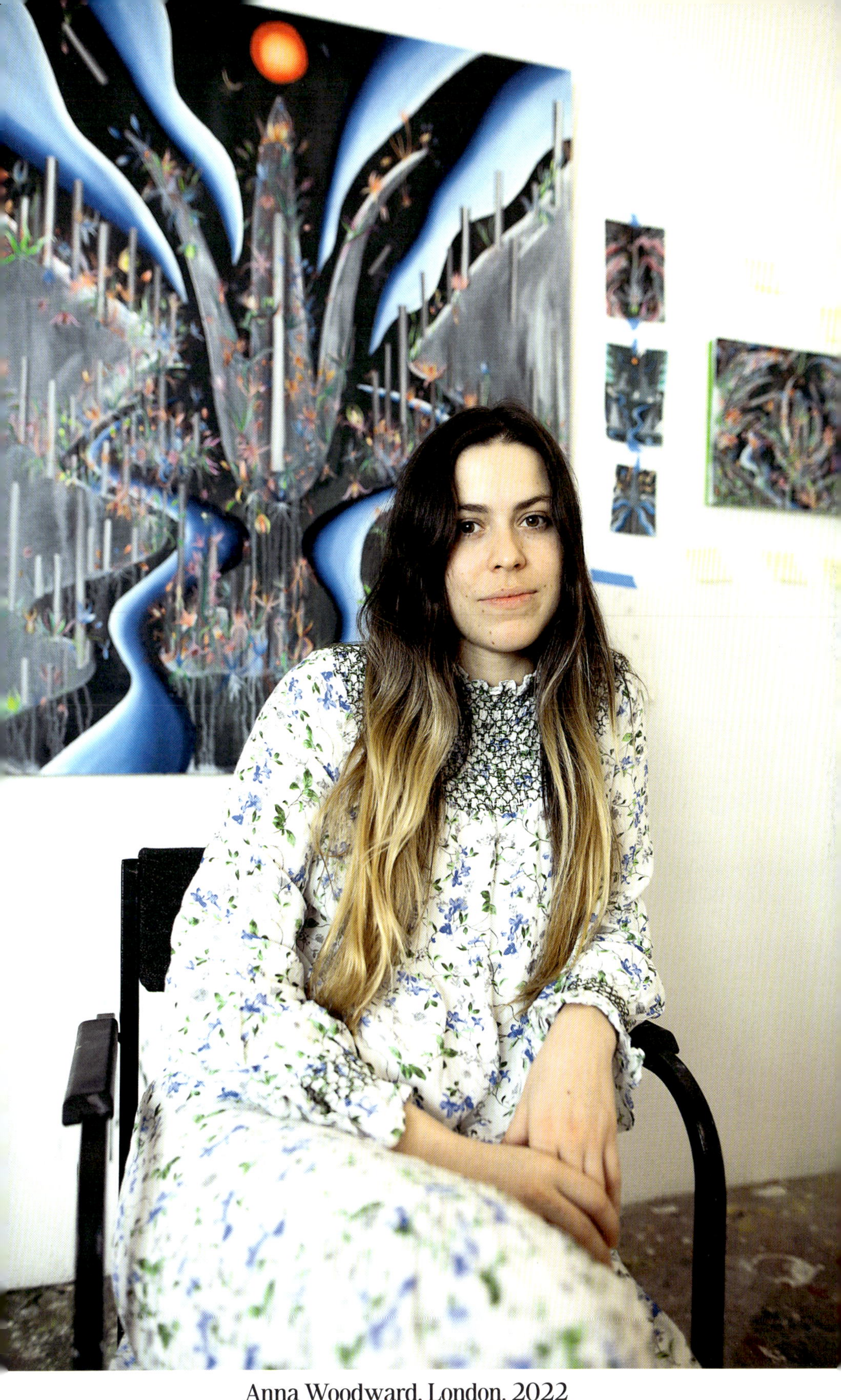

Anna Woodward, London, 2022

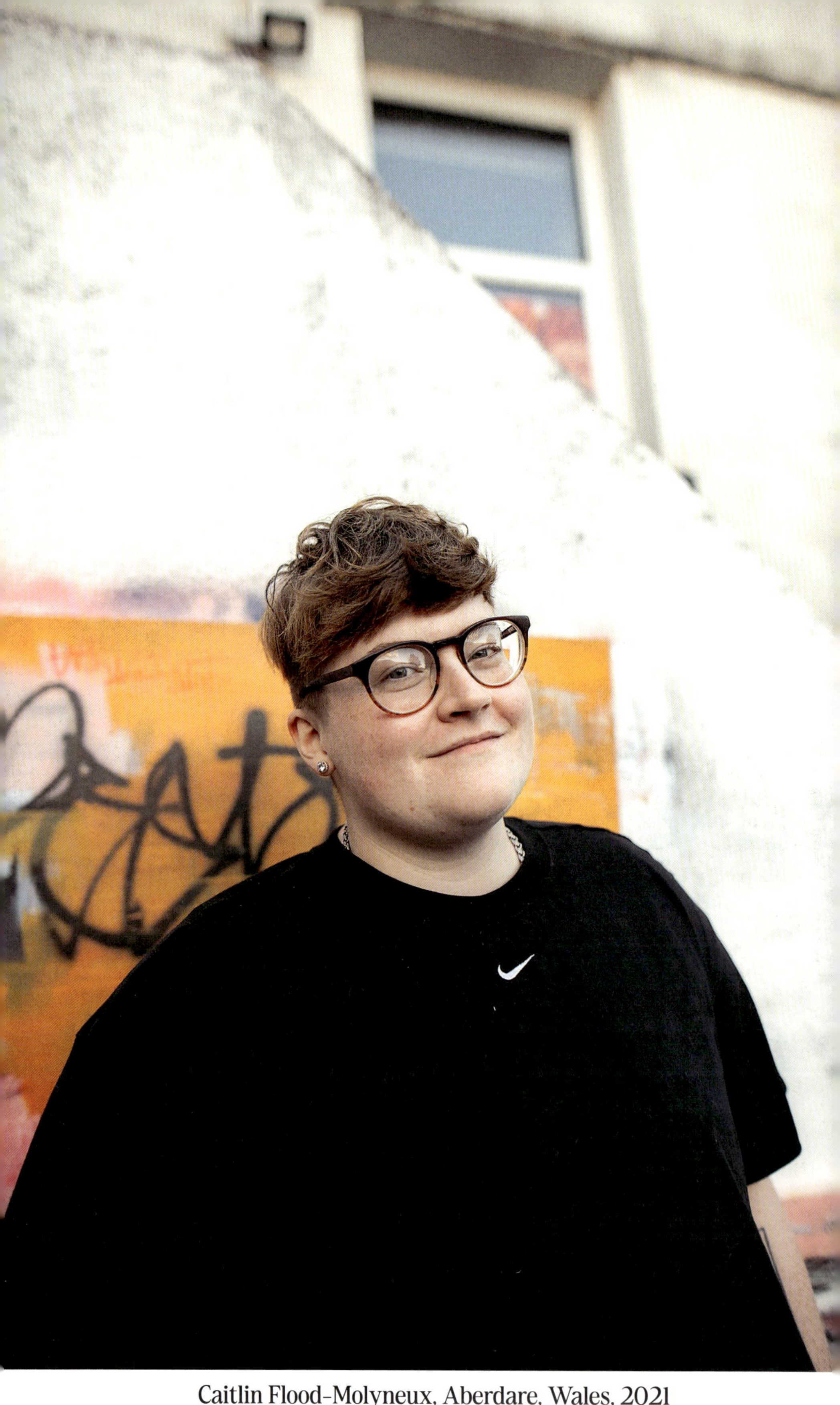

Caitlin Flood-Molyneux, Aberdare, Wales, 2021

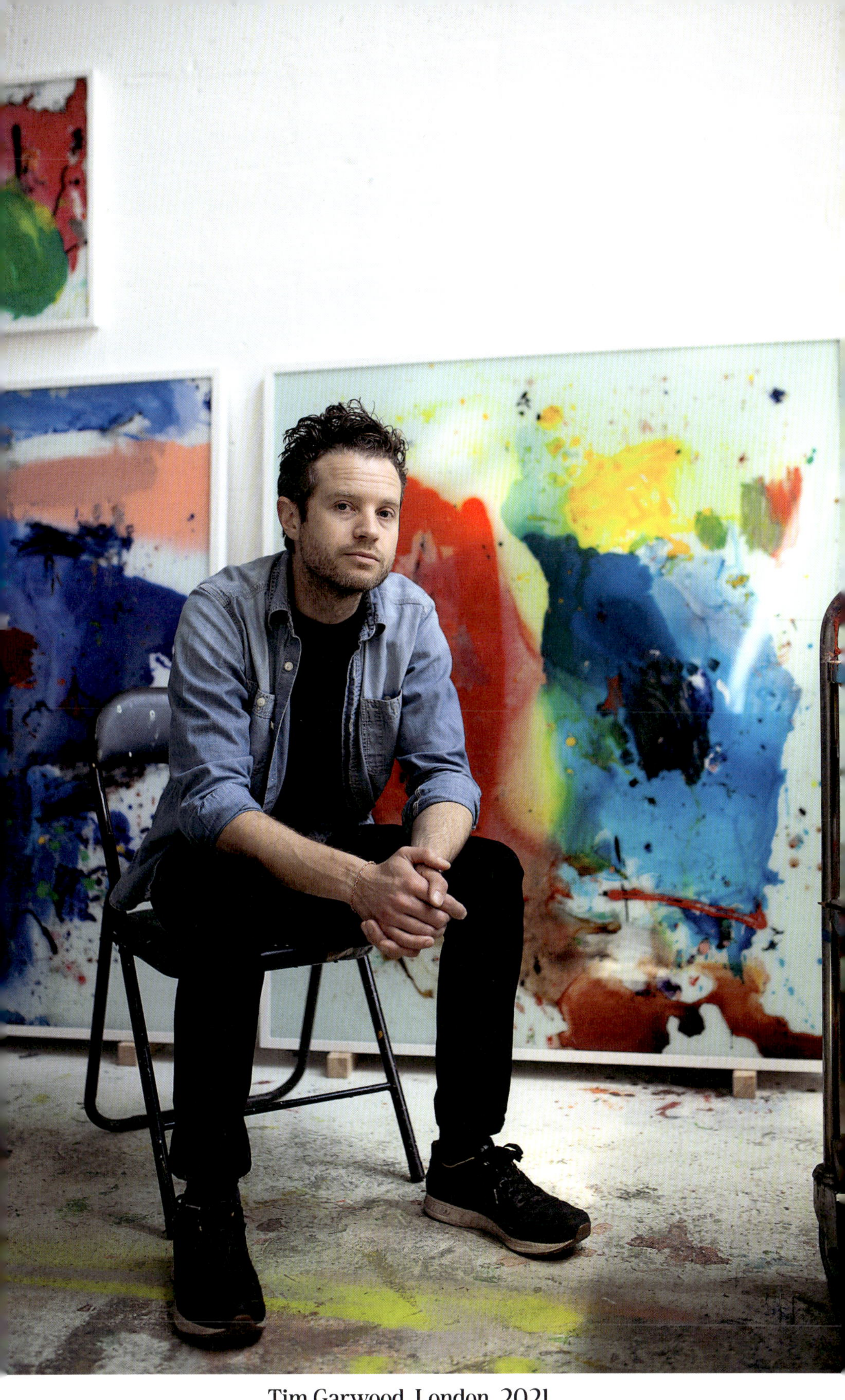

Tim Garwood, London, 2021

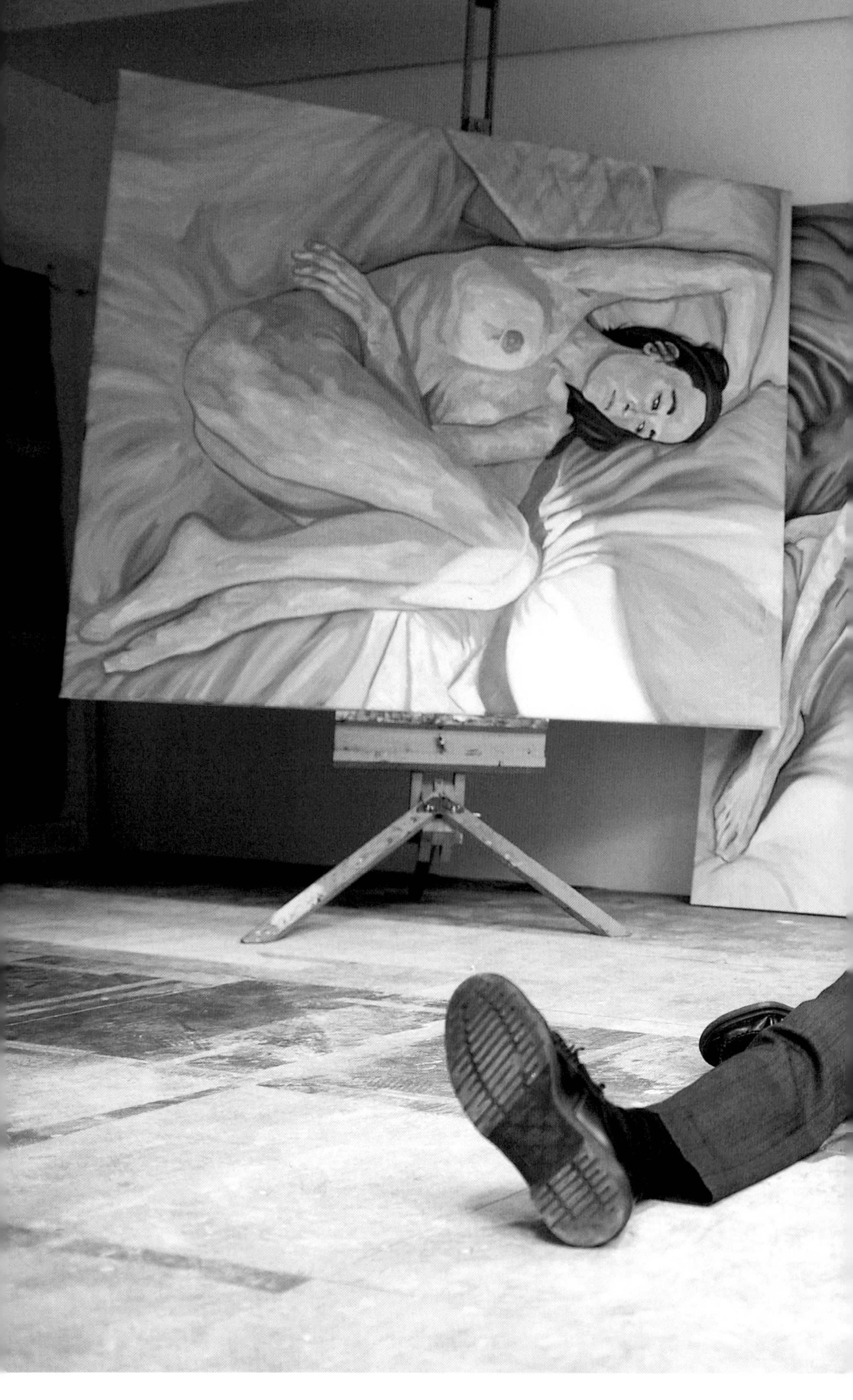

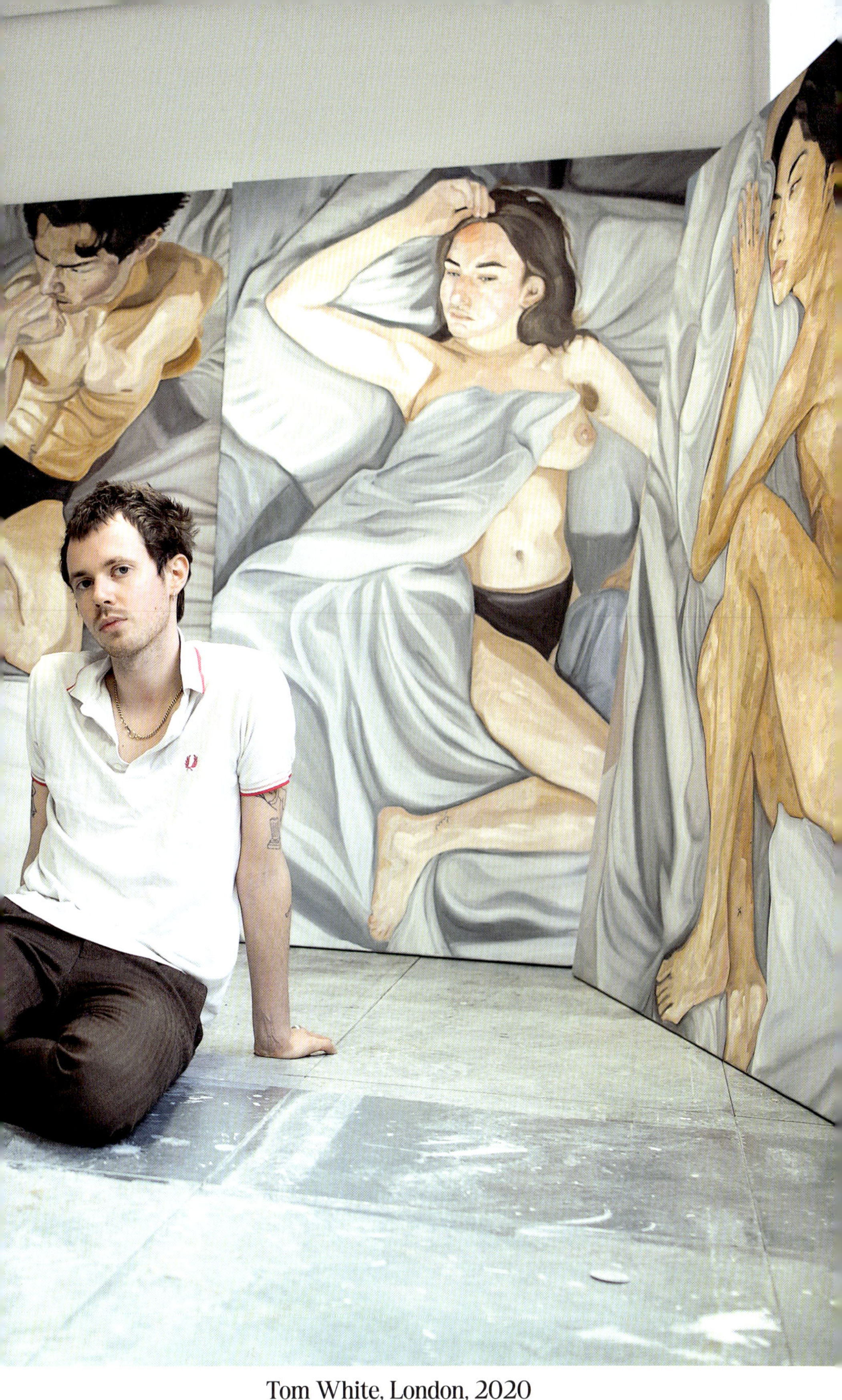

Tom White, London, 2020

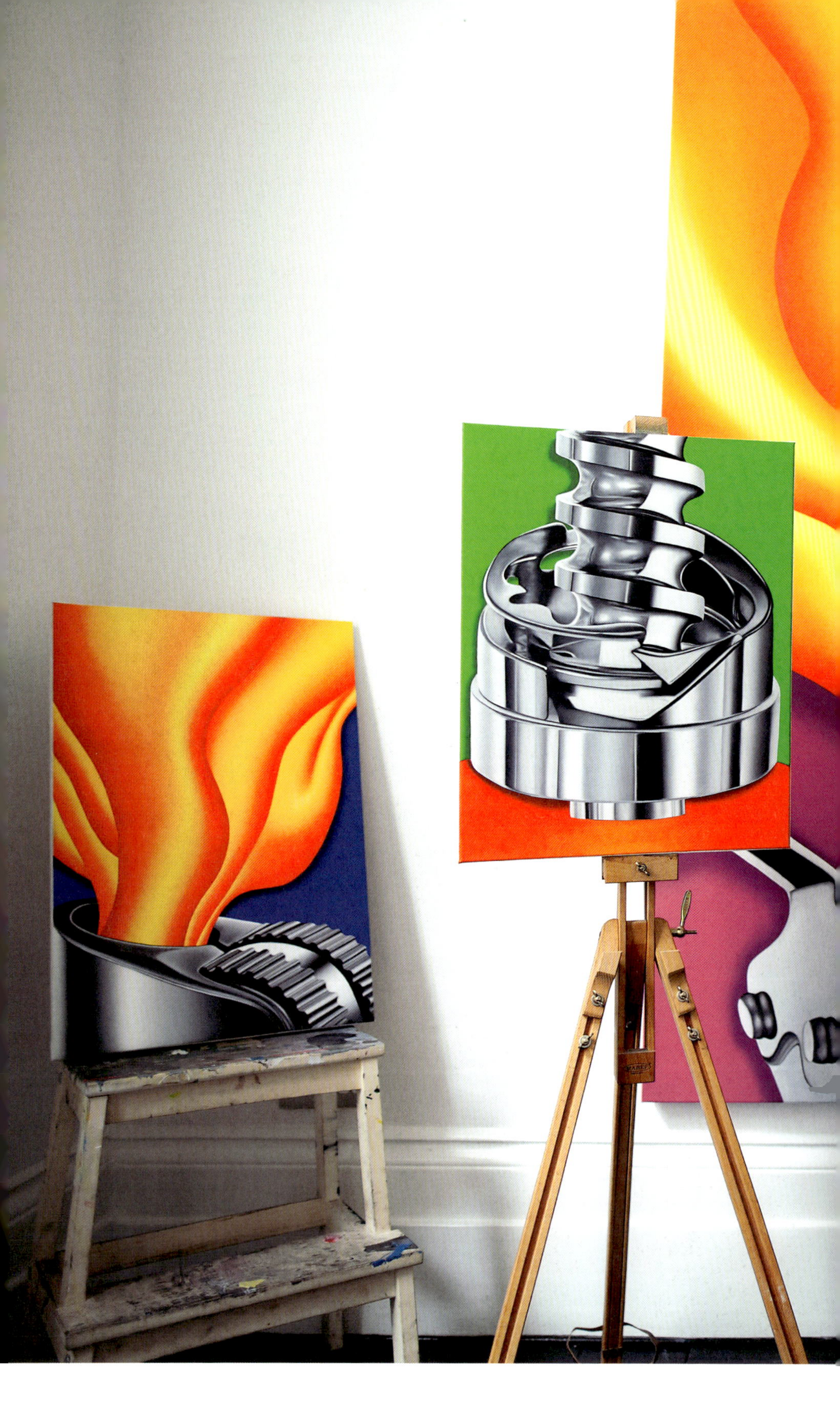

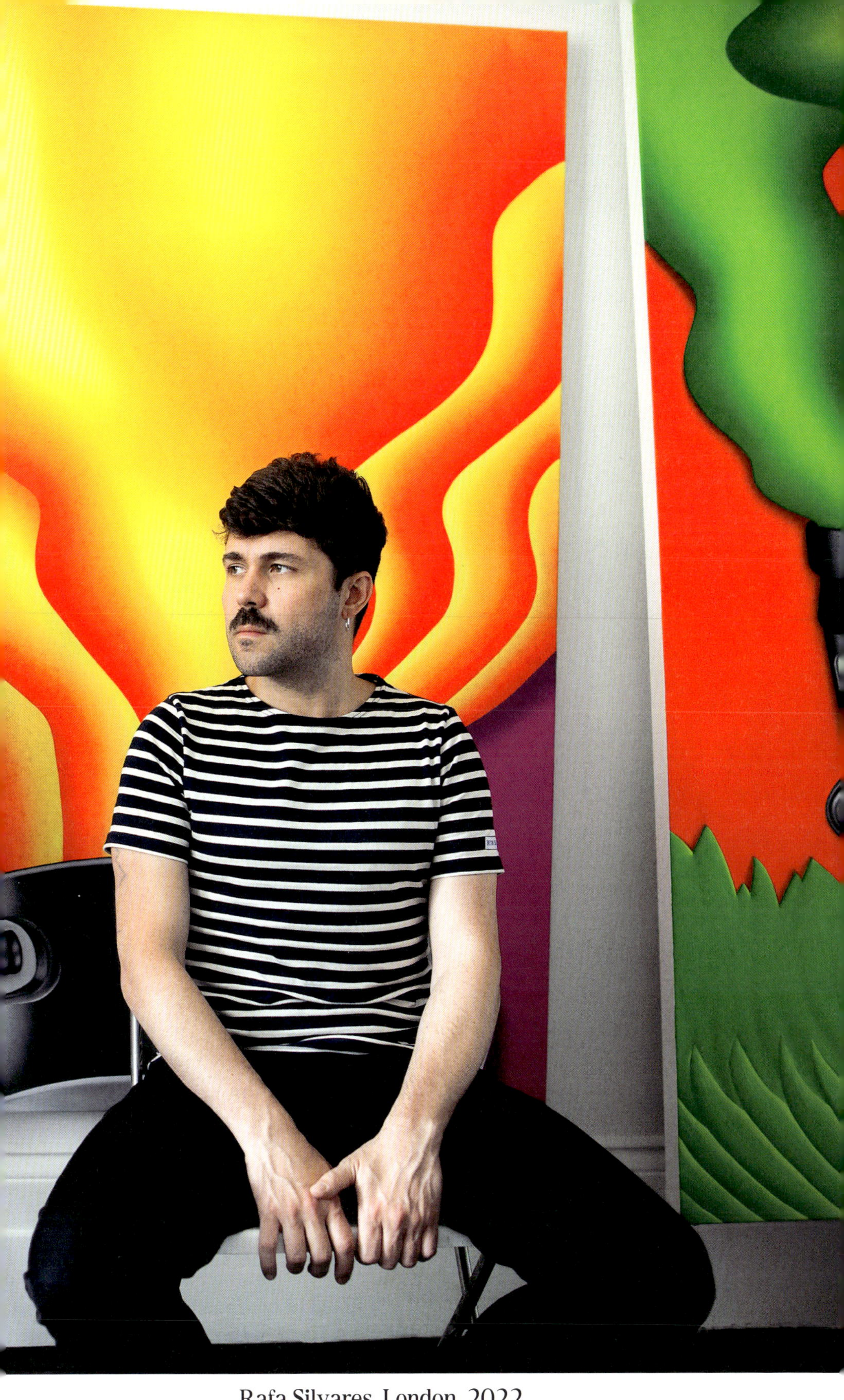

Rafa Silvares, London, 2022

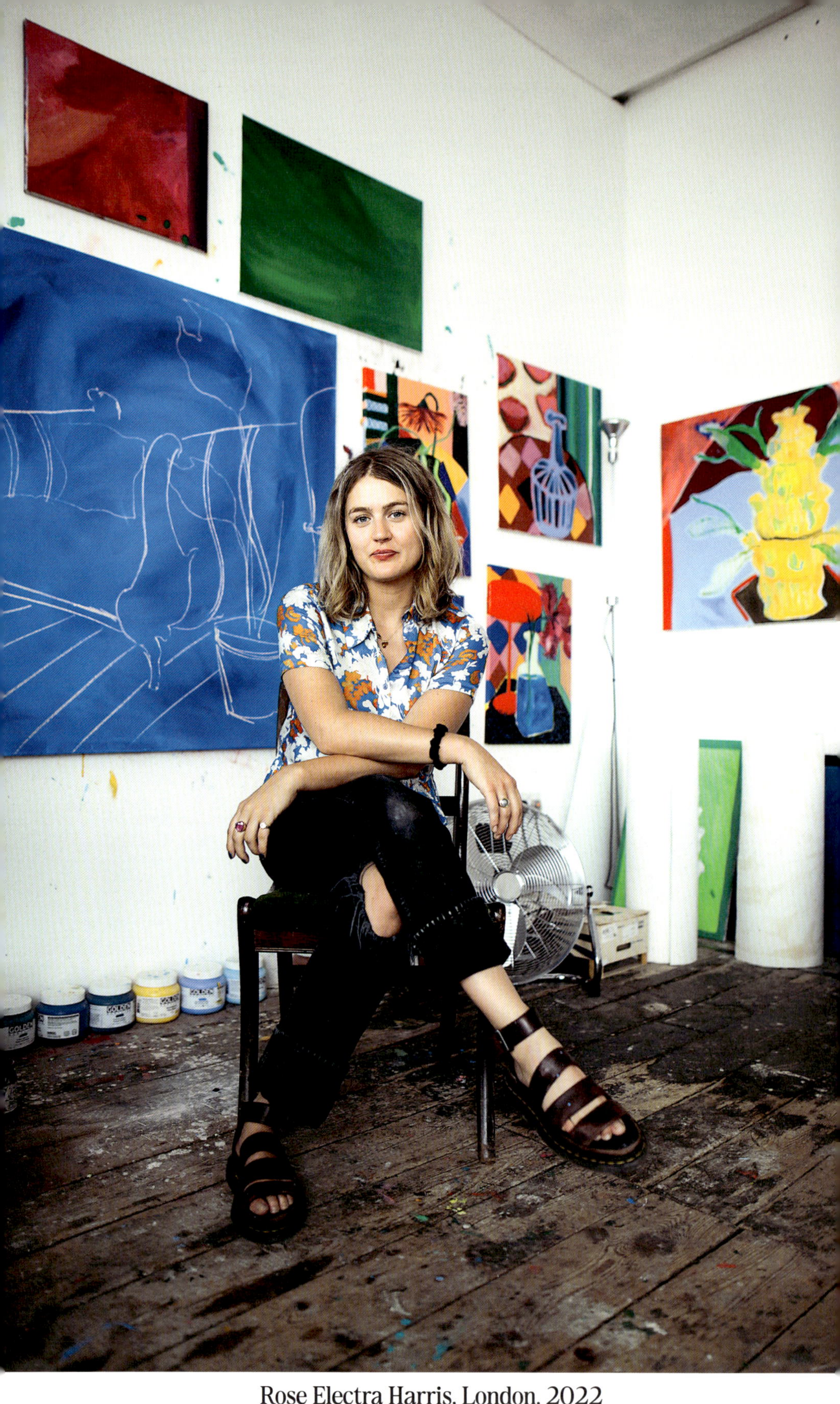

Rose Electra Harris, London, 2022

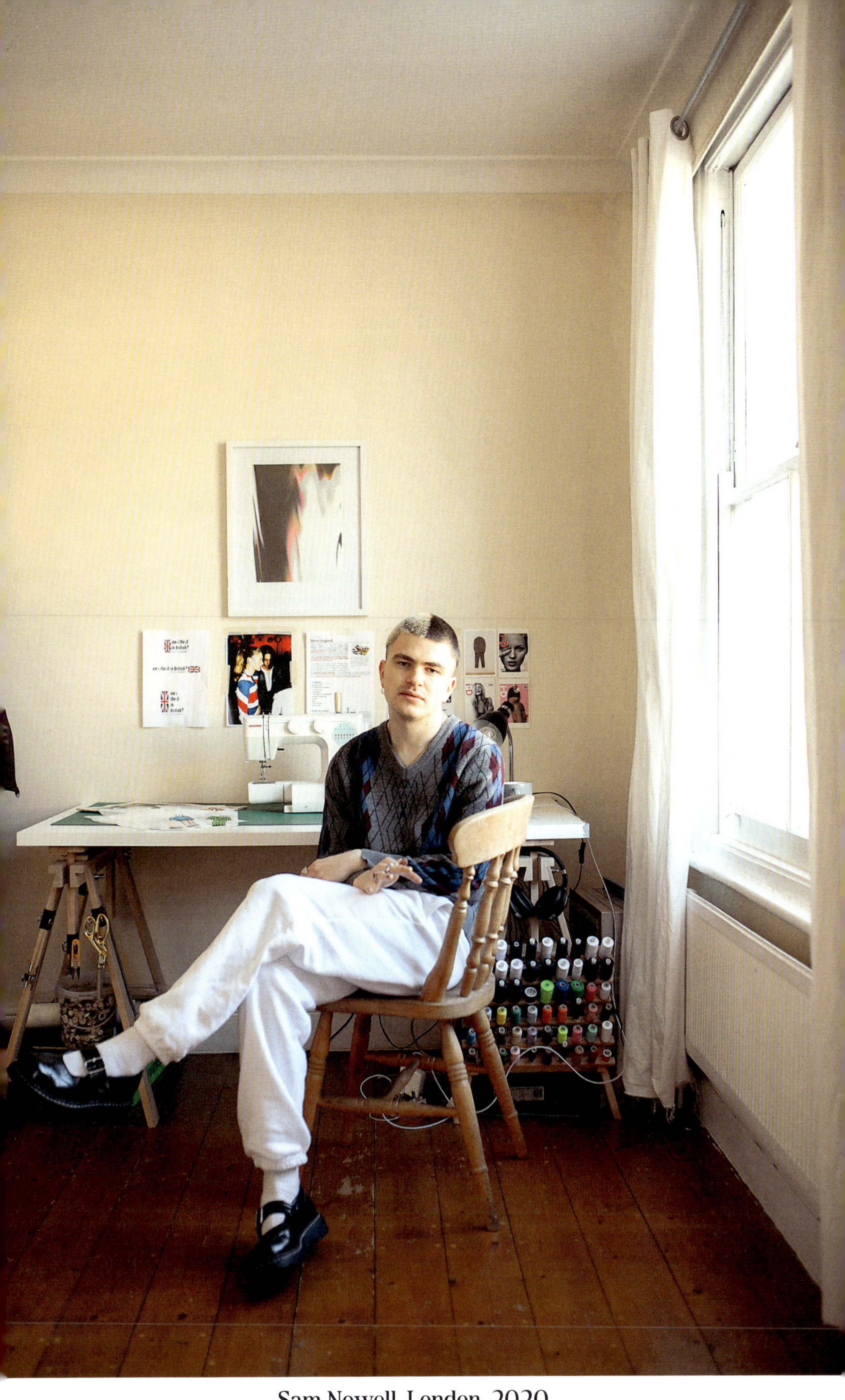

Sam Nowell, London, 2020

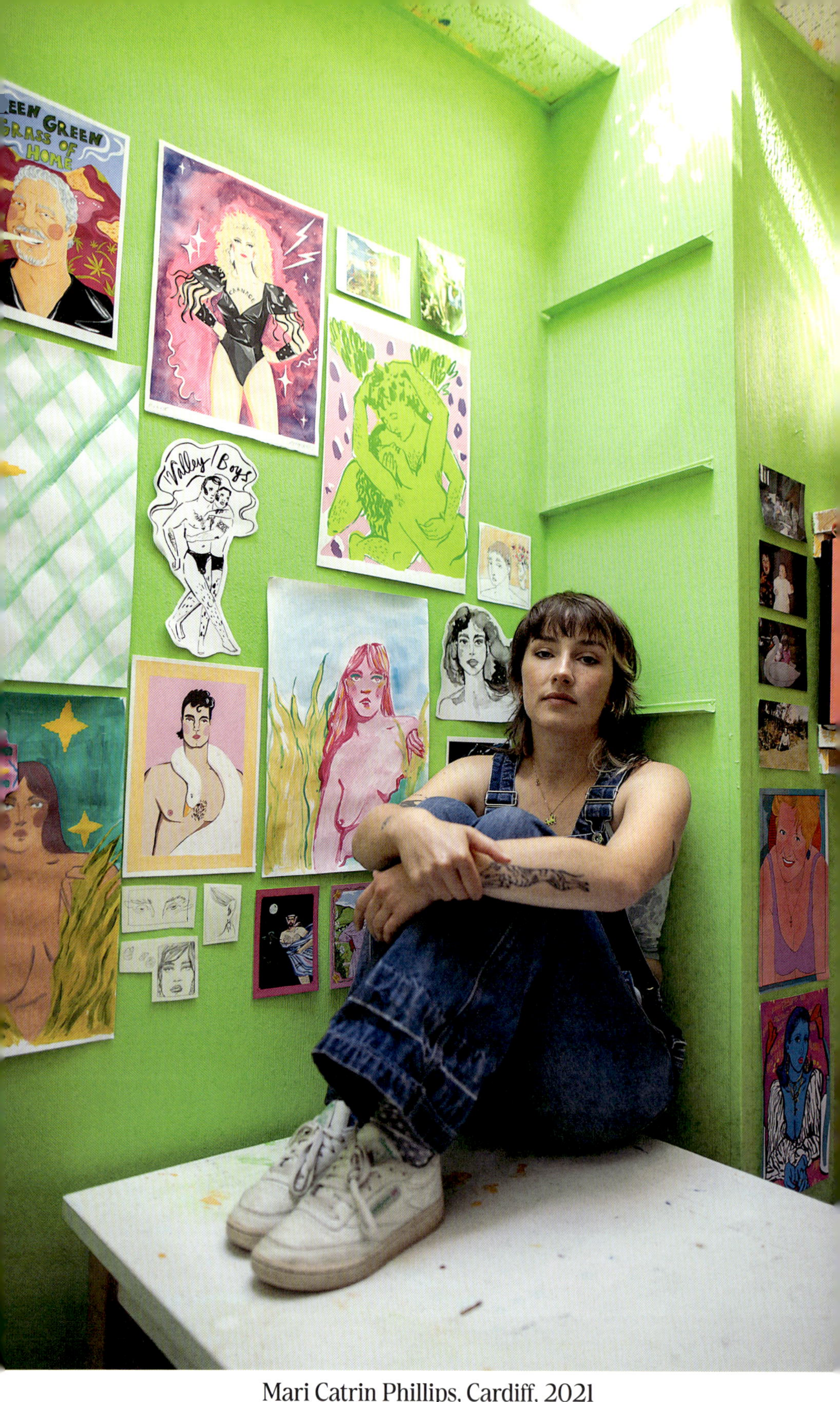

Mari Catrin Phillips, Cardiff, 2021

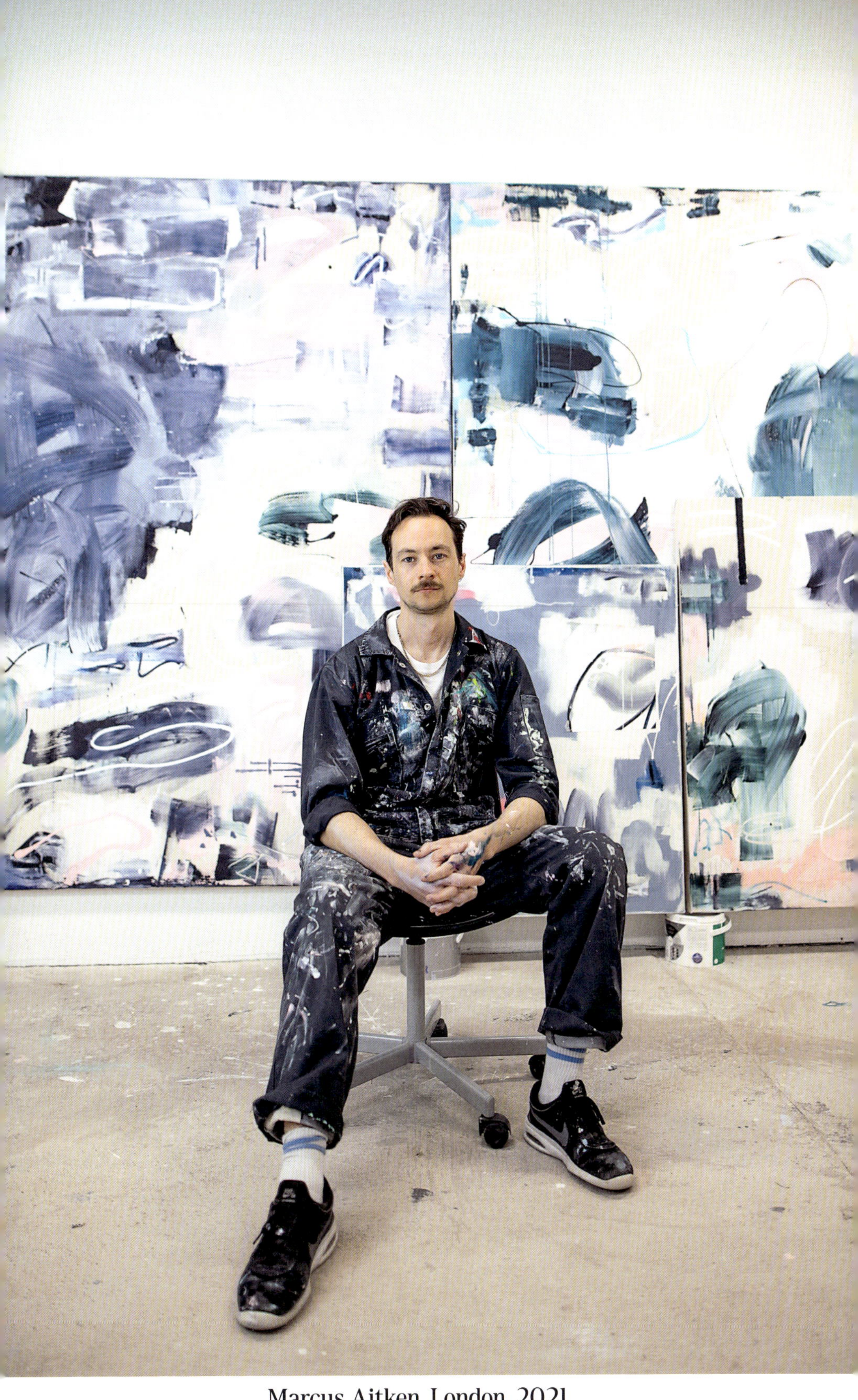

Marcus Aitken, London, 2021

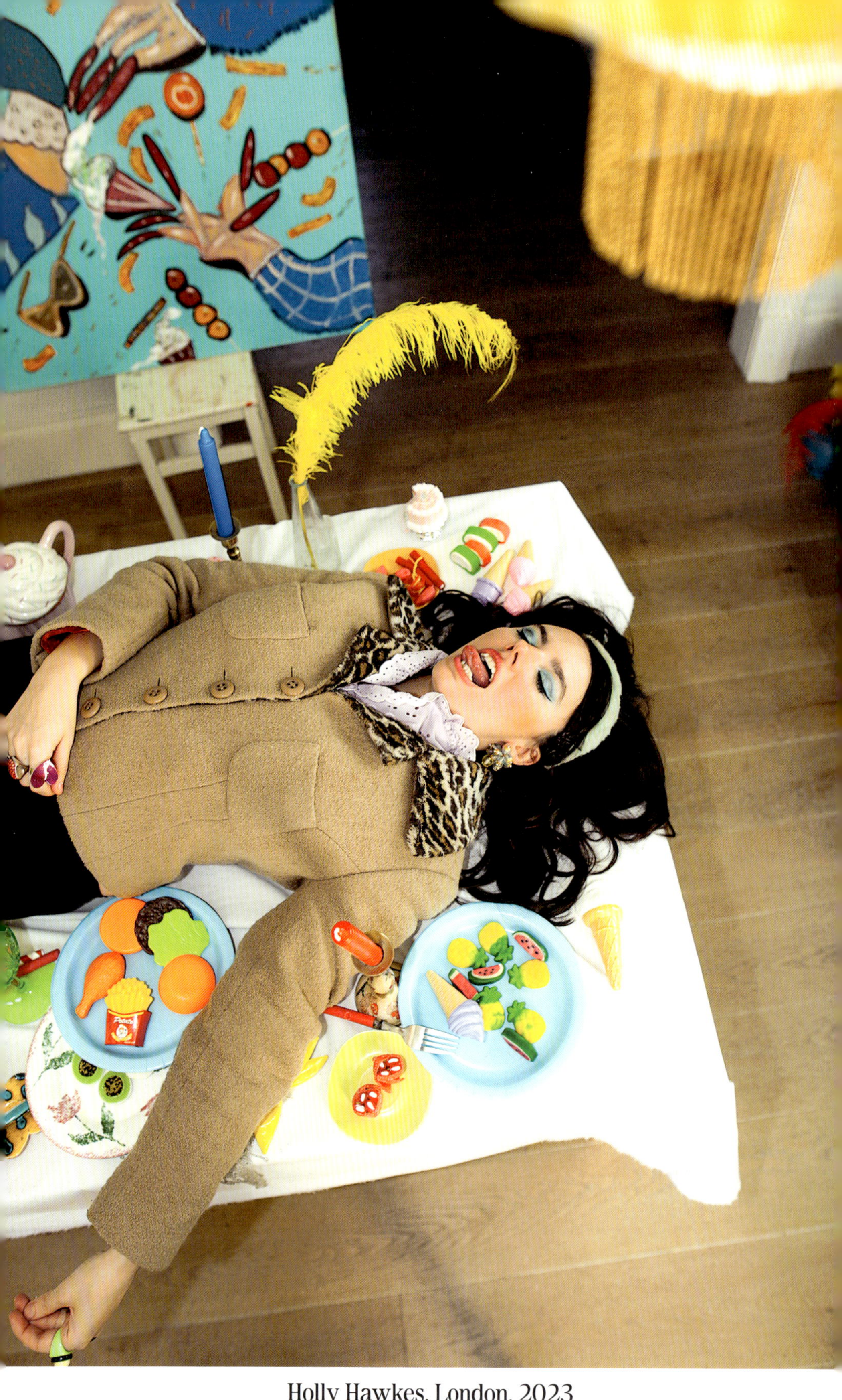

Holly Hawkes, London, 2023

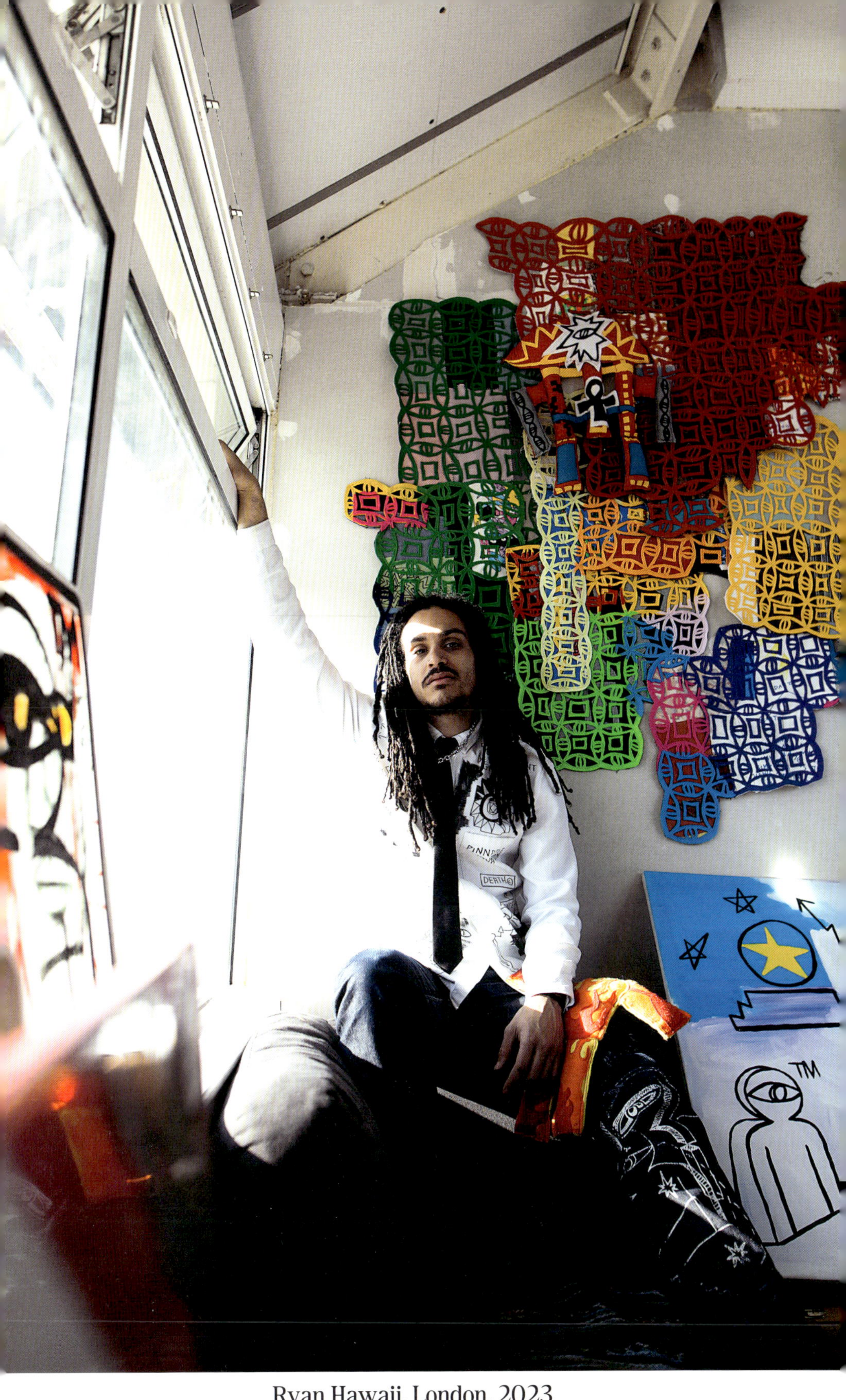

Ryan Hawaii, London, 2023

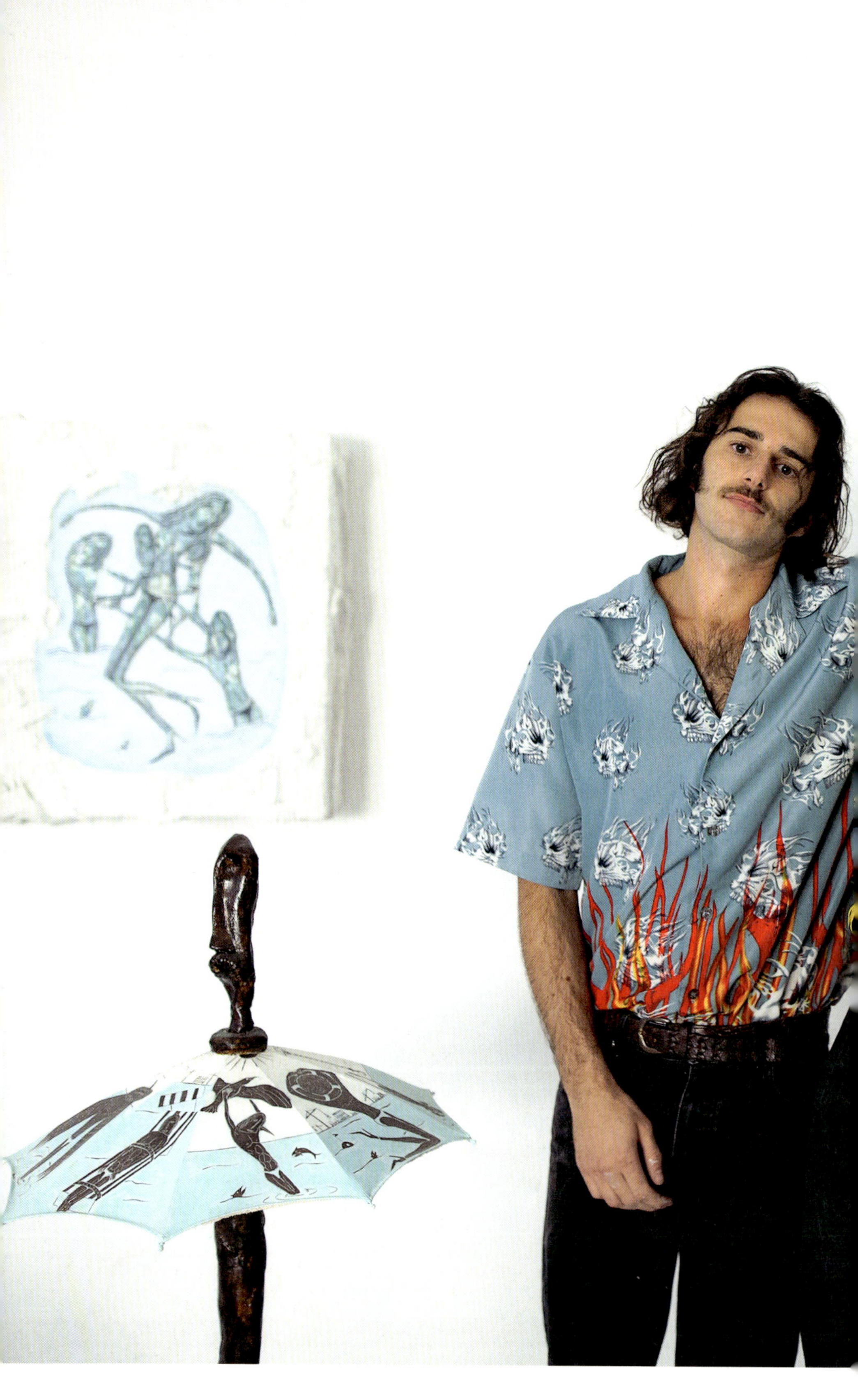

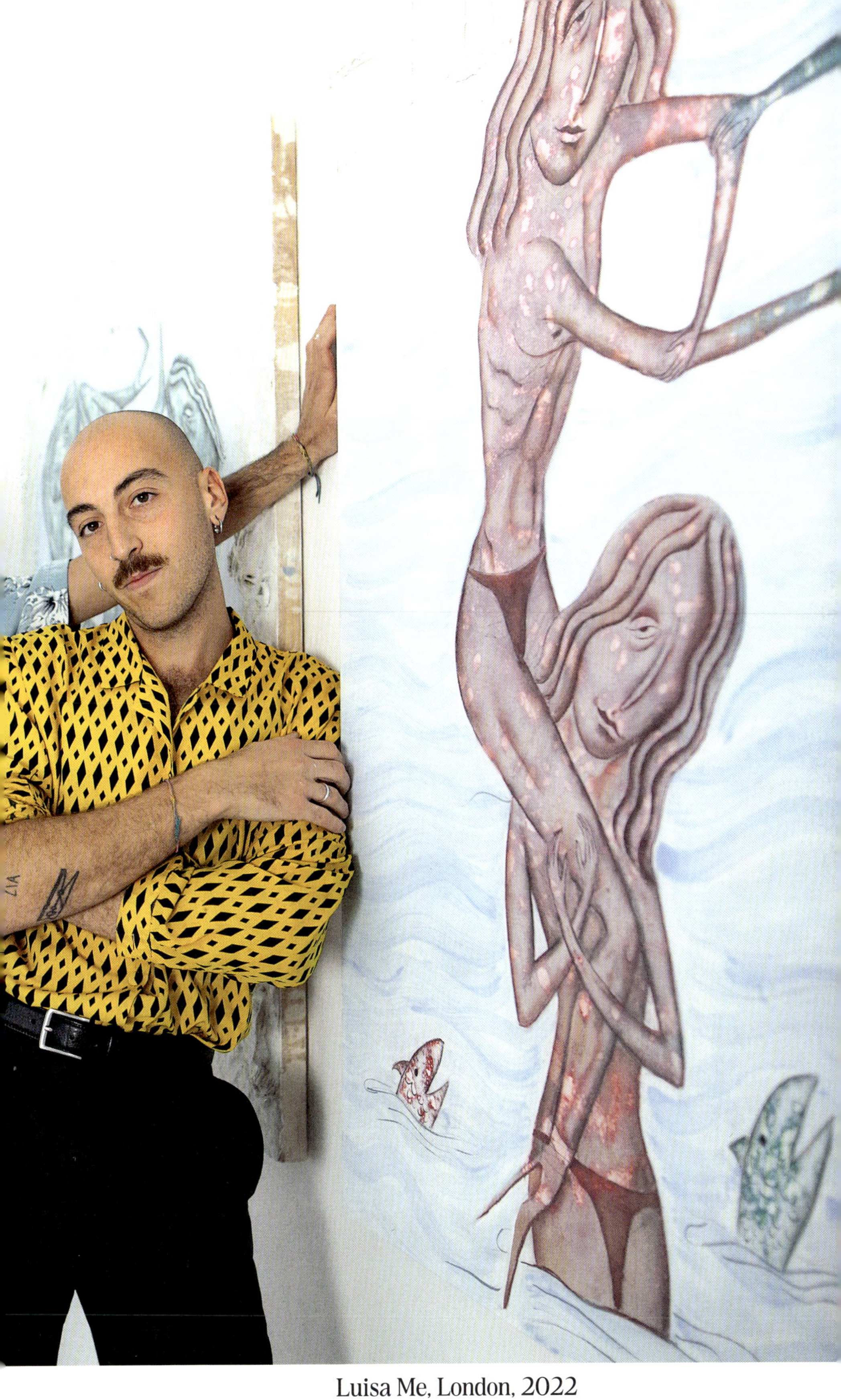

Luisa Me, London, 2022

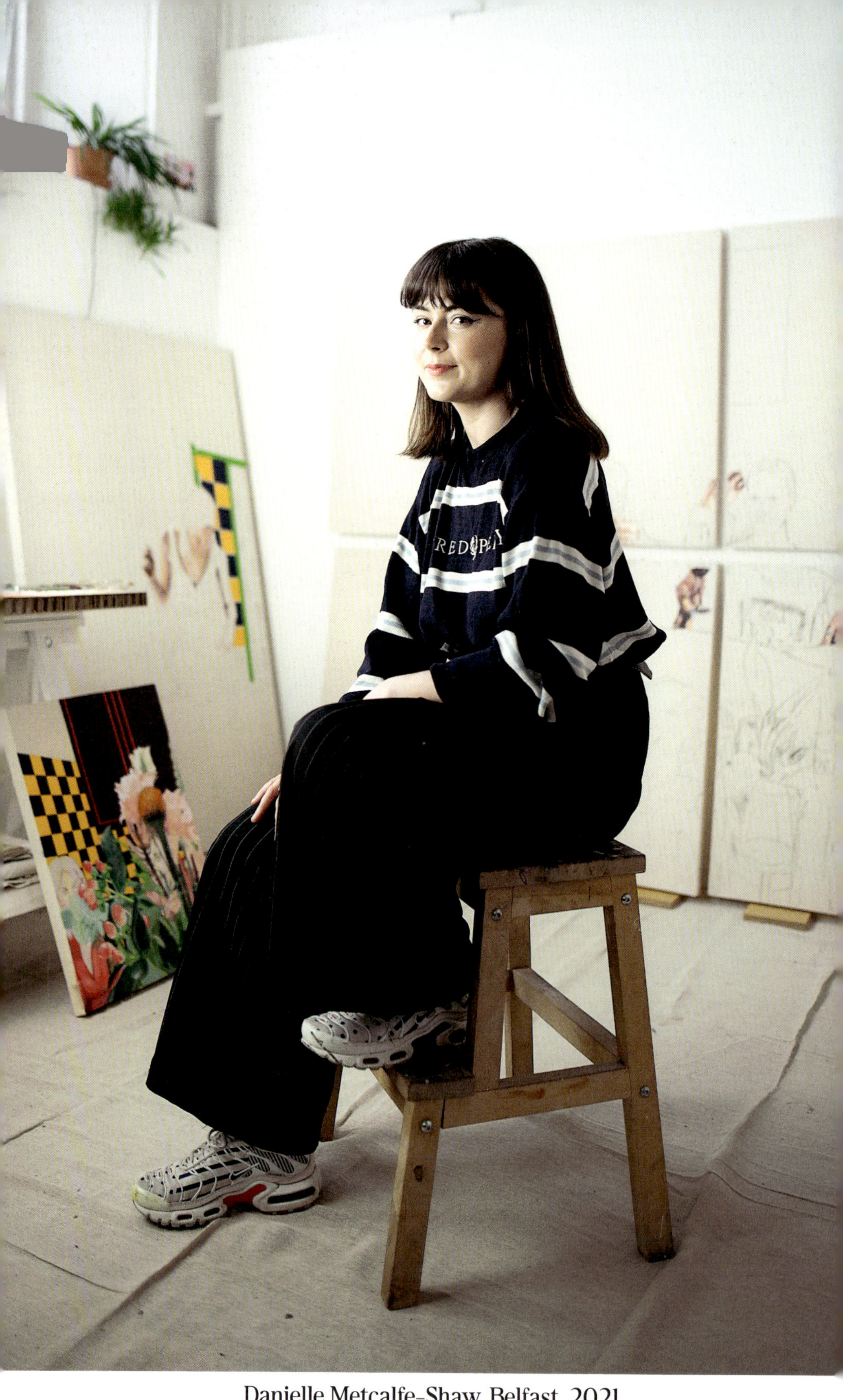

Danielle Metcalfe-Shaw, Belfast, 2021

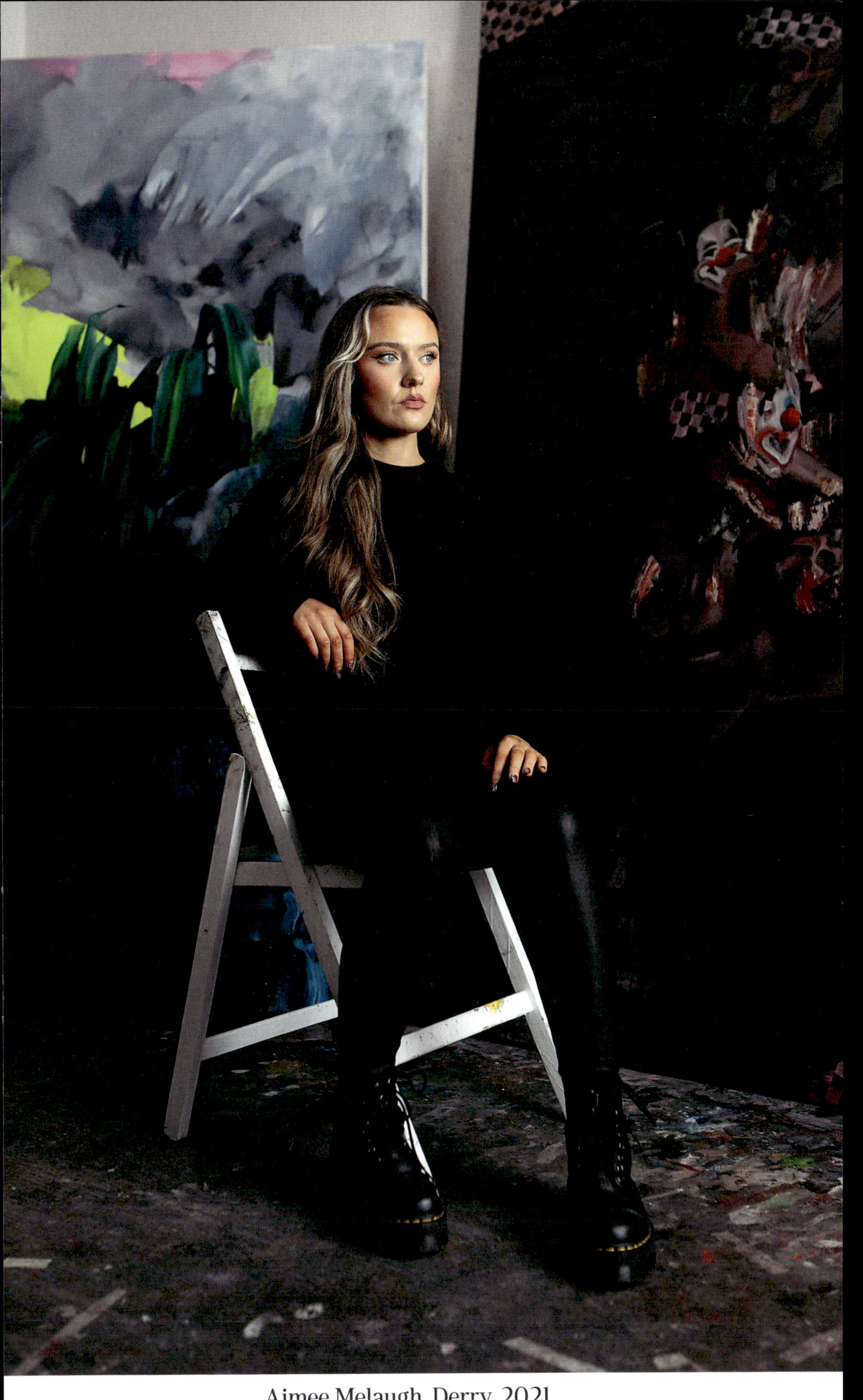

Aimee Melaugh, Derry, 2021

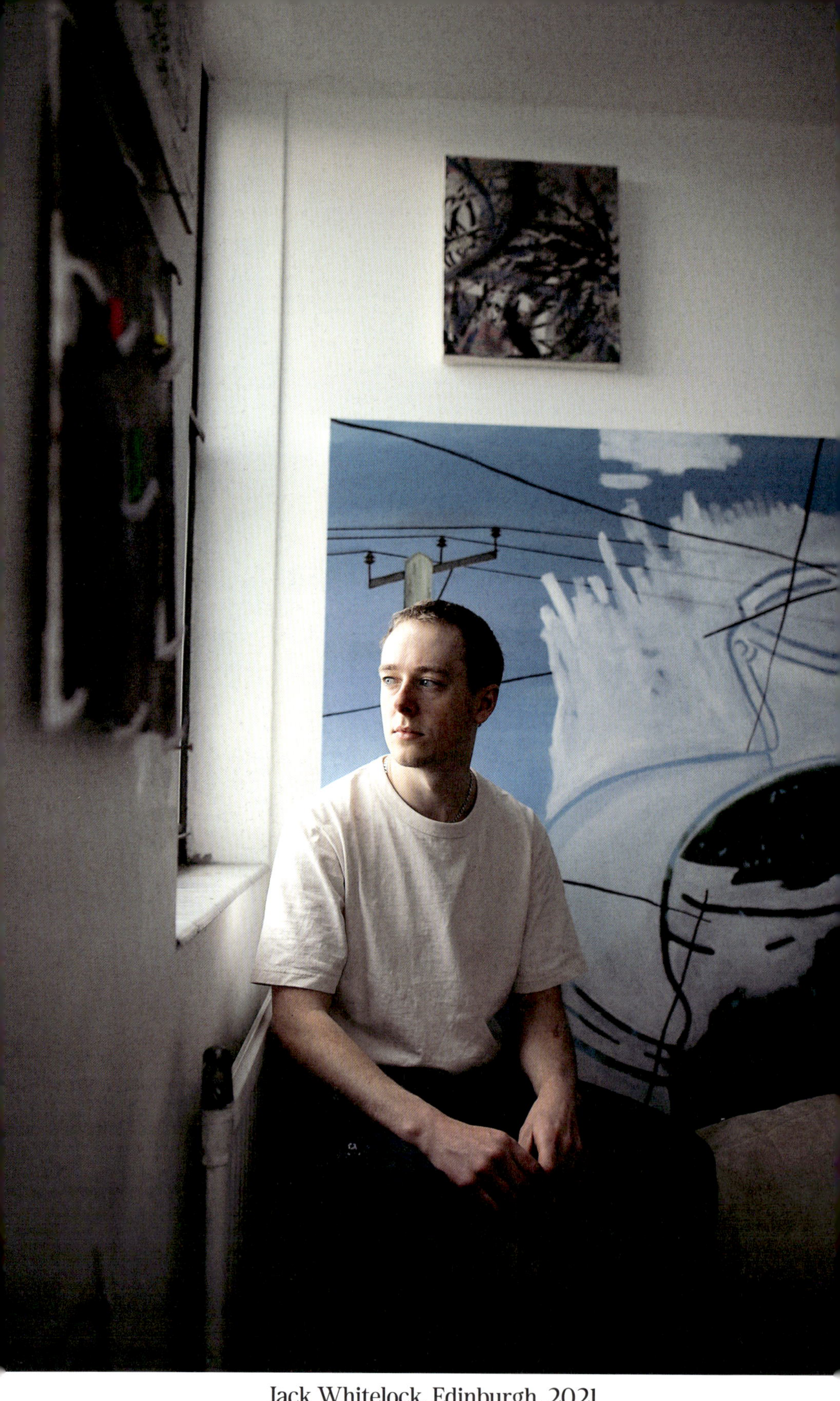

Jack Whitelock, Edinburgh, 2021

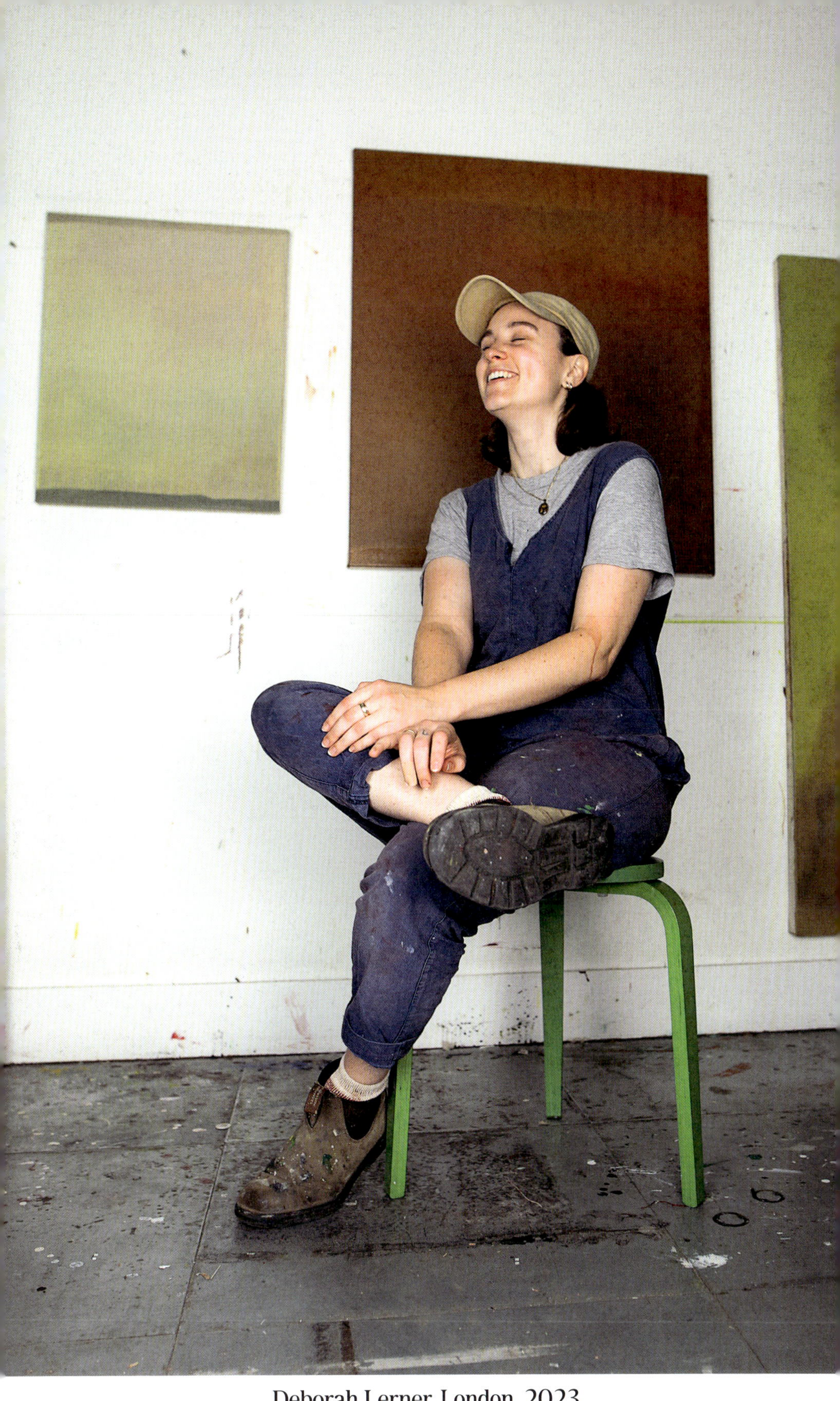

Deborah Lerner, London, 2023

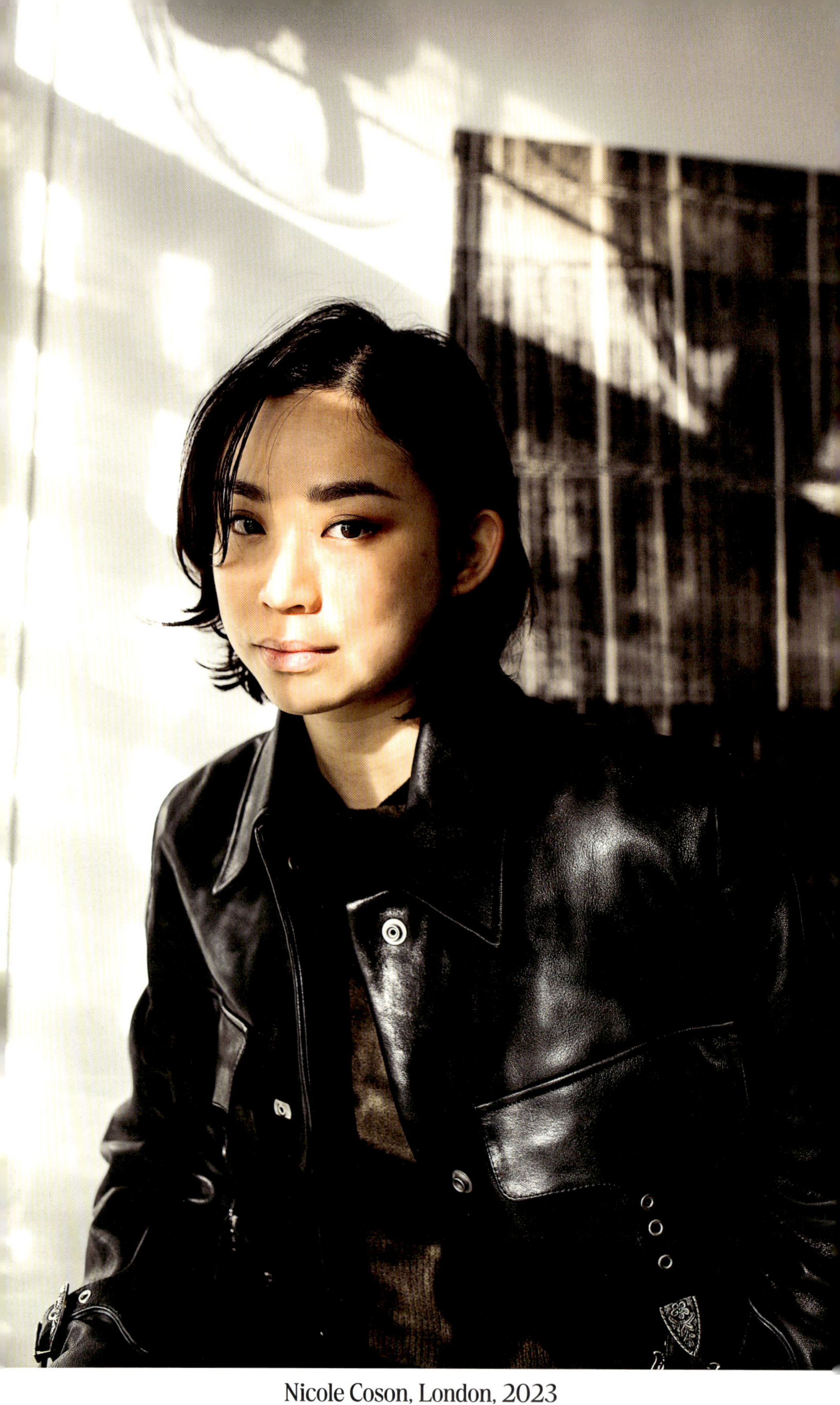

Nicole Coson, London, 2023

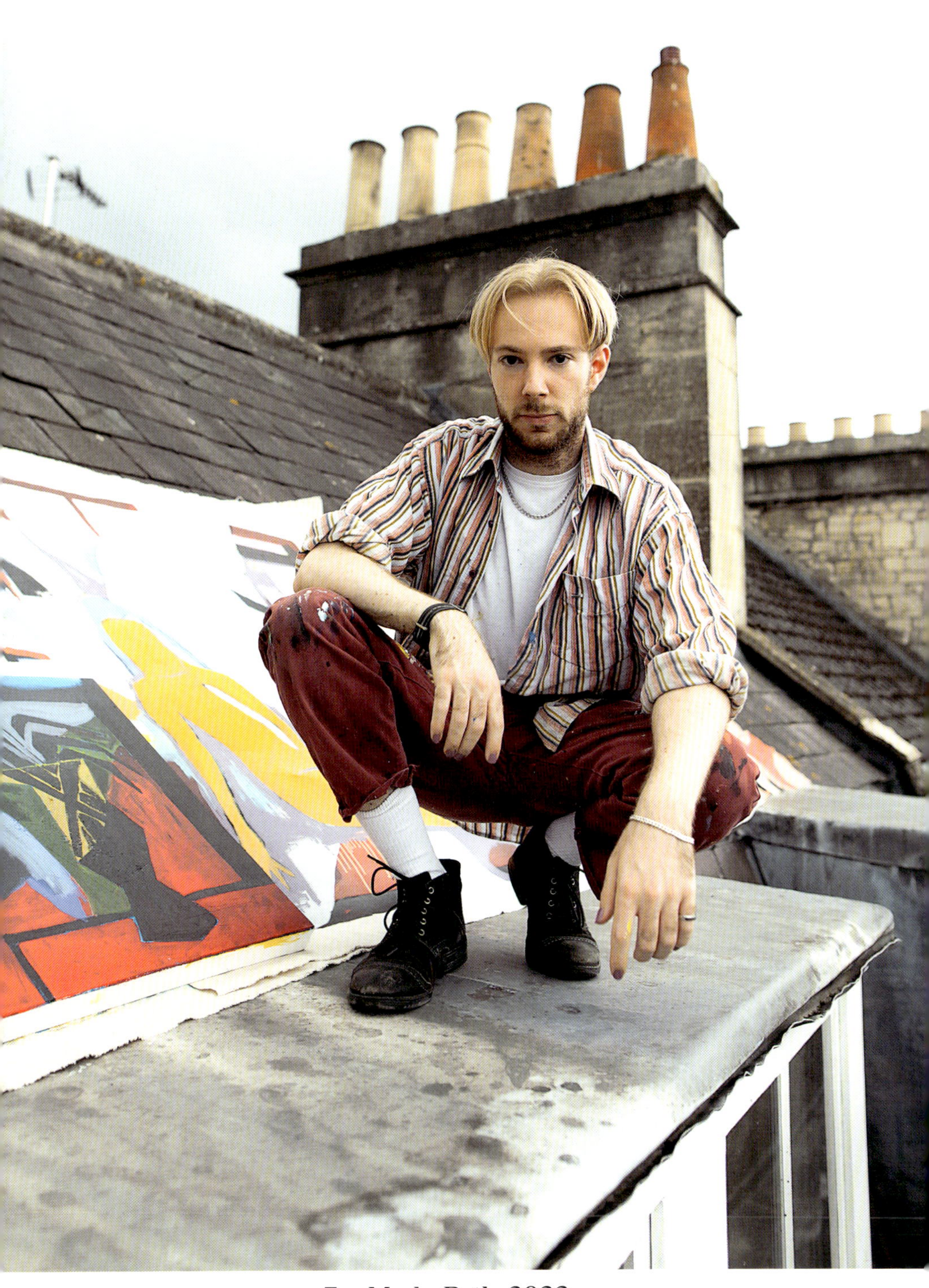

Zac Merle, Bath, 2022

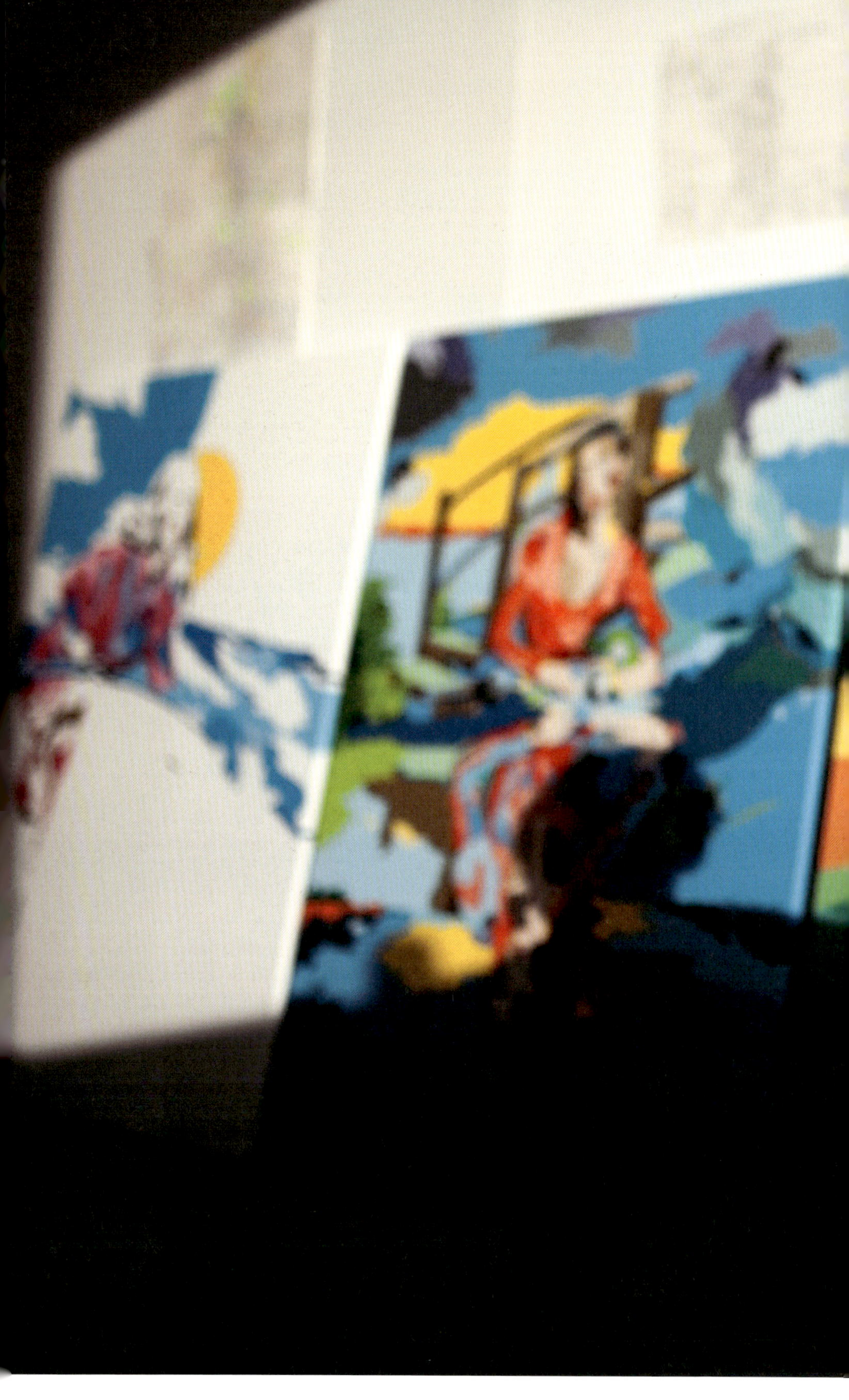

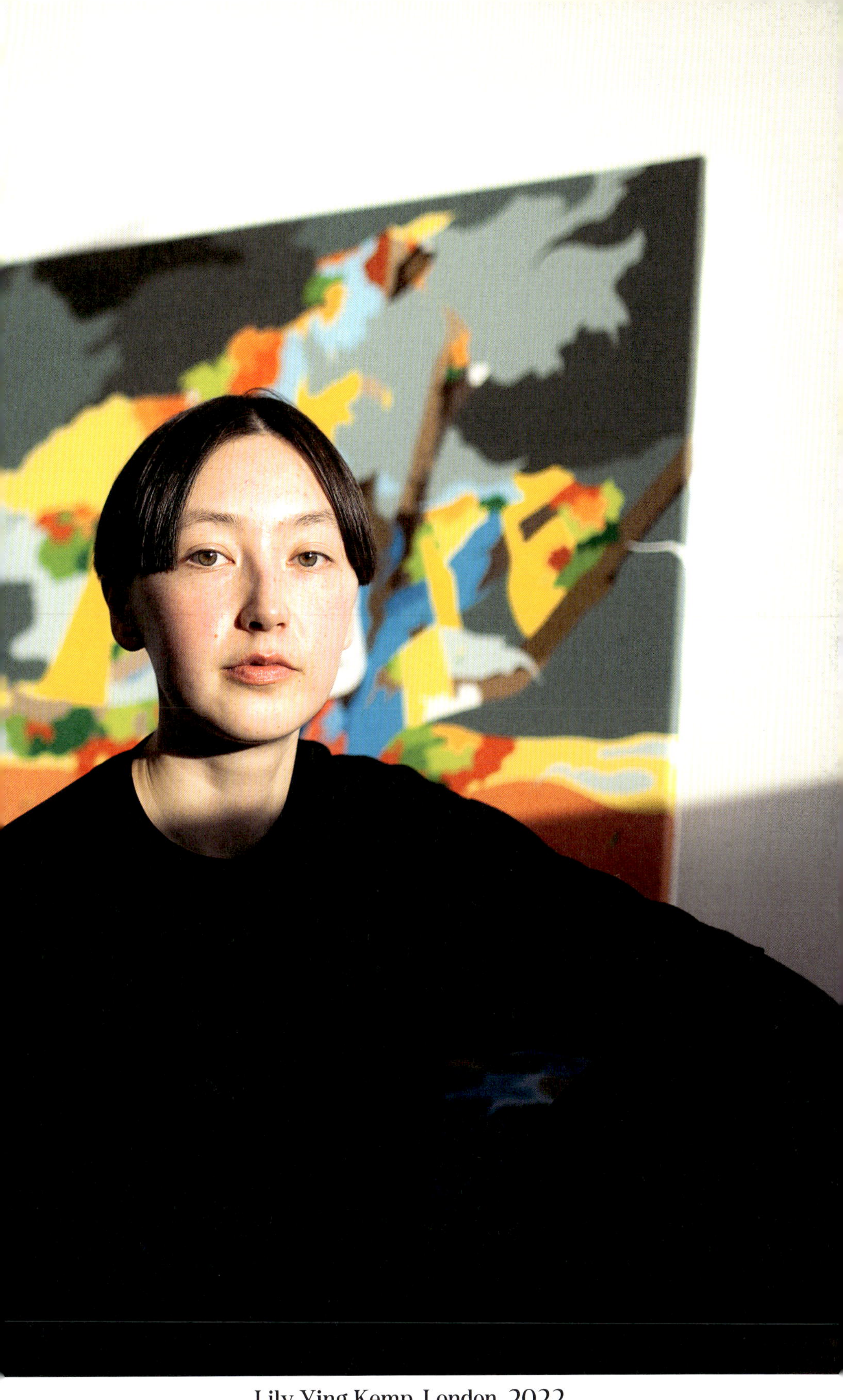

Lily Ying Kemp, London, 2022

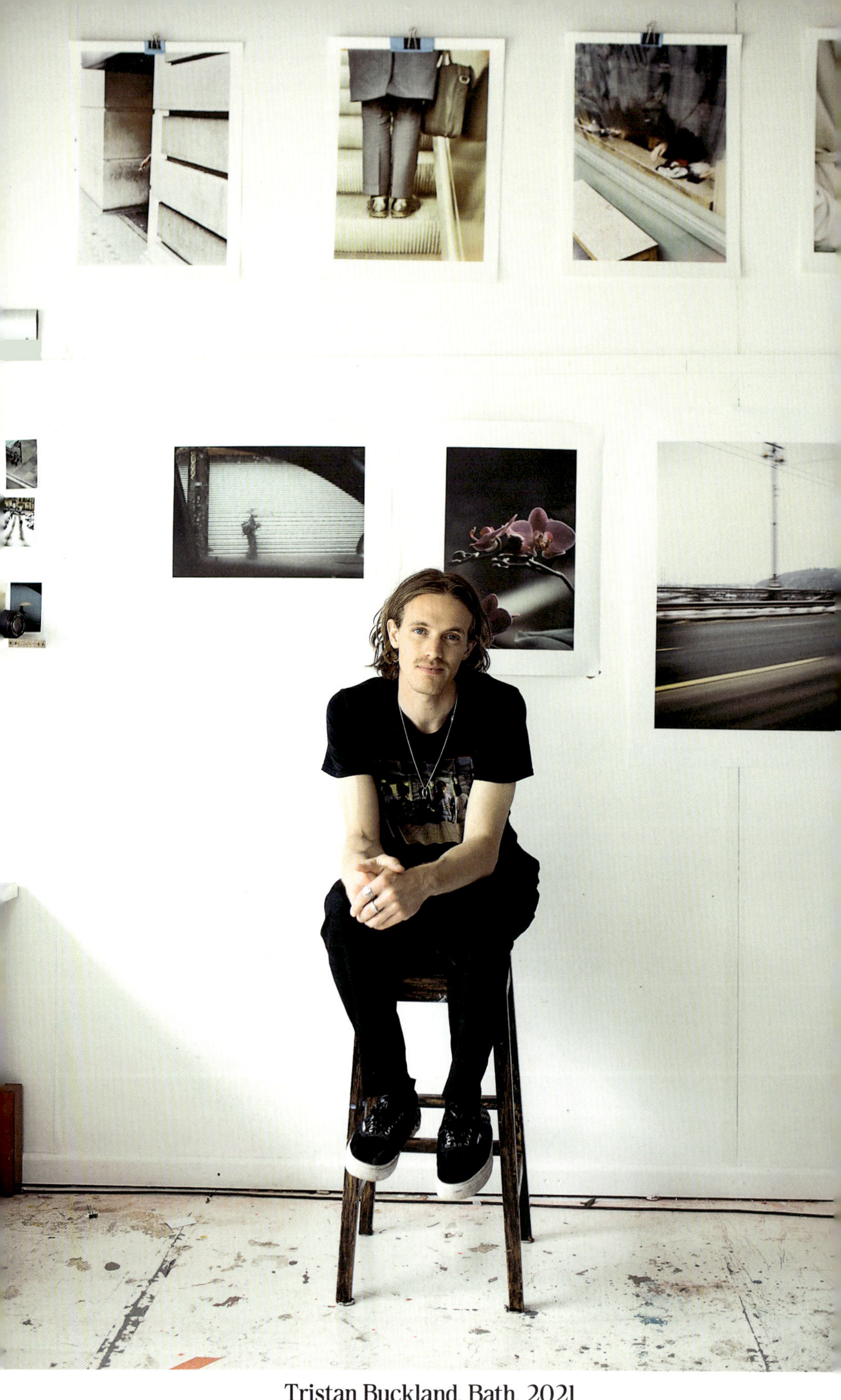

Tristan Buckland, Bath, 2021

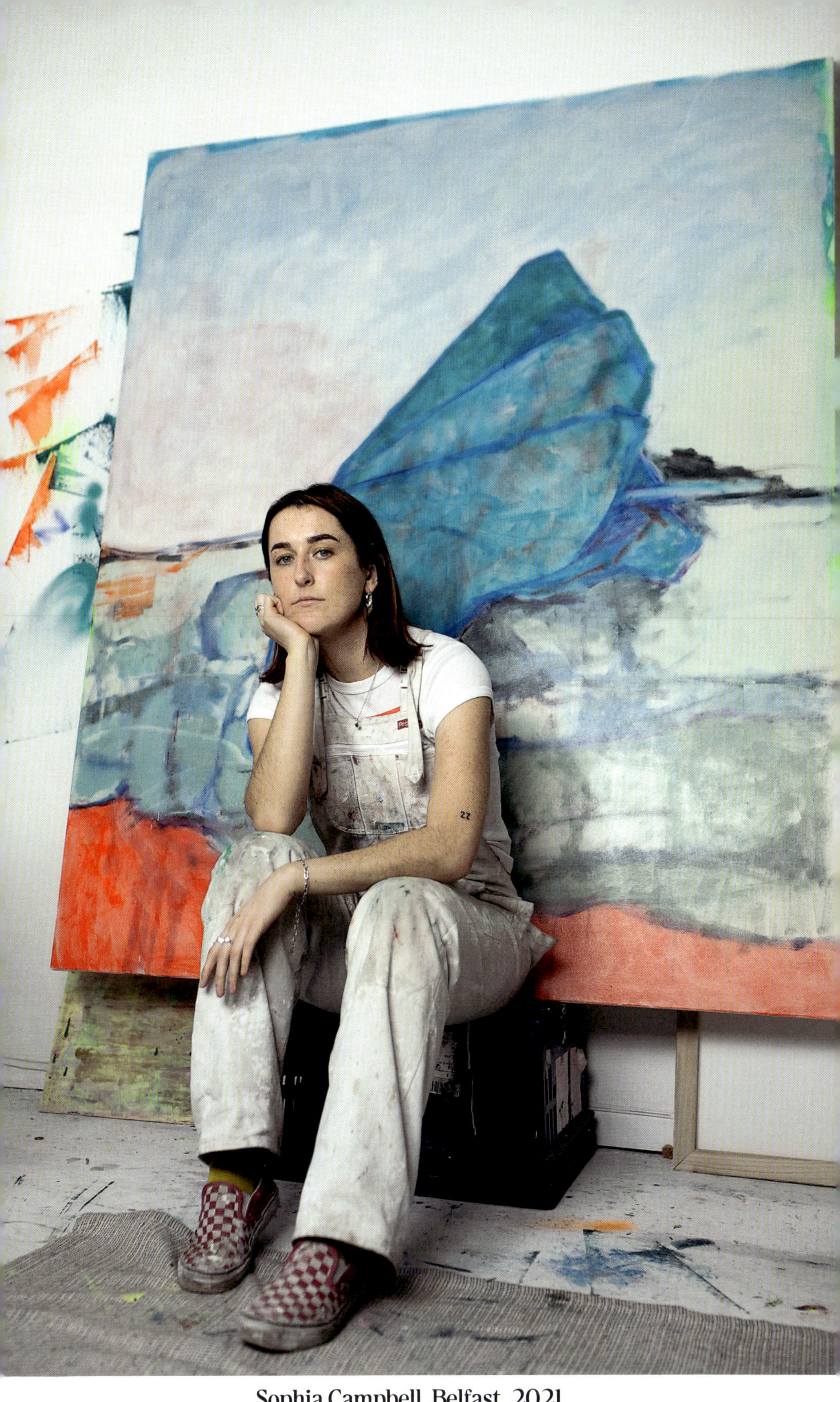

Sophia Campbell, Belfast, 2021

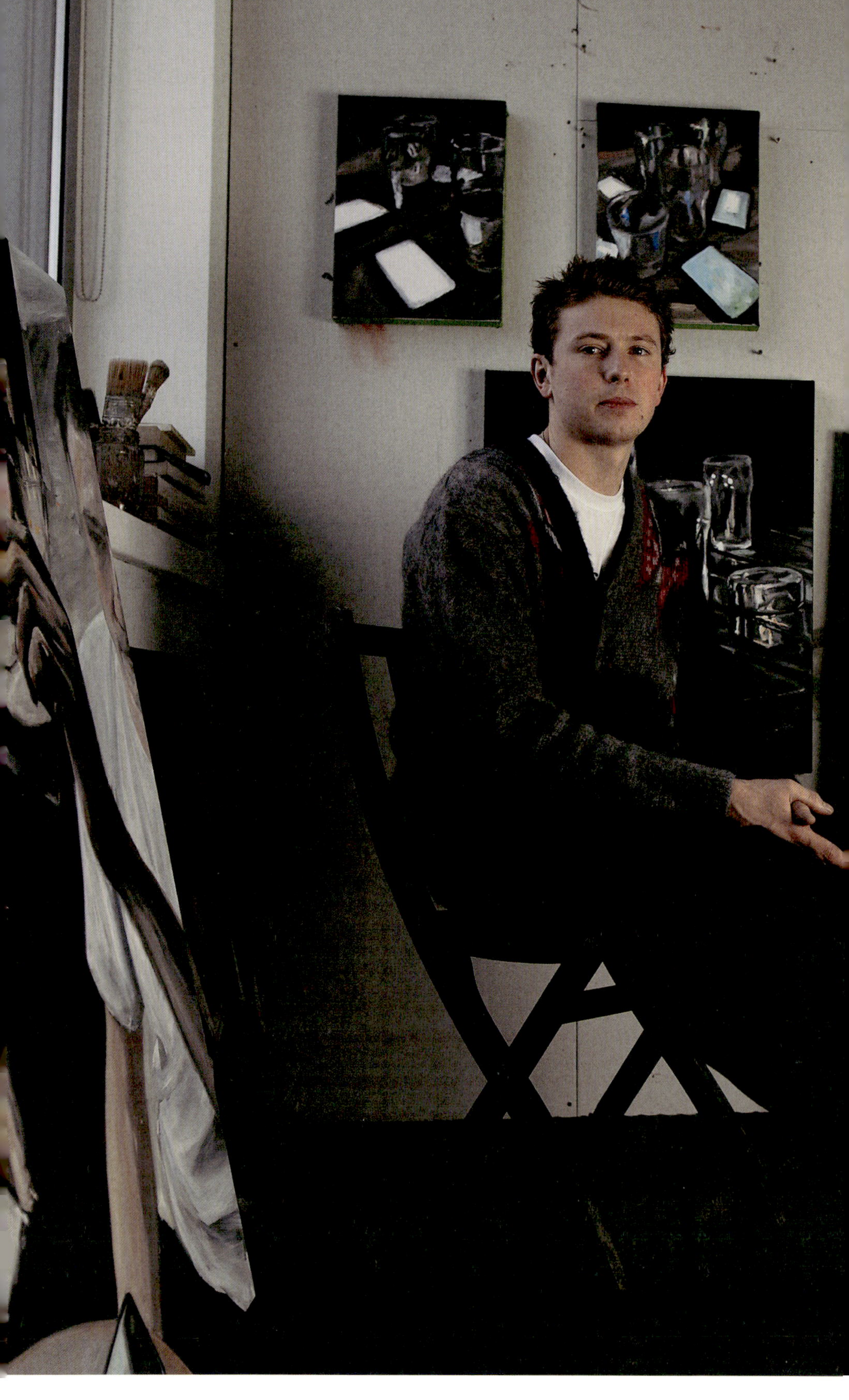

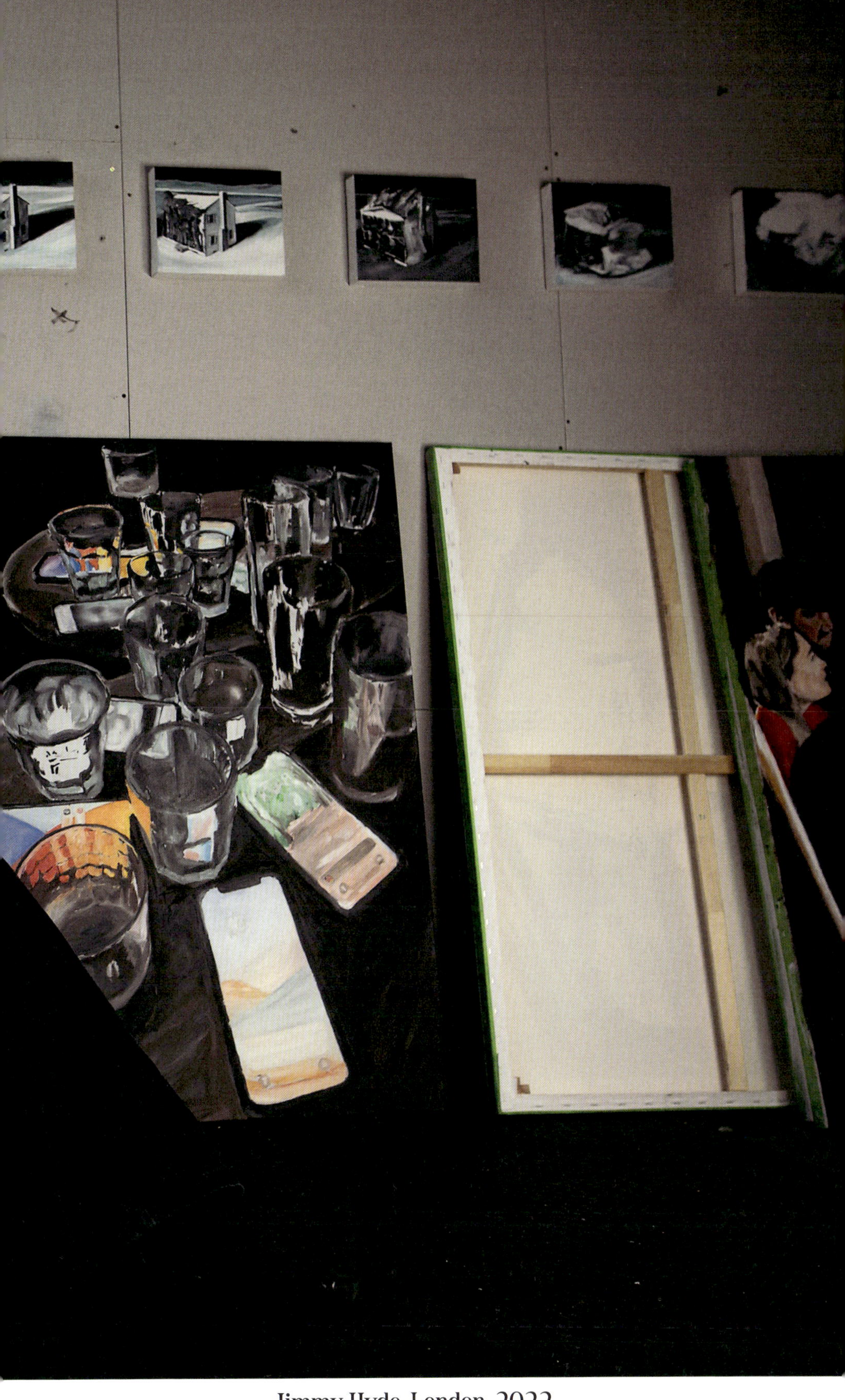

Jimmy Hyde, London, 2022

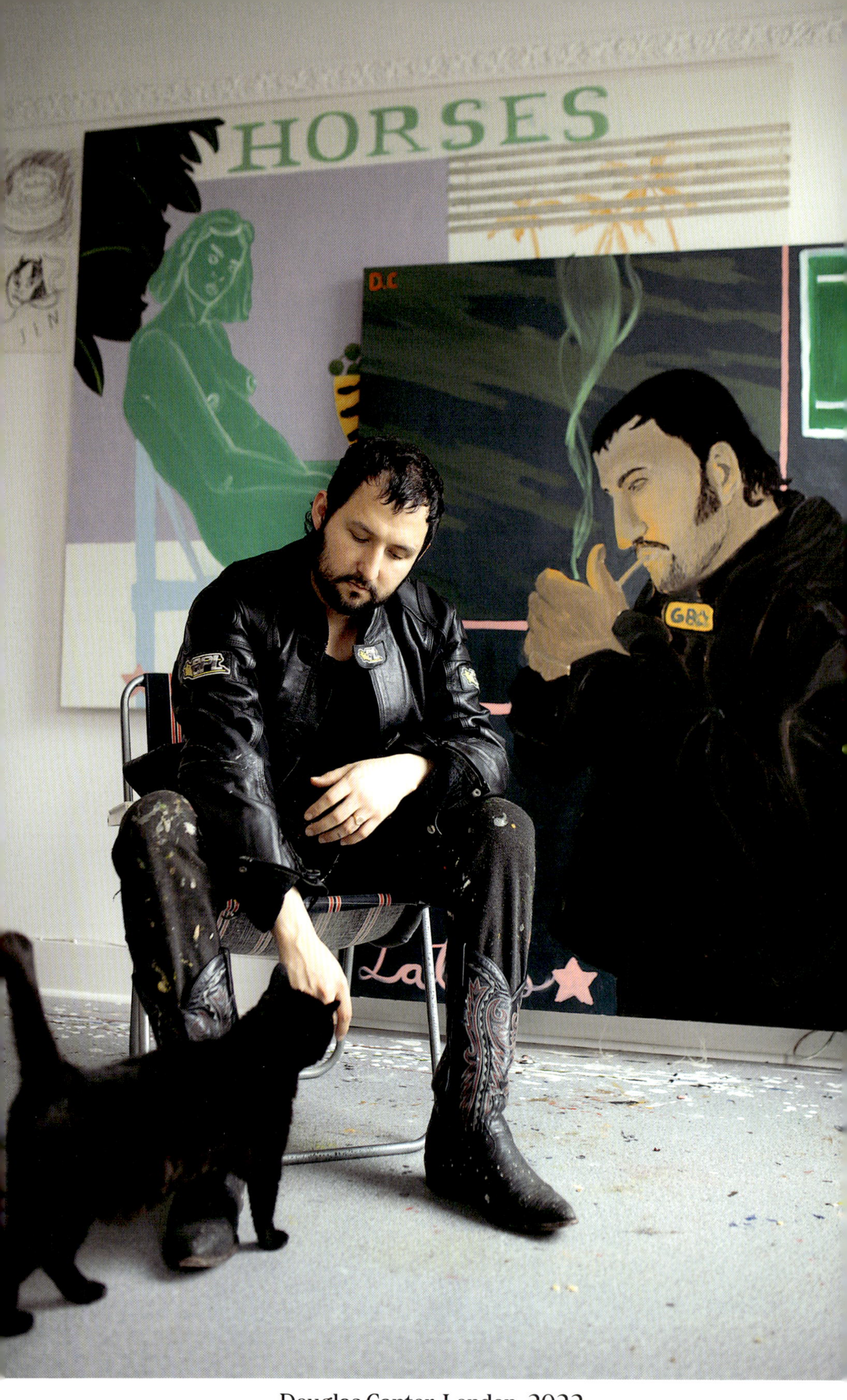

Douglas Cantor, London, 2022

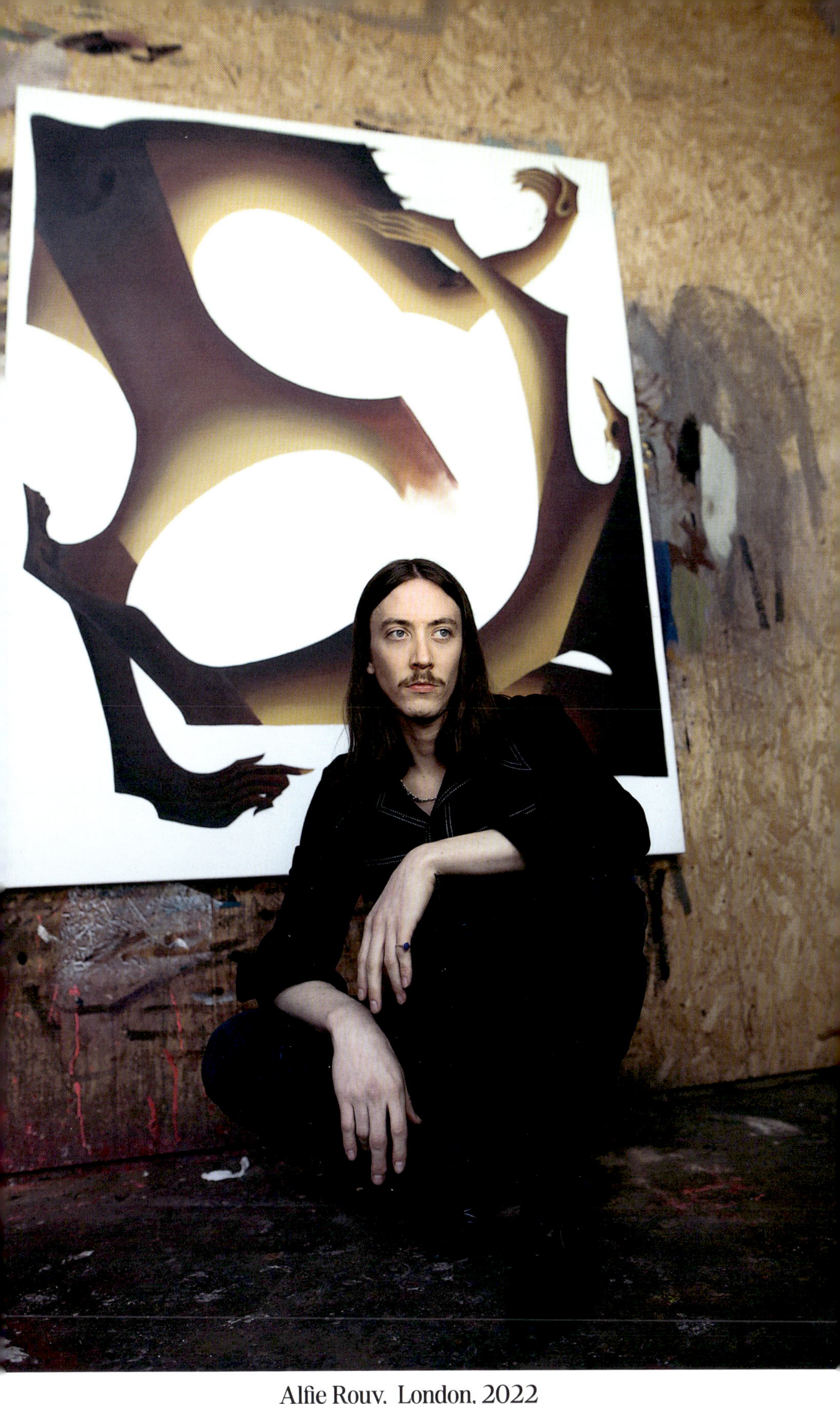

Alfie Rouy, London, 2022

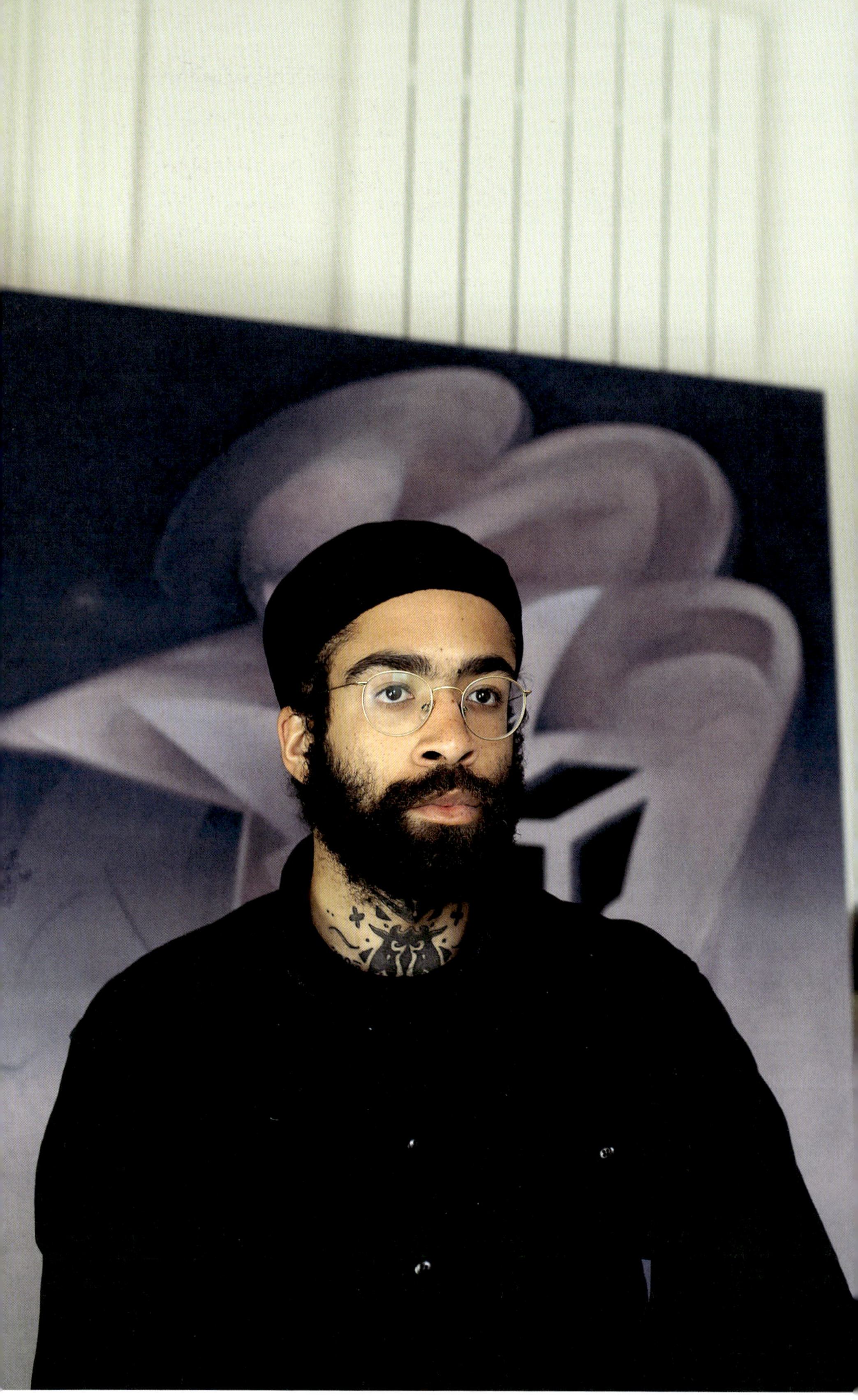

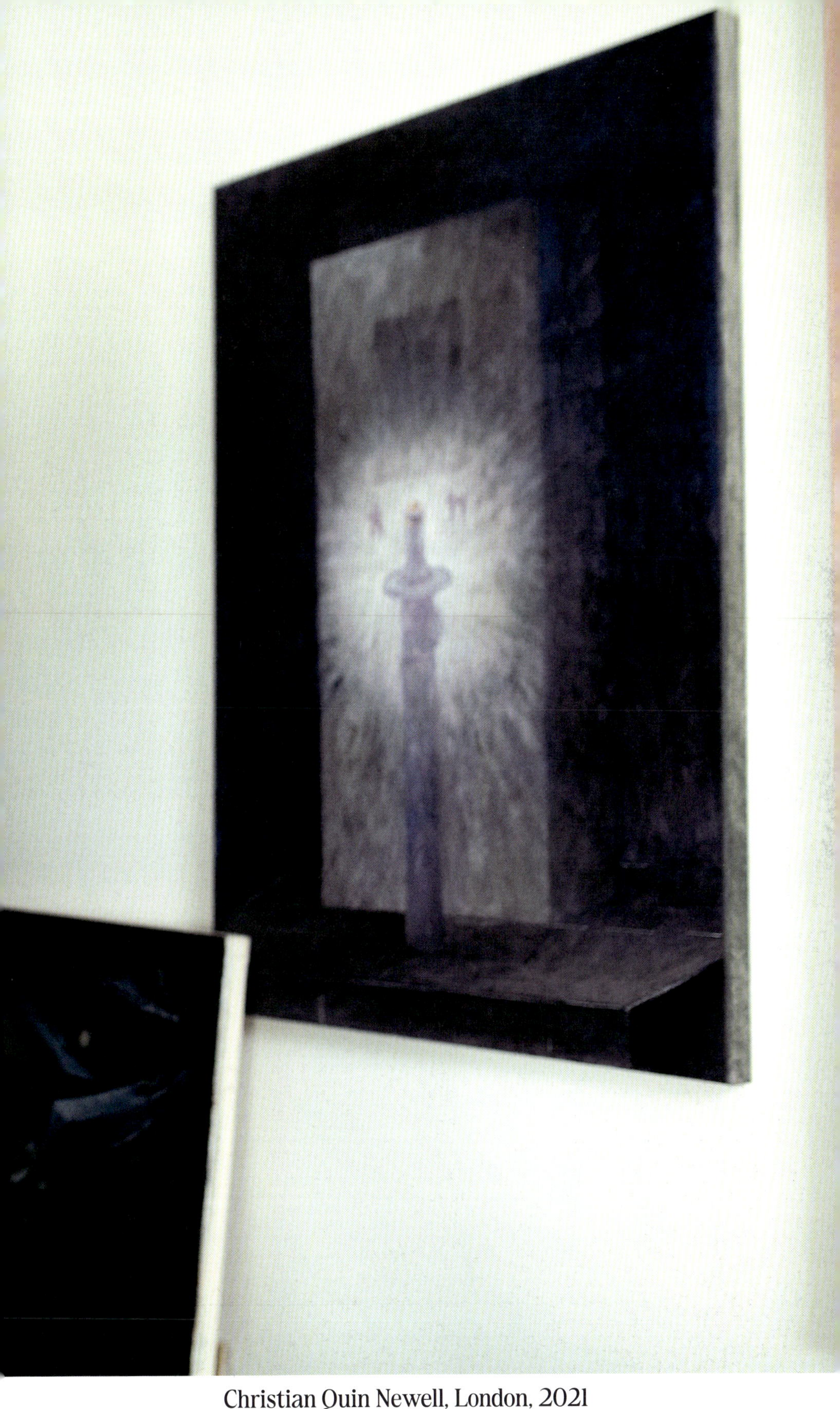

Christian Quin Newell, London, 2021

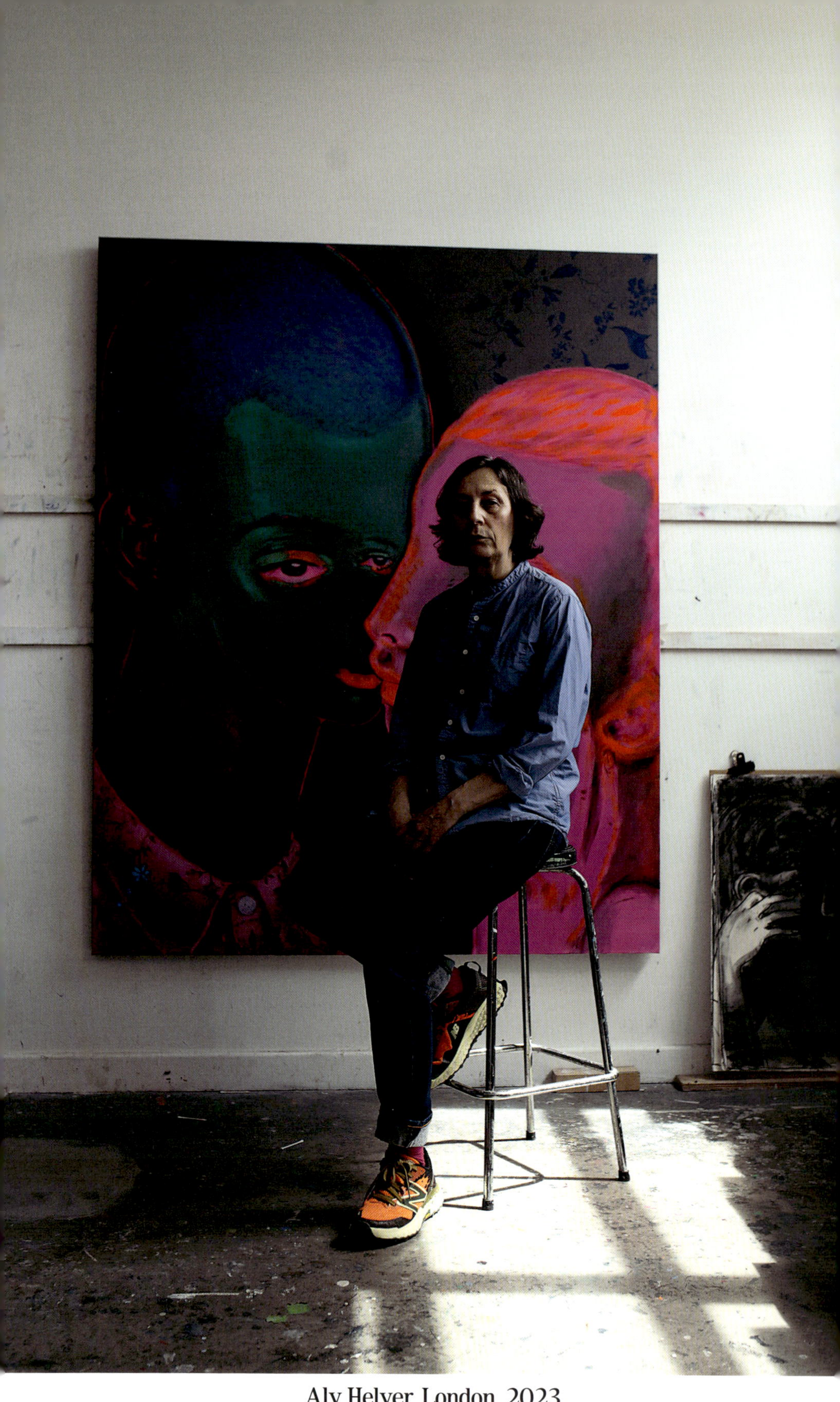

Aly Helyer, London, 2023

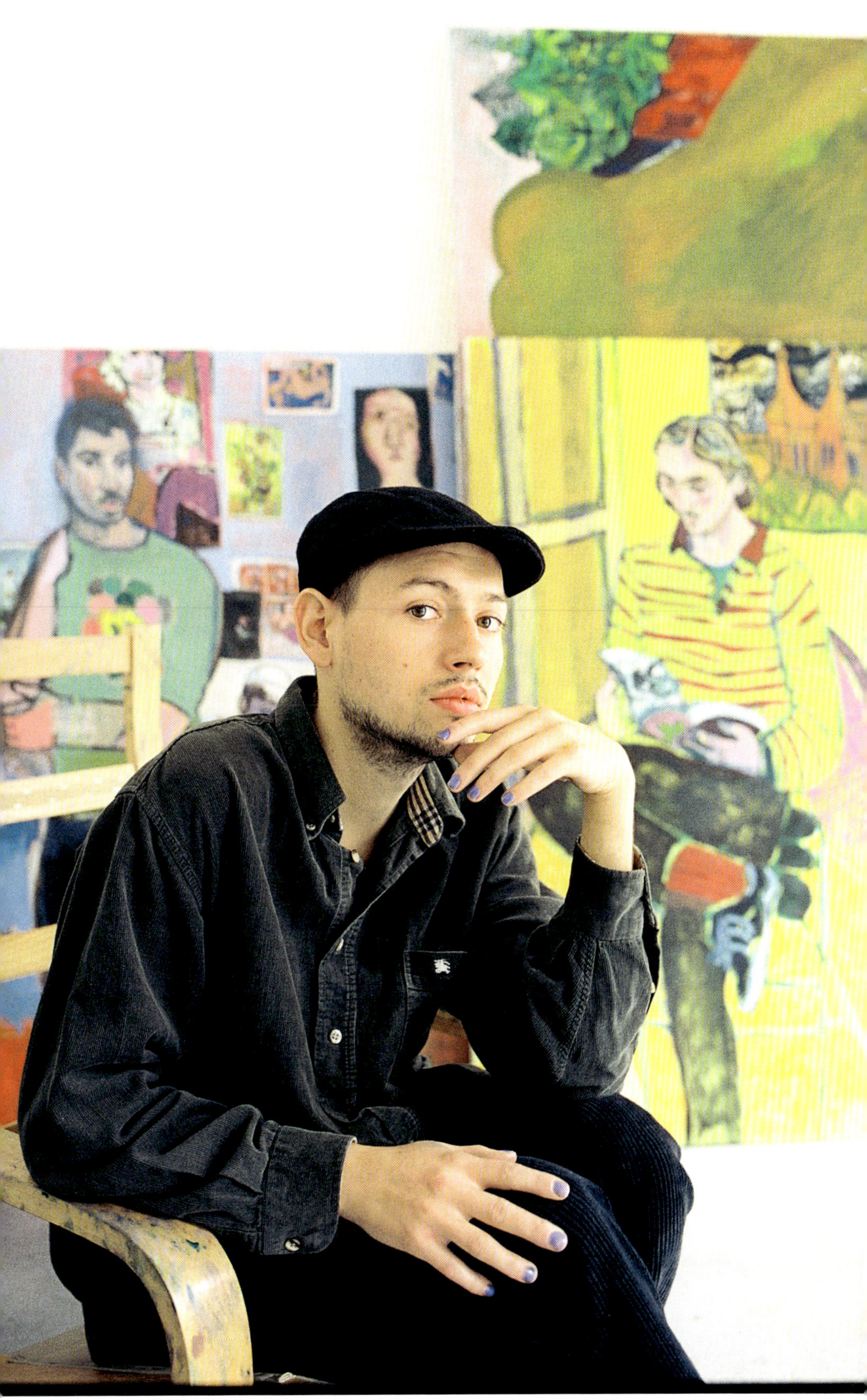

Igor Moritz, London, 2020

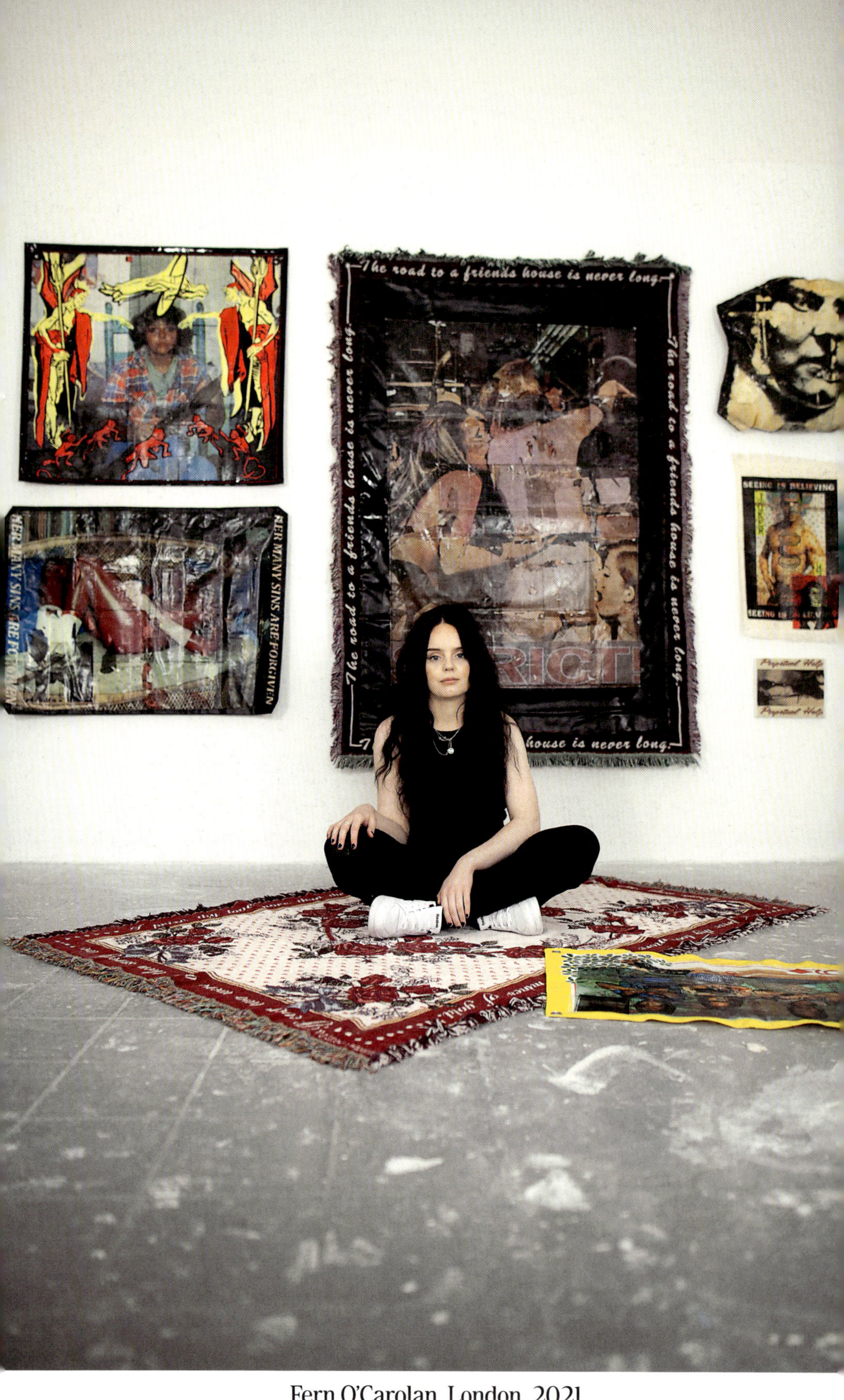

Fern O'Carolan, London, 2021

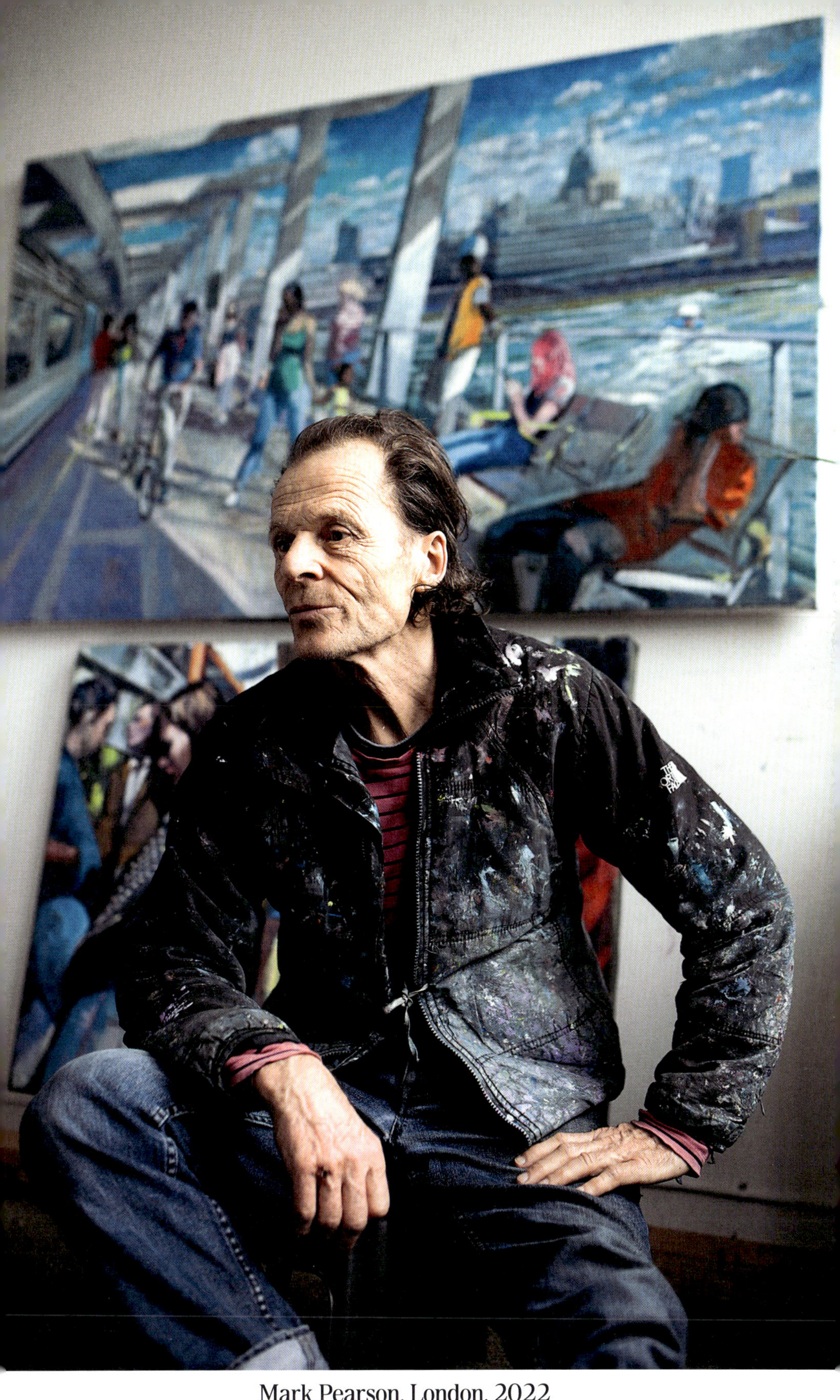

Mark Pearson, London, 2022

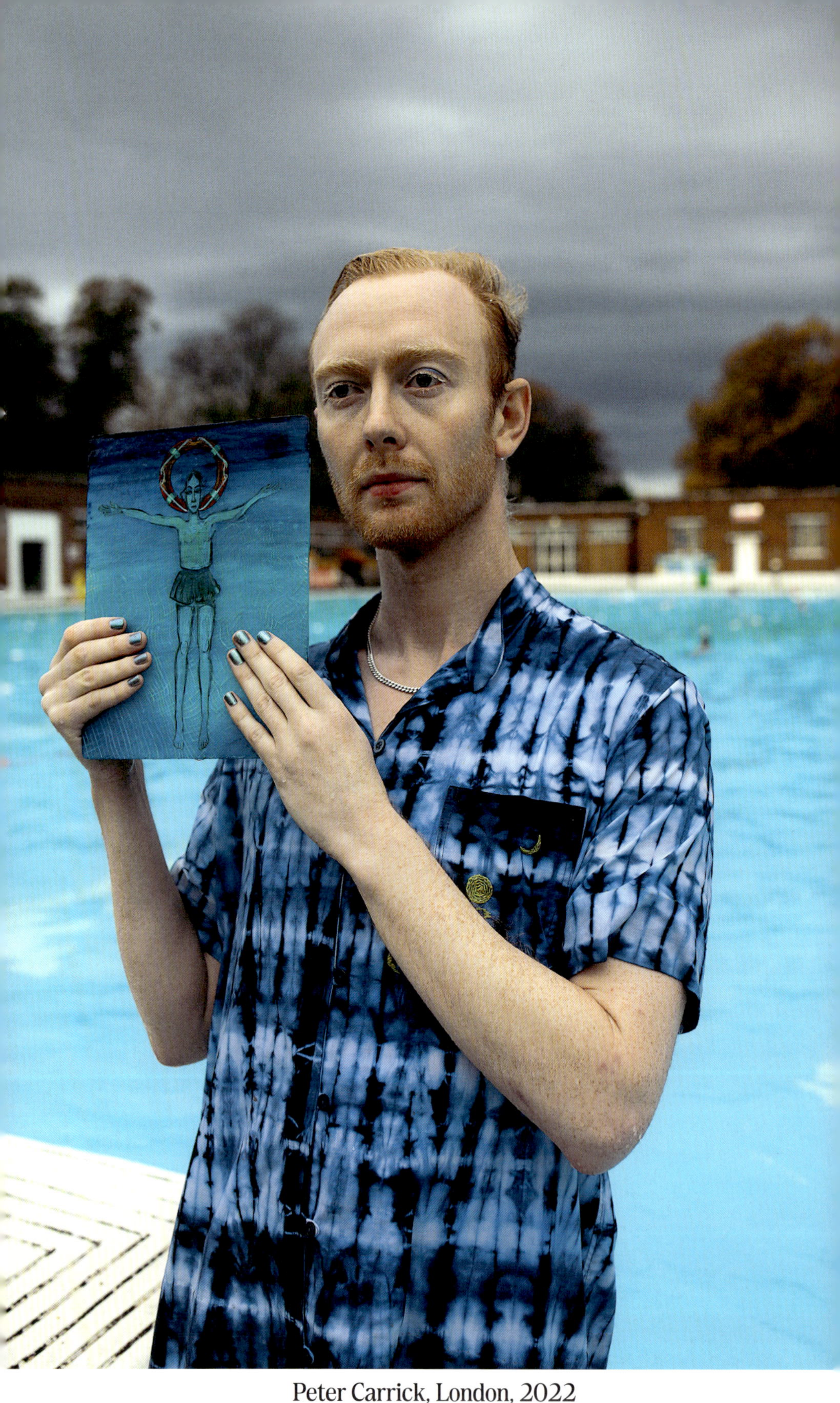

Peter Carrick, London, 2022

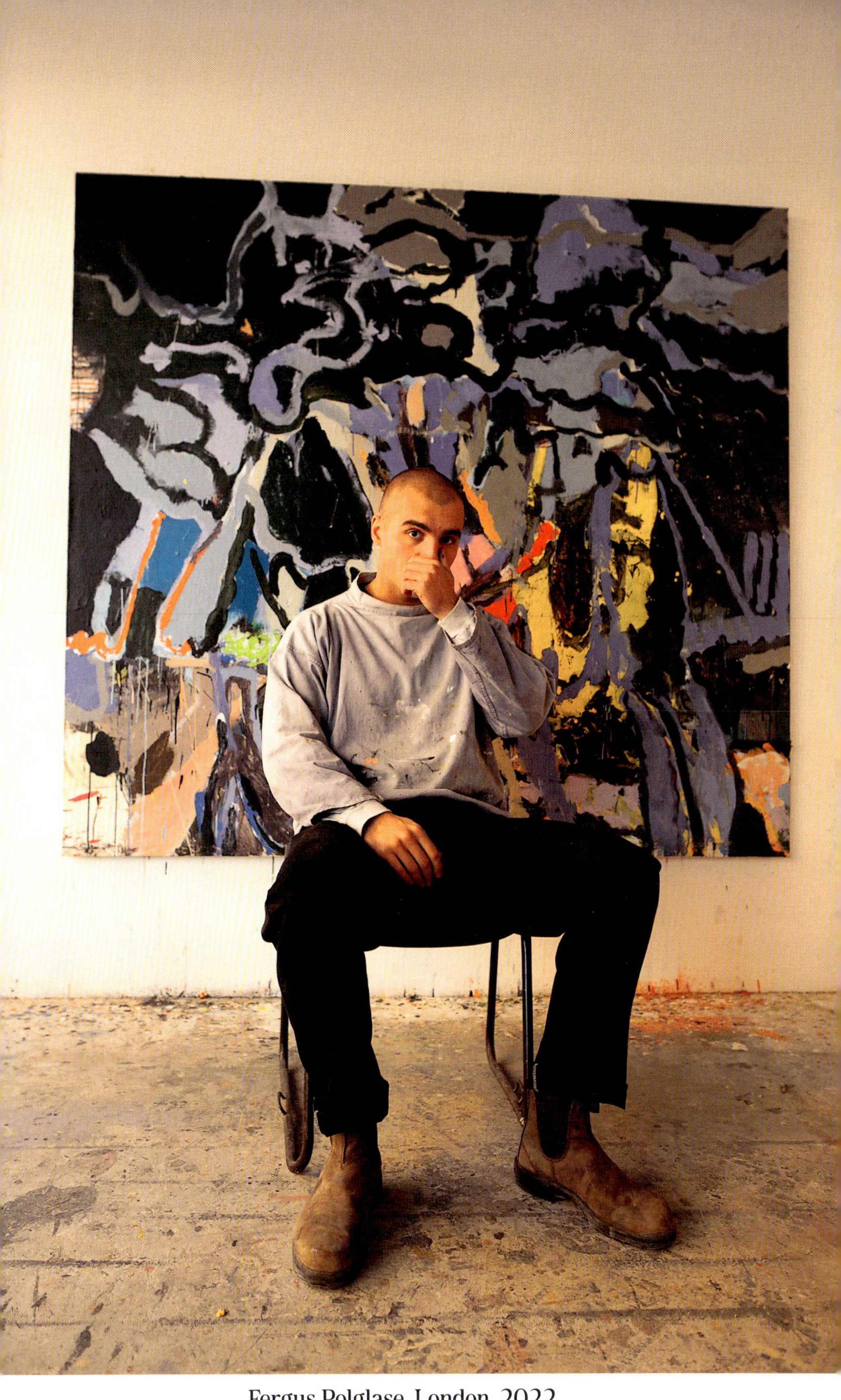

Fergus Polglase, London, 2022

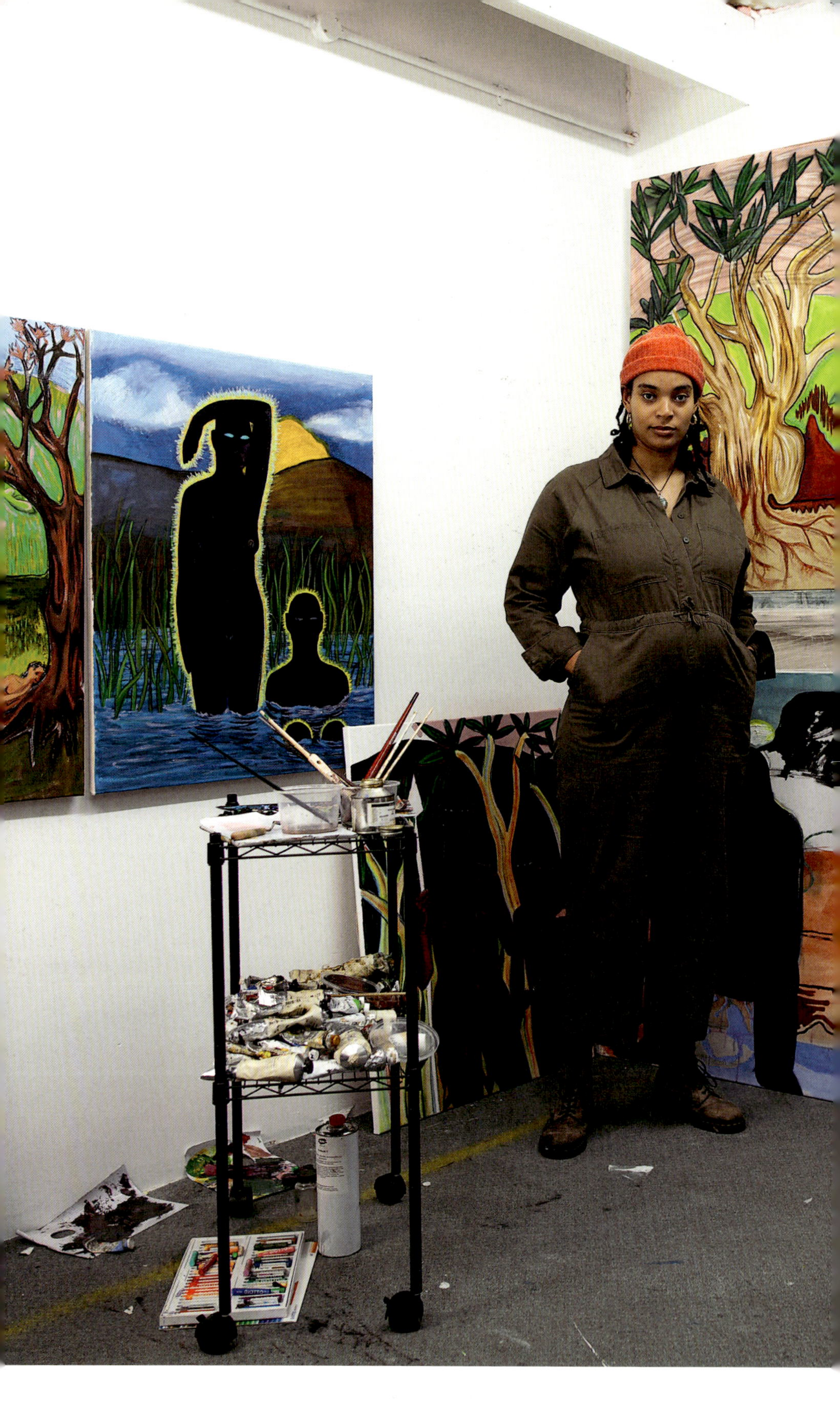

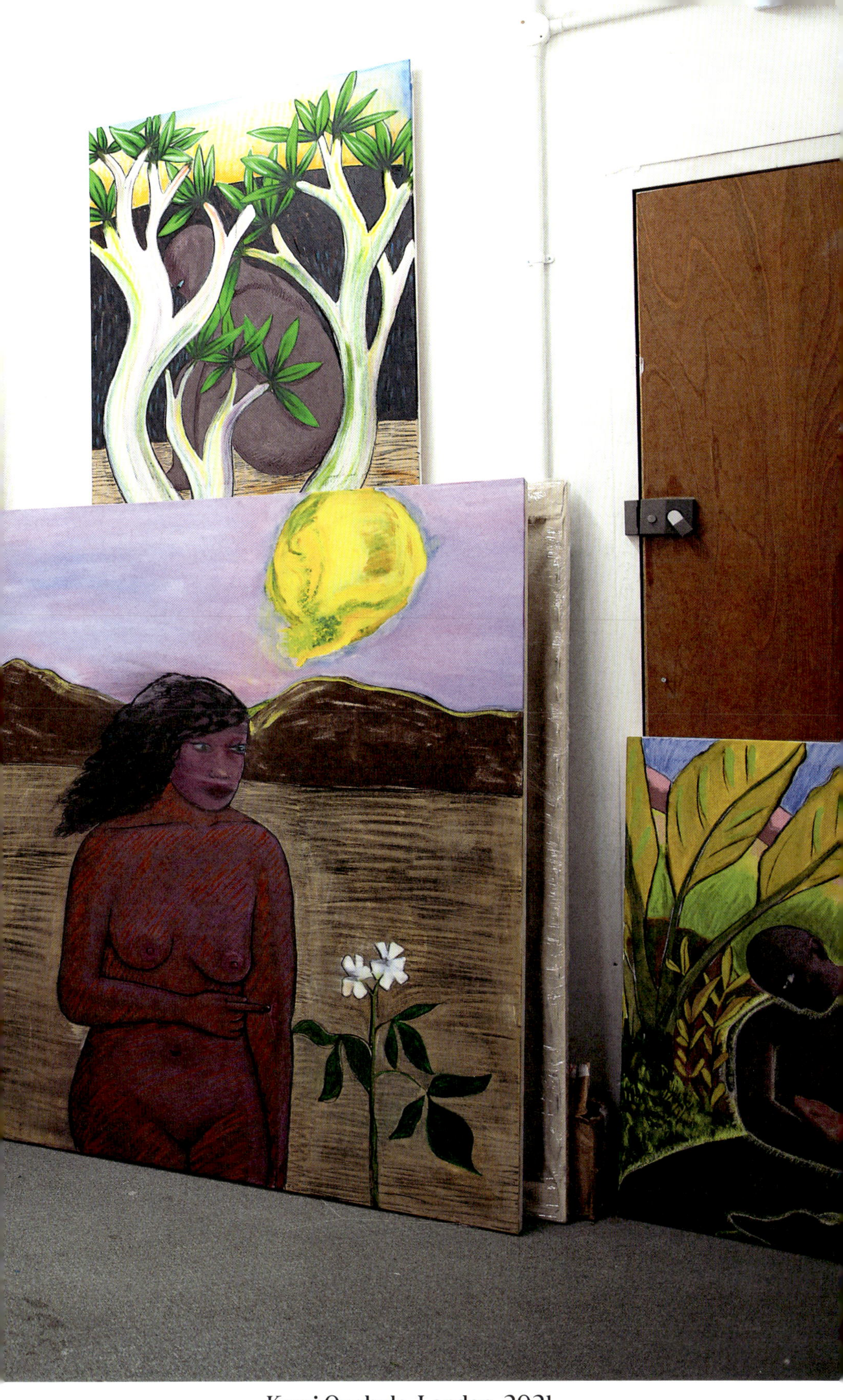

Kemi Onabule, London, 2021

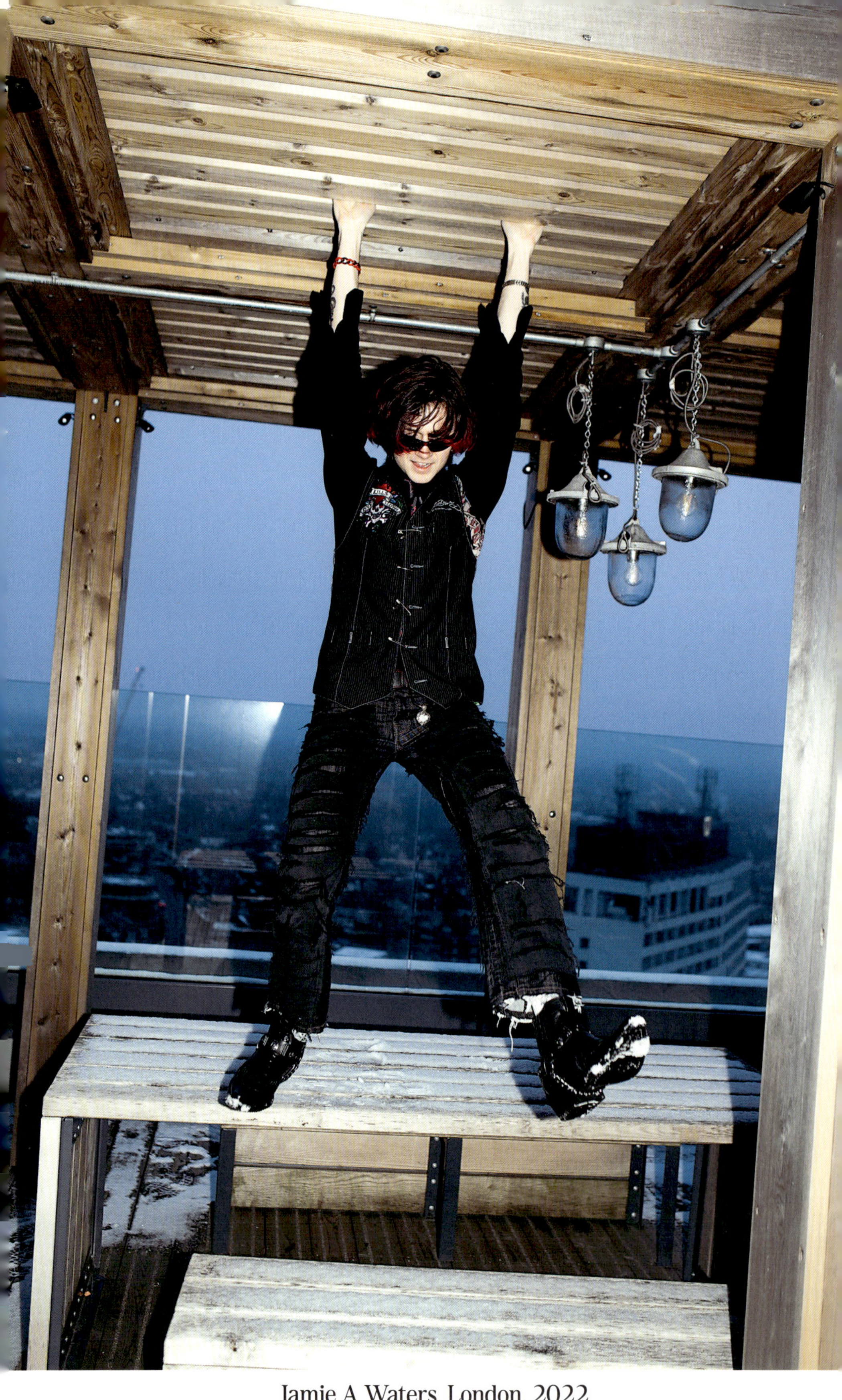

Jamie A Waters, London, 2022

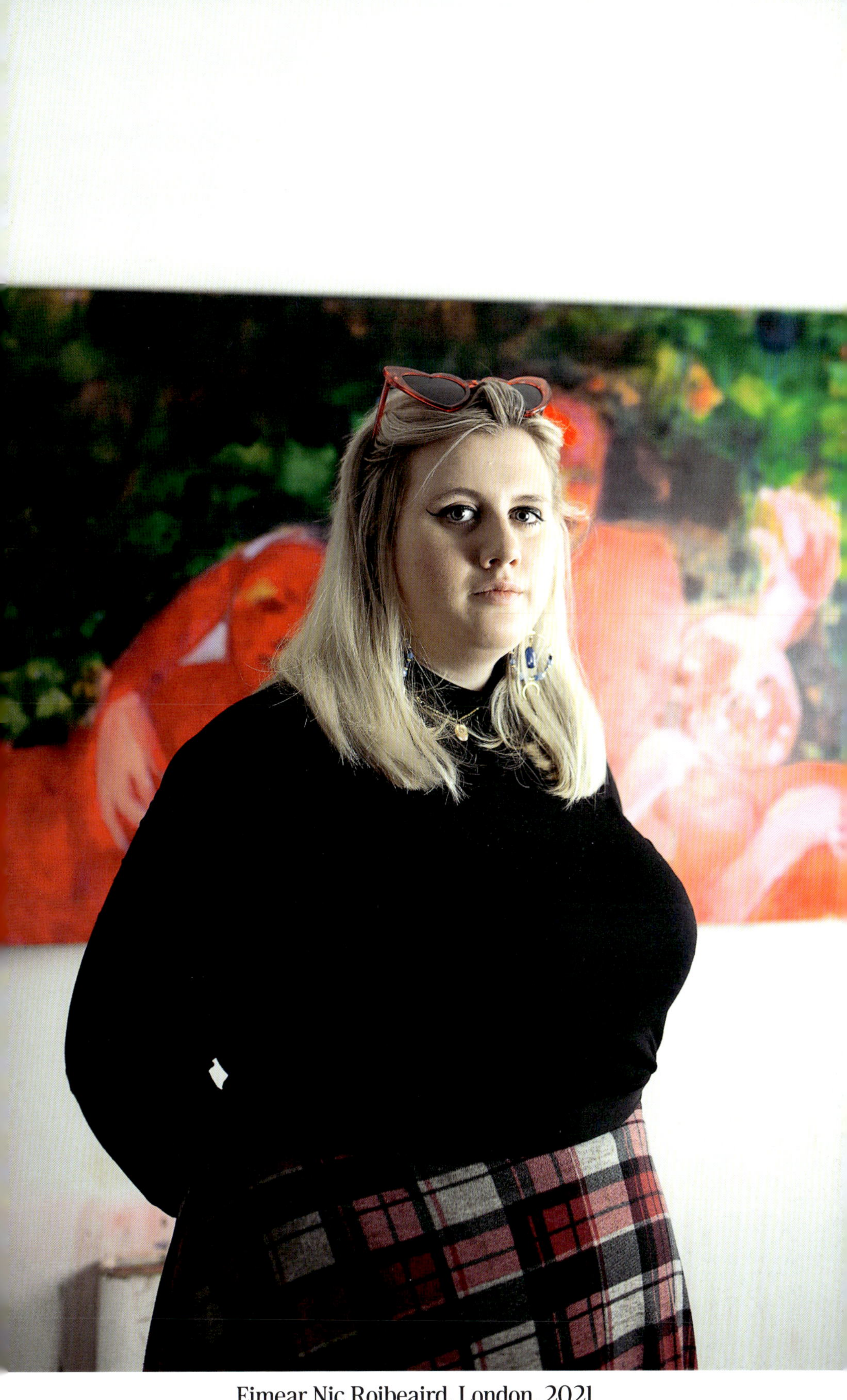

Eimear Nic Roibeaird, London, 2021

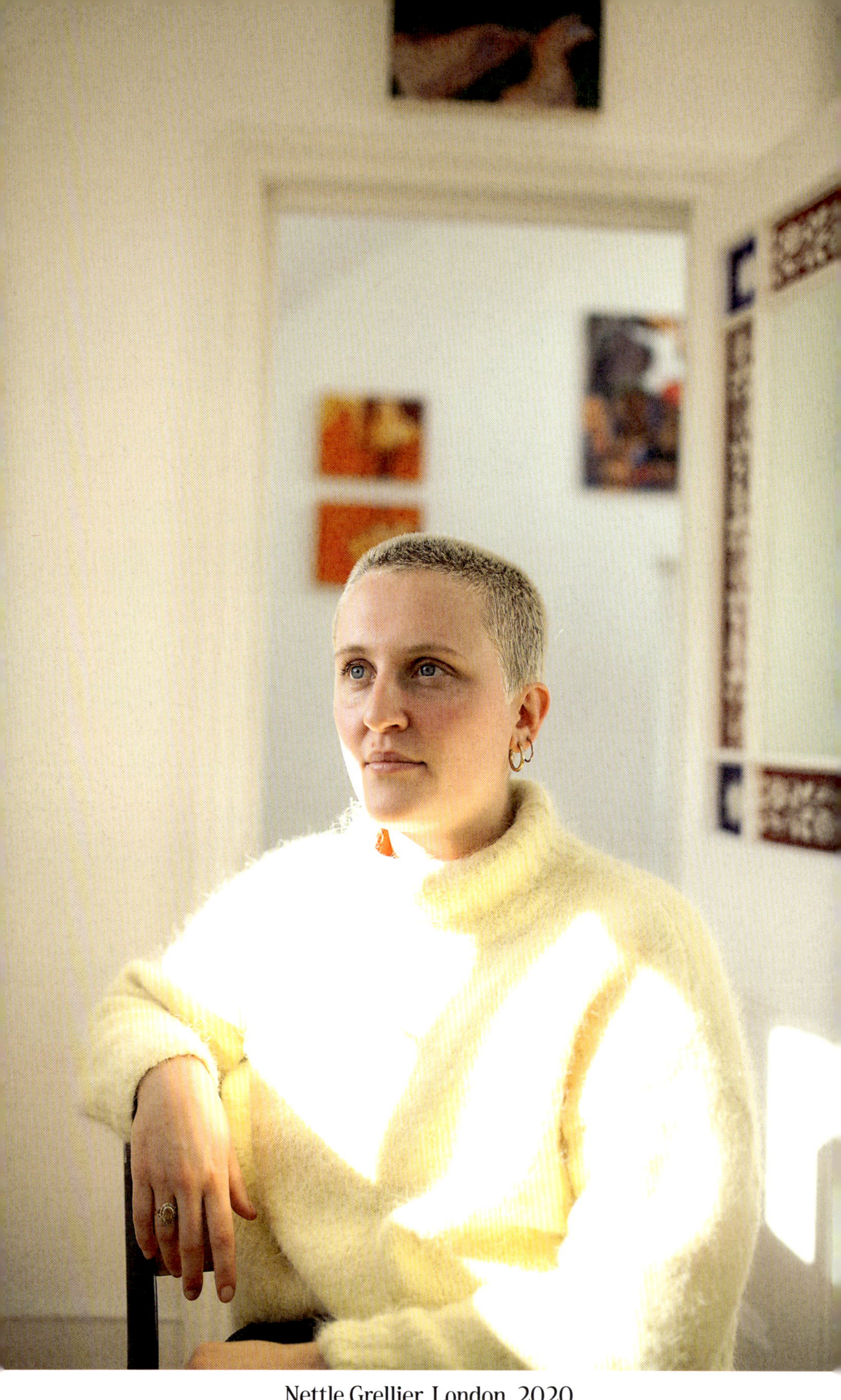

Nettle Grellier, London, 2020

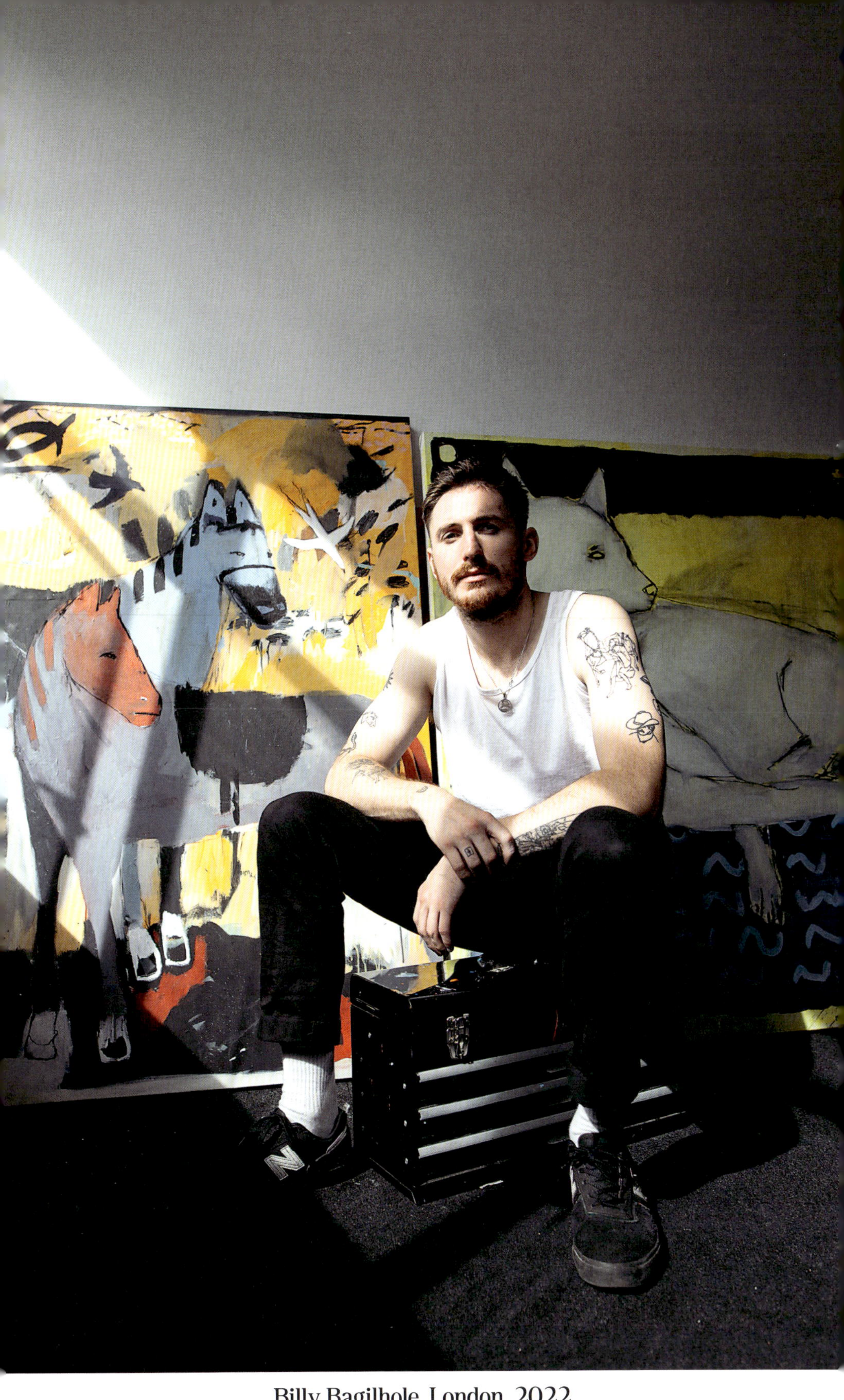

Billy Bagilhole, London, 2022

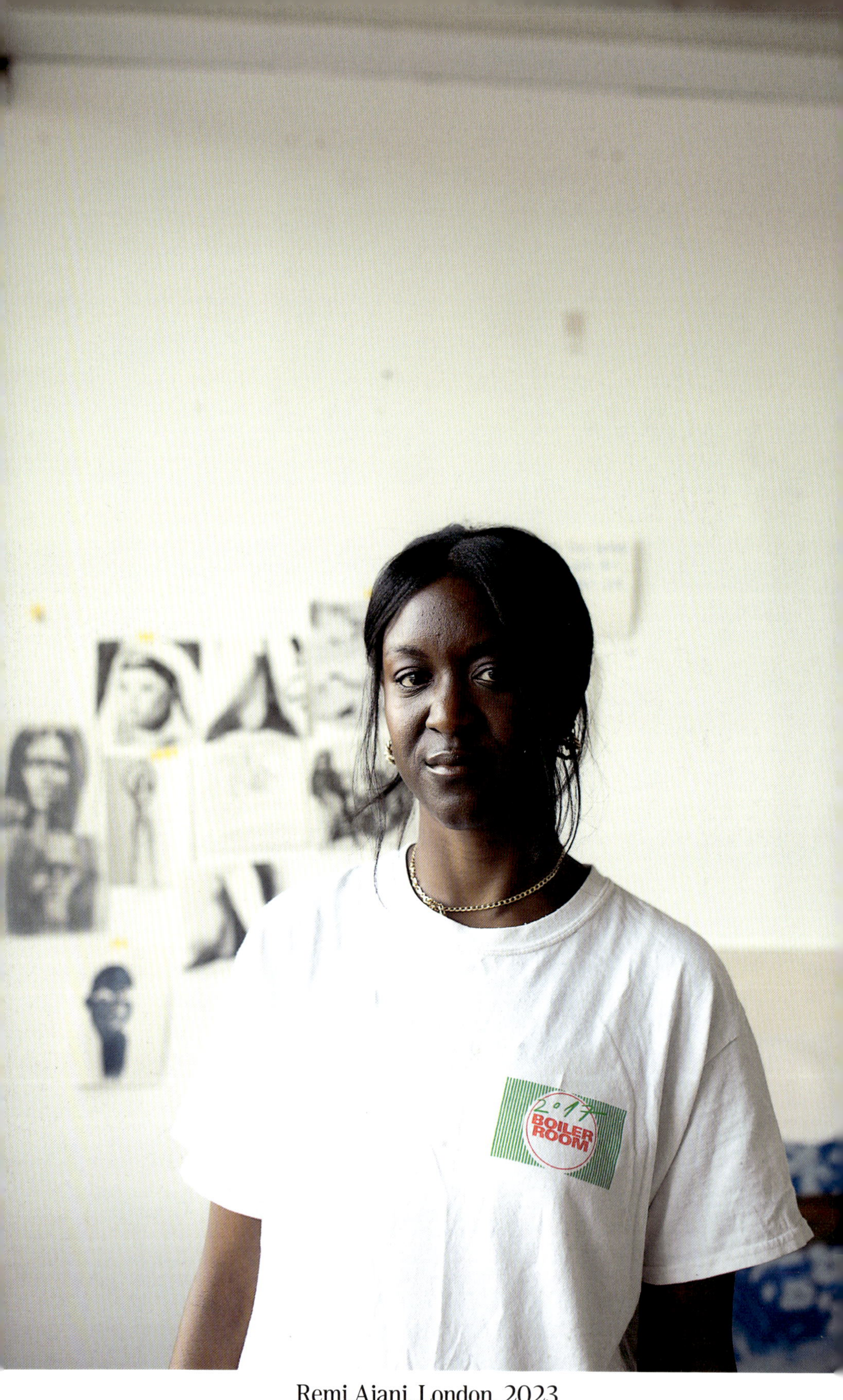

Remi Ajani, London, 2023

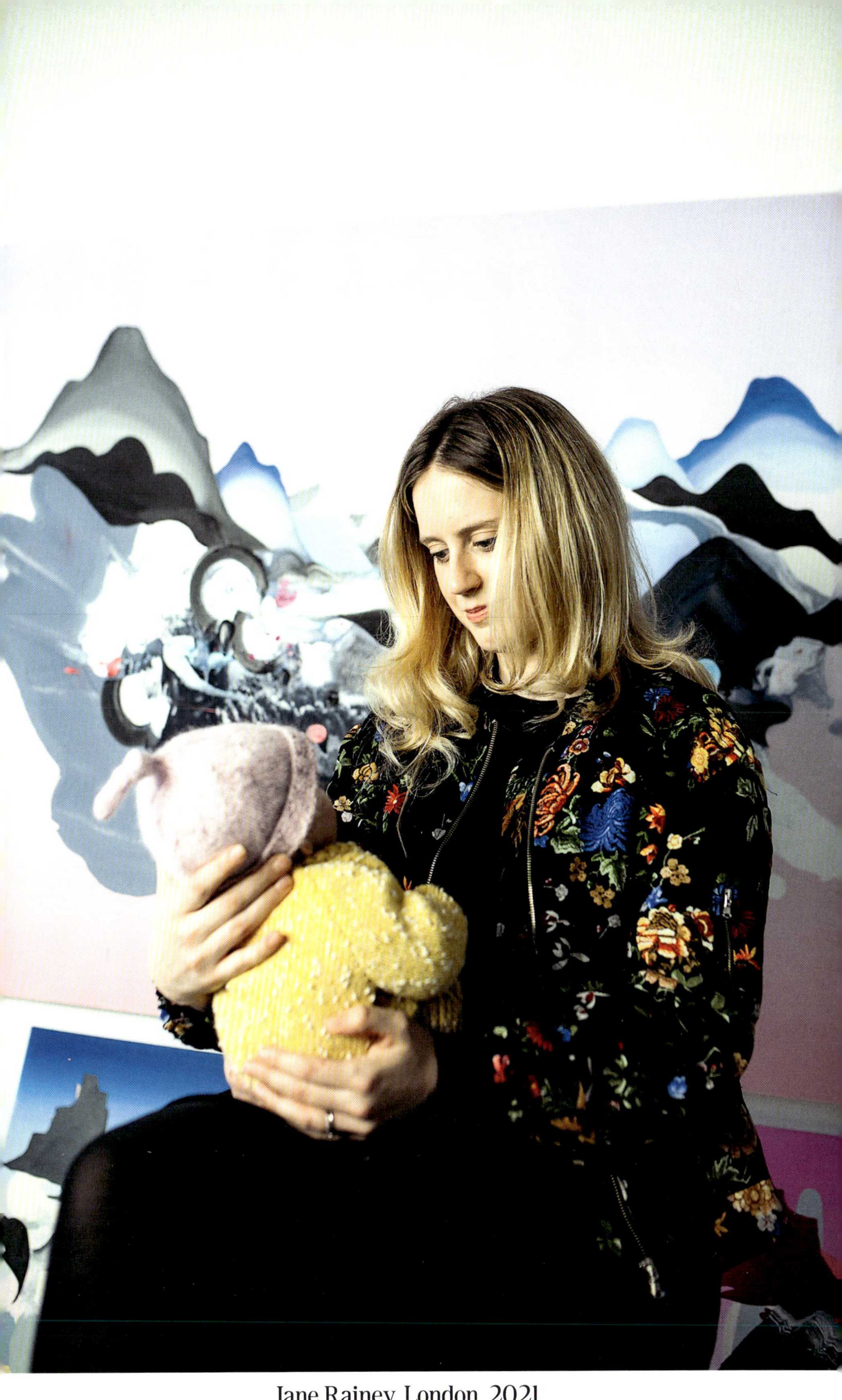

Jane Rainey, London, 2021

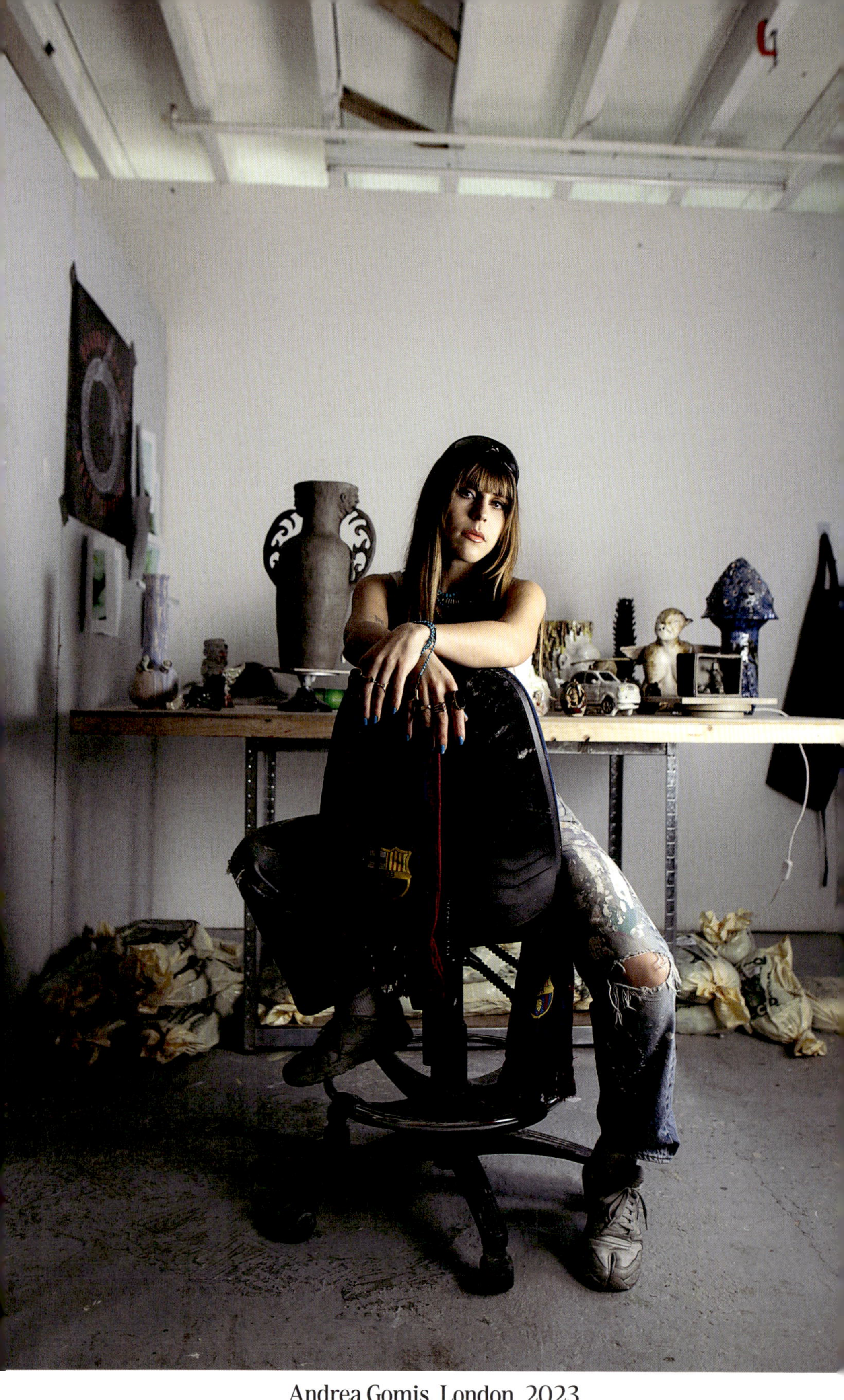

Andrea Gomis, London, 2023

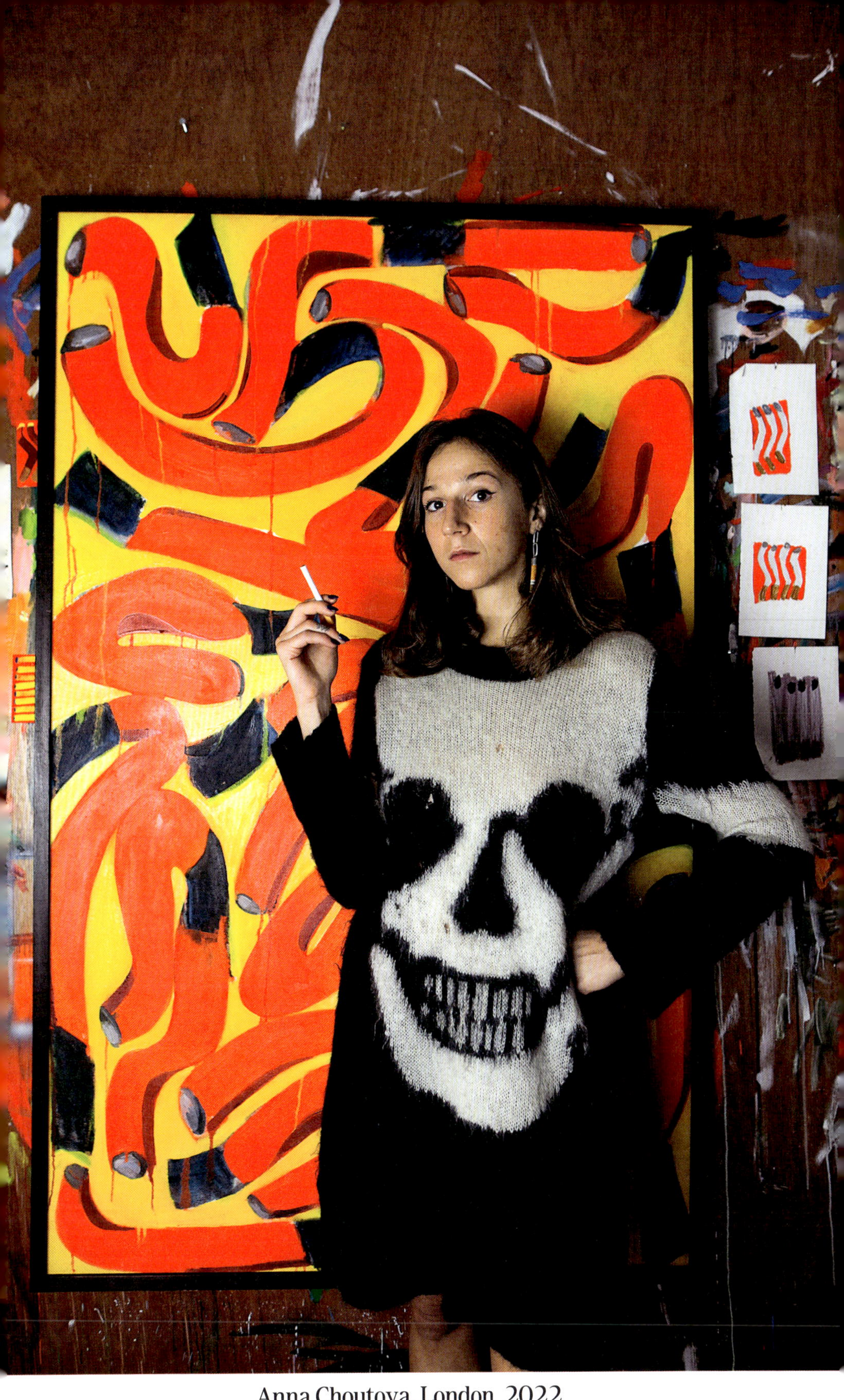

Anna Choutova, London, 2022

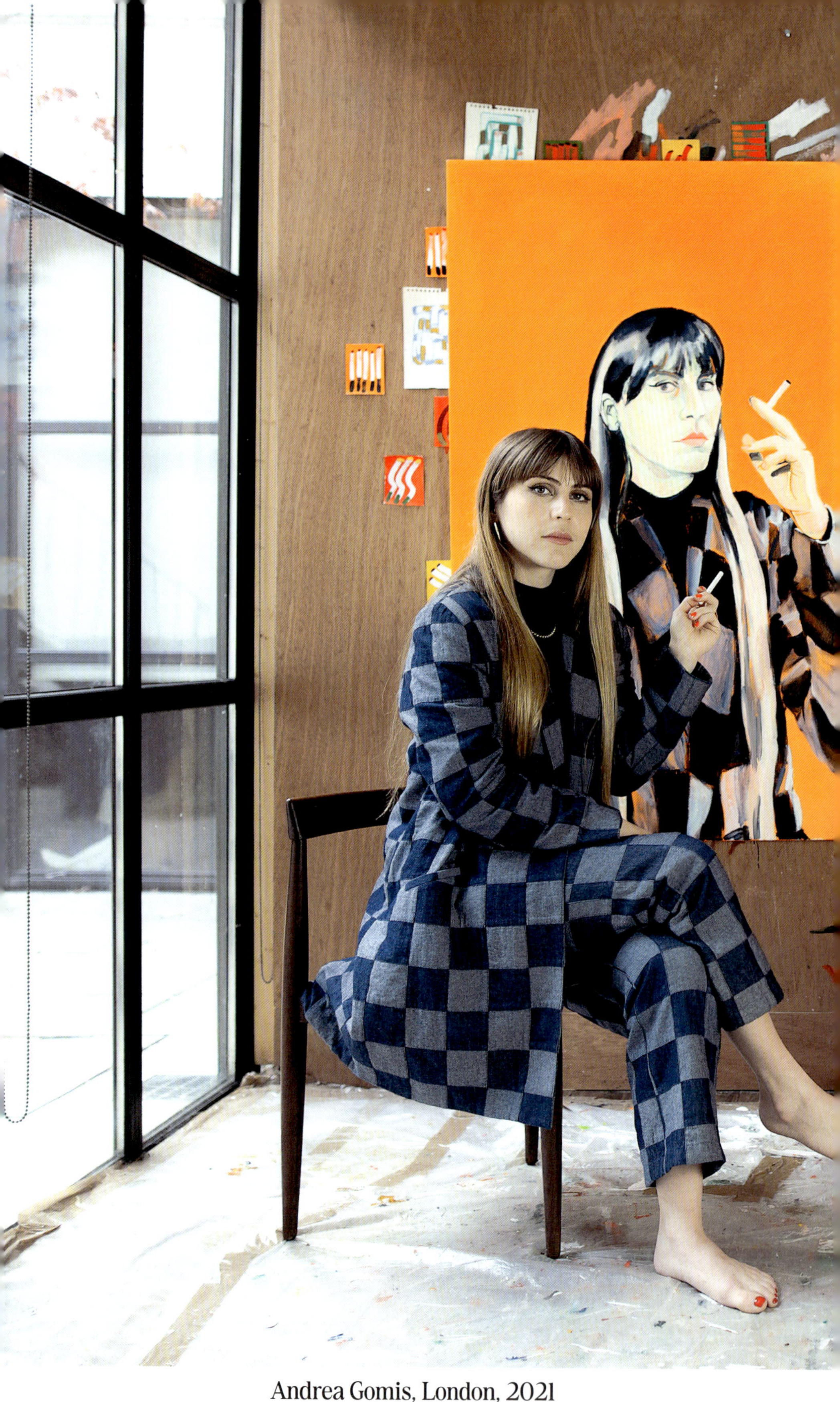

Andrea Gomis, London, 2021

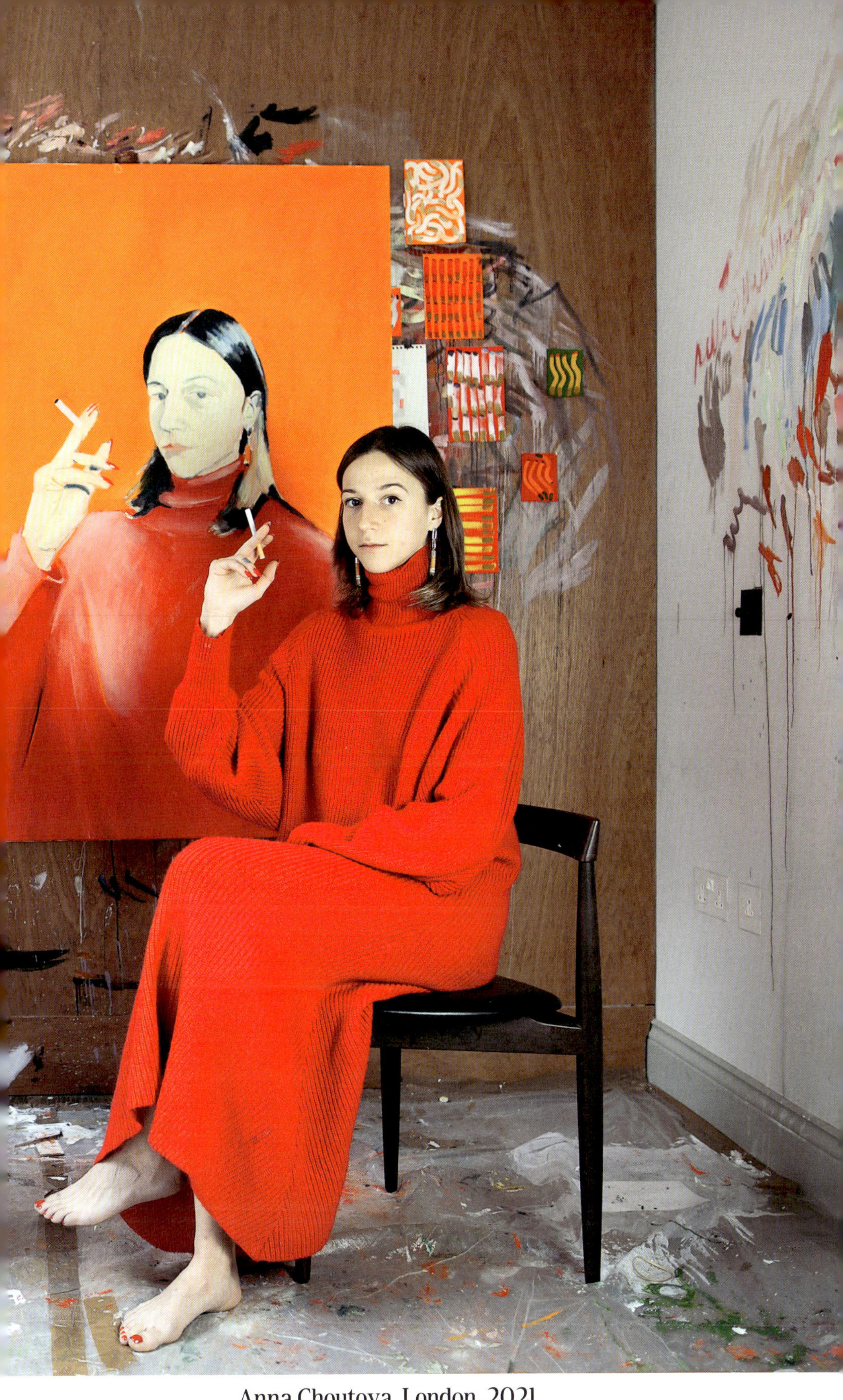

Anna Choutova, London, 2021

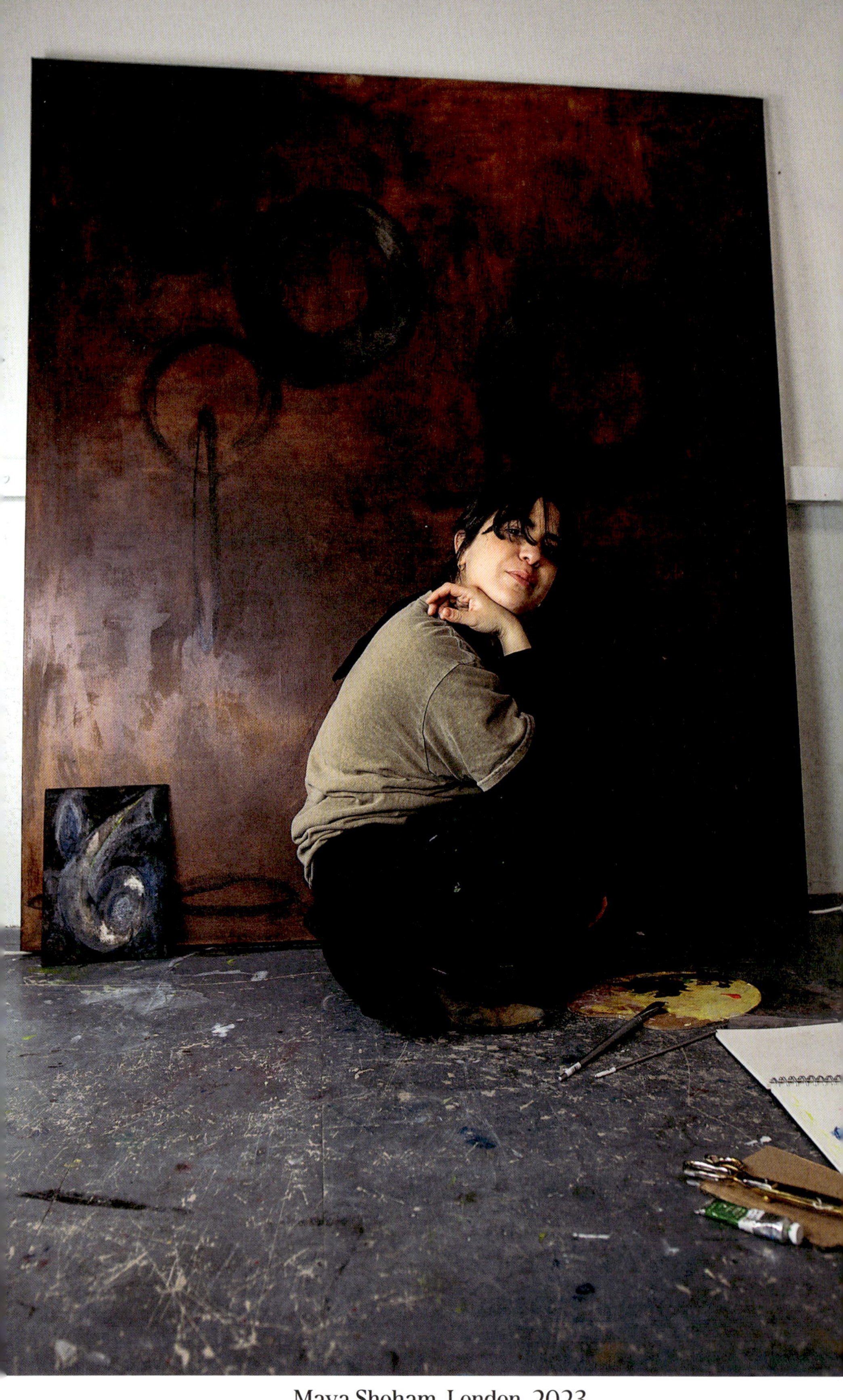

Maya Shoham, London, 2023

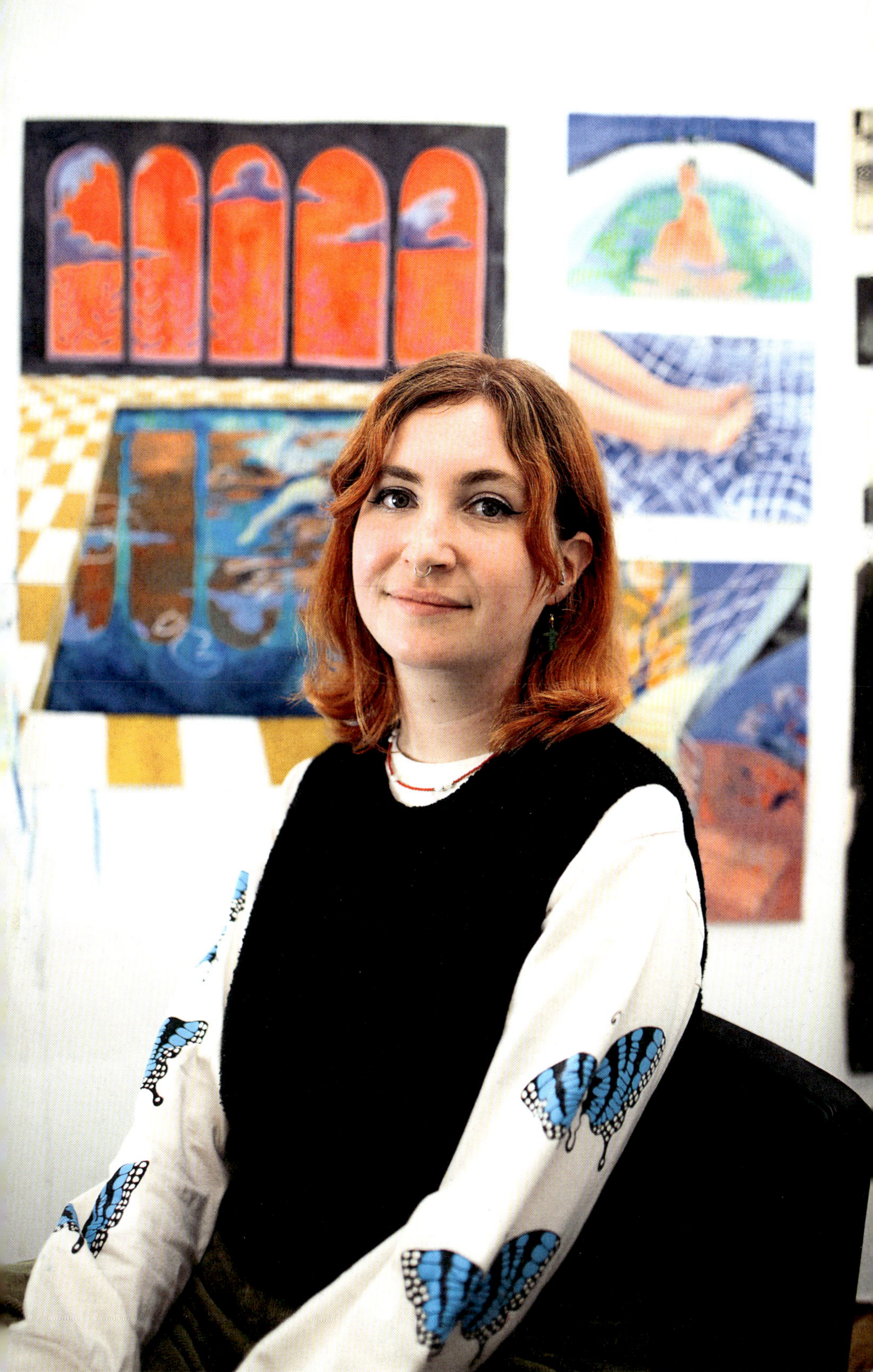

Cecilia Reeve, London, 2021

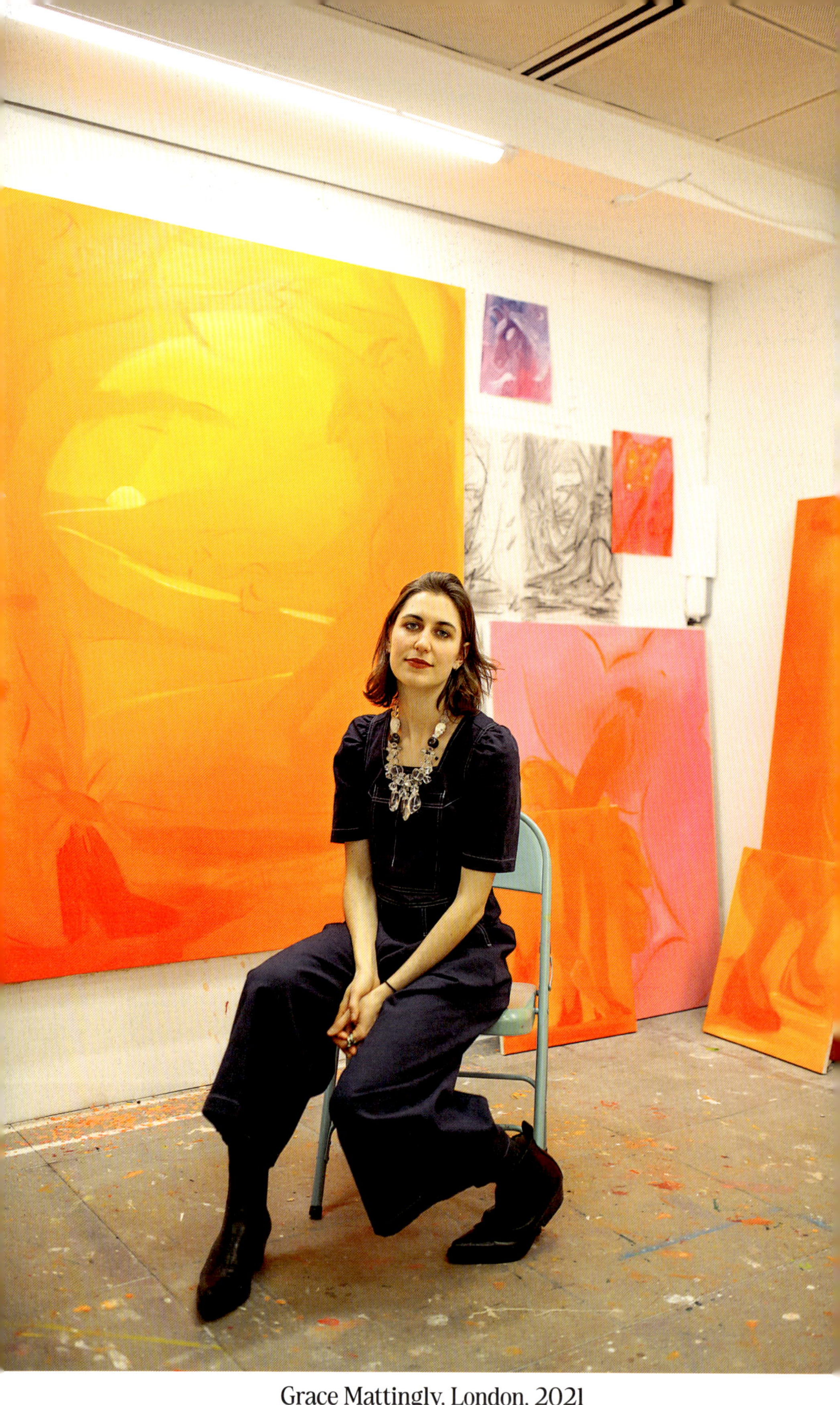

Grace Mattingly, London, 2021

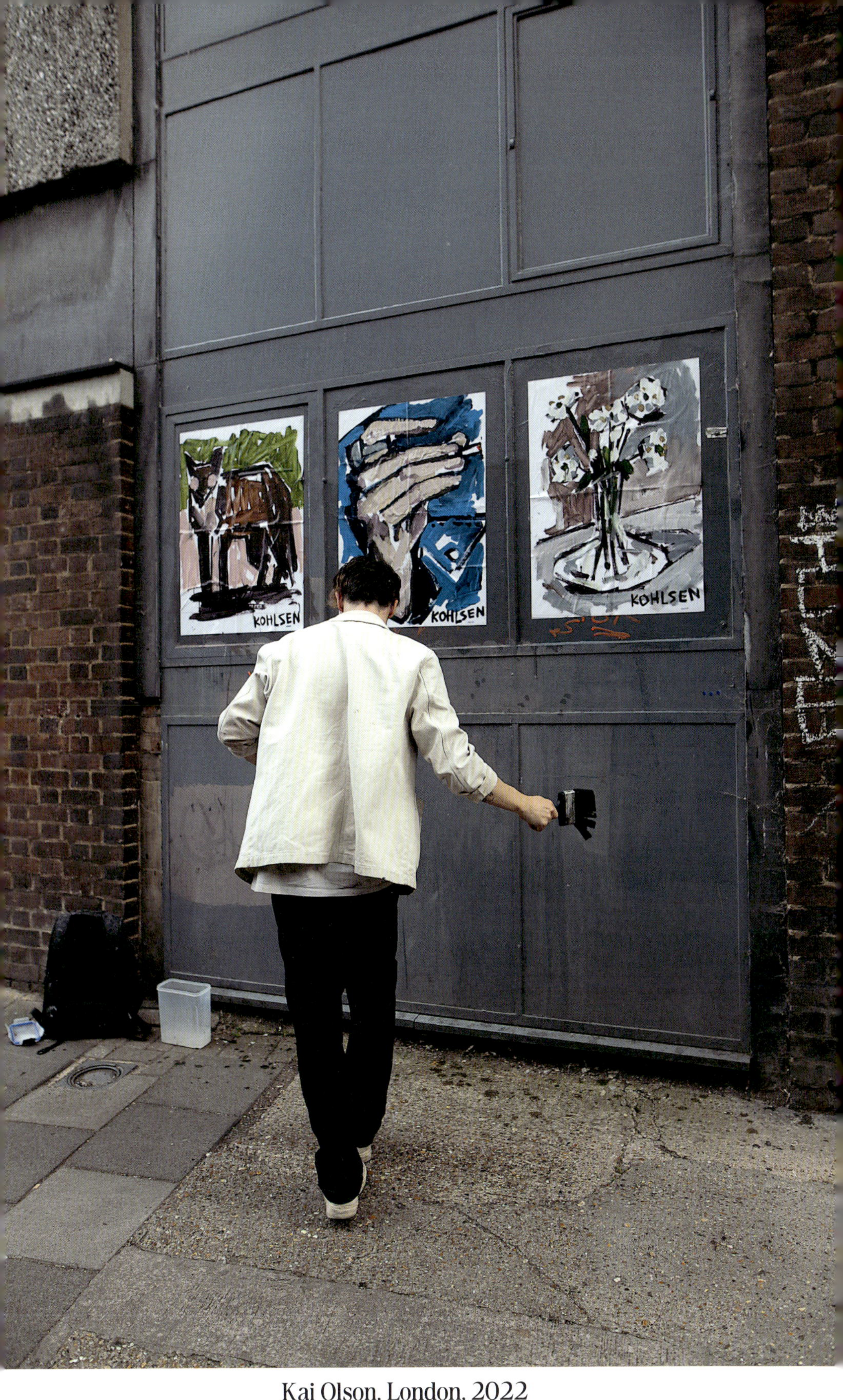

Kai Olson, London, 2022

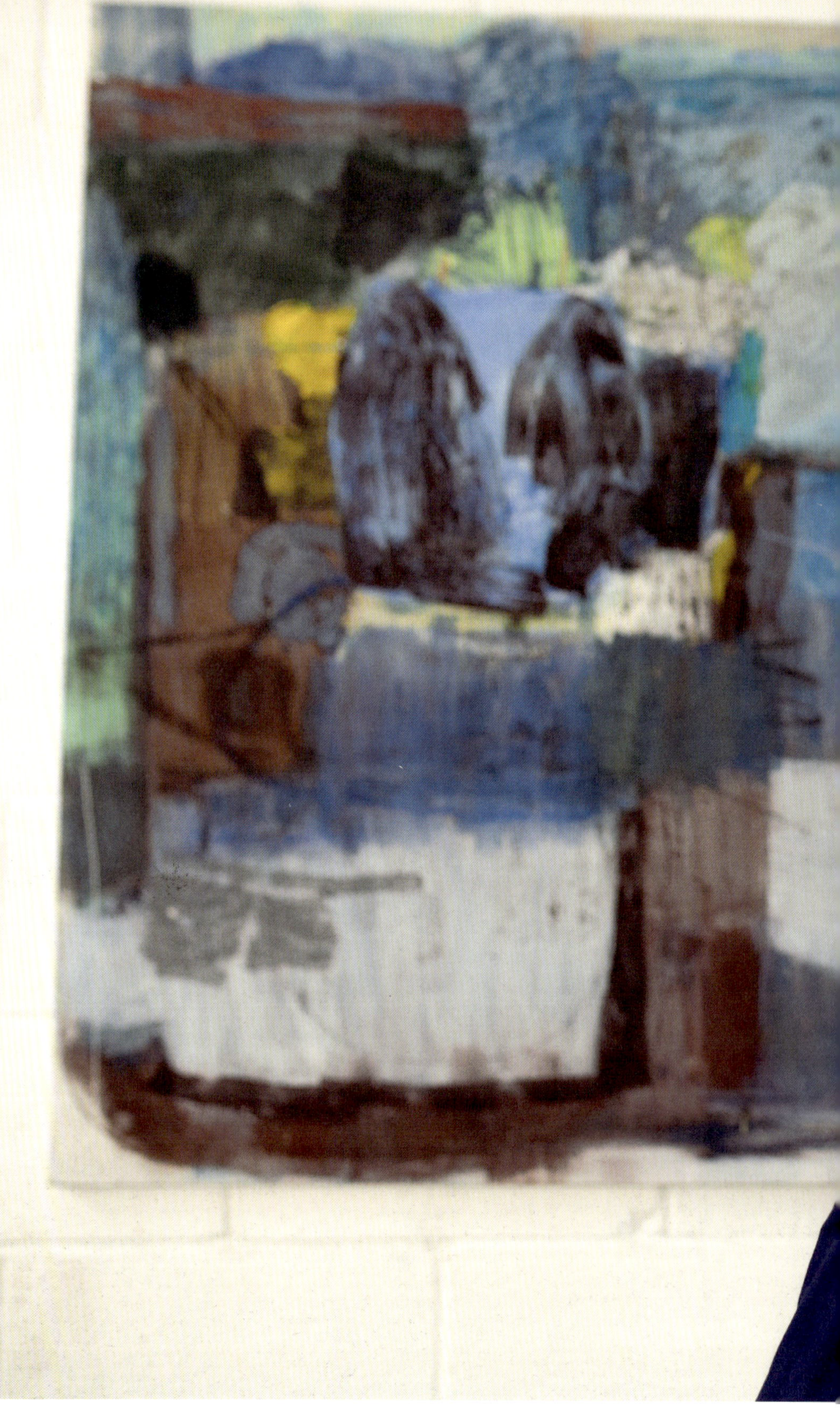

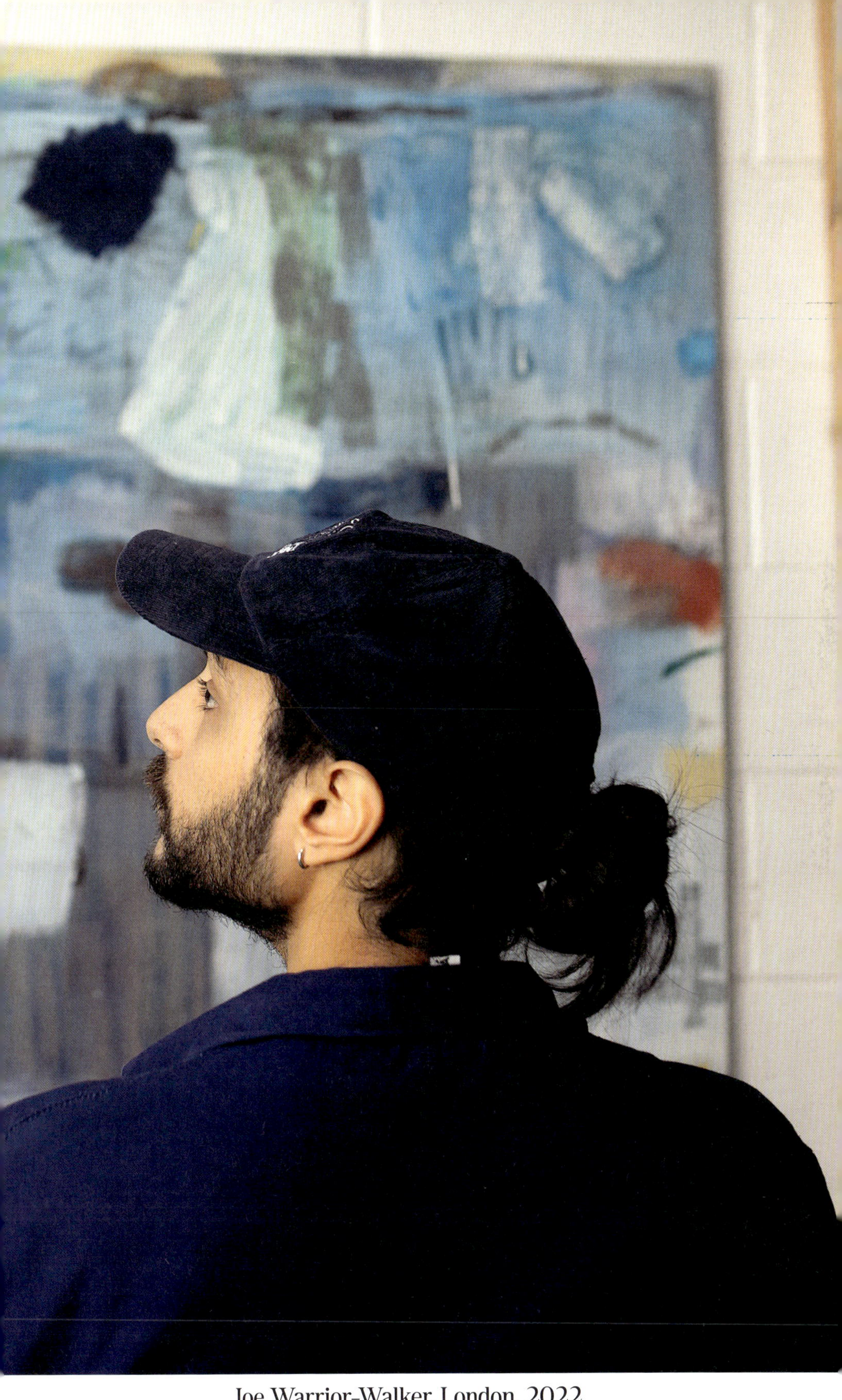

Joe Warrior-Walker, London, 2022

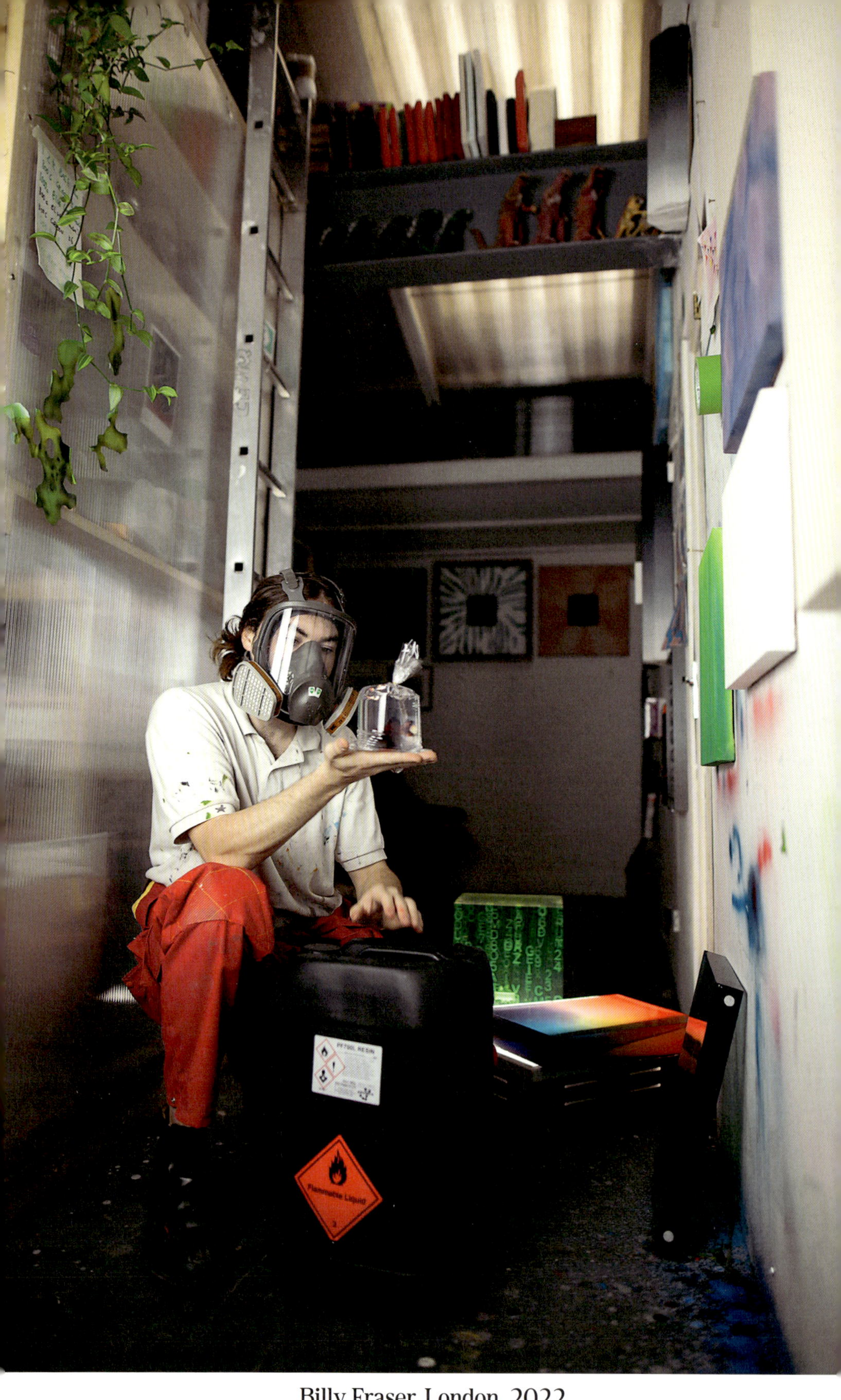

Billy Fraser, London, 2022

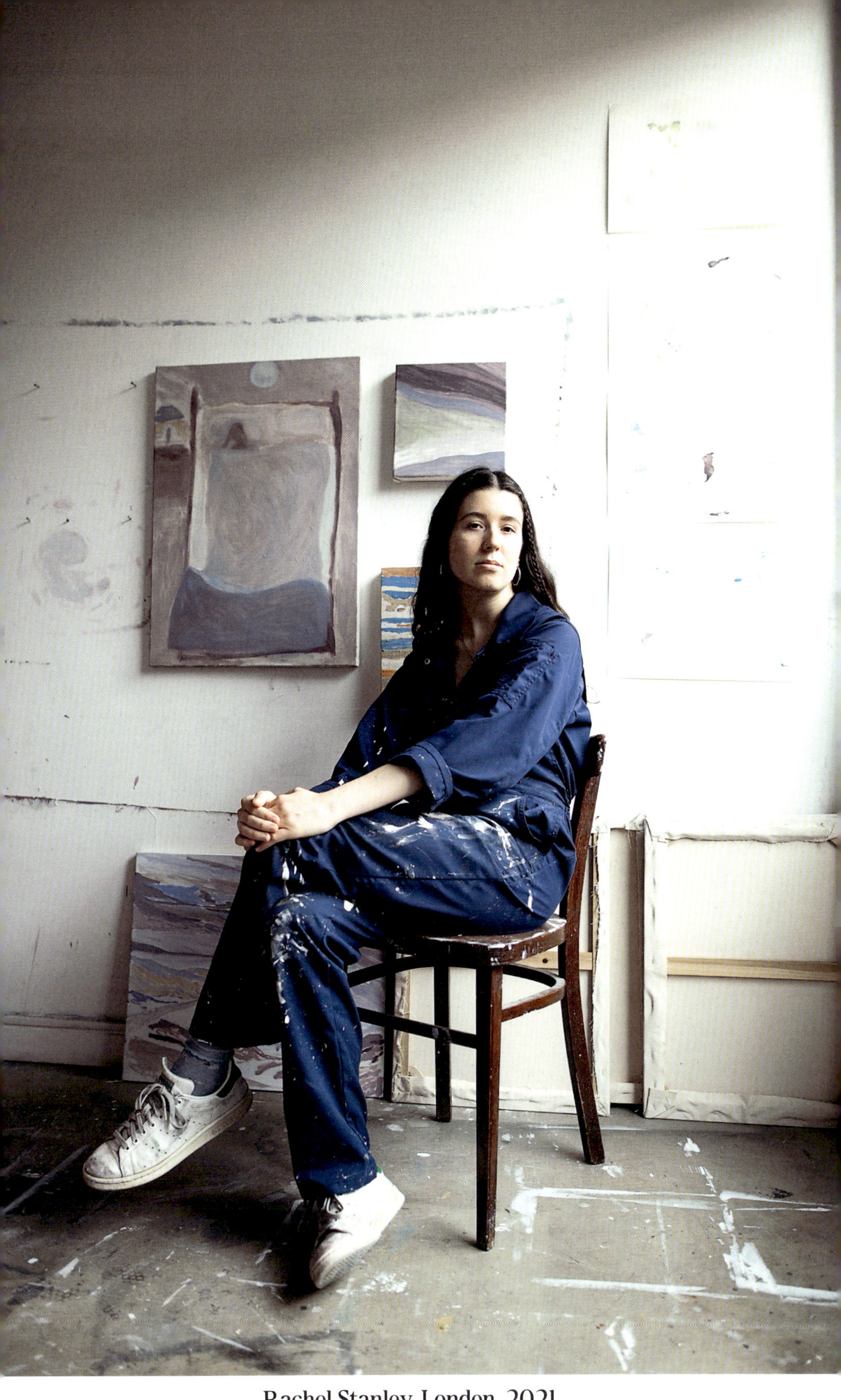

Rachel Stanley, London, 2021

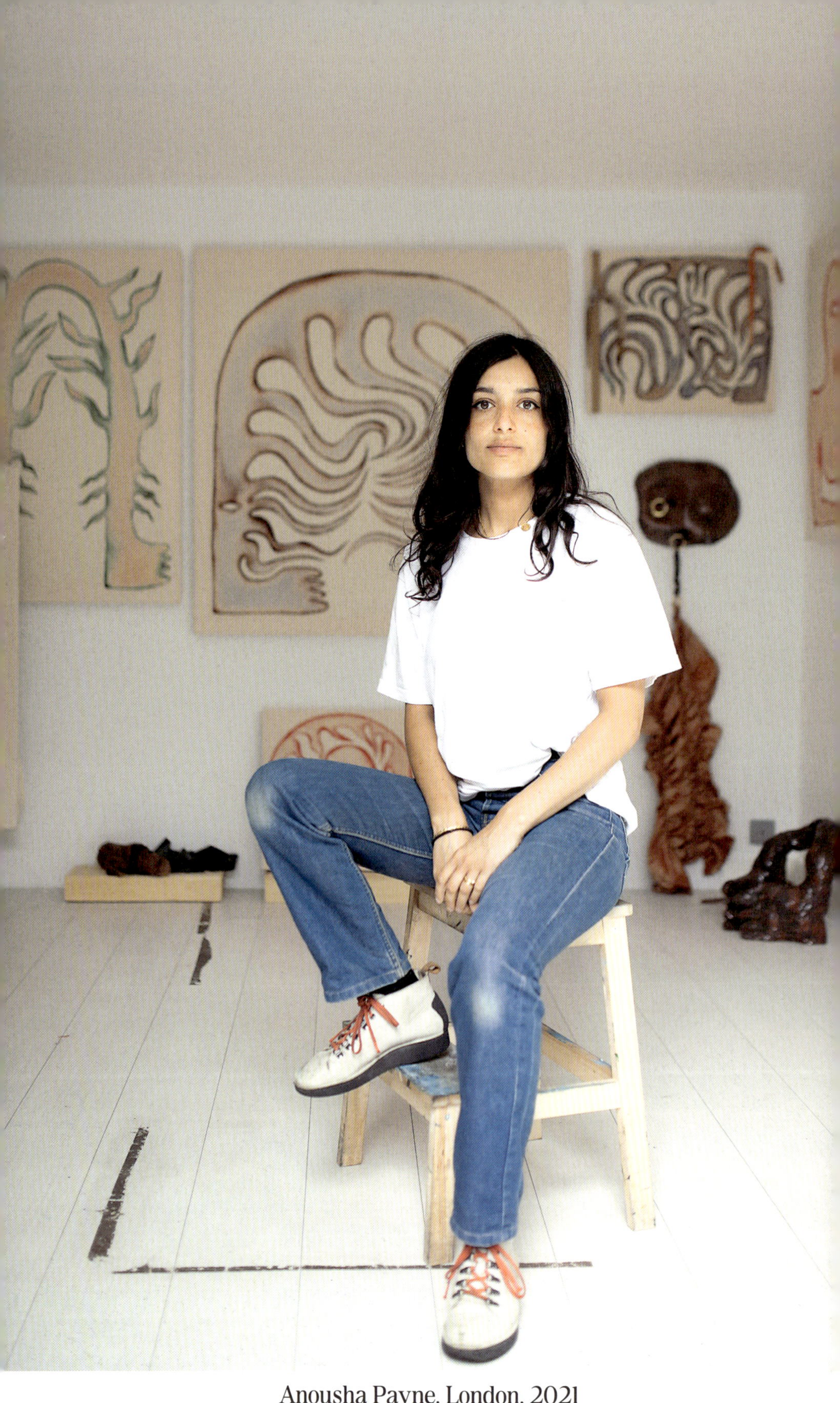

Anousha Payne, London, 2021

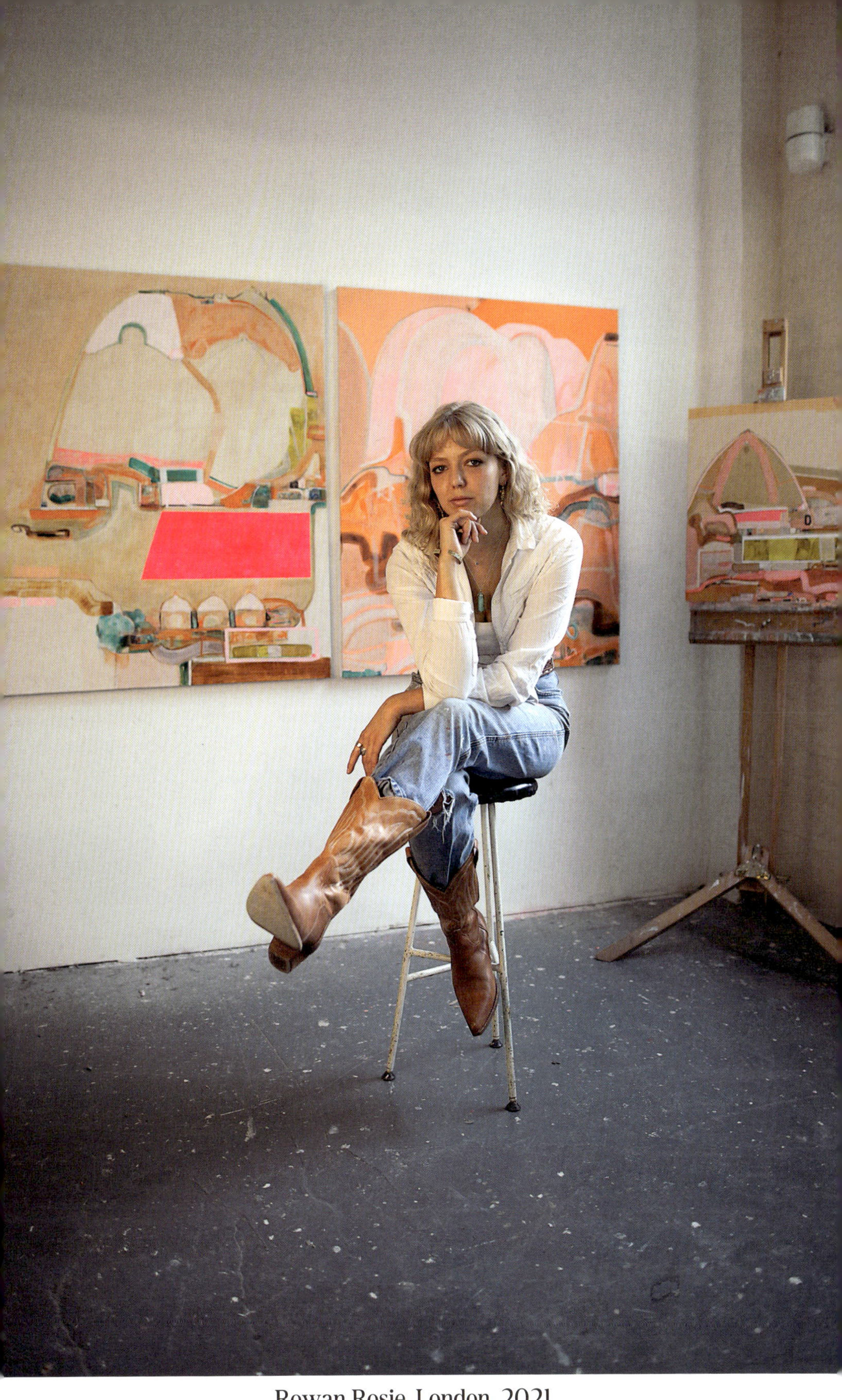

Rowan Rosie, London, 2021

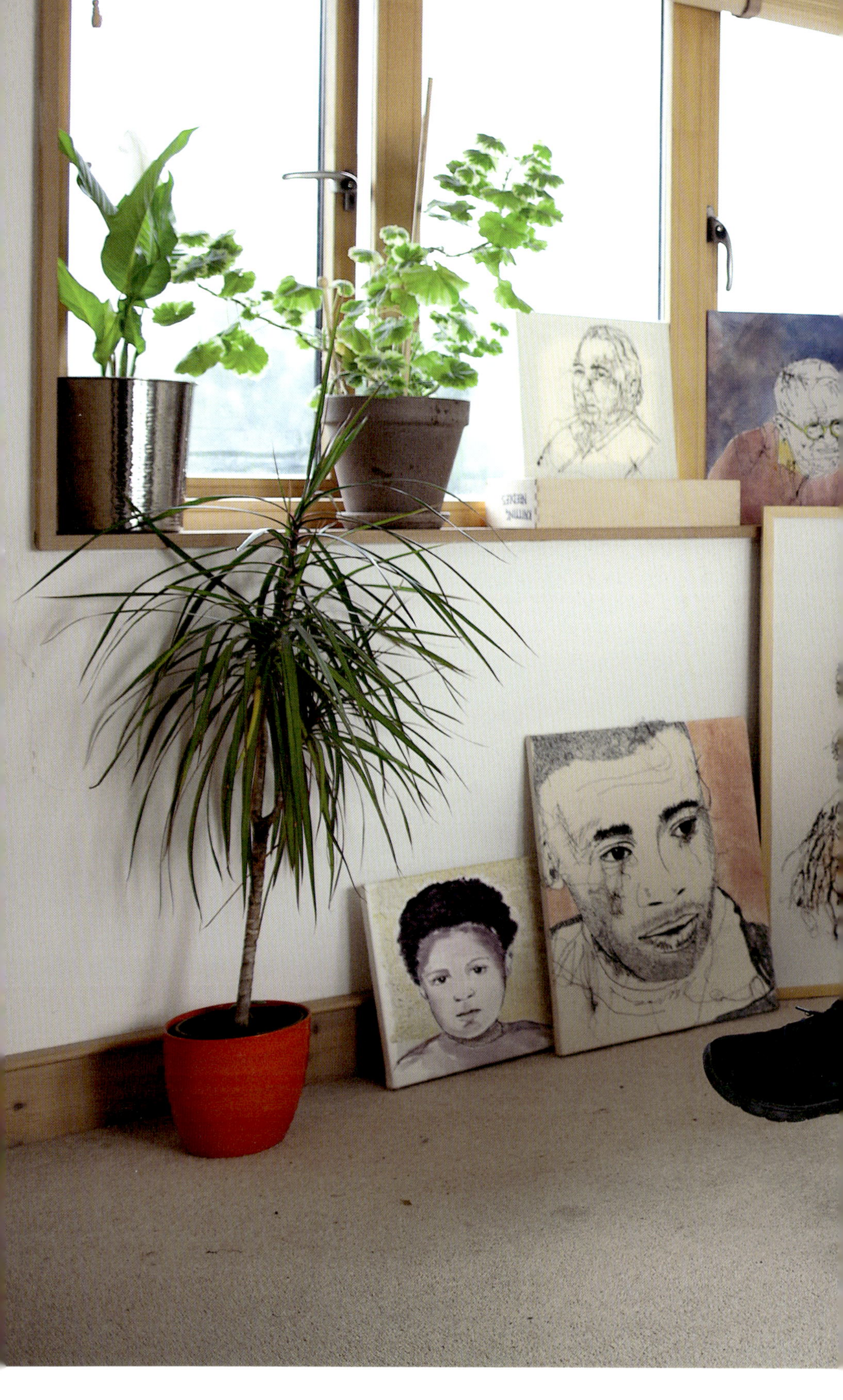

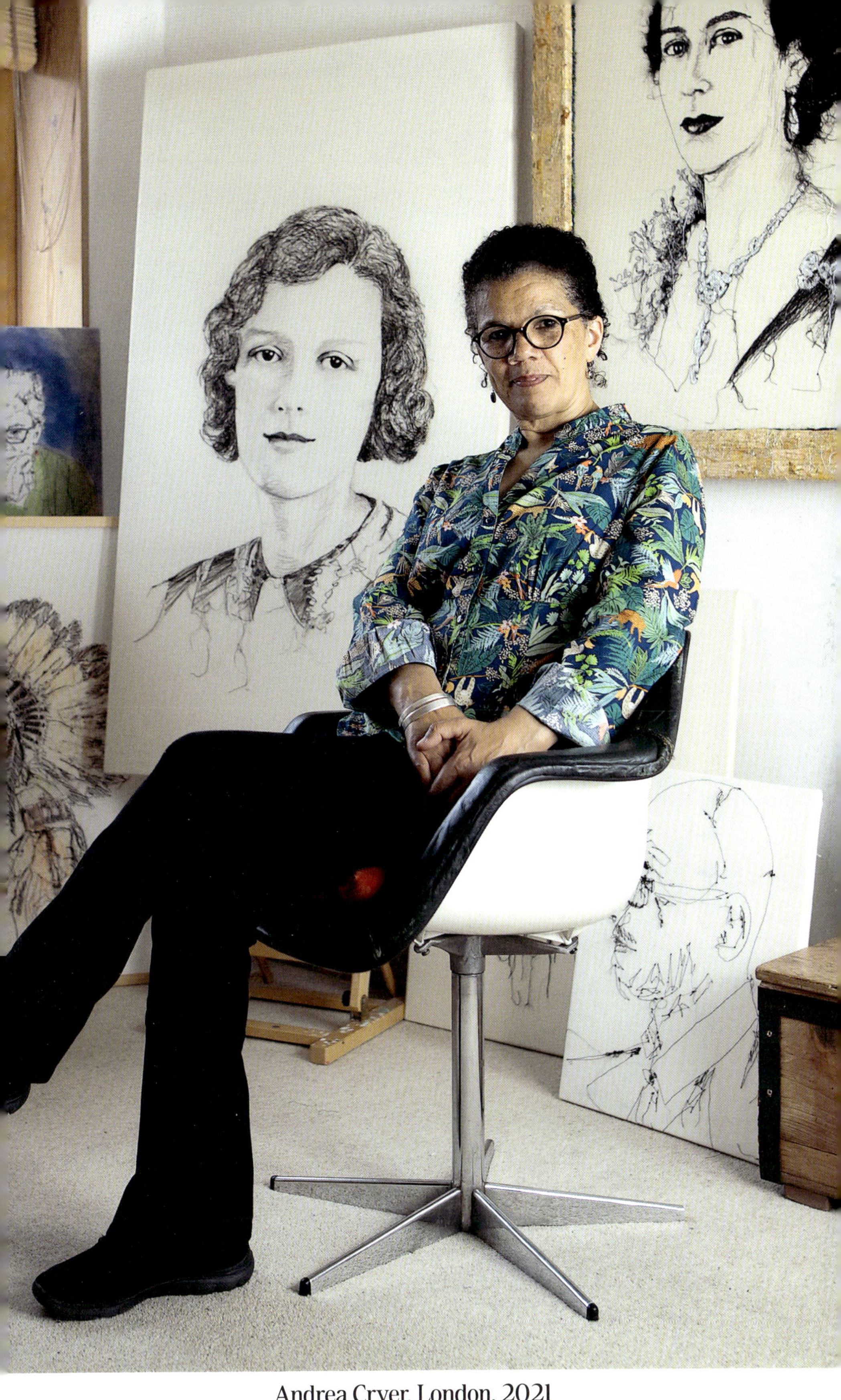

Andrea Cryer, London, 2021

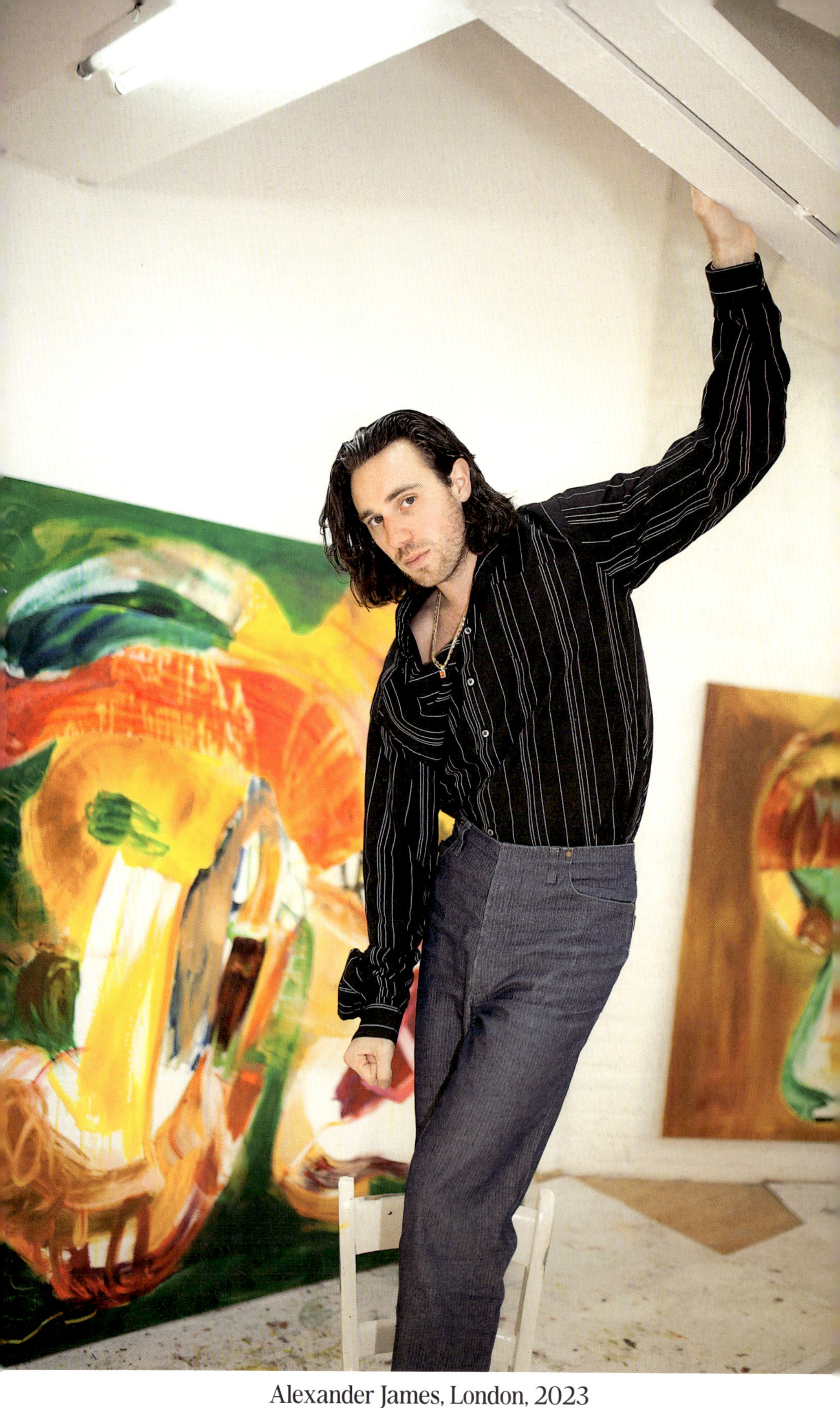

Alexander James, London, 2023

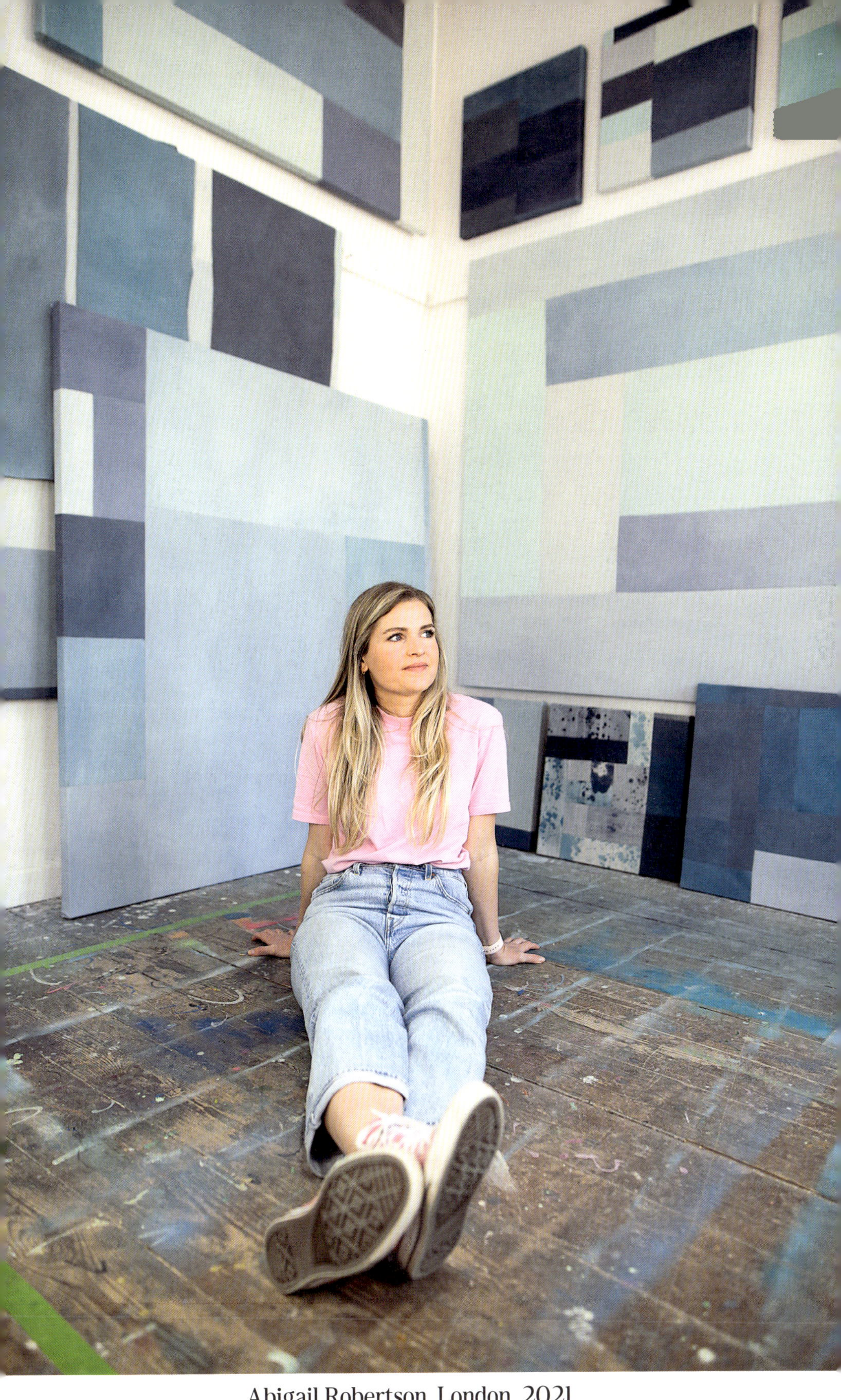

Abigail Robertson, London, 2021

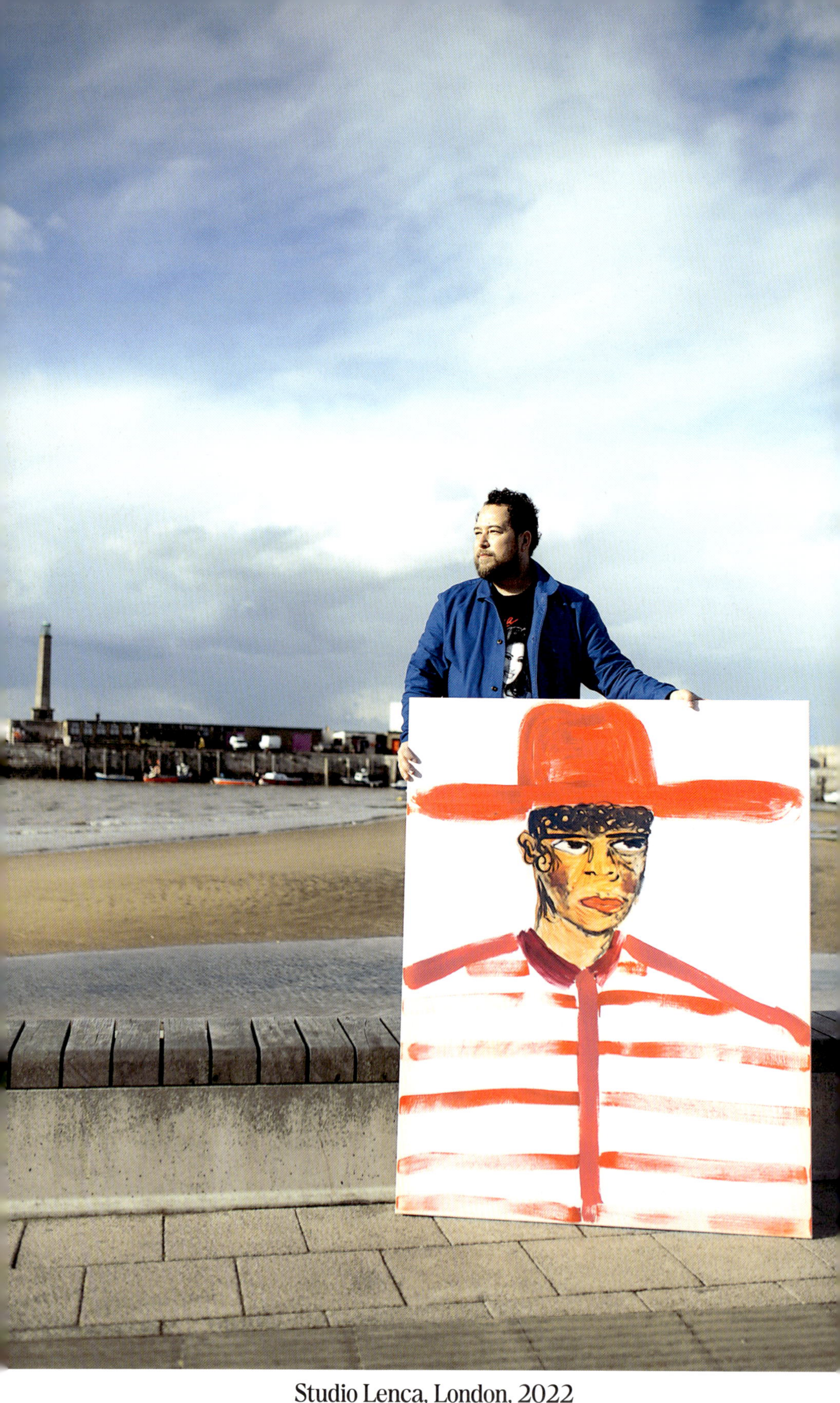

Studio Lenca, London, 2022

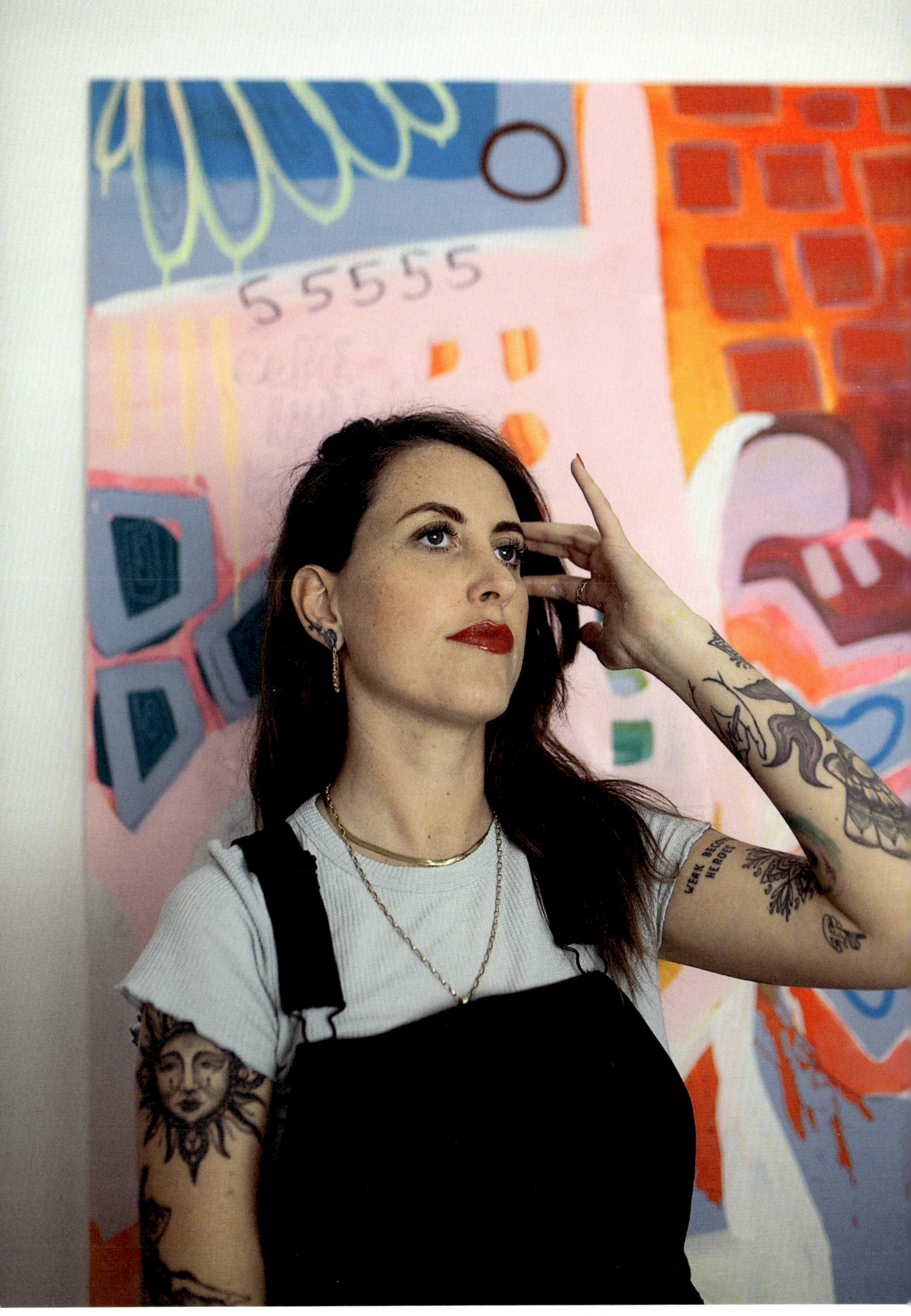

Charlotte Archer, London, 2022

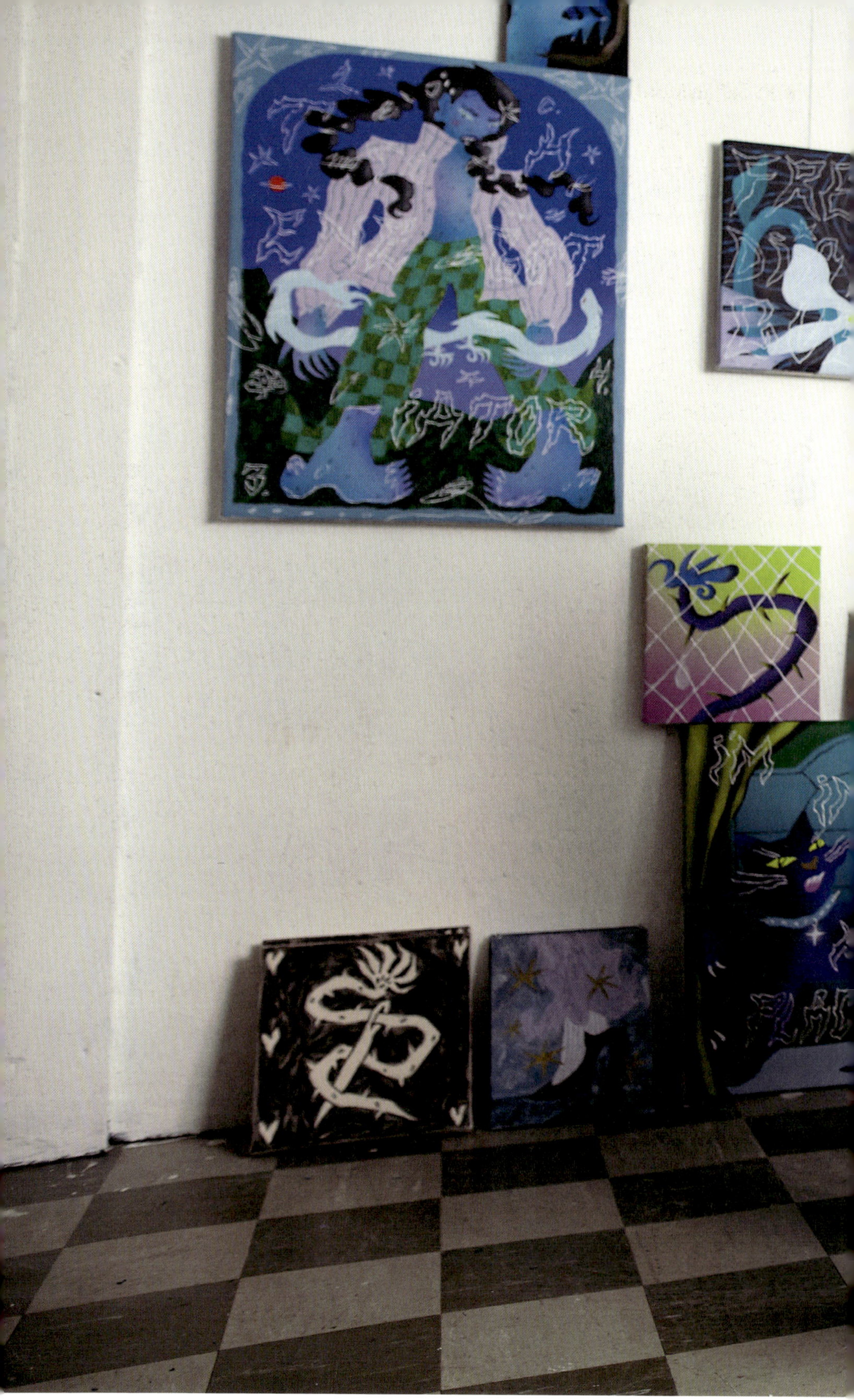

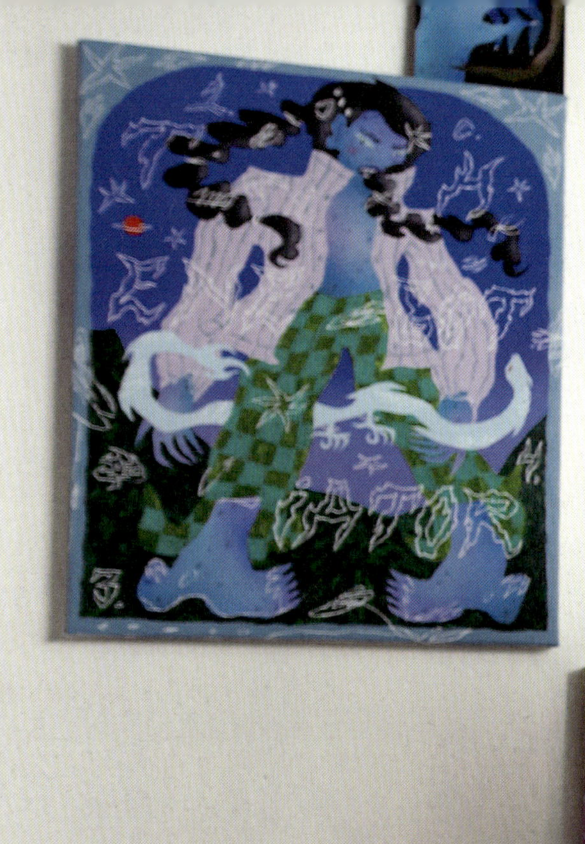
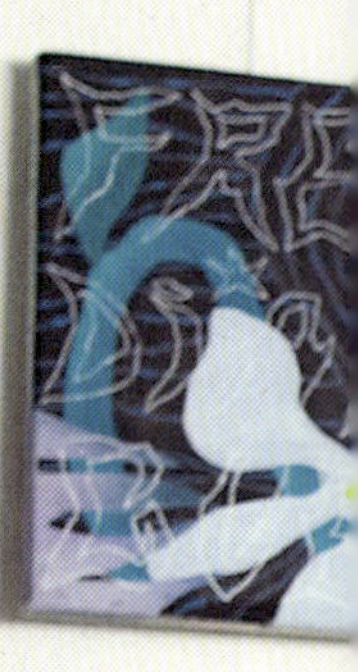

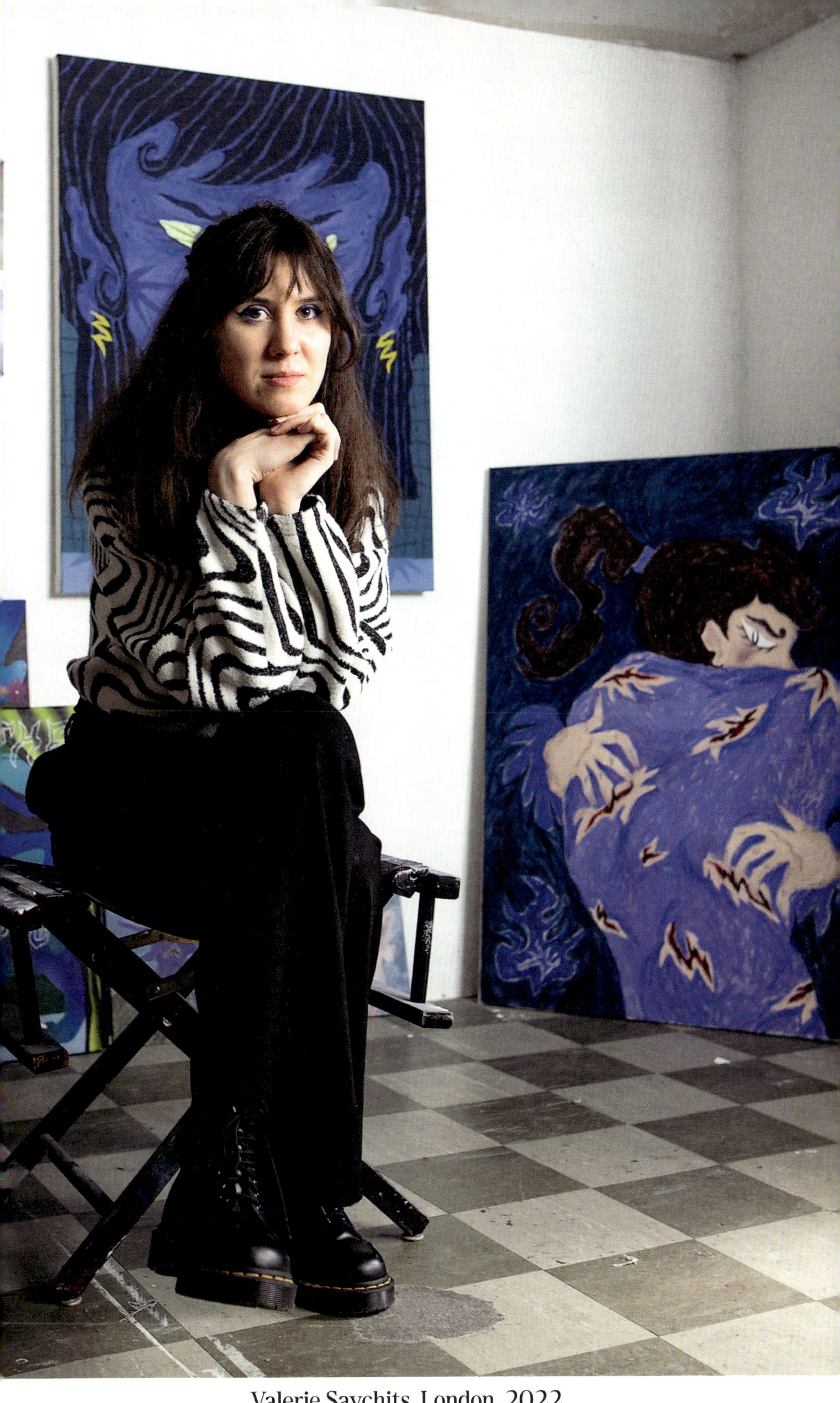

Valerie Savchits, London, 2022

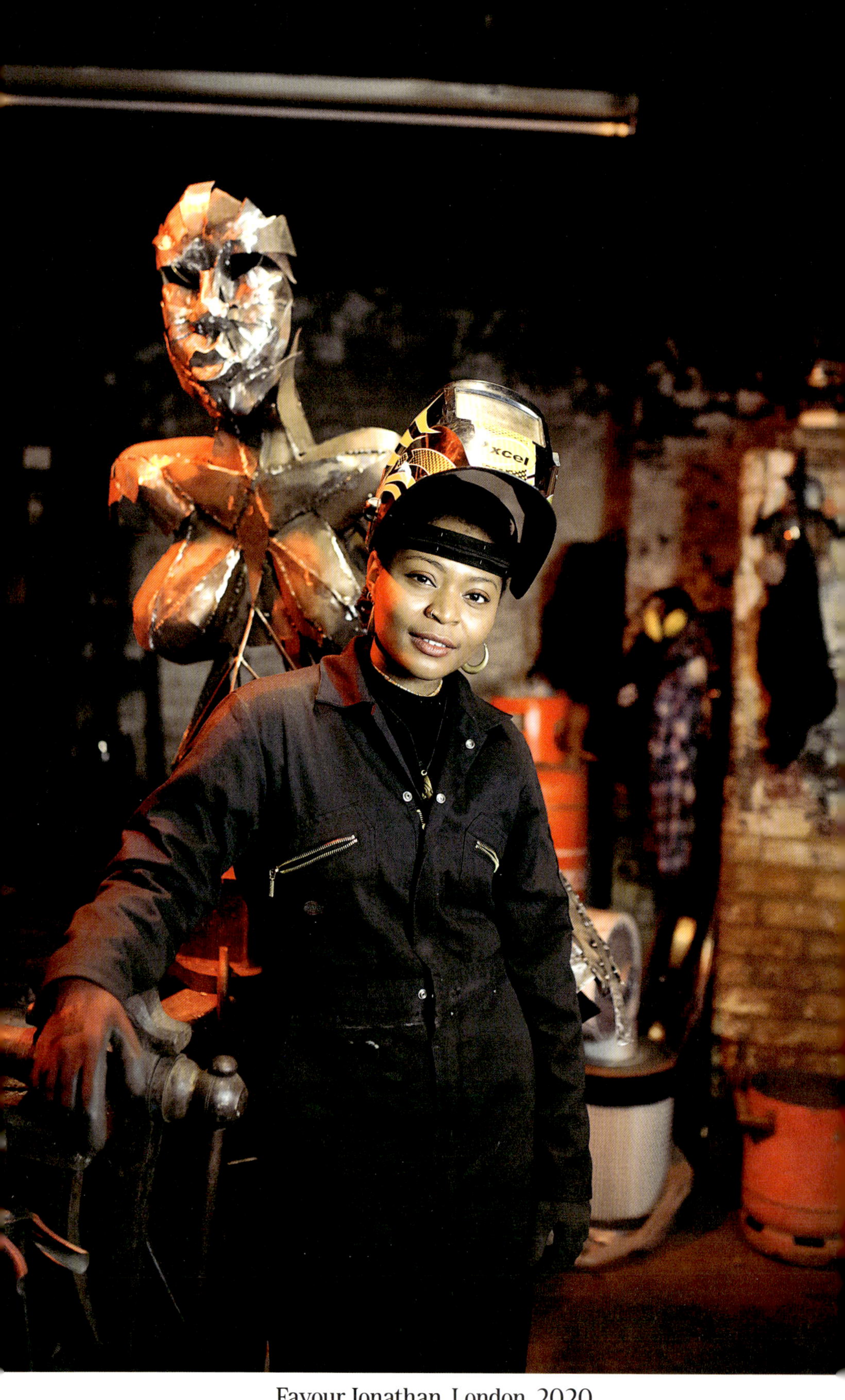

Favour Jonathan, London, 2020

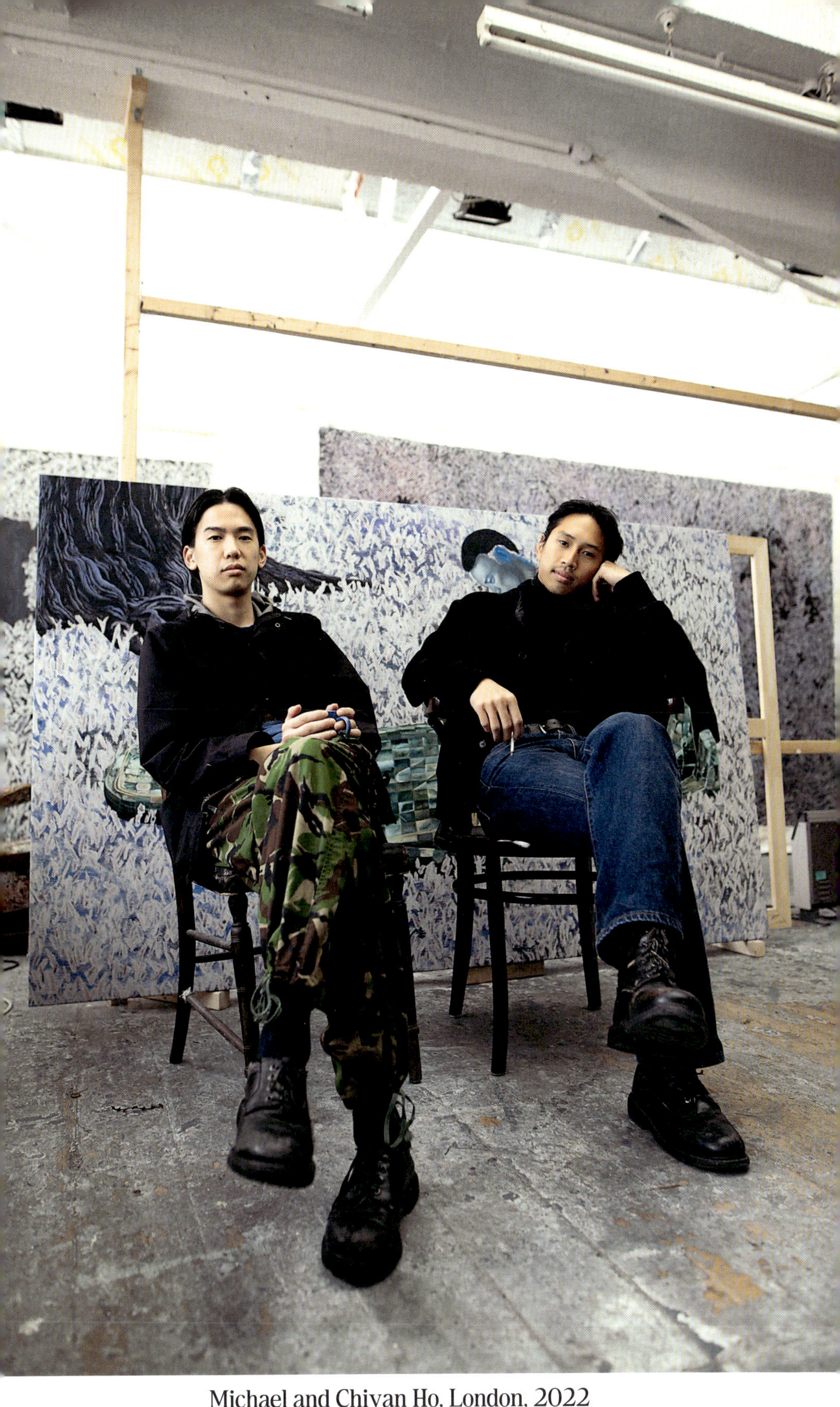

Michael and Chiyan Ho, London, 2022

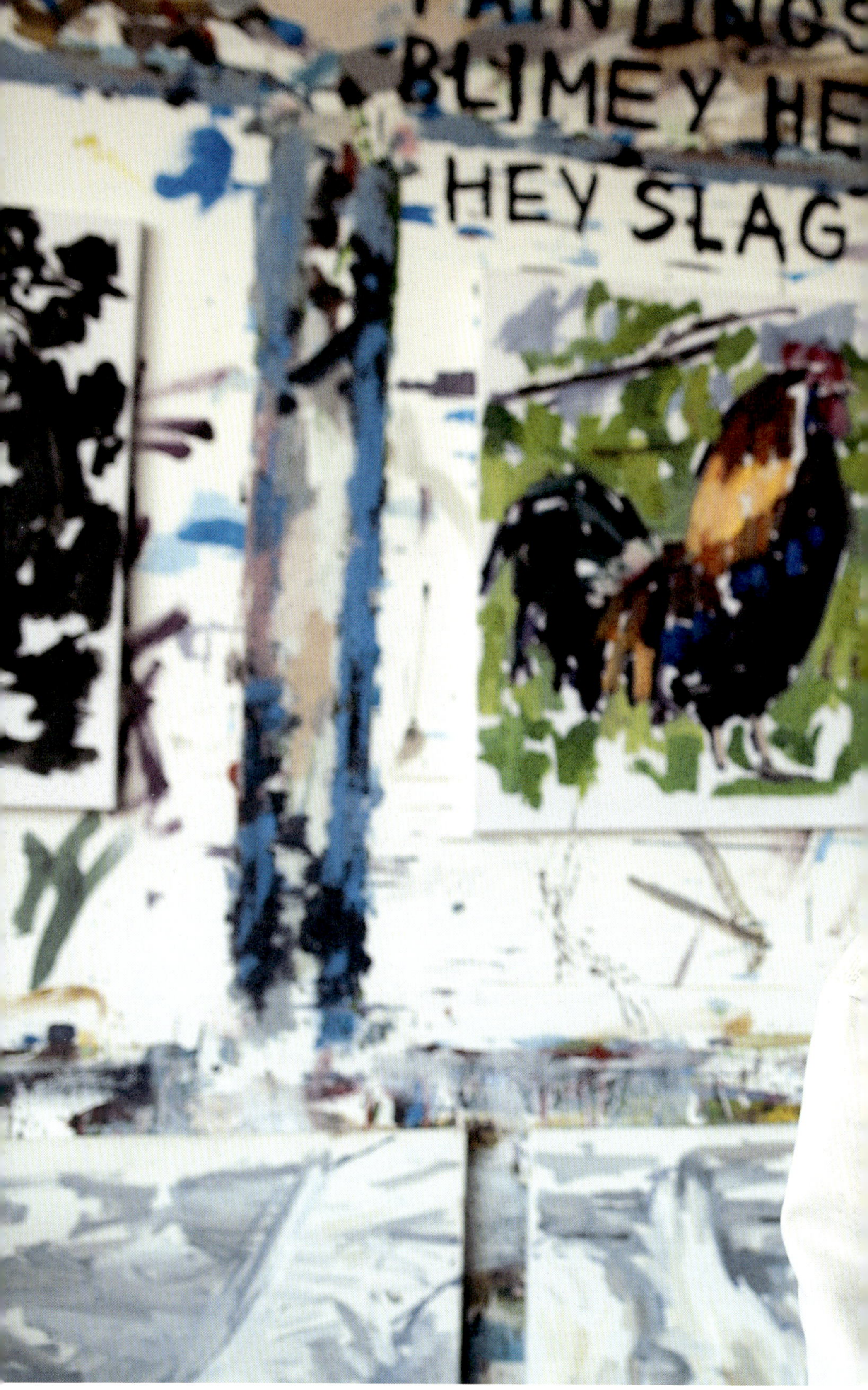

PAINTINGS
BLIMEY HE
HEY SLAG

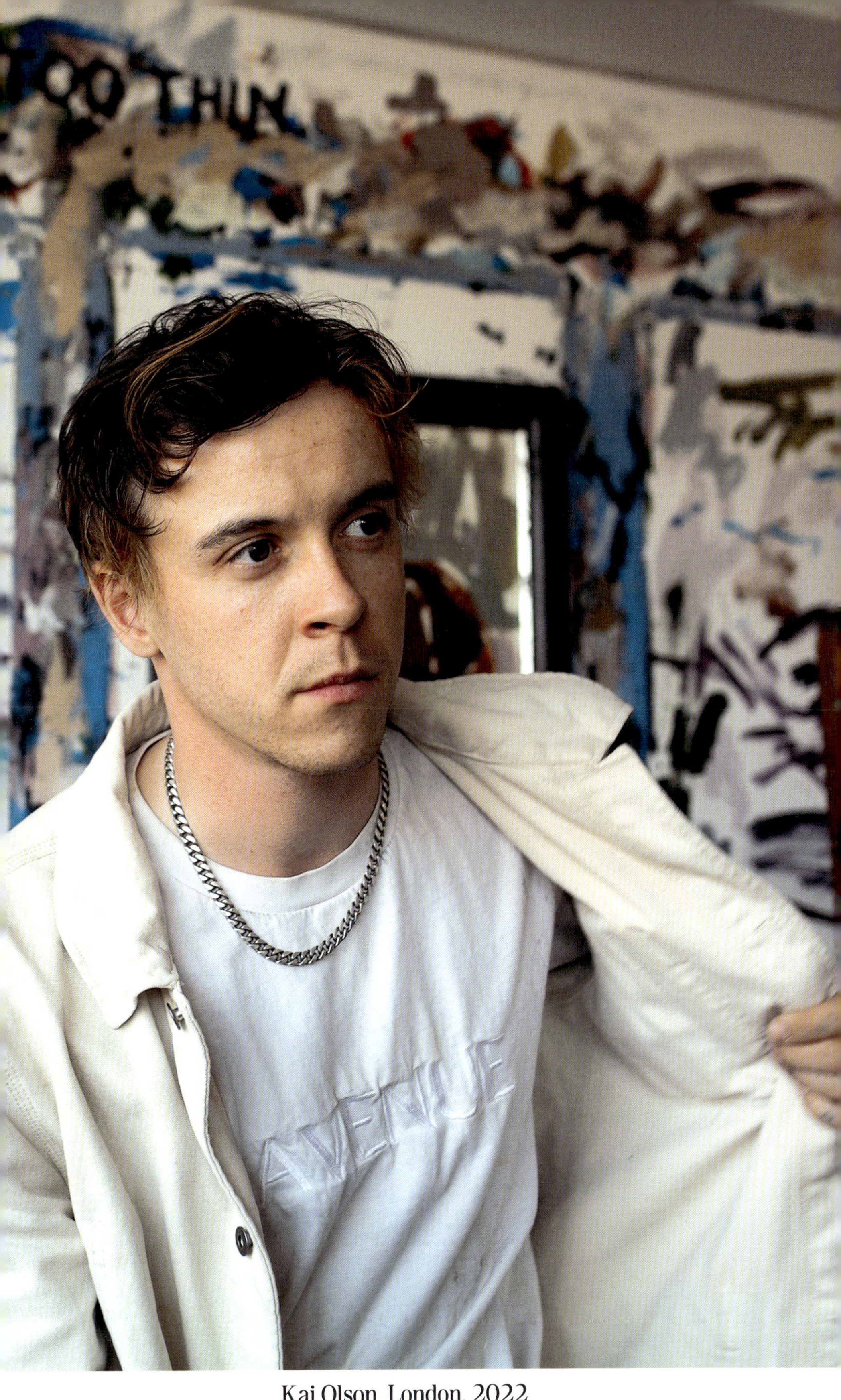

Kai Olson, London, 2022

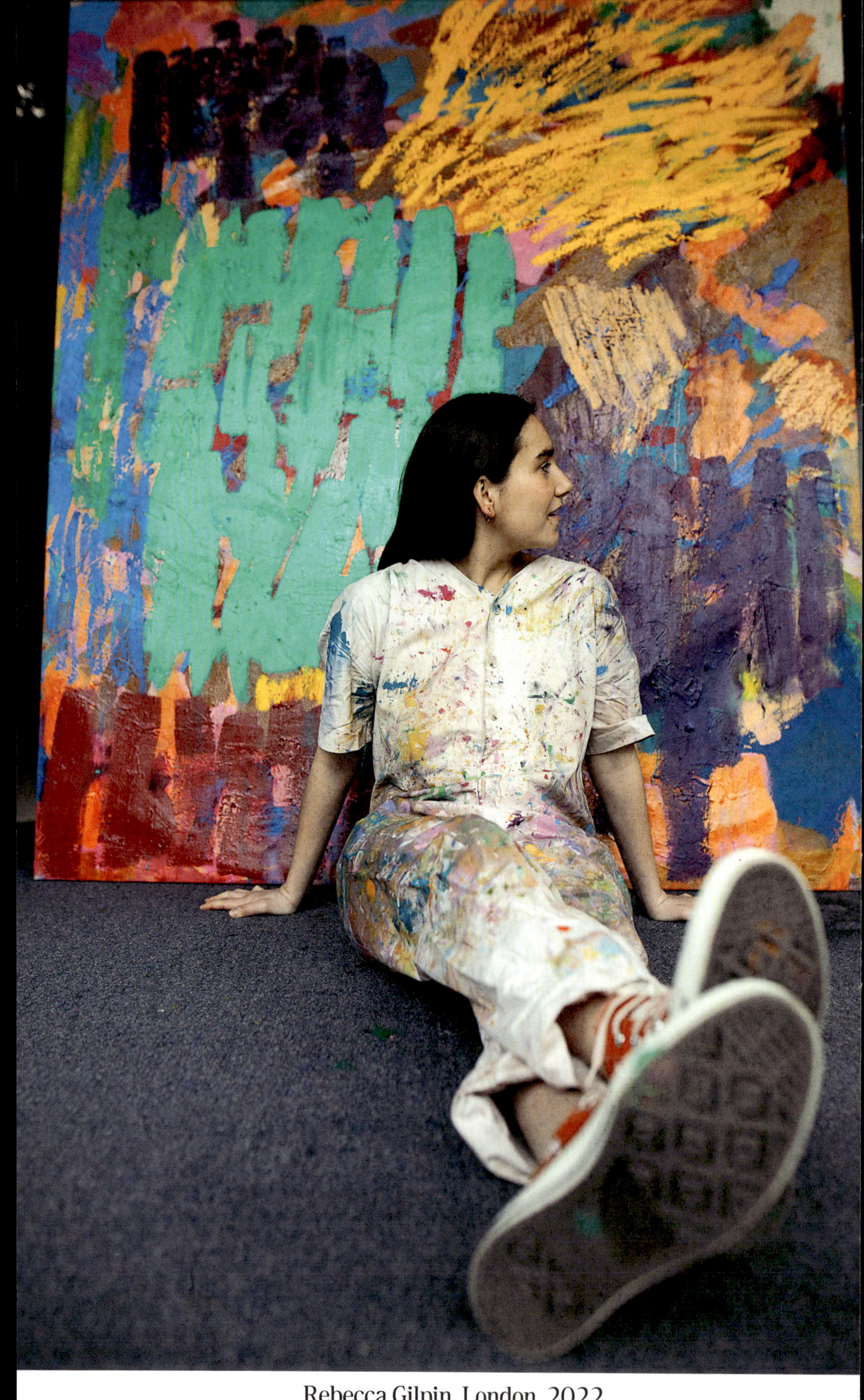

Rebecca Gilpin, London, 2022

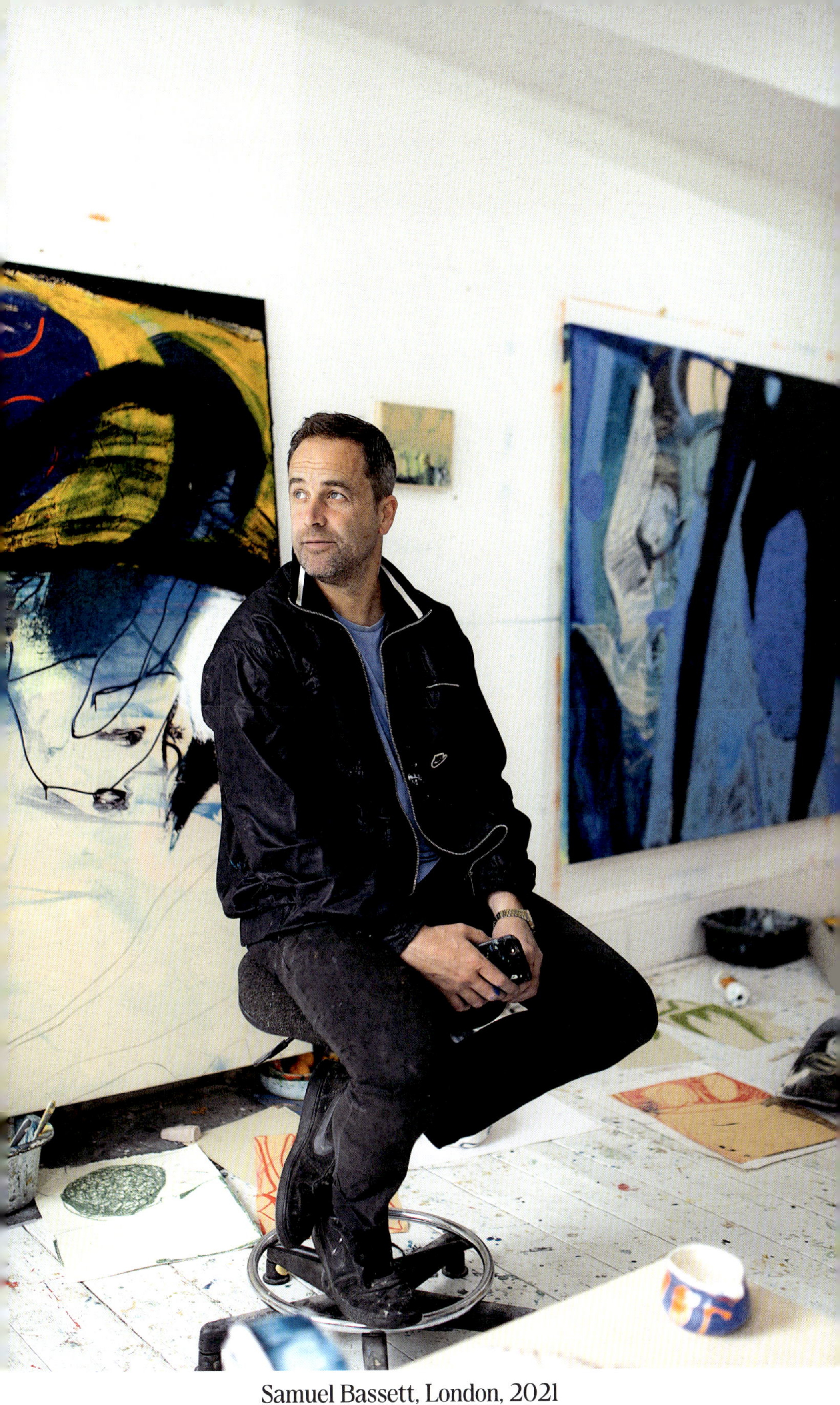

Samuel Bassett, London, 2021

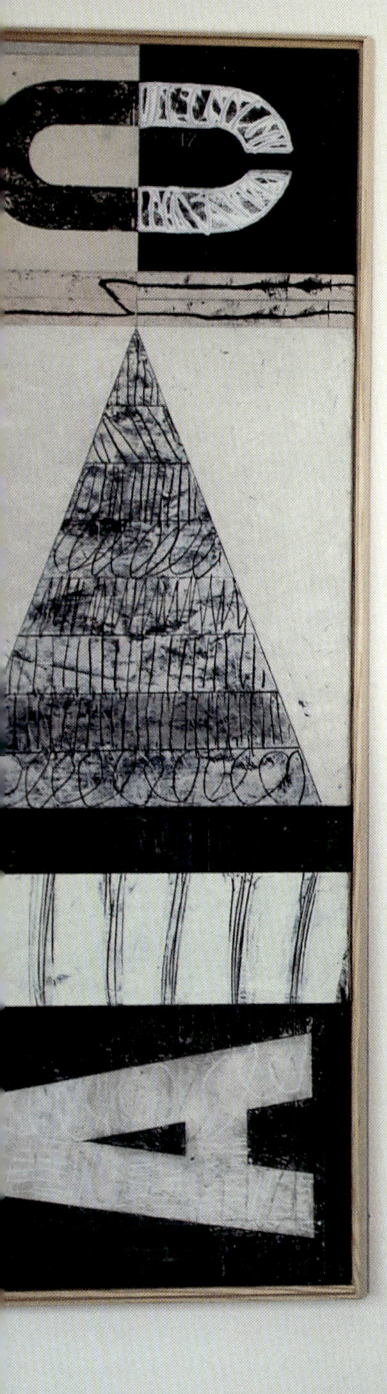

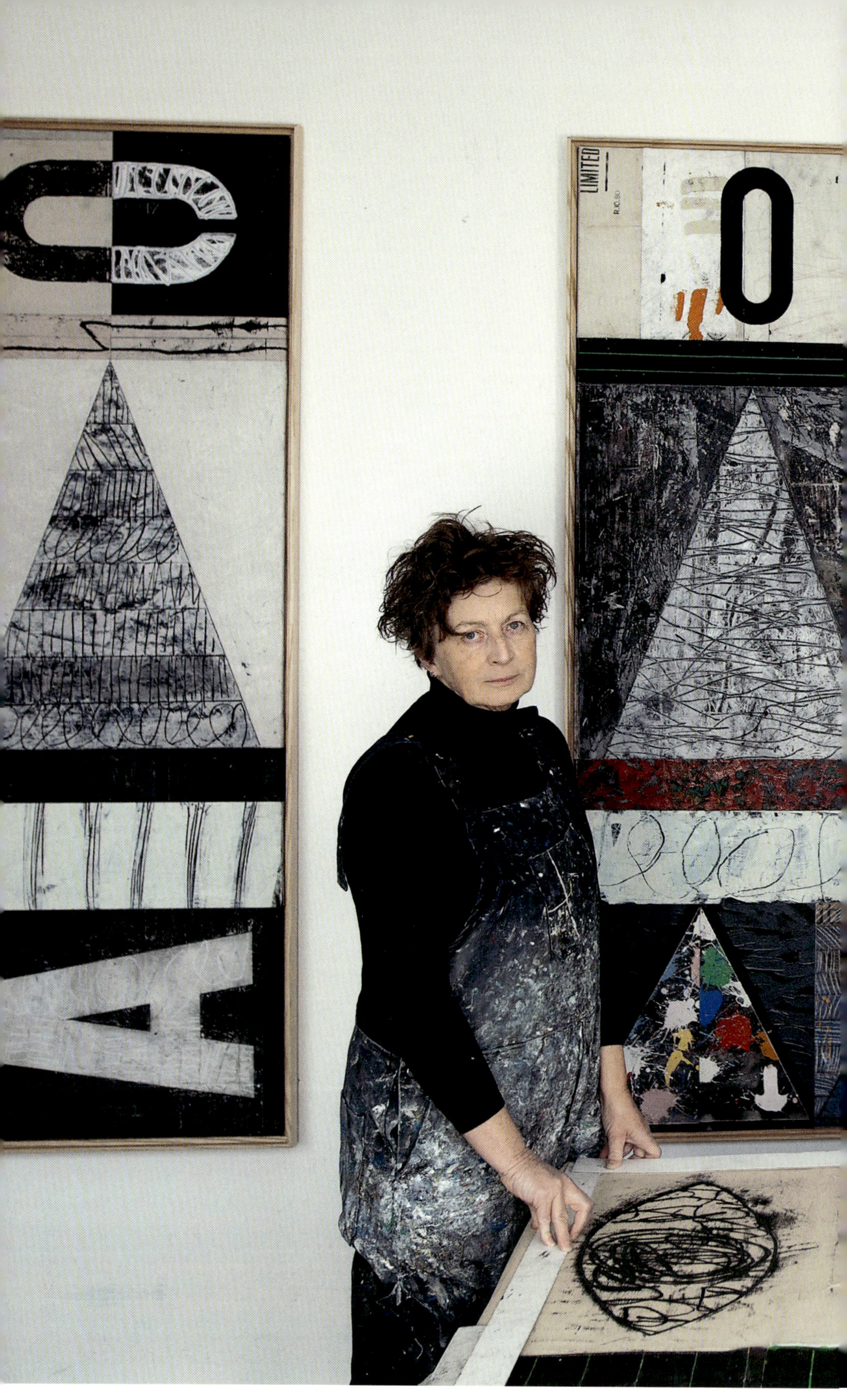

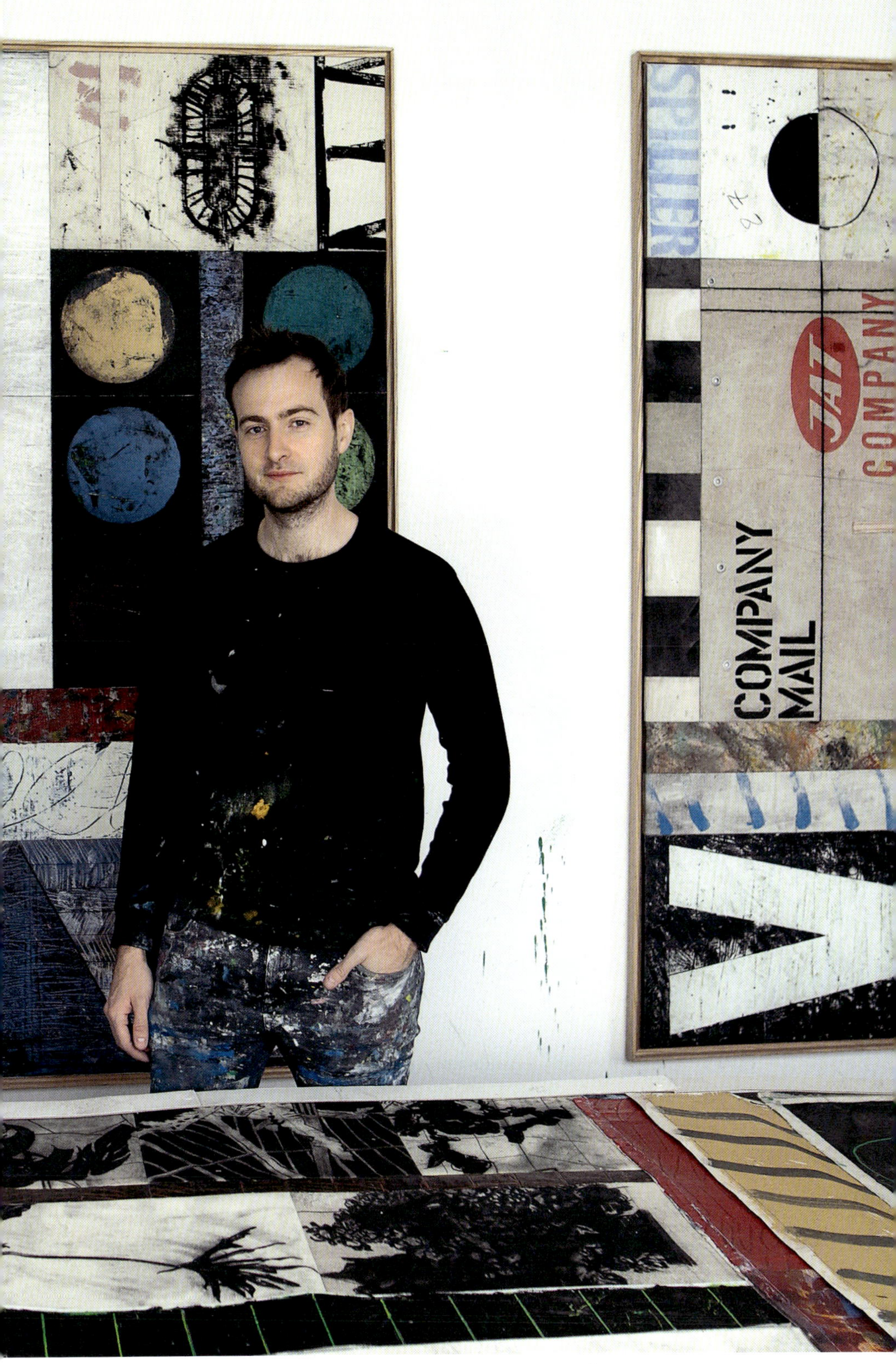

Spiller + Cameron, London, 2021

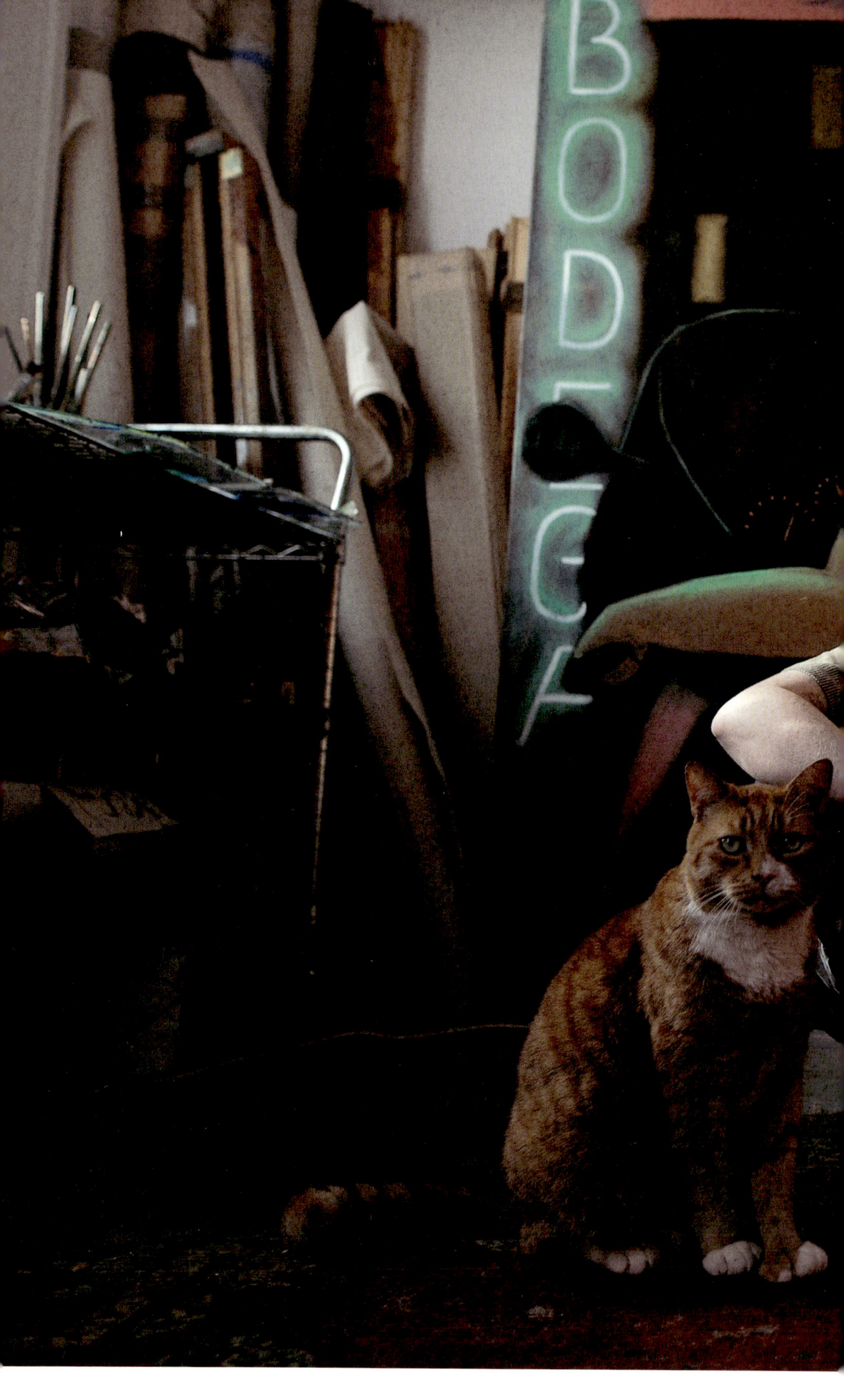

BODLEIGH

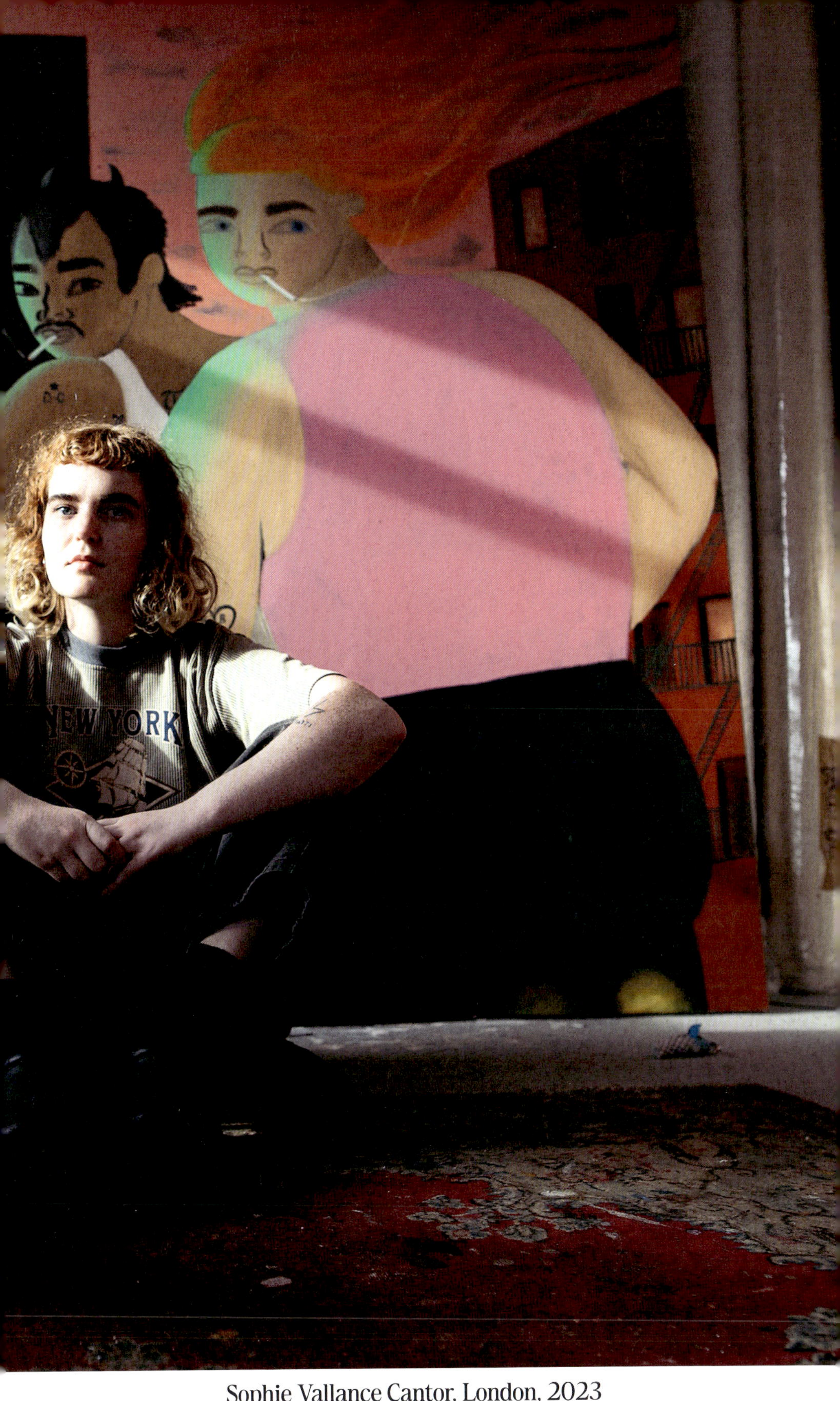

Sophie Vallance Cantor, London, 2023

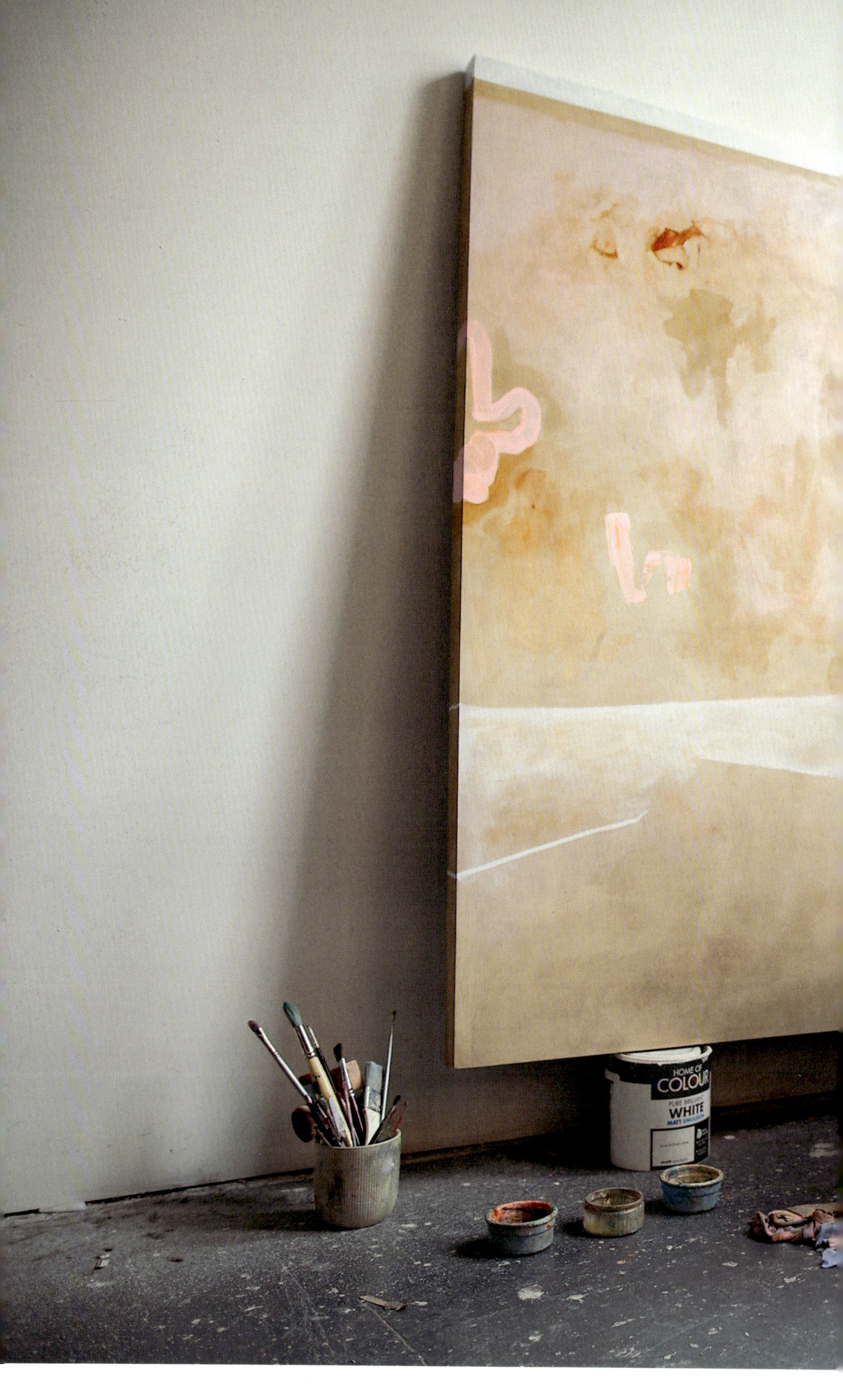

HOME OF
COLOUR
PURE BRILLIANT
WHITE
MATT EMULSION

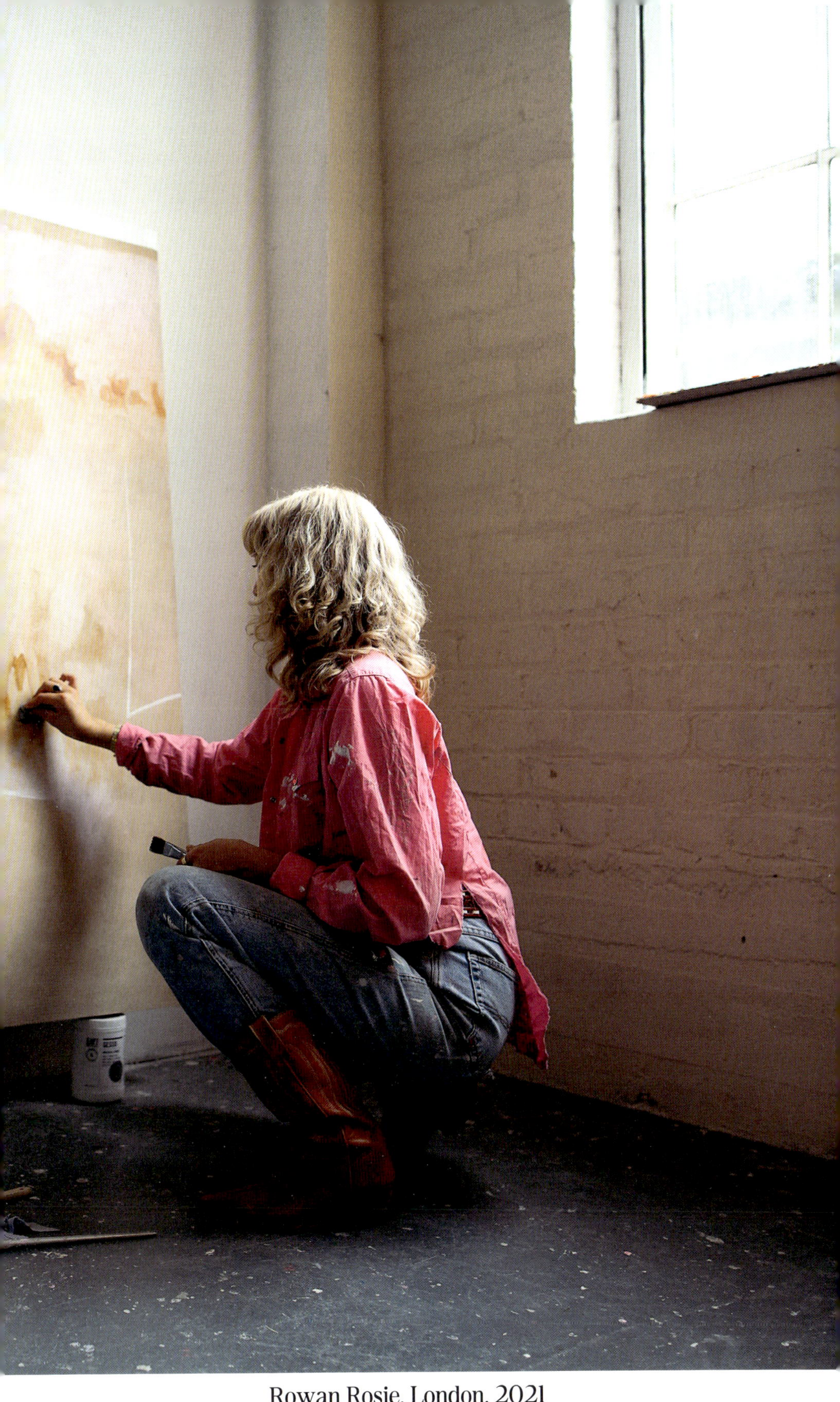

Rowan Rosie, London, 2021

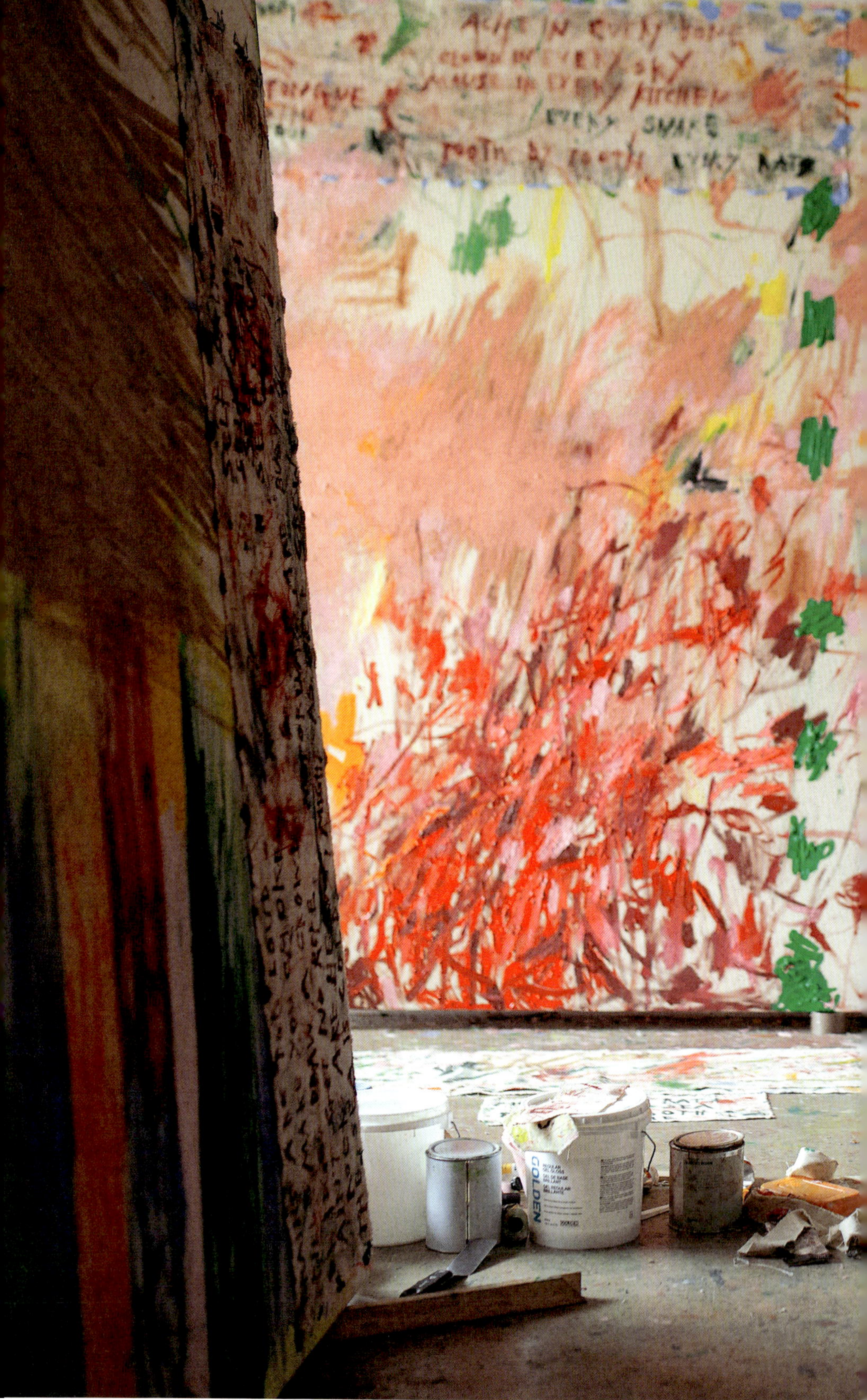

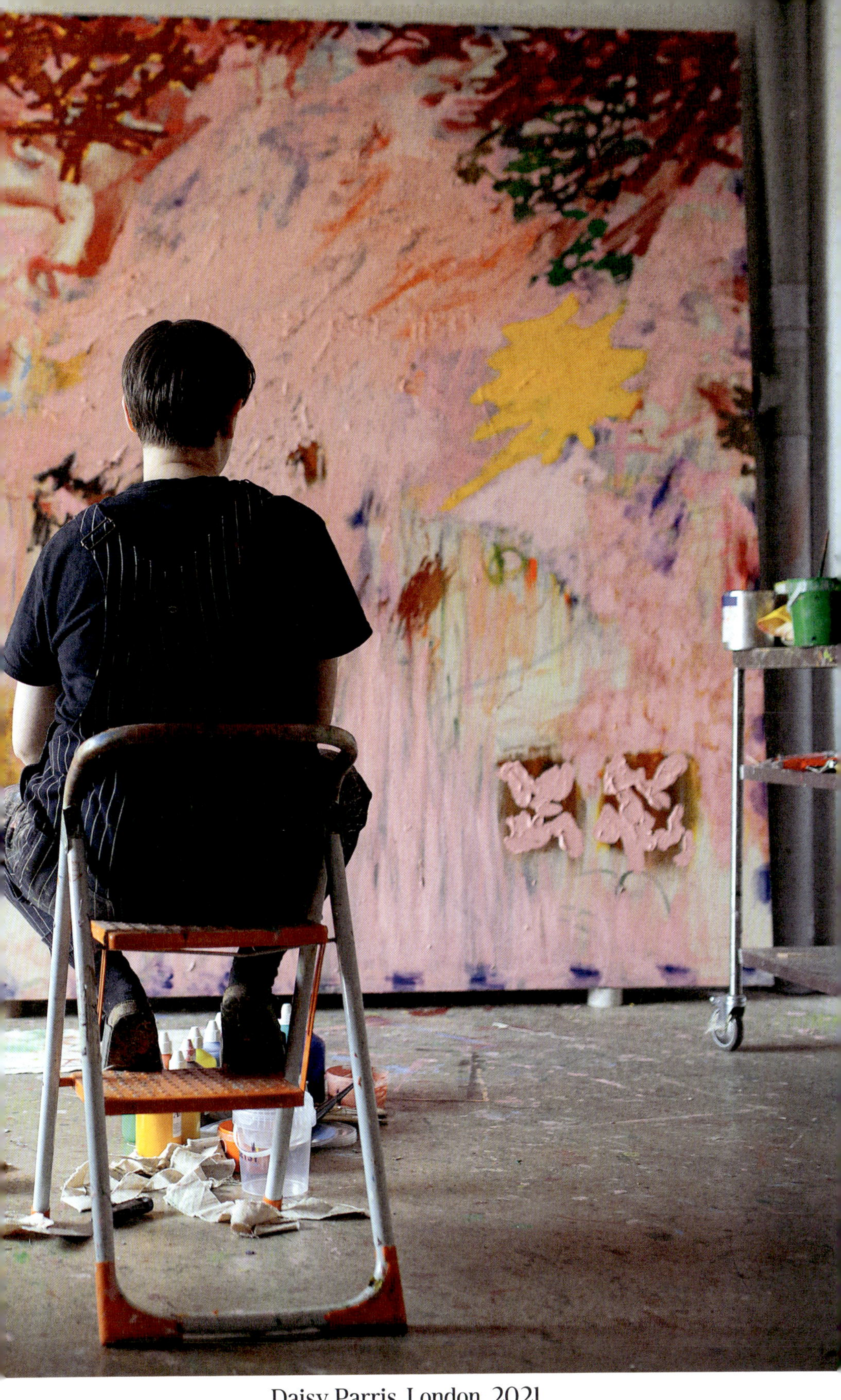

Daisy Parris, London, 2021

In memory of Paul Adrian Davies and Chiyan Ho

with immense gratitude to

Elizabeth Brooks
Soo Hitchin
LondonArtRoundup.com
Marion & Christoph Trestler

I would like to thank a number of people for the creation of this book.

Firstly I would like to thank Ell Pennick for believing in the vision as well as Mai Harris for helping make the vision a reality with their fabulous design work.

Secondly I would like to thank Hannah Watson from Trolley Books for helping make this book happen.

I would also like to thank my uncle, Paul Adrian Davies, for viewing the images as I made the project and for always being such a positive role model and guide in my photographic life.

A special thanks also goes out to Hannah Curley, without her support none of this would have been possible. Thank you very much Hannah.

A big thank you also to all of the artists, who allowed me into their worlds with open arms. It has been a pleasure of a lifetime to get to know all of you and to now count you as my friends.

Photographs © Brynley Odu Davies
Text © Hector Campbell, Ellie Pennick
Design Mai Harris
Proofreading Aleksandra Moraś

ISBN 978-1-907112-70-6

Printed in Italy 2023 by Grafiche Antiga 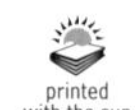

Published in Great Britain in 2023 by Trolley Ltd
www.trolleybooks.com

GUTS GALLERY